The Monkees, *Head*, and the 60s

PETER MILLS

THE MONKEES, *HEAD*, AND THE 60S
PETER MILLS

A Jawbone book
First edition 2016
Published in the UK and the USA by Jawbone Press
3.1D Union Court
20–22 Union Road
London SW4 6JP
England
www.jawbonepress.com

ISBN 978-1-908279-97-2

EDITORS Tom Seabrook and John Morrish
JACKET DESIGN Mark Case

Printed in China by Everbest Printing Investment Ltd.

1 2 3 4 5 21 20 19 18 17

CONTENTS

THIS BOOK IS FOR THOSE WHO LOOK FOR MEANING IN FORM AS THEY DO FACT.

INTRODUCTION

Why write about The Monkees? That's a question I've been asked a few times since embarking on this study. My answer, at least in part, is this book, but the shorter version I've come to use is that whichever way you look at it The Monkees and their story provide a direct route into the centre of the popular culture of the last 50 years, be that music, film, television, live performance, marketing, and advertising … you name it. In heated moments I have even been known to claim, to the amusement of my friends, that popular culture as we recognise it would not exist if it weren't for The Monkees. So, I'm partial.

Like everyone else of my age group, I first heard the records and saw the TV show as a child, and although I'm primarily an advocate of the music and the movie, it is undoubtedly the TV show that has kept their name alive to new generations of fans. For me and my school friends, it was the 1974 repeats on the BBC – an episode a day during the long summer holidays – that got us into the series and sent us all out to spend our pocket money on the only Monkees album available in the UK at that time, an 11-track compilation simply called *The Best Of The Monkees* on an offshoot of EMI's budget 'Music For Pleasure' label, Sounds Superb. It cost £1.25 at a time when, say, *Band On The Run* or *Dark Side Of The*

Moon would have cost you £2.99. It offered all the best-known hits and also introduced its young listeners to 'Listen To The Band', which at that time was a virtually unknown song in Britain. Watching and listening to the show, it was clear there was a lot more music to be had – in the days before Google searches, heritage reissues, and online discographies, it was almost impossible to find out what a defunct band's output had been, once those records were deleted. So began my habit of browsing second-hand record shops.

At first I had to make do with the ones closest to me, but they delivered – notably Project Records on Roundhay Road in Leeds, walking distance on a Saturday morning from our house and directly opposite the legendary and near-notorious Fforde Grene pub-cum-music venue-cum-roughhouse. Project was where I found most of my Monkee albums, usually mono copies, sleeves a bit battered but the discs fine to play, and usually located in the cheapest section of the shop at the back, where albums sold for 30 pence. It's important to understand that at this time in the mid 70s, with a few obvious exceptions, the music of the 60s and even the late 50s was not fashionable and sometimes even considered an embarrassment in a world where prog rock ruled and Led Zeppelin and Pink Floyd were too cool to release singles because the pop charts were, like, *nowhere*. So my Monkee albums were in those bargain bins alongside titles by other acts who seemed to have been left behind by progress: The Young Rascals, The Lovin' Spoonful, Every Mother's Son, Eddie Cochran, Wayne Fontana, Cliff Richard & The Shadows, The Association, The Spencer Davis Group, The Troggs. At 30p a time, even paper-round money stretched to letting me try out the unknown on the strength of a half-recognised name or an interesting sleeve. I've still got them all.

The shop also sold used singles (5p to 30p, depending on title and condition) and I found most of my Monkee 45s there too. My original black-label RCA of 'Alternate Title' was from the sleeveless 5p bin and in such bad condition that I was shocked the first time I heard a 'clean copy' – where was all that noise? This was how second-hand record collections were assembled by kids in the mid 70s. It was a couple of years later that I found out about *Head*, while looking for a copy of *Headquarters*, which – probably because it's the best Monkees album – fewer people had dumped after their fall from favour and was therefore harder to pick up at the kind of prices I could pay. I found my mono copy of the *Head* soundtrack in the punk summer of 1977, while Micky and Davy were starring in Harry Nilsson's *The Point* in London and around the time that *Head* got its UK debut at the Electric Cinema Club in Notting Hill in August. I picked it up at Gerol's, a little second-hand stall in the covered market hall in the Merrion Centre in Leeds at the relatively lofty price of £1.50.

So I've been listening and looking a long time. To return to our opening question, why write about them? Compared to The Beatles, Bob Dylan, or The Beach Boys, there are remarkably few books about The Monkees; there were scores of quickie fan books and annuals in the 60s, but if we look at 'real' books about them, even including the memoirs of Jones and Dolenz, I count no more than seventeen. This is and remains a great mystery to me, as once you begin to dig into the story you see how their tale connects up quickly and closely with the much wider spread of popular culture since the mid 60s. Thus they pop up not only in heavy-duty cineaste tomes like Peter Biskind's *Easy Riders, Raging Bulls* and musical memoirs like Neil Young's *Waging Heavy Peace* but also in works on the history of television, marketing, and bubblegum pop music.

The books we do have seem to fall into four distinct categories, which we might call 'archival', 'analytical', 'biography', and 'fan memoir'. In the first group we find the mother of all Monkee reference works, Andrew Sandoval's *The Monkees: The Day-By-Day Story Of The 60s TV Pop Sensation* (2005). This work is and will most likely remain the definitive text on the archival side of The Monkees story, primarily because it had the great advantage of access to both all the main players in the tale and the tape archive itself. Indeed, it grew out of the deep mining into that archive by the staff of Rhino Records. Rhino began as an enthusiast's dream as much as a record company; their role in The Monkees' story over the past 30 years can hardly be overstated, and we look in detail at their contribution in this book. Clearly taking its cue from Mark Lewisohn's similarly structured *The Complete Beatles Recording Sessions* (1988),

Sandoval's book is a meticulously constructed diarising of The Monkees' career and has proved very useful in the composition of this book both in the trustworthiness of its information (taken direct from source) and the forensic clarity of its presentation. All the session information cited herein, unless clearly specified as being found elsewhere, is drawn from this impeccable source. With so much ground to cover in a single book, the detail by necessity squeezes out sustained analysis of the music and its wider contexts, but it is an invaluable work and a must-read for anyone interested in the group.

The other book to draw on an archival element is older, being the Chadwick, McManus, Reilly, and Schultheiss volume *The Monkees: A Manufactured Image: The Ultimate Reference Guide To Monkee Memories And Memorabilia*, published in 1993. The book's introduction notes that it grew out of a frustration with the lack of books acknowledging the group's success and as a response to their enduring 'underground' popularity and benefits from the contributions of Bill Chadwick, who worked with Michael Nesmith in the folk clubs of LA pre-Monkees and was a stalwart of the organisation until the end, even writing a number of tunes for latter day Monkee albums, such as 'Zor And Zam', and the original, scorchingly acerbic 'You And I' with Davy Jones. Where Sandoval focuses on the hidden world of Monkee studio recordings, this book sweeps across the world of fan memorabilia, discographies, variant record releases, and precious ephemera. Bill Chadwick also writes a short but fascinating memoir of his experiences in and understanding of the Monkee phenomenon. It's the perfect companion volume to the Sandoval, and together they cover the 'archival' approach to the group in a way it is hard to imagine being bettered.

Poised between archival analysis and memoir are two invaluable works by Rhino Records co-founder Harold Bronson: *Hey Hey We're The Monkees* (1996), a lavishly illustrated oral history of the band in which we hear from all the key players, and *The Rhino Records Story* (2013), a fascinating slice of pop-cultural history delivered directly from experience and which, amongst much else, contextualises the relationship between group and label brilliantly well.

In the 'analytical' bag we have two excellent volumes, both pioneering and coming well ahead of the game: Eric Lefcowitz's *Monkee Business* made it into print in 1985, just ahead of Australian pop scholar Glenn A. Baker's similar volume from 1986, *Monkeemania*. Baker was also the man responsible for the original piece of Monkee archive vinyl, the Aussie-only double album that shared the title of his book and was issued in 1979. Both volumes communicate their enthusiasm as well as their knowledge, and I hope this book catches some of that spirit. In here too we find Andrew Hickey's *Monkee Music* (2011), which takes the route established by books like Ian MacDonald's Beatle book *Revolution In The Head* (1994) by being a track-by-track commentary on the recorded works. I really like Lise Ling Falkenberg's *The Monkees – Caught In A False Image* (2012); while it is hard to find other than as a download, it is worth seeking out, developing as it did from a long telephone interview with Peter Tork.

In the book-box marked 'biography' we find some volumes from the horse's mouth: Micky Dolenz's memoir *I'm A Believer: My Life Of Monkees, Music, And Madness* was first published in 1993 and then in an updated edition in 2004. Like all showbiz books, it tells certain well-known stories in certain well-known ways but is written in a style that is both original and intuitively creative, and as such is distinctly Dolenz. Davy Jones published two books, both equally unconventional. His first, *They Made A Monkee Out Of Me*, arrived in 1987 and was followed in 1992 by (deep breath) *Mutant Monkees Meet The Masters Of The Multi-Media Manipulation Machine!*, both co-written with his friend Alan Green. Despite being uneasy on the eye at first, these books are bursting at the seams with stories and humour and a fantastic array of documents, private correspondence, and publicity materials which really allow the reader into the world in which Davy lived for so many years. I also like how he gives plenty of room in the first book to what happened before and after The Monkees – his was a full, exciting life. The audiobook version, originally issued on a double cassette tape, is still available as a digital download and is a great listen, even though we miss out on the pictures and documents.

Away from the autobiographical works, Randi Masingill's book on Michael Nesmith, *Total Control* (1997), does a fine job of working through a revealing Nesmith biography, especially as it was constructed without the co-operation of its subject. Fragments of a Peter Tork autobiography can be found online, and hints at a longer version persist, but up to today nothing has emerged. The best source for information about Peter's early life remains the articles in the fan magazines from the original era and comments he has made in interviews over the following decades; though these are widely dispersed and often obscure, they proved useful to me in writing about his life pre-Monkees.

Few bands have commanded loyalty of the kind Monkee fans have shown over the decades. In fact it's arguable that it is the fans who have made The Monkees what they are. Not just in the sense that the enduring loyalty of the fans keeps someone like, say, Peter Noone or for that matter Fleetwood Mac in work, but The Monkees, perhaps more acutely than any other band of the pop era, have existed most fully in the hearts and minds of their fans. It was there that the true identity of the group was cast. For example, once the TV show was cancelled in 1968, the set and props were disposed of in the way they would be for any other finished project. Somehow, certain artefacts survived and became cherished, coveted items – most notably, one of the original Monkeemobiles came up for sale at auction in 2008, and, in a frenzied sale, went for $360,000. I suspect the price would be much higher today.

This is spectacular, but the loyalty most usually operates at a more intimate level. Initially connections began to grow with the fan clubs and bespoke magazines like *Monkees Monthly* in the UK and *Monkee Spectacular* in the US; then in the 70s and 80s came fanzines like *Monkee Business*, *Band 6*, and *Head*. Out of these grew the networks that led to the long-established fan conventions (1986–present) and then, with the advent of the world wide web, came a proliferation of websites dedicated to the group and all aspects of their career, some archival and encyclopaedic (see Monkees Live Almanac), some quirky and hilarious (see psycho-jello.com). From this quarter came 'fan' books such as *A Little Bit Me, A Little Bit You* by Fred Velez (2014) and Edward Wincentson's earlier *The Monkees, Memories & The Magic* (2000), both of which reflect upon the experience of the Monkee fan and the central role of the group in their lives. There are also some very readable books that sit between analysis and documentation, such as Scott Parker's comprehensive *Good Clean Fun* (2013) and Melanie Mitchell's original, funny, and focussed *Monkee Magic* from the same year. There are also a handful of academic articles about the group, usually from the viewpoint of 'television studies'. As hinted at earlier, the group also turn up in a great number of music-business memoirs, most obviously in Bobby Hart's superb *Psychedelic Bubble Gum* of 2014.

All these books have enlightened and entertained me, and I recommend them all to you. However, certain themes and ideas that seemed to be central and fascinating to me have felt under-explored, and in that sense I have been waiting for someone to write the book I wanted to read about The Monkees. In the end, it seemed that if I was ever going to read it, I had probably better write it myself. The original manuscript for this work came in at nearly three times the length of the book you're holding; much of the writing about the music and the marketing that has been held back for reasons of space will emerge in a sister volume I intend to publish in the future. Of course, this book still has plenty to say on The Monkees before *Head*, and likewise on the group after it, but as its title suggests it is constructed on the principle that everything that preceded the movie somehow fed into the shape and workings of it, and equally that everything that followed it was in effect a consequence of the film.

The first section deals with matters arising from the band's history, the TV show, the live shows, and the music up to *Head*. Then the text looks at the roots of the film and its place in the tradition of innovation within pop and rock filmmaking. Next we look at the film itself, scene by scene, to try to tap into the internal riddles of the film and how they sign back into the group's story and forward out into their future. We attempt to shed a little light on the infamous marketing campaigns that surrounded the film, and finally we consider the soundtrack album as an innovative 'sound collage' that corresponds to the movie's structure in some ways but also stands alone as a work of art in its own right. In the book's final section, we examine the 'Aftermath' – the end of The Monkees, the solo careers, and the comebacks, while also examining the influence of Rhino Records. A short conclusion considers the two final statements we have on TV and on disc: 1997's TV special and 2016's *Good Times!*

What quickly became apparent was that writing a book about The Monkees quickly spreads away from music or TV or film into much wider and more subtly connected areas of culture and society. That's one of the many reasons why the group were, are, and will remain so special. Yet in other ways it's not complicated at all; they were just *brilliant*. This book was written out of a fan's enthusiasm and a scholar's interest in text and context; an acknowledgement of all the pleasure and – yes – wisdom The Monkees have given me since I was a child. I suppose in the end it is written out of love. As the line runs in 'For Pete's Sake': 'Love is understanding – don't you know that this is true?' I hope there's something in here for you, too.

PETER MILLS
LEEDS, ENGLAND
MAY 5 2016

CHAPTER ONE

PRE-HISTORY: THE ROAD TO 1334 NORTH BEECHWOOD DRIVE

The way The Monkees came together is the stuff of pop music legend: on three consecutive days, September 8, 9, and 10 1965, an ad was placed in *Daily Variety* and *The Hollywood Reporter*, the village pump titles of LA's showbiz world. Headed 'MADNESS!!' (huge point size, bold type, two exclamation marks) it called for 'folk & roll musicians–singers' to audition for acting jobs in a brand new television show. It also specified the age range (17–21) and that they should be 'insane', the second reference to the borderline craziness of youth in the ad. Becoming ever more focussed, it said these spirited boys must be courageous and would ideally be 'Ben Frank's types'. This has conferred legendary status on Ben Frank's, a funky 24-hour cafe and diner at 8585 Sunset Boulevard, where the young and hip and skint would convene to dream about the future and make coffees and grits last all night. It's still a restaurant, and the space-age modernist architecture is still striking. Decoding the message would have been easy for the dreamers who frequented the cafe – they wanted real young hip kids, not ersatz Hollywood versions – as would the sly reference to the need to 'come down for interview'. Any number of stories circulate about who auditioned, some true, some apocryphal – a British documentary team located four of those who did walk up, Love's Bryan MacLean among them. Stephen Stills was also in line. Jerry Yester – then in The Modern Folk Quartet and later to join The Lovin' Spoonful – claimed to Pat Thomas that he had been offered a part:

> **Yester**: Bert Schneider called up and said, 'Well, you're in!' and I said, 'I can't do it, Bert. I've been thinking about this and I really don't want to leave The Modern Folk Quartet. I've got an idea, why don't you make the MFQ, The Monkees? That kind of stuff really goes on with us on the road.' He said, 'No, no, we've got the other three and we've got a lot of money invested.'
> **Thomas**: Well, the only question you have to answer if you know it, is which Monkee you would have been?
> **Yester**: Absolutely. Peter Tork replaced me.
> **Thomas**: Oh, OK. You would have been Peter! Well, Jerry.
> **Yester**: Yeah. Well, they had the other three and so they got Peter after I said no. Bert and I, he said, 'Well, let's talk about it.' He picked me up and took me to Barney's Beanery and talked about it for an hour and a half and I just said, 'No, I can't do it.' I don't know if that was a bad idea because MFQ broke up six months after that.[1]

Here we see the interesting idea that The Modern Folk Quartet – perhaps the most important single 'other group' in The Monkees story, as they also featured producer-to-be Chip Douglas and future in-house photographer Henry Diltz – could have been the foursome. The idea that Yester could have 'been Peter' is a curious one, too, and tells us something about this process. Ads and auditions for castings were entirely standard fare in papers like *Daily Variety* and *The Hollywood Reporter*, and the daily reality of Hollywood and showbiz at entry level for young hopefuls. Applying that process to the relationship between pop music and television was something brand new. As it turned out, only one of the final four cast in the show came down for interview in response to the original ad, despite the myth and legend that surrounds the early days of the group. So, as

David Byrne would ask much later of a once in a lifetime moment like this, how did they get here?

DAVY JONES

In 1976, Davy Jones looked straight down a TV camera and said:

> There's things you can recapture, and there's things you can't, and it's lucky for me that I'm an entertainer, I capture some of the same moments, over and over, and that's performing … basically I'm an entertainer, so whether that's The Monkees or whether it's … the school play, or whether it's Dolenz, Jones, Boyce & Hart, it all feels the same to me because that's what I do, *for life* … I live off entertaining and going fishing and bowling and a lot of other things … it's a very important thing to me, Dolenz, Jones, Boyce & Hart, it's a new cast, and a new show.[2]

There are two key moments in this apparently unscripted monologue – the smile on his face when he mentions the school play, and how he resists saying that entertaining is what he does for a living – he stops himself, and says 'that's what I do for life' instead. If there was a boy born to entertain, it was David Thomas Jones, who was born on December 30 1945 in Openshaw, Manchester, in a house that no longer stands. His autobiography tells us that the house at 20 Leamington Street was a two-up, two-down back-to-back typical of the northern industrial English city, and accommodated six: his parents, Doris and Harry; and his sisters, Hazel, Beryl, and Lynda. Manchester then as now was a tough town, and no one expected life to come at them easily. In his autobiography, Jones recalls that he went to Varna Street Secondary Modern: 'They called the loser's schools "Modern" as a consolation – but I knew better.' As he noted in an interview with Sam Tweedle, his early experiences in the school play and beyond were mindful of the rough and tumble of 'the new show', illustrating the same mindset as on the *DJBH* special:

> I left home when I was fourteen. Obviously I missed out on

> those normal things; school proms if there is any such thing in England, which there wasn't. I missed out on all the early dating and that kind of thing. I was thrown straight into a dressing room on Broadway and on the West End Stage.[3]

Jones is probably reflecting upon his stage debut in London's West End, as the Artful Dodger in Lionel Bart's *Oliver!*, a stage musical adaptation of Charles Dickens's 1838 novel of life at the margins of society in Victorian London. This is the usual starting point for synopses of the pre-Monkees career, but earlier work led to it – all evocative of a Northern English black-and-white world, of angry young men and tightly packed terraces of back-to-back houses. Most notable was a cameo in the legendary British soap opera *Coronation Street* in an episode broadcast on March 6 1961, where he played Colin Lomax, grandson of the Street's 'grand dame', Ena Sharples. Skipping back a little further, he was cast in a TV version of *June Evening* by Bill Naughton, who wrote *Alfie* and later *The Family Way*, both successfully adapted for the cinema, the latter with a famed soundtrack by Paul McCartney. Impressing in this, he was invited by Alfred Bradley, the BBC's 'Drama/Features Producer, North Region', to participate in a radio play, an adaptation of the 1957 novel *There Is A Happy Land* by Keith Waterhouse, author of *Billy Liar* and *Whistle Down The Wind*.

The credentials of all these productions is clear, and although the radio play – available in full as a download from Jones's own website – is certainly of its time, it still strikes the listener with its charm and invention, and the energy of its performances. In his 1987 memoir, *They Made A Monkee Out Of Me*, Jones notes that it was at the time the longest part ever written for that newest of cultural creations, the teenager. It's a tale of a world lost in time to us but also full of detail of a way of life long-gone, and the first stirrings of adult feelings and social interactions making themselves felt. His Leeds accent is pretty good, too. For your interest, it was recorded over three days, January 6–8 1961, in the building next door to where I am writing these words, in the large, echo-y BBC studio of the old Broadcasting House on Woodhouse Lane,

Leeds 2, now occupied by various offices of Leeds Beckett University.

His other great passion was riding, and with the enthusiastic advocacy of his racing-loving dad, he spent eight months from late 1960 to May '61 working at Basil Foster's stables in the great Suffolk horseracing town of Newmarket. Foster was also well connected in theatre-land and gave his contacts there the nod about the young boy. The recommendations clearly worked, because after briefly playing Michael, the youngest of the Darling children in a regional touring production of J.M. Barrie's *Peter Pan* alongside the Wendy of future nearly-Mrs-McCartney Jane Asher, Jones went to the West End to play the Artful Dodger in *Oliver!*. It was this role that really kick-started the public phase of Davy's life, which, once it had begun, never really ended. Jones never forgot the debt he owed to Foster in the short or the long term: in 1967, he set him on to care for and train his own horses, and in 2011 paid for his sheltered housing costs in Florida.

Davy joined *Oliver!* at the New Theatre (now the Noel Coward Theatre) on St Martin's Lane, the Mississippi Delta of London's theatre life, on May 7 1962; he was 15, also the number of English pounds he was paid a week for his trouble. Directed by Peter Coe, the play had been running since 1960; the original Dodger was the similarly impish Martin Horsey, and it is he, rather than Jones, who can be heard on the album of the original production, although Jones licensed a recording of his era's cast and sold it as a limited edition via his website in 2005. *Oliver!* ran to well over 2,500 performances before closing, at that theatre, in September 1967, just as The Monkees were at the zenith of their success. Jones left the London company in late '62 to open the play on Broadway, debuting on January 3 1963 at the Imperial Theatre only nine months after he opened in the West End. In that natal interlude a new star was born. Jones was propelled right into the Broadway scheme of things, but another world gleamed on the horizon. In a delicious twist of fate, the cast of the Broadway *Oliver!* was featured on the same edition of *The Ed Sullivan Show* that first featured The Beatles (February 9 1964), which provided the seismic shock which seemingly changed the music world overnight. He looks right at home singing 'I'd Do Anything', with sweet

Georgia Brown also reprising her West End turn as Nancy – and yet suddenly new possibilities rose into view.

Within a year Jones had fatefully attracted the attention of Columbia Vice President Ward Sylvester and Colpix boss Lester Sill when a touring production of another Dickensian musical, *Pickwick*, came to California. Jones played opposite Harry Secombe's Pickwick as Sam Weller, a part created by Roy Castle in the London original. Quickly signed to Colpix, he issued three singles through '65 and an album in September of that year. Colpix was the record label that issued material from Columbia Pictures and Screen Gems; it would be superseded a year later by Colgems, the label created to issue Monkees music. This contractual tie would provide a fast track into the auditions for *The Monkees* TV show just months later; the *David Jones* album was the final release on the label before it mutated into Colgems. The album strives to cover the bases of his perceived appeal at the time, a mix of Broadway tunes, Brill Building-style teen pop, and picks from the new catalogue of self-composed pop. This leads to unusual juxtapositions – the vintage British music-hall stalwart 'Any Old Iron' cheek by jowl with Bob Dylan's 'It Ain't Me Babe'. Jones would later try very hard to synthesize these two distinct styles into what he characterised as 'Broadway rock' toward the end of the Monkees' 60s recording career, with some success (think of 'Dream World' or 'Changes'), but here the contrasts are striking. For all its apparent ephemerality, the album is truthful in at least one major way – it documents where the young hopeful had been and hints at where he was headed, and tackling Dylan early on will certainly have helped him make such a memorable job of a tune like Boyce & Hart's 'I Wanna Be Free' a year later. There's a great photograph of Davy standing by Neil Sedaka as he works the piano and Carole Bayer Sager stands finger poppin' beyond him; I suspect the number on their minds is 'When Love Comes Knockin' (At Your Door)'.They are in a theatrical rehearsal space, mirrored walls, blonde wood floors. This is the kind of space and situation Davy knew well – it's the world of musical theatre, the songwriters and arrangers bashing out the chords to teach the actors how to deliver the song to best help the show go on. This little image sums up the early days of The Monkees, and how well suited Davy was. It's also a substantial tribute to his boldness of spirit as well as his professionalism that he took the risk and got behind the push for change in The Monkees 'revolt' of early '67 into a new kind of working and creative environment for him.

Jones quickly became a favourite at Screen Gems and appeared in one episode of *The Farmer's Daughter* as leader of the kids' band Moe Hill & The Mountains, who were rehearsing a version of Boyce & Hart's 'Gonna Buy Me A Dog'. So by the time he stood before the cameras and Rafelson and Schneider for his screen test for a new TV project in September '65, he was already a shoo-in for the project, as his employers were looking for a vehicle for their young prodigy's talents. As Steve Blauner noted in a 1997 documentary about those who auditioned for the show:

> Screen Gems put Davy under contract after seeing him in *Oliver!*. I didn't know what I was gonna do with him but thought we'd find a show for him. So when Rafelson and Schneider came knocking I said, 'Well, we've got one of your group.'[4]

It was indeed Rafelson and Schneider's brainchild that was to offer that way in. Of course initially it was just another role, another cast, and in the famous screen test, he seems good-naturedly vexed by the vibe and line of questioning. He is definitely still sporting some of the Artful Dodger's Cockney accent alongside best-behaviour long English *a* sounds – 'dahrnce' – but throughout he is very charming and funny and self-deprecating, and his willingness to admit he is 'uncool' and to look perplexed and say 'I don't get that!' to one of the wise-ass questions from the producers only adds to the appeal. Even being teased by Rafelson and Schneider after he shows off a quick stage-school tap-shuffle – 'Davy, you wanna know something? I really think you shoulda been a jockey' – elicits a charming response, as he laughs and claps in delight, finally covering his face with the inner crook of his arm in mock despair. He would surely have got the role, shoo-in or not, with his comeback to the question, 'Do you make a rock sound or a folk sound?' 'I make a TERRIBLE sound.' The laughter from Rafelson and Schneider is loud and genuine, and no wonder; that's *funny*! If proof were needed, this shows it – he's a natural. He also says, with commendable honesty that reflects forward onto the mix of the 'authentic' and the 'role-playing' that would become so beautifully confused by the project's success, 'They made me grow my hair over my ears and all this schtick, I'm really a clean cut kid.' He's an actor, and he's willing to take on the role. Only this time, the mask was going to stick. But back then, who knew where this was going? It was all terra incognita. That's one of the key reasons why The Monkees are so special.

In the show, from the off, Jones played the part of the pinup – in the pilot, 'Here Come The Monkees', it is him that the businessman's daughter falls for. Davy, somewhat uncomfortably, wrestles with a hollow-bodied Gretsch in the live sequences, as they blam through the then-unissued band version of 'I Wanna Be Free' and later 'Let's Dance On'. An early version of the gentle acoustic arrangement of the former, soon to become familiar to millions, appears in contrast, mid-episode, accompanying shots of Davy looking soulful by the surf. At this stage, The Monkees were no more a real group than Moe Hill & The Mountains. The difference being that where the Boyce & Hart song in *The Farmer's Daughter* had been a light-hearted (if undeniably charming) thing, the songs they pitched in for this pilot were 'real' songs that in any other context would have passed for the contemporary pop of the time. That's because the songs actually were the real thing: as Bobby Hart told me, 'As far as we were concerned, we were cutting an album.' This is the point missed then and, amazingly, still by the band's detractors – Boyce & Hart provided the alchemy between the Brill Building model and the new era of self-expression, and having someone as naturally gifted as Davy Jones helped substantially in the doing of it.

This extended to the way he accommodated and extended his character, the role of 'Monkee Davy' as opposed to David Jones of Openshaw and Broadway. A couple of years later, his friend and co-writer Steve Pitts would describe him in a magazine article entitled 'Davy Jones: An Actor Who Never Acts', as someone for whom all representations are authentic, even if they are not his own.

> Davy was perhaps speaking for all the Monkees when he said, 'I was Davy Jones long before I was a Monkee, and I'm still the same Davy Jones. Even as the Dodger in *Oliver!*, I was really just being myself. I was always a mischief maker in school so playing the Dodger seemed quite natural. I felt comfortable in the part because in many ways my background was similar to the Dodger's.'
>
> Remember this statement of Davy's next time you watch the show or hear a Monkee song on the radio. Davy, Micky, and Mike are strong personalities: they are real people who refuse to be anything but themselves.[5]

Pitts puts his finger on a key element of Jones's gift and – as he suggests – perhaps even one of the secrets of The Monkees' success overall. In this sense, Davy provided the key part of the matrix that allowed the group to stay together, and in doing so created the space in which they could develop beyond their original remit and become even better than the real thing, the actors who never act.

MICKY DOLENZ

If any of the group embodied the mix of media and cultural practice required from the four Monkees, alongside the contradictory impulses that made the group so special, it was George Michael Dolenz. When the show was cast, Dolenz was already a showbiz veteran, having had great success as a child star of the TV show *Circus Boy*, which ran for 49 episodes in 1956–58. Pretty much the same number of episodes and screen life as *The Monkees*, in fact. In *Circus Boy*, billed as Mickey Braddock, he was cast as a golden-haired boy living every child's dream of working in a circus. Good practice for the world of pop, some might say. But as Dolenz has said many times, he was also protected from Hollywood, despite his parents, Texan beauty Janelle Johnson and Slovenian émigré George Dolenz, both being working actors. Born on March 3 1945 in Los Angeles but by no means a Hollywood brat, he lived out in the countryside, where he learned to love the landscape, and – like his lifelong comrade Davy Jones – learned to ride horses. He was also a musician, having swiftly ditched the 50s pomade for a Beatle front-comb style and fronted a raucous bar band called The Missing Links – a serendipitous name if there ever was one, and a happily accidental connection acknowledged in the series of *Missing Links* albums issued by Rhino in the late 80s and early 90s, which really got the whole Monkee reissue machine off the ground.

Micky's *Circus Boy* character, Corky, was an ingénue, a child sadly freed from parental control after his parents, The Flying Falcons, perished in a trapeze accident. As a consequence, he was informally adopted by the circus clown Joey, played by Noah Beery Jr., and lifted gently into showbusiness, on the back of his pal Bimbo the baby elephant, into the limelight of a travelling circus in the 1890s – which may sound positively Dickensian to us reading today, but in 1956 was within living memory of the grandparents of the kids with whom they will have watched the show. In all this it shares a similarity with the key detail of the Monkee setup: Dolenz and Tork have both spoken of the significance of the absence of an authority figure in the series, and how there was no one to say you can or you can't, or to circumscribe adventure or indeed save them from its consequences. The manager briefly seen in the pilot was quickly dropped because – parochially – it connected the show backwards to programmes like *The Farmer's Daughter* and *Gilligan's Island*, where young people always behaved and lived within the confines of the nuclear family. Perhaps more significantly, as much by accident as design, the absence of such a structure, and the replacement of it by a new one – the band, like the circus 'family' of *Circus Boy* – was introducing itinerant, marginal social structures into mainstream entertainment and, thereby, into the minds of the people watching as a possible future for themselves. So *The Monkees* would be Micky's second go at playing out a young person's fantasy of a kind of freedom.

After *Circus Boy* finished, Micky went back to school and college and combined a period of mild delinquency with learning his musical chops in bands like Micky & The One-Nighters, aka The Missing Links. It's notable that Dolenz's screen test for *The Monkees* was the only one to feature other people, and indeed two guitars and a harmonica. He seems to have slightly misunderstood the nature of the event, which took place in a different place to the other three: he didn't answer the *Variety* ad but was invited to a private audition.

In the show, his character was pitched midway between Peter's obligation to be 'the dummy' in the cast ('Mr Schneider' excepted, of course) and Mike's group leader, wise-guy persona – Davy was always the unchallenged pinup. Micky's character took everything as it came – not unlike the real young man, but not wholly him either. Dolenz has speculated about what difference it might have made to their futures had the four been given screen names, like any 'regular' TV show, such as *Bonanza*, *Gilligan's Island*, or indeed *Circus Boy* and *The Farmer's Daughter*. One consequence may have been a shift in the dynamics between audience and act. Using their real names made these conventional connections far more complex – it's Micky, but it's not *really* Micky – but the spirit of the age forbade it. *A Hard Day's Night* showed us John, Paul, George, and Ringo being themselves, or versions of themselves, so who wanted playacting anymore? Lester's Law demanded the real made manifestly fab. Yet this was difficult for them, too, or for George Harrison at least:

> The Beatles exist apart from my Self. Beatle George is like a shirt that I once wore on occasion and until the end of my life people may see that shirt and mistake it for me.[6]

Micky, Davy, Peter, and Mike's shirts were eight-button and similarly enduring. So real names were chosen, and were perhaps even essential; once this decision had been made, there was no turning back for the four. Regardless of the varying disputes and turbulent years that lay ahead of them, they *were* The Monkees, now and in perpetuity. Look, they're there on the back cover of the first album, with their heights, birthdays, place of birth, everything! Marked and ID'd as if by their passports.

When recalling the difficulties he encountered finding acting work after the dissolution of The Monkees in 1970, Dolenz reflected on this:

> I started to regret having used my real name on the show instead

> of a character name. To this day I wonder if it had made any difference to the success of the show; I know it certainly would have made a difference to my credibility as an actor.[7]

Indeed, the show as originally drafted did give the characters different names ('Biff', 'Jerry', 'T.J.', and 'Suds'), just to identify them before the show was cast. As soon as it was cast, these 'stand-in' names were replaced by the young men's own real names, but the characteristics of each remained in place as scripted. *The Monkees* is an unusual hybrid in this, as in much else, and it's possible that in this simple detail lies a key to the whole Monkee phenomenon.

Micky was certainly the best and most intuitive actor of the four. His understanding of the visual dimension of performance and, specifically, of physical comedy served him well. He took to the multiple environments of the character, adapting as gangster, child, cowboy, acid freak – Hollywood archetypes, yes, but given a gloss for the Summer of Love. The character rarely had the love action – that was always Davy, starry-eyed and loving – but he often drove the plot, collared it, and took it for his own in a way the others did not. Look at how he both sticks to the script and improvises in the unicycle scene in the middle of 'The Spy Who Came In From The Cool', or the way he leads them out of their 'Fairy Tale' with a goofball improv on their own 'Theme', long before the same blameless little tune was brutally deconstructed as part of *Head*. By that stage, of course, they were *out there*, and the series had changed tremendously, acquiring the quality of their wilder extrapolations – as the very quality they had been employed for in the first place became the uncontrollable energy at the centre of the show that would eventually destroy it.

PETER TORK

Micky Dolenz had a tough acting job to do in learning the drums – going from 'pretending' to actually playing them – but in another way the job Peter Tork had was just as tricky. How does a smart, sensitive soul with a real concern for the state of the world around him play dumb? Well, as he said in his screen test, 'I'll do anything you want me to.' This would be music to a TV producer's ears, no doubt, but it also shows how keen he was on getting the gig. It's notable that the two musicians, Tork and Nesmith, are the 'highest', as in nervous excitement, for these tests, whereas the two seasoned actors are, while keen, aware that it's just another audition. The young Tork looks more startled than anything by this sudden looming up of good fortune and opportunity.

Although he would eventually blossom into the quintessential Laurel Canyon flower child, he was actually born a long way away from those idyllic groves. He entered the world on February 13 1942 in the nation's capital city at the exclusive and pioneering Doctor's Hospital, whose letterhead of the period gave its address as 1815 Eye Street NW, Washington 6, D.C., and which represented a great leap forward in hospital planning, practice, and architecture. As the name suggests, it was a place designed by doctors with a revolutionary aim in mind, to create a 'hotel for the sick'. When Peter Halsten Thorkelson was born there, the place had been up and running at full strength for only two years, and he arrived in one of the building's quartet of delivery suites.

It's somehow appropriate that a child who went on to participate in a new way of imagining America through progressive popular culture should arrive in such a forward-looking environment. The place of his birth also tells us something about his family – not everyone in D.C. had access to this facility, and it was the child's good fortune to be born to a comfortably off family. His father was an economics graduate from the prestigious private liberal arts college in Northfield, Minnesota, Carleton College. After graduating, he worked for a year in industry and entered the University of Wisconsin's graduate school in 1939. He worked in the Department of Agriculture and the Budget Bureau in Washington, D.C., from 1941 to 1943 (which is why his son was born at the Doctor's Hospital), and for the education department of the United Auto Workers in Detroit from 1943 to 1945. Thorkelson was drafted into the U.S. Army in 1945, during World War II, and then commissioned as a second lieutenant. He served in the military government in Berlin, Germany, from 1946–48, locating housing for many displaced people. The young boy went with his parents and saw the ruins of Europe for himself. Returning to the US, he enrolled at his father's *alma mater*, Northfield College, but didn't find the scholarly life as fulfilling as he might have wished. In a 'hometown' radio interview with Scott Peterson for Northfield radio station KYMN in 2011, he recalled:

> I kind of misused the school and flunked out twice. I'm kind of academically inclined but not for college. I grew up in an academic family, my parents were both academics, but for some reason I'm constitutionally incapable of dealing with the rigours of college. I learn more by osmosis rather than actual studying. So what I got out of college was much more the auxiliary stuff, I played French horn in the college orchestra, I did some DJ'ing, the social side, of getting along with people in the dorm situation, all those things were much more important to me than the actual academic stuff. As I say I misused the school but I'm awfully glad I was there.

No doubt his view of his early days has changed as the years have piled up, but this paints a picture of a boy both sociable and lonely, who had been transplanted from the US to Germany and back again, never quite making a fit with his peer group until music provided the common language that gave him a sense of enthused purpose and direction, which had previously been lacking in his work and leisure. In some ways he came to things from the opposite end of the continuum to Davy – the latter was working class and lacked financial security but was secure and successful, with a real sense of identity and belonging, and indeed embodied that feeling so well that most of his early roles called on him to represent those values, where Peter was from a comfortable background but felt insecurity keenly and struggled to find an outlet and an expression, a place where he could truly flourish and grow as a person.

Music was that space, the place where the tedious piano and French horn lessons he had dutifully completed suddenly paid off, expressed through the five-string banjo he clutched in his hand as he arrived in Greenwich Village in 1963, playing in a folk duo with Bruce Farwell at the same time Davy Jones was illuminating Broadway as the Artful Dodger. In a vintage piece published under the name of Catherine McGuire Straus, Peter's beloved 'Grams', his maternal grandmother, recalled being alongside Peter's father, whom she calls Jack, when he first met his new born son at the Doctor's Hospital, and that he was born at 11pm on February 13, thereby just missing becoming what she calls a 'Valentine's baby'. She lovingly cites this as evidence of his being a 'go-go boy'.[8] Grams' role in mediating Peter's public image is instructive of her importance to the young boy but also to the construction of a wholesome and family-friendly image for the group, the more effectively to market them to a young audience, all of whom loved their grandparents too in the way that children do.

Tork joined a folk group, Casey Anderson & The Realists, who would later issue a brace of 45s on ATCO, and also teamed up with Bruce Farwell as Tork & Farwell. The duo worked the Llewyn Davis coffeehouse scene, earning only from 'pass the hat' tips; they were occasionally joined by Carol Hunter and billed as Tork & Farwell + 1. In June 1964, Tork's search for connection led him into a passionate gesture – he married his 16-year-old girlfriend Jody Rabb in the highly cultured 'village' of Nyack, New York ('Art and Soul on The Hudson'). It was a union entered into sincerely but destined to last only until the autumn leaves fell – they separated three months later.

The high point, publically, of his stint in the Village was as band member behind Peter La Farge on the stage at Carnegie Hall as part of the first (and, according to Lance Wakely, last) New York City Folk Festival to be held in the hallowed hall. Like Tork he came from an intellectual family (La Farge's perhaps even outdoing the erudite Thorkelsons on that score) but he was less inclined to sunniness, and his music reflected that lugubrious view of existence and human nature. Musically it's a hard sell nowadays, but nevertheless La Farge was a major figure in the scene, straddling the old and the then-new waves, working with a very young Bob Dylan ('As Long As The Grass Shall Grow') and having his song 'The Ballad Of Ira Hayes' recorded by Johnny Cash. La Farge was older than the new wave of folkies, and playing with him was a considerable feather in the young Tork's cap. In a way this topped out his NYC time – the ever-decreasing circles of the basket circuit must have started to feel like a trap rather than a home, and 'something' made him feel the pull of the West Coast. Wakely recalled a chat and filled in some of the blanks for the young reader:

> In mid-July I started working with [Village stalwart and early Elektra signee] Bob Gibson, and I was on the road all the time. I moved out of the apartment. Shortly after I left, Peter gave up the apartment, because he couldn't afford the $90 a month rent. One night we were sitting in the Kettle Of Fish talking, and Pete was really down. He told me he thought California was the only answer. 'I mean, Lance, like I am never going to get anywhere in the Village. I hear it's really starting to swing out there. I guess I gotta hitchhike out there and try my luck.'[9]

In some ways, Tork is the Monkee who left least of a trail before the band – no formal showbiz CV, no dynamic arrival on a scene, no singles on regional labels – just growing up and working his way toward musicianship and that big moment. It was a friendship with a young songwriter called Stephen Stills, who had come to New York at the same time as Peter, that provided some business background stories to his arrival on the nation's screens and record decks. Not only did they frequent the same scene, the physical resemblance between the two was strong enough for mutual acquaintances to remark upon it, and eventually they met and became friends. Stills came from a military family and spent most of his youth being hauled around army hotspots. This kind of statelessness found something of an echo in Tork's younger days, too – he was never too long in one place.

Stills had his sleeve tugged for a comment in the high summer of Monkeemania:

> I first saw Peter Tork in Greenwich Village at a coffee house called the Four Winds, which stands on West Third Street …

> Peter played guitar and banjo and sang songs of social import, big, heavy ballads, Phil Ochs tunes and, occasionally, a show tune.[10]

This seems a likely mix. Songs of social import (a category which would readily accommodate anything from the Phil Ochs songbook) have always held a draw for Peter, who believes in the redemptive power of music, and while 'big heavy ballads' are a less obvious fit, buried among his folk tunes and band try-outs in the Monkee archive are a bunch of demos of 'Who Will Buy?' from *Oliver!*. Similarly, he would try out versions of the old-time jazz tune 'I Wish I Could Shimmy Like My Sister Kate' in his folk set, and performed it during The Monkees' debut show in Honolulu in December '66.

Aside from being Tork's entree to the coffee scene, Stills's place in Monkee lore is that he put himself forward for the interviews and screen tests for the new show in September 1965. According to who you read, he was turned down because of his thinning hair and bad teeth, or because he was contractually obliged elsewhere; whichever, the producers weren't interested in paying out to fix either situation, so they passed. Stills recommended his friend Peter Tork, as he later told Harold Bronson:

> I said, 'Listen, I know another guy that's a lot like me and he's probably a little brighter, and he might be a little bit quicker and funnier.' That's when I suggested Peter Tork.[11]

Music, girls, and sunshine wasn't such a bad life for a young man but, by means not unlike the claw that hauls out the aliens in *Toy Story*, he was about to be plucked from the pot-washing and the scraping a living and propelled into a dream. Peter's audition is with Micky's in the 'less-seen' half of the draw – it's Davy and Michael's that are the best known. Tork's screen test is the hardest to watch in a way as we see how much the young man wants the gig, quite unlike the showbiz-savvy 'just another audition' manner of Jones and Dolenz and the wise-beyond-his-years Nesmith, answering back and besting the hipster producers. Peter isn't afraid to show that he wants it and that he is willing, as he says, to 'do anything'. He is also the only one to bring a musical instrument with him. Dolenz is interviewed somewhere else with some buddies, and cradles a guitar, but Peter holds onto his for dear life and uses it – and the occasional musical phrase – to communicate and to emphasise. He's not messing about – this is his chance and he's going to take it. Wouldn't you?

There was a double set of hoops from them to jump through – first being chosen via the screen tests and then, once these were complete, via the audience ratings of the pilot episode, which took place in November 1965. So even though the quartet were 'Monkees' from September, that particular bloom may have been destined to remain unflourished had the audiences, and the studio execs who looked to them for their cue, decided it wasn't to be. In the first viewing, a dangerously low number of 600 was scored, mainly – according to Jackie Cooper, chief of funding at of Screen Gems, because the material was so unlike the standard US programming of the day: 'They didn't do anything. They had never seen anything like it before, and didn't know whether they liked it or not.'

This tells us a lot about how the show broke the rules, or simply evaded them all together in delivering and embodying something new. So, even though they were The Monkees, they were still living the same life – they socialised, looked out for each other, but were still actively seeking employment – and couldn't have possibly anticipated what was to come and were still pretty much broke. Davy recalled that Peter was living at Mike and Phyllis Nesmith's house, staying in a small guest room: 'Michael was very kind to me at the outset. He put me up through the entire process of shooting the pilot. He and his wife had a wonderful little apartment just big enough for a guest on the day bed.'[12] The news that the series had been green-lit was not issued in an *X Factor/American Idol* manner, all staged suspense, but was instead somewhat dribbled out, with Jones claiming he was on the brink of splitting LA and had to be called back by Nesmith when he heard the news. Dolenz found out not in person or over the phone but courtesy of a small feature in Hollywood trade daily *Variety.* Tork will have found out via Nesmith – the group's de facto leader – too. Once he became a Monkee, his musical and public image stopped belonging to him. Unlike Jones and Dolenz, who were used to being convincing while being someone other than themselves, this was new territory for the young musician, described in 2014 by director Jim Frawley as 'a quiet, sensitive guy – and he still is'.[13]

MICHAEL NESMITH

When we're watching The Farmer's Daughter, *I'm gonna say, 'Do you know what's in that drawer?'* MICHAEL NESMITH EXPLORES THE SET DURING HIS SCREEN TEST FOR THE MONKEES

Walking into the set of *The Farmer's Daughter* like he'd just burst through the swing doors of a saloon, the young Michael Nesmith already seemed like he was just pausing awhile on the road to somewhere, something. The comfortably settled voices of Bert Schneider and Bob Rafelson behind our side of the camera start off, as they did, teasing and probing their specimen, but by the end of the clip – free for all to see online – Nesmith has effectively turned the tables, and is inviting the pair to question their own motives and assumptions. He is sufficiently aware of his situation to acknowledge, charmingly, that he is indeed the young hopeful here – 'I think I'm out of work … and I hope I get this job' – and, earlier, 'I was a failure'. That swooping between candour and cockiness shows him to be the real thing while not out of his depth. It's impressive. I play a little game with my students, showing them all four screen tests and ask them who their favourite is – Davy gets the *aah*s but Nesmith usually wins. And so it proved. Nesmith usually won. But let's backtrack.

Born in Houston on December 30 1942 to Bette (nee McMurray) and Warren Nesmith while his father was stationed in Hawaii, just a year after the attack on Pearl Harbour, Robert Michael Nesmith was named for his paternal grandfather but his mother, his sole carer while his father was at war, called him Michael. As a Christian Scientist, her beliefs opened up and closed down elements of his childhood, and frequent moves between homes, schools, and cities make any child adaptable and self-possessed. This book is about music, but we're not unaware that the music doesn't come from nowhere – Nesmith grew up in Texas in the

1940s and 50s, where country music in general and Hank Williams in particular was king, while blues and R&B blew from the bars.

His musical roots were in those bars and cars of Texas – remember in the 1966–67 shows his solo spot was not a Hank Williams tune but Willie Dixon via Bo Diddley – and these two strands, country and R&B, run together throughout his early work, sometimes in parallel, sometimes entwined. His musical epiphany came at a Hoyt Axton show while he was in the air force at Sheppard Air Force Base, located eight kilometres north of Wichita Falls in Texas. Nesmith watchers need not have the connection made here – that singing train whistle may have been located further south than we might have guessed. So, for example, the coltish canter of 'The Kind Of Girl I Could Love' marries these two elements, country-pop melodies, vocal inflections, and arrangement in a fruitful encounter with driving R&B rhythms.

After experiencing his generation's apotheosis of seeing The Beatles on *Ed Sullivan* in February 1964, Nesmith dropped out of San Antonio College and became engaged to his college girlfriend, the beautiful Phyllis Barbour, in April of that year. He had found the windows of possibility swung open by the music and he was in a hurry. While at the college he had begun to play regularly as part of a folk scene – like Peter Tork was doing up in the North West – and as this was a boom period in record labels and affordable recording, he dove in to make something happen. He recorded a bundle of originals himself and also placed a fistful of songs with the Trinity River Boys, a duo of his friends Michael Murphey (who later wrote 'What Am I Doin' Hangin' Round?' with Owen 'Boomer' Castleman) and John Kuehne, aka John London, who was his close friend for many years, as well as his 'body double' on *The Monkees*. Around this time they co-wrote the beautiful 'Don't Call On Me' from *Pisces, Aquarius, Capricorn & Jones Ltd.* (Kuehne also played bass on later Monkee recordings, which were effectively Nesmith solo demos, and in The First National Band.)

Like Tork, Nesmith plied his trade in what was going on at the time – and that was the folk revival. In common with his musical peer group he took the path of the folk revival, an open scene and, until

Dylan's commercial breakthrough, one satisfied to play to itself, with every college town having its own version of The Kingsmen. It was such a signifier for that generation that it was the only other musical style spoofed by the team responsible for the greatest rock picture ever made, *This Is Spinal Tap*, in a film called *A Mighty Wind*. Nesmith was both the right age and possessed of the determination to drive his ambition forward. So he was there among the gang at the hootenannies and parties and folk-club gatherings, but also striking out as a solo act, his name on the label, his songs in the grooves, rather than subsuming into the ensemble and performing 'Green Green' and the other stalwarts of the repertoire. After he met Kuehne he started to find a way forward with his own material, mixing his originals with Woody Guthrie- and Burl Ives-style folk standards and, once the guitar and double bass were hooked up, the heat and pace of this transition accelerated – the duo picking up their college's 'Headliner Of The Year' contest. Doing nicely, Michael and Phyllis married on June 27 1964 at the Father Sam Houston Chapel on New Braunfels Avenue in San Antonio.

They left the town that had been so important to them almost immediately, heading for California in an Austin-Healy Sprite to join Kuehne and mutual friend Charlie Rockett who were already in LA. Aside from a dispiriting return to Texas in October '64 for a misfiring tour of school halls, this was Nesmith relocated for keeps, not least because Phyllis was already expecting their first child. He started to work in the local music scene, notably as part of The Survivors, a baggy ensemble with a fluctuating personnel, in the folk-group way, including Michael Murphey and Owen Castleman. Another member, Nyles Brown, appeared as an extra in three episodes of the TV show ('Monkees Marooned', 'Monkees In Texas', and 'The Frodis Caper').

By this time, The Byrds were poised to leave their 'pre-flyte' days behind them – 'Mr Tambourine Man' was recorded on January 15 in New York – and the mercury was rising on folk-rock. Nesmith, as always, was keenly aware of what was coming and beefed up his sound with drums and recorded some sides as Mike, John & Bill, two of which emerged on the Omnibus label as 'How Can You Kiss Me' and 'Just A Little Love'.

They are impressive facsimiles of the Byrds sound, in musical shape and vocal style, the A-side with its 12-string ringing melancholia and McGuinn/Clark vocal echoes, the flip more Dylan-esque, complete with harmonica blasts – both are not at all bad. Nesmith later told Andrew Sandoval that he recalled being ripped off by the deal with Omnibus and being less than impressed by the sessions' producer, one Chance Halladay – 'Awful'[14] – but the surviving music is surprisingly assured, and no doubt the experience did the young songwriter several favours in the longer run.

The straitened nature of the circumstances he found himself in is demonstrated from a detail in Sandoval's calendar when he reports that Nesmith sold a song to Frankie Laine's publisher, Melo-Art Music, for $50. This is where Nesmith was when he heard the casting call for the proposed new TV series, the place he candidly described as the one occupied by 'a failure'. By his own standards, it seems – looking at the young man's life up to this point, it bears the shape of a series of successes against adversity and overcoming difficulties by dint of energy, skill, and the force of will – what Blake meant when he wrote, 'Energy is eternal delight.' It was in there, Nesmith knew it, and it was his responsibility to find a way to let it out. So when he burst through the door onto the set of *The Farmer's Daughter*, he plugged in.

Watch him in the clip, loping about, feet up on the table, cowboy boots with the dust of the street still all over them, harmonica bracket hanging loose around the neck, empty but fully symbolic – 'I am a musician, and have a mind of my own' – wool hat already on his head, checked shirt, denims torn around the backside … he was relaxed but full on, Dylan-esque one might say, simply being himself but a conspicuously heightened version of himself. You've done it probably in job interviews, or on dates, and so have I. The difference here is the camera and the rich possibilities of reward to be earned by doing the right thing at the right time. How to get around that little bend in the road? By simply being yourself in a situation that demands you be more than that – that's a real test of nerve and Nesmith had and has plenty of that, cast in steel.

Checking his 'reflection' in the stylised old-timey portrait on the wall, Nesmith must have felt he had walked into another world – a room he'd never been into which he had seen into many times on the small screen, so he knew where everything was. Nesmith made it when Rafeslon claimed that his 'strong and silent type' and his 'girl' were the same, and he replied, 'Well that's your hang-up man.' He'd turned the tables. This was the equivalent of Dolenz's crying 'Checkmate!' as he outdid the stylised goofing of Schneider and Rafelson with the coffee cups. Looking at the silents that preceded the famous screen test, he seems to be trying harder to cover the performative bases, pulling 'silent movie' moves and – as he was bidden – showing right and left profile. It's appropriate that these first rushes are silent – after all, they were casting for a look first, a sound second. The sound was negotiable, while the look circumscribed – within the variety inferred by the 'Ben Frank's types', of course, but a narrow range. The music was, at this stage, most definitely a secondary consideration.

A less well-known story is that Nesmith already had connections with Colgems, having recorded a single for the pre-Monkee imprint Colpix, a label given primarily (as the name suggests) to TV and film related releases – issuing hit singles by Paul Petersen and Shelley Fabares of *The Donna Reed Show*, a big hit for ABC and Screen Gems from 1958 to that key year of 1966. It also issued spoken word albums (including some by Woody Allen) and cartoon sound effects (Hanna-Barbera); in the eclecticism and range of its output, it was uncannily like Parlophone, EMI's outlying comedy label to which a certain Liverpudlian quartet were signed in 1962. His first Colpix single featured two tunes produced and co-written by no less a figure than Bob Krasnow, who also gave him the stage surname 'Blessing': 'Blessing is a pseudonym,' he tells Schneider and Rafelson in a direct and business-like tone during his screen test.

Entitled 'The New Recruit', the A-side is a bit of tinny folk-rock à la Barry McGuire, sung in a stagey manner and backed with the undistinguished instrumental 'A Journey With Michael Blessing'. It's not especially noteworthy in itself but was issued in the first week of September 1965, just days before the publication of the ads asking for spirited Ben Frank's types who are also 'folk & roll musicians–singers'. On the evidence we have, who, we may well ask, was better suited to that description than Michael Nesmith? Plenty of people maybe – but it was Nesmith's time. His second 45 for Colpix, issued in November 1965, was a cover of Buffy Sainte-Marie's 'Until It's Time For You To Go', which won him a November 11 TV appearance on *The Lloyd Thaxton Show*, a kind of *American Bandstand* on LA's KCOP station that was shown in syndication across the country. The footage still survives and can be viewed online.

Despite such exposure, the record did not provide a breakthrough, but it connected Nesmith to the wider audience through the medium of television – one which was to prove so central to his career and his creativity over the next 30 years or so. The single's B-side gave him a co-credit with Bob Krasnow on the admirably titled 'What Seems To Be The Problem Officer', which proves to be an outrageous Dylan take-off, right down to the faux-Woody Guthrie diction and wheezing harmonica blasts. The writing credit won't have made him any money, but it was grist to the mill, coming as it did in the lacuna between the auditions and the show being green lit. The Colpix 45s also made him a labelmate of David Jones. The stars were aligning.

A stray single, giving A-side status to 'Just A Little Love', the flip of 'How Can You Kiss Me', slipped out on the Edan label in December '65, by which time the waiting was almost over – although it didn't feel like it to the foursome. Michael made Peter welcome in his home over this period and carried on presenting and organising folk clubs in LA, getting the experience, making the contacts, digging deeper into his work. Come early February, the news was out – the show was go. The Monkees were coming!

CHAPTER TWO

MADE FOR TELEVISION? THE MONKEES AND THE ART OF TV

It was based on The Beatles' A Hard Day's Night *– four rock'n'roll musicians trying to make it – living together in a house on Malibu Beach – sea, sand, surfboards. Replace the Pierre Cardin suits with bathing costumes … the two-up, two-down terraced houses of Liverpool with a rambling, California beach house … well, maybe it was nothing like* A Hard Day's Night. *Four guys in matching suits, I'll give you that.* DAVY JONES[1]

Although this book is primarily about The Monkees as a musical entity, it's impossible to write about them without writing about television. As Davy observes above, nicely bursting the bubble of received opinion about the show, the root of *The Monkees* TV show lies back much further than the big bang of *A Hard Day's Night*, its commonly accepted catalyst.

BERT AND BOB

Berton 'Bert' Schneider was born on May 5 1933. Though born a New Yorker, he arrived into a family who would become Hollywood royalty. His father was Abraham (Abe) Schneider, who worked for the Cohn, Brandt & Cohn Film Sales company; that firm later became Columbia

Pictures and moved to California. Abe rose through the ranks and when founder Jack Cohn died in 1958 he was appointed his successor as company president. This was undoubtedly helpful to his sons, one of whom, Bert, had taken up a post in 1953 with Screen Gems, the company's arm for producing content for the new medium of television. He plugged on with this role, gaining experience and making contacts across the industry until, while working on a sitcom called *The Wackiest Ship In The Army* in 1965, he encountered what must have been a rare thing: a dynamic producer his own age.

Robert Rafelson was born on February 21 1933, also in New York. Like Schneider's, his family had strong connections with the early days of Hollywood and, more pertinently, in the marriage of music and the moving image: his uncle, Samuel Raphaelson, had written the screenplay of the first ever widely seen talking picture, Al Jolson's *The Jazz Singer* (1927). Rafelson had lived a wilder, freer life than the somewhat cosseted Schneider up to that point, serving in the army in Japan and travelling and gathering experience in a way that suggests a child of Kerouac (his accounts of dropping out of Dartmouth College at 15 to go riding in rodeos, work on an ocean liner, and gig with a jazz group in Mexico in the mid 50s have more than a touch of life *On The Road* about them).

When they collided, Schneider and Rafelson found kindred spirits and a useful pooling of talents and capacities. Rafelson encouraged Schneider to quit New York and come and set up a production company with him in Hollywood; and, in early 1965, that's what he did. They were fired up, like so many of their peers, by The Beatles, and in particular *A Hard Day's Night*, which could bring the Fab Four right to your town even if they actually were thousands of miles away. In fact, they were so fired up that they decided that with the first project for Raybert, their new company, they would try to translate that success and that kinetic energy to the size and shape of the form with which they were then most familiar – the weekly television show.

As is often the case when a new idea breaks through, it turns out that plenty of people had had a similar thought; sure enough, when *The Monkees* was in production, a claim came in that the idea had been effectively plagiarised from a proposed show called *Liverpool, USA*, which had been pitched to and declined by Screen Gems in late 1964. The two claimants were David Bordon of United Artists – whom, lest we forget, had already made and funded *A Hard Day's Night* earlier that same year – and David Yarnell of the venerable RKO, who would later helm such teen-targeting titles as *The Mini-Skirt Rebellion* and *Hit The Surf*. This case went under the radar aside from mentions in the trade papers like *Daily Variety*, but it eventually went to court; pre-broadcast injunctions were applied for and denied, and it all spun on well into 1967. Such wars of attrition are not uncommon over intellectual property, but in the world of pop, the moment is all – this summer's hot tamale may quite possibly be cold potatoes next spring – and, once cast, the more the four Monkees grew into themselves the further away from the original concept experience and success took them, reducing any traction the litigants may have had. Their claim may well have had some truth in it, but by taking on Raybert, Bordon and Yarnell were taking on a giant of Hollywood (Columbia and Screen Gems) – and, secondly … that's showbiz.

JIM FRAWLEY

James Frawley is the closest thing the series had to an in-house director, the Texan's work accounting for 28 of the 58 shows and straddling the two series, accommodating and helping to visualise and represent the changes. Before being recruited, he had been working not only in mainstream theatre in New York, including a role alongside Laurence Olivier and Anthony Quinn in a production of *Becket* at St James' Theatre, but also in improv companies, most successfully in a piece entitled *The Premise*, which Rafelson and Schneider saw and liked enough to approach Frawley to work with them on *The Monkees*. Frawley effectively schooled the quartet into behaving like an ensemble, like a cast, working differently but making distinct contributions to the common goal. He clearly found a workable common ground between theatrical improv and the requirements of a weekly TV show on a mainstream network. He would claim that the show was less improvisational than it seemed, and this is no doubt true – it had to fit a certain template – so whether we're watching 'Too Many Girls' or 'The Devil And Peter Tork', there is a script to be worked with, and the narrative has a lodestone which draws it toward the required dimensions. Yet Frawley's imprint is right across the series, not just in the episodes he directed but everywhere else, too, in the spirit as well as the matter of the enterprise, and this was rewarded when he was awarded an Emmy on June 4 1967, for Outstanding Directorial Achievement in Comedy for 'Royal Flush'.

THE MUSIC AND THE SHOW

For the first heady phase of the group's life – effectively the period from the show being green lit to its cancellation 30 months later – The Monkees were balancing a TV identity with a musical one. At first, the latter was designed to reinforce and support the former, but very quickly the music overtook the show in popularity and, ergo, earnings. Every Monkees album, 45, or piece of merchandise had an individual price tag and an individual owner; the TV show 'belonged' to everyone who watched it. The musical brand proved stronger than the visual one, in sales terms, but in truth neither could function as efficiently separately as they could together. This took everyone by surprise: *Monkees Monthly* reported that the band had sold 27 million discs by its launch issue in February '67; 16 million of those had been albums, 11 million 45s. This is in itself testament to the depth of quality in the musical side of the project – it hadn't been so long since albums were eight or nine tracks of filler padding out two hit singles. The need for speed in musical production to match the output work rate of the TV episodes ensured an abundance of material, but equally it ensured that little fell below the standards expected from the range of significant investors in the project; things were done fast, but not on the cheap.

I asked Bobby Hart how he viewed the role of music in the show; whether the music helped the show, or the show helped the music:

> Well, the power of television can't be denied. There were other shows; *The Partridge Family* made it work because they had a great lead singer, *The Brady Bunch* not so much. But I think both are true; we knew the power of television would help the sales of

records, but The Monkees were able to deliver really good music. These records were able to stand on their own because they had that platform, so instead of selling maybe half a million they ended up selling multi-million copies. The television show had been playing around the world continuously and it continues to do that, so there are a lot of audiences that came along that way, especially in '86 [during the first major revival of interest in the group], and in countries like Japan there have been several 'Monkee manias' over the years. One was spurred by a commercial that used 'Daydream Believer', and then all the records hit the charts again. Australia has been very supportive of The Monkees as well, and England the most, apart from the US. This shows that when you marry music with visuals it will always be shown somewhere because, you know, you gotta put *something* on the air; what do you got? It works because it's got the four guys, it's got the slapstick that goes across centuries; it's funny stuff, how can you not love it?

Who chose which song went where in each episode, I wondered?

The producers and the directors of the show. We just handed in songs, we wanted to make hit records, so we handed them in and they cut them in wherever they would work in the show. As far as we knew, we were just cutting an album, and that they would make it worth our while. I actually think that was the downfall of other music TV shows since they all tried to cut songs too literal to the scene or were writing music *for* the scene; we weren't doing that. We were trying to make a hit album.

The high quality of the music in the show was down to this determination that the songs should not be too literal, and that the same standards would apply as if they were cutting a 'sound-only' album. The music was embedded into the show by the opening and end titles – the 'Theme', just like a real TV show's – and, usually, two songs in between. Sometimes, as in 'The Spy Who Came In From The Cool', the band are seen performing to an audience – in that case, we hear Nesmith's 'The Kind Of Girl I Could Love' – and sometimes tracks would play over the 'romps', as in 'Royal Flush', where Davy and the boys wreak havoc at a Ball for the royal family of Harmonica to the strains of Goffin & King's 'Take A Giant Step'. There's no problem with the quality in either 'homegrown' or 'Kirshner'd' material there; the shows proved to be promotional material for the records, and it isn't surprising – the record can be taken home, cherished, played over and over again. The TV show, though delicious, was a once-weekly treat that could not yet be reviewed at leisure.

THE PILOT

While it was undoubtedly the combination of Schneider and Rafelson who hustled The Monkees into being, the original idea was conceived by two young screenwriters, Brooklyn-born Paul Mazursky and Larry Tucker from Philadelphia. In his memoir, Micky Dolenz called them 'co-creators of the show', while Jones noted that 'they had the show – which *they* wrote – which they had the original *concept* for yanked away from under them'.[2] They had been hired by Schneider and Rafelson after the show was 'sold' to Screen Gems via Raybert in April '65 and been commissioned to write the pilot, so while it's not the case that they had the idea and took it to Hollywood where it was bought and changed, à la 'I've Got A Little Song Here', they did make a key contribution to the early days. Things rapidly turned litigious, however, and the contextual notes in Jones's 1987 memoir observe that while Mazursky and Taylor did indeed write the first episode, there were other claims to the original idea:

> [Raybert] then assumed complete control. Mazursky and Tucker then retaliated by filing suit, claiming they were integral to the whole conception of the show. Schneider retorted by claiming he had been working on the idea himself since 1962. Eventually it was settled out of court and nobody but the parties concerned knows how much Mazursky and Tucker got. But they were never again seen in connection with The Monkees.[3]

They were absolutely instrumental in the show getting off the ground in the first instance and should be given due credit for their contribution, but we should also note that the end titles of every episode included the caption 'Developed by Paul Mazursky and Larry Tucker' (over shots of Davy in and out of a little 'fuzzy felt' hat), second in line only to 'Produced by Robert Rafelson and Bert Schneider'. It may not amount to a weekly cheque, but that seems like a decent credit, and one that must have helped their future prospects. The pair went on to great late-60s success together with the screenplays for *I Love You Alice B. Toklas* and *Bob & Carol & Ted & Alice*, and also they had hits separately – Mazursky with *Down & Out In Beverly Hills* (1984), and Tucker with 80s TV shows like *Stir Crazy*.

'Here Come The Monkees' is an exception to the rule in the catalogue of the shows, and not just because Mazursky and Tucker never wrote another episode. In this pilot – which possibly proved confusing for viewers when it was first broadcast as episode 10 of the series, a year after it was made, on November 14 1966 – the group are shown as having a manager. Rudy Gunther, played by Bing Russell, owns Rudy's Record Rack and is seen in this episode only – he tells the band of a gig at the Riverdale Boat Club and despatches them over there.

We can see how this would have gone had the manager stayed as part of the setup; gigs and booking would have cropped up more often and, most vitally, the show would have more closely resembled the sitcoms that had preceded it. Rudy was the parental authority figure, whose patience would be tried and tested by the scrapes the band got into, and who would be obliged to intervene and forgive and preach the lessons learned. Once that parental figure was eliminated from the equation the show was much more socially radical, and much more appealing to a younger audience, imagining a world of freedom beyond curfews and parental control. Peter reflected on this to Lise Falkenberg:

> It was the most radical aspect of the show, the no-parent figure, because it was a first. We were presumed to be teenagers, but teenagers on our own and that was radical. I mean, people weren't adult in TV-shows until after they had graduated from

> college and gotten married. And that didn't happen until 24 or 25 or something, and we were supposed to be 18 or something, so it was quite unusual.[4]

The symbol of their independence, especially as they 'were supposed to be 18 or something', was their house or 'pad', located at 1334 North Beechwood Drive in Malibu, California. The telegram delivered to the pad in *Head* bears this address, but it too changed between the pilot and the full series. The pad in this episode is a kind of precipitous construct hanging over the beach with an outdoor staircase that had to be climbed to get into the building; the beach, seen in so much of the first series at least, was Westward Beach on the west side of Point Dume in Malibu, just a few miles along from Neil Young's Zuma. The programme-makers were right to focus on the way the immediate environments in which they lived could add to and express the personality of the band and the programme as a whole, and the redesigned pad – courtesy of set designers at Columbia – has become iconic in its own right. It features a spiral staircase, the dynamic and comic potential of which was frequently exploited – think of the old-school 'cream pie in the face' gag, which is so familiar from the opening titles – alongside four separate bedrooms for the group – Davy and Peter downstairs and Micky and Michael up in series one, with everyone upstairs by series two, best seen in 'The Frodis Caper' – and a fascinating array of clutter, expressive of the good-natured disorder that reigned. What else? A jukebox, a dining table with four chairs; random objects like a totem pole, a typewriter, and a 'monkey chair'. In the slightly raised bay window area, the band's gear is permanently setup. Most famously, and most visibly, a stitched artwork reading 'Money Is The Root Of All Evil' also hangs on the wall. This phrase harmonised with the optimism of the 'young generation' – the promise that there might be a different future, one that was not a duplicate of their parents' past – but is also of course a joke played on the show by its creators. *The Monkees* was at first at least simply an update on an old TV formula – one already proven to monetise the energy, passions, and leisure time of young people. It became something else once it was made real, but that's where the show is rooted. The quote is actually Biblical in origin, coming from Paul's first Letter to Timothy (6:10), where he writes that 'the love of money is the root of all evil', rather than money itself.

In the post-pilot absence of a parental authority figure, that convention of the standardised US TV show was playfully subverted by the presence of a dummy who was known as Mr Schneider, after the show's producer Bert and, lest we forget, Bert's father and head of Columbia Studios, Abe Schneider. He wasn't one of Kraftwerk's anonymous 'showroom dummies' (although one of that band's original members was, amusingly, Florian Schneider, who also lent his name to the David Bowie track 'V-2 Schneider') but a kind of adult-size marionette or ventriloquist's doll who sat and silently observed, only offering advice when asked via a string-pull which permitted him to speak and even turn his head. He was voiced by series director James Frawley, and is usually shown slumped under the 'Money Is The Root Of All Evil' sign; occasionally he is sat at the table and sometimes drawn into the nonsense, dressed in orange clothes or held hostage, but never shown outside the pad, and AWOL from the 'pad' scenes of *Head*. Despite this, I think of Mr Schneider when Peter is reminding Micky that he is 'always the dummy' after the riotous conclusion to the boxing scene in *Head*. It's a play on common usage, of course – tailor's dummy, 'class dummy' – but also links in with that theme of plasticity, and of being an imperfect copy of the real thing, one that will only speak when spoken to or when something is required of them. That is clearly how the four Monkees felt they were being treated in the run up to the revolution of '67, and this was a key theme explored imaginatively in *Head*, and also – far more crudely – when carried over into *33 1/3 Revolutions Per Monkee*. By including the dummy they are cheerfully subverting expectation but also taking a knowing court-jester's shot at the authority figure. Surely every child at some point wishes they could do figuratively what The Monkees can do here literally and pull the parental strings when and only when they need to; that is, to be the one in charge.

The Monkees depended on so much more than the four young men; beyond them lay a huge ensemble caught in a famous team photograph. Factor in the car – a customised Pontiac GTO in blazing red – and the clothes, designed by master tailor Gene Ashman, alongside the pluck and the philosophy. These all mingled and marbled together to make the show turn into the revolutionary success it became. The show ran for two seasons and, in the brief gap in filming between them, they 'became a real group' through the recording sessions of February–April 1967, which produced *Headquarters*. So, by the time the second series began filming, the changes offscreen inevitably affected events onscreen. They looked different, acted different, and the show went off in a much more spontaneous direction, less dependent on scripts that could have been written for any four young men and more expressive of their own real personalities. So much so that The Monkees (TV show *and* group) became as legitimate a target for satire as any other media text – see the 'outro' of 'Fairy Tale', for example, with Micky leading them off the cheapo-cheapo cardboard set in a goofball version of the 'Theme'. This kind of thing – a meld of self-flagellation and a dance of freedom – was of course writ more viciously throughout *Head*, but it had its roots in their strike for autonomy, and that included setting themselves apart from their onscreen characters in a way that the decision to use their real names in the show had not allowed them to do.

At the outset, the shows were driven by good-natured if flimsy plotting; in fact, the plot was probably the least important part of all – it was the fizzing energy of the execution and the mix of fast cutting magical images and the first class musical content that really counted. There are 58 complete episodes, none of which substantially repeats the same plotting, but all are unmistakably the kind of stories that would happen in the world of *The Monkees*. The shows were written by a group of writers who one way and another had become attached to the Raybert operation – to repeat, the initial idea was Mazurksy and Taylor's, but they only wrote the first filmed pilot. In total, 25 people wrote for the show, all subject to the script editing of Neil Burstyn. There were also 15 directors, including Tork and Dolenz.

The show was brazen about its being a TV show, frequently breaking the fourth wall and probably the fifth and sixth too, should they exist. It routinely confronted the viewer with the unreality of what they were seeing – in a classic example, Micky is seen walking off the set and toward a door marked 'Writer's Room' in episode 14, 'Dance, Monkee, Dance': the camera cuts to four men of Southeast Asian extraction, sat at typewriters and dressed as Hollywood Chinese, accompanied by a man with a whip, as Micky asks them for something that would be fast and groovy enough for the show. In another episode, we see a room full of chimps (monkeys?) at typewriters, no doubt hard at work on the works of Shakespeare. So it wasn't only the band that found itself the target of the show's satirical intent. But what was that intent? These shows are brimful of ideas and flashes and moments, but apropos of what? Perhaps there is complex satire on the substance of popular culture, or perhaps just the pleasure of watching cityscapes pass from a fast moving train. One thing it certainly did was explore various established genres of movies and TV that were by the mid 60s so well established that they were ripe for satire. Not in a vicious or angry sense; the satirical tone of *The Monkees* has more in common with the insider humour of *This Is Spinal Tap*. These were styles and conventions widely known and recognised, and fun could be had using them and sending them up, rather in the way children do: 'Let's play cowboys!', 'Let's play space!', 'Let's play pirates!'

So many genres and styles are borrowed and variously employed across the 58 episodes. Often they just appear for a moment rather than providing the hook for a whole episode but are nonetheless integrated. Again, what *The Monkees* does is bring ideas and styles in from the edges of things and make them part of the ever-changing centre – 'There's no time to get restless: there's always something new' or 'Always changing inside, what does it become?' You can decide.

SHOWTIME #1: THE FIRST SERIES

The first series began with 'Royal Flush', a stall-setter in a number of ways, with Davy falling in love, the band uniting to defeat the bad and duplicitous adults. The girl actually is a princess, and Davy her knight in shining armour. It's a love story but one that would be easily understood by the young as coming straight from the fairy tales read to them in their earlier childhood. There again we see the satire that works only if your audience is already familiar with the form being used. So *The Monkees* is at one level TV that satirised itself from the off, casting the later more hard-hearted self-analyses into the same chain of events rather than as something unconnected with and in opposition to the early days.

Likewise, episode 2, 'Monkee See Monkee Die', is a story of a kind familiar to the target audience, being a cross between a kid's mystery story with a dash of Haunted House (and a sweet girl for Davy to fall for) with the staples of inheritance denied and adults trying to cheat the young out of what is rightfully theirs. 'Monkee vs Machine' proved something of a turning point for the series and gave it its first 'classic' scene. It has its roots in glorious word-game nonsense from variety and the music hall, and most obviously Abbot & Costello's 'Who's On First?' sketch, and I recall that the first time my sister and I saw Peter's scene we laughed so hard that our stomachs ached. In the *Hey Hey We're The Monkees* documentary, Peter makes reference to this scene as the first real evidence of his onscreen character being revealed as 'the dummy', and how he had mixed feelings about that:

> I apply for a job … or rather the Peter Tork character does … [*appealing to the camera*] there is some difference here … he applies for a job and is interviewed by a machine.

The scene begins as follows:

> **Computer**: Your name please.
> **Tork**: What?
> **Computer**: Thank you, last name What. And your first name, Mr What.
> **Tork**: It's not What!
> **Computer**: Not What. Mr Not What What.
> **Tork**: Wait a minute, that's not my name at all. My name is …

And so it goes on. The four Monkees had their roles and their characters; members of successful pop acts are sometimes assigned individual characteristics, usually by others, but it is often helpful to the 'brand value' of the group. George was 'the quiet one' in The Beatles, and the success of The Spice Girls was embedded when they were given nicknames by *Smash Hits* magazine – Baby, Sporty, Ginger, and so on. It adds to the palette of ways a band can be understood, discussed, and enjoyed but it's not always the truth. The Monkees, as in so many other ways, complicated this formula by fulfilling their roles as required by the script but also by being themselves – so in a single episode we might have Peter as 'dummy', Mike as parental figure or 'wise guy', Micky as 'the funny one', and Davy falling in love at first sight, suffixed by an interview in which the 'real' people talk candidly about the experience of playing live.

The plots in the first series map a range of kid or teen-friendly adventure and anxieties – adventures involving dating and money troubles, dastardly adults and wicked step-relations, fantasies of stardom and success. Episode 12, 'I've Got A Little Song Here', combined the latter two categories, with Nesmith being swindled by a phony music publisher. In some ways it's a very modern sounding story, perhaps surprising for the young viewers (who knew that singers and musicians got ripped off?) but it also has the ring of a Golden Age of Hollywood musical – the little guy triumphs over The Man. There's even an old-school vaudeville routine by Dolenz and Jones, just to reinforce what kind of story this is. They were not above delving into their own story for good value plotlines, with 'Find The Monkees' (episode 19) being also known as 'The Audition', and with good reason. A TV producer is looking to cast a band for his new pop TV series and, by an improbable series of coincidences, he hears and loves a tape of them playing 'Mary, Mary' – but has no way of identifying the band on the recording. So, in a neat twist, the search is on for The Monkees on the strength of the music – the reverse of the 'real' process, where the band was cast before a note had been heard.

By the far end of the first series, the group had indeed remade themselves, using the same basic formula but heading for the freedom that would see the second series veer off into a beautiful swirl of surrealism that would change the mainstream. A great example of this is episode 29,

'Monkees Get Out More Dirt', the deliberately vague and ambiguous title actually referring to the adventure being connected to a Laundromat and, more particularly, the beautiful girl who worked there. April Conquest, played by Julie Newmar, is adored by all four who vie for her attention and as an object of desire she is several leagues away from the chaste, sweet young things Davy was falling for in other episodes. Amazonian and naturally sexy, Newmar is a sight to behold in this episode, her beauty leaving each Monkee dazed and confused; to add to this, we learn that she loves cycling, chamber music, ballet, and – ah! – Pop Art. Newmar's luminous presence is evidence of how these later stories were able to accommodate more volatile emotions and elements. Davy also, unusually, quotes from someone else's song, namely Roger Miller's 1965 hit 'England Swings', when he observes over the phone to April, 'It's terribly true … England does swing like a pendulum do.' Symbolically, the 'romp' in this episode is to The Monkees' freedom song, 'The Girl I Knew Somewhere' (listed as '*A* Girl I Knew Somewhere' in the end titles), but this sequence also introduces the possibility of a situation in which the four would not only not support each other but actively try to out-do one another. An agony-column spoof follows in which the idea of falling out over a girl is mooted and discussed; it ends in the revelation that April is experiencing similar confusions over which one she likes the best, which the fans could sympathise with – who is your favourite Monkee? (Mimi Jefferson tries out all four in *Head* and is left unmoved overall: 'Even.') Here, April chooses Peter, kissing him full on the lips but – dashing the cup from those same lips once more – she is last seen going off on a date with another guy, Freddy Fox III, clearly modelled on Sonny Bono, with the 'III' maybe borrowed from Monkees casting agent Eddie Foy III. Adding insult into injury, she cries that she'd never met a singer before. This gives Davy the rare opportunity to quote T.S. Eliot: 'April is the cruellest month', the opening line of his modernist classic poem *The Wasteland*, and a punning usage by writers Gerard Gardner and Dee Caruso that deserves a little ripple of applause all to itself. Mike attempts to quote Shakespeare (from *Hamlet*, as it happens) before Micky cries, 'Please … no morals!' It's an interesting line, acknowledging they are 'in a story' but also that morals are the rules laid down by authority figures, and part of the point of *The Monkees* was to picture a young life free of such restraints. The four-way lonesome blues are dispelled by four single girls arriving and announcing they are the boys' new neighbours, and off they all go to fresh adventures, happiness restored just in time, but they fall into each other's arms with an ease that may just have troubled any watching parents. This episode is key in that it allows the head-spinning reality of adult sexuality into the world of the show, as opposed to the stars-in-the-eyes storybook kind of love Davy had routinely experienced thus far, and that such feelings could destabilise the internal harmony of the group. It's worth recalling that it was at almost precisely the same time as they were making this episode that they were asserting themselves into being as a real group, and the dose of realism among the romping fun of 'Monkees Get Out More Dirt' speaks to that parallel narrative. *And* it's got Julie Newmar in it.

Episode 23, 'Captain Crocodile', takes on their role as arbiters of TV and, specifically, agents of kid's entertainment; they are booked to appear on a children's TV show, *The Captain Crocodile Show*, and it emerges that said 'captain' is an embittered old man who hates the children. This isn't uncommon, sadly – a whole generation reeled in the UK when it was posthumously revealed that the much-loved stalwart of the BBC's *Crackerjack!*, Peter Glaze, despised children – but tallies with the motif of the dastardly adult that runs through the show's plots. He humiliates them onscreen by encouraging the kids to pelt them with 'custard pies' and on successive episodes of the show finds ways to thwart their efforts to actually sing for the children, even tricking them into performing 'Valleri' (in its original recording, unreleased for two decades) after the show had gone off the air. To cheer up the despondent Peter they spoof a whole host of TV styles, types, and specific shows, including *The Huntley-Brinkley Report*, which always preceded *The Monkees* on the air, and later, Dolenz as a Nielsen ratings analyst. This is a show all about the making of an alternate reality through television and the distance between what we see onscreen and what the reality is or might be: the kid's entertainer who is a malicious child-hater, the ease with which a Monkee can 'become' a weatherman, a six-year-old child, or a media analyst. It's funny and fun, but it is also a kind of covert whistleblowing job – don't believe in everything you see. This is a theme that would return in a much more overt manner in the very last episode of the show, 'Mijacogeo', aka 'The Frodis Caper'. There, the malign influence of TV as a form of mind control is made obvious, The Monkees cast as heroes defending us against such manipulation, whereas here they are simply seeking justice for themselves; it's no accident that, in a scene where Micky reads to the children to quell a riot (not a demonstration) directly after a 'romp' to the tune of 'Your Auntie Grizelda', he begins the tale, 'Once upon a time in the land of Kirshner, there was a handsome prince in love with a frog and three little pigs!' They were ripe for kicking back at the men who had 'made' them.

The season's final episode – and the one that scored highest out of all 32 on those Nielsen ratings – was 'Monkees On Tour'. Providing incontrovertible evidence of the project's success, it captures what happens on the day of a concert without intervention or direction – the boredom, the excitement, the radio studio takeovers, the humour, the irritation, the infamous tunnel of darkness leading to a brief period of blinding light onstage. It is all the better for being in a more 'vérité' handheld style, which immediately connotes documentary in particular and 'truth' in general. It is also shot in Kodacolor, unlike the more stagey, saturated colours of the series. In the time it has taken to make it through the series, they have gone from being the cast of a TV show to a real-life pop phenomenon, live on stage tonight! Something had happened which spun the whole project far, far beyond the control of those who instigated it, and even those who were actually living it. The brief 25 minutes of 'Monkees On Tour' shows the level to which the project had succeeded commercially as well as creatively, and how powerfully reality had supplanted fantasy – or was it the other way around?

The episode opens with a short, sincere-sounding 'thank you' from Jones in the pad, which is soon hijacked by the other three. Beyond this opener, 'Monkees On Tour' is a mix of on-the-road antics, horses, a swan, radio station stuff, and music, music, music, and is the best insight we have into what it was like to be at the centre of that storm. In an innovative and still-influential touch, the film features no voiceover, with the footage presented 'straight' (although obviously sifted through and edited to achieve a particular effect), with the only dialogue being unscripted 'real' conversations and four 'candid' personal voiceovers from each Monkee. It is purely documentary in nature, and as such makes the claim on truth that the form seeks. In the opening scenes, the group arrive at an airfield in their private jet, demonstrating the level of their success – a private plane! – and we see typical Rafelson quick-cutting across the multitude of bright, hopeful faces behind the very modest chicken-wire fencing, as they eagerly drink in the glimpses of their heroes. Peter looks cool in his Buffalo Springfield sheepskin; Micky wears a white knitted sweater that predates the 'Star Collector' outfit and the clothes they would wear in the live sequences of *Head*; Davy looks funky-smart in his wine-dark jacket. All three interact with the throng, Peter gentle and funny, Micky generous, Davy clambering up a fence to wave and shake a few hands. Mike isn't pictured. They pile in to a waiting limousine and speed away. They are no longer the faces of a TV show called *The Monkees* – they *are* The Monkees, in the John, Paul, George, and Ringo sense of it. As Davy said years later, 'The Monkees is like the mafia – once you're in, you can never get out.' The trap had already been sprung.

The show, recorded at the Phoenix Memorial Coliseum, was actually very early on in the story – their first ever show had been in Hawaii, far from the eyes of the pop and TV mainstream on December 3 1966, and this show on January 21 1967, was only their 12th gig as a live act. They were surging forward at – to borrow from the lexicon of *Star Trek* – warp speed, and there was no way back. That moment they make their entrance by bursting out of the huge Vox speakers into the blinding light in Phoenix, vivid spots and flashes of brilliant light in among the inky-blue of the evening, it's like the genie escaping from the bottle.

The show does not contain the whole set – which would run to over an hour, much longer than any Beatle set, ever – but opens with 'Last Train To Clarksville', as did every show in this year, alongside the soon-to-be dropped 'Take A Giant Step', while 'You Just May Be The One' is introduced by Peter as 'a song you would have heard a couple of Sundays ago', referring to its inclusion on an earlier episode of the TV show. A few moments of 'Sweet Young Thing' are seen and heard, and then Davy gets behind the kit, allowing Micky out front, for 'Mary, Mary'. The bit of business between him and Mike – culminating in Micky being awarded the wool hat – allows Peter to nip downstairs and change. We go with him, giving us that treasured backstage access but also an illustration of contrasts – quiet, empty corridors and dressing rooms. Micky announces him, the stage now deserted, and he piles back on, now changed into a white sweater, and dives, joyously happy, into his banjo number, 'Cripple Creek'. This old Appalachian tune is no doubt precisely the sort of tune he used to perform on the coffee house circuit. Here he doesn't need to pass the basket; they already paid. (How much of that sum Peter saw is another question.)

The 'solo' spots – which we see each of – are quite unusual in a conventional pop show most probably designed to reinforce and build up the group identity, rather than the separate talents of the involved individuals. These spots are a cue for short thoughtful 'interludes', with each Monkee reflecting on the scale and nature of their success. Even Davy has something to say about how different being on the road is to being in the studio or on the set, 'where everything is planned out, hour by hour, even minute by minute'. What is remarkable, in retrospect, is how like themselves the four young men are. They are nobody's puppets: Peter is hippie-reflective, Mike amusedly incredulous, Micky very mindful of needing to create something that will last, and Davy tasting the freedom that a rock band gives that life in the theatre doesn't. Then, back in Phoenix, it's the finale, in which a climactic 'Steppin' Stone' can be discerned above the roaring crowd. Once The Monkees are back in the car, there is genuine concern for the safety of the band and for that of the crowd as the vehicle is besieged, the roof and doors pounded upon and the windscreen wiper blades grabbed and pulled away. If you have seen *Head*, this 'real' encounter will seem strangely familiar.

Watching the live footage in the show is fascinating; it illustrates the uniqueness of each member but also that, against the odds, they were a band with logical internal functions. Each contributes to the group sound – this sounds like a truism, but is in some ways overlooked in reflections on the group. As Nesmith said on *The Hy Lit Show* nearly two years later, the 'real' Monkees sound was only ever really heard at their concerts. The drums could be plashy, the guitar atonal and rudimentary, the bass and very occasional keyboards toppy, the vocals wayward. But there is undeniably a great energy and verve to the playing, and what it lacks in finesse it more than makes up for in sheer power-trio drive – the energy from the audiences informs the music, taking it to a wilder place. The Monkees had to learn to be a band in public. As 'Monkees On Tour' shows, from the very beginning they stood or fell by their own efforts onstage, and they stood pretty good, putting no one on. They were already a real group, expecting to fly.

SHOWTIME #2: THE SECOND SERIES

By the time the second series dawned, that is precisely what they had done, and the 26 episodes that followed both created and mapped this brave new world. The series behaved like the post-*Headquarters* albums in that they were assertions of identity and, to some extent, creative control, but also interesting mixtures of the original elements and wilder, freer stuff. So although in the second series the music was treated differently, often placed as a standalone performance at the show's end, as well as or instead of the plot-related 'romps', the development of the musical content was commensurate with the growth of their visual identity through the episodes of the show. Furthermore, separating performance from plot was a way of illustrating that the show and the music, though complementary elements, were now also distinct.

It's not true to say that the second series is completely 'out there' and the first wholly 'square' as both runs have episodes that could have been swapped over – 'Monkees Get Out More Dirt' could be from season two, for example, and a yarn like 'Everywhere A Sheikh Sheikh' could sit comfortably midway through season one. What is beyond dispute, however, is that all the changes that the band were propelled through in less than a year would have made the second run different regardless of their relations with the studios and their music team. It's the use of music in the second series that marks out the differences – think of how the amazing solarised film of Micky singing 'Goin' Down' uncompromisingly opens 'The Wild Monkees', even before the initial scenes or title sequence. The show – and The Monkees – had become so popular and recognisable at this stage that they literally needed no introduction. Not only is the music front-loaded, but the job is given to one of the least 'Monkee-like' tracks of the original era; it's a bold statement of their stellar success but also evidence of their willingness to do interesting things with that success rather than stick to a winning formula, a policy which is always favoured by the culture industry.

The second series opens with a skit on America's views of her immediate neighbours, and also on the en-vogue 'spaghetti western' (something they had already done briefly in the opening sequence of 'Monkees In A Ghost Town' in series one), namely 'It's A Nice Place To Visit', aka 'Monkees In Mexico'. It also marks the debut of 'For Pete's Sake' as the end title music, but Monkee fans will have known the song from *Headquarters* by the time the episode was shown; the musical changes impact upon the show in a way that, here at least, does not destabilise it while showing that things are moving on. It's in the second season too that the mixed-up confusion over The Monkees' names in the title sequence arrives, evidence again that the four were by this point so well-known that they could play with the conventions of TV credits and have some creative fun with the fame of their faces. This episode showed their audience that, despite all the convulsions, they were still themselves, and indeed had actually become more of a coherent unit, so much so that their individual identities had part-disappeared into the group one – the point being made lightly but pertinently in the credits mix-up. It's got the dressing up and the silliness of the first run – look at the bullet belts and the extravagant moustaches, direct from Sergio Leone's prop store – but also has the sense that the four now function almost intuitively together, with the onscreen rapport reflecting the then-contemporary shared musical goals.

The climactic scene, where El Dolenzio takes on El Diablo, is both a brilliant kid's fantasy but also a bridge into a knowing satire on the conventions of the spaghetti western, with the fast-zooms, the tumbleweed, the beautiful girl looking fine and proud alone on a balcony, and the impassive cruelty on the bandit's faces being edited to the beats of the town's bell striking noon. The sequence brilliantly devolves into silliness as the chimes go on and on, cutting in the shot from the opening titles of the first series where Davy's head hits a 'Test Your Strength' bell, a donkey braying, and, on the last stroke, Micky emerging dressed all in white – the signifier of the 'good guy' in western movies. El Diablo, brilliantly played by Peter Whitney, is surely in part the prototype for the unhooked and dangerous Lord High and Low portrayed by Timothy Carey in *Head*, both characters sporting rough sheepskin jackets and coming on armed to the teeth. Behind the dialogue in the square between Dolenz and Whitney we hear some brilliant faux-Mariachi music. The 'hidden' music ofThe Monkees series was by Stu Phillips, and this is a nice bit of work, borrowing from strongly identifiable conventions of musical representation of the land 'south of the border' in film and TV, setting the tone at an ambient level, almost unheard but still very effective. Phillips made a substantial and underappreciated contribution to *The Monkees* with his mood music and short bursts of the theme-linking scenes. He also endorsed an easy listening album of Monkee tunes, credited to The Golden Gate Strings, while his skit songs in 'Monkees At The Movies', of which he was particularly proud, are a real treat, showing he understood both the potential and the limits of pop perfectly well.

Episode 52, 'The Devil And Peter Tork', was directed by Jim Frawley and written by serial contributors Gerald Gardner and Dee Caruso. The theme of the show is an ancient but pertinent one, especially for The Monkees. When Nesmith was told to 'look at your contract' by lawyer Herb Moelis in the Beverly Hills Hotel, he was being reminded that, professionally at least, he was 'owned' by Screen Gems. For years after the end of the original Monkee era there would be wrangling over the rights to the various logos and devices associated with the group – even the name itself. One of the defining myths of pop music is that of Robert Johnson, the itinerant blues musician who supposedly sold his soul to the devil at a crossroads in Mississippi in the early 1930s in exchange for his musical talent – and this relates to the impact that a musician can work on our emotions and responses. They can work a kind of magic on their listeners; it's a great power and could be used for good or ill. Is it 'Sympathy For the Devil', or is it 'American Pie'? Which way will it go? This is in itself part of the continuing debates around music censorship, seeking to control music's power – but the central idea is that something is traded in exchange for the ability to achieve mastery of an instrument and the power to move people through music, and the idea of selling one's soul to get an earthly power is a primal myth found in popular culture and also in classic literature, philosophy, and religious texts. The legends of Faust and Robert Johnson are the same story, and 'The Devil And Peter Tork' introduces these grand themes into a bit of primetime television. Long-time Monkee baddie Monte Landis finally gets to play the Satan figure, Mr Zero, who buys Peter's soul in exchange for a harp and the ability to play it. Like the Faust/Robert Johnson stories tell it, Peter's new talent is incorporated into the act and brings great commercial success – there's a splendid spoof news montage with screaming fans (from 'Monkees On Tour') and whirling newspaper headlines declaring 'Monkee Harp Is Happening'. Eventually, Mr Zero calls at the pad to collect on his side of the deal – Peter's soul. His bandmates refuse to let this go unchallenged and there follows the episode's chief musical production number, a very daring 'romp' set in Hell, to 'Salesman'. It is unusually lusty for a Monkee episode – perhaps even more obviously saucy than the harem scene in *Head.* The challenge is taken to a court scene in Hell, where previous soul-sellers are called to the stand by Mr Zero, among them Billy The Kid, Al Capone, and Attila The Hun. I always think of this scene while watching the *Night At The Museum* movies, another example of strange bedfellows working well together. Nesmith speaks for Peter and persuades him that he can in fact play the harp without the 'black magic' of Mr Zero to help him. He sets to and, wonderfully, begins to play 'I Wanna Be Free' without intervention of any kind; it looks authentic, but as Peter later recalled, 'I never did get to play the harp – all I did was imitate what I'd seen

Harpo do in the Marx Brothers movies. I knew how to fake the look … I promise it's all imitations of Harpo Marx.'[5]

Because he had paid attention to the art and craft of someone else, Tork 'knew how to fake the look'. That's the essence of performance right there – just as an actor might 'fake the look' of Hamlet or J.F.K. onstage or in a movie. That doesn't come quickly, by – for example – selling your soul. It takes much longer, much watching and learning. Peter's performance gets everyone teary-eyed, and one of the 'jury' of hoodlums asks him if he knows the old vaudeville hit 'Melancholy Baby', a song that is also asked for in 'Find The Monkees'. The episode closes back in the Rainbow Room with 'No Time', and is one of if not the most audacious in the entire run.

The idea of mind control dovetails so well into the final episode of the series, Dolenz's own directorial debut, that their juxtaposition cannot be accidental. However, where this episode wears its philosophical content lightly, blending it in seamlessly to a superior but standard Monkee episode, 'Mijacogeo' makes very different demands of and suggestions about its audience. Whereas in the first episode it was The Monkees who blew their minds, in the next it is our turn – the viewer is in the front line of the media wars.

By the time this episode aired, the series had already been cancelled – there would be no third run. The shows that went to air after the cancellation take on another feel in the light of this. 'Monkees In Paris' – where they finally say 'no' to the original TV formula, as they had done to that of the music a year or so earlier – was the last show broadcast before the news broke. So 'Mind Their Manor', 'Monkees Blow Their Minds', 'Some Like It Lukewarm', and 'The Frodis Caper' were the final foursome, and by the time they were broadcast, everyone knew they were. Thus it is entirely appropriate that much of what we get in these episodes deals with being outsiders and the consequences of striking out for freedom and, ultimately, the power of the media.

Much of what people say about *Head* I think you could also say about 'The Frodis Caper' – it's not easy on the eye (no pun intended), and it is more than a little fried. Directed by Dolenz, it's a fable about the responsibility of the consumers of the media to remain aware that what they are watching, hearing, or reading is not necessarily 'the truth'. It's crude – a blunt development of the 'hypnosis' model we see in 'Monkees Blow Their Minds' – but is nevertheless effective, especially within the limits of the available 25 minutes. What is also striking about the episode is that it *looks* very different to the typical Monkee show. Light, colour, set, clothes – all are changed. The opening shot of the show alarms me for a reason I've never quite been able to characterise – a kind of weak, dry-mouthed, and bleached out sunrise that cuts to shots of the Monkees bedroom, itself rarely seen. Strange radio static crackles, oddly lit and shaky close-ups of contraptions dance about, and a cockerel crows. Sounds familiar? That's because it is from The Beatles' 'Good Morning, Good Morning', track four on side two of *Sgt Pepper*. Dolenz recalled that Lennon and McCartney graciously gave him permission to use the tune in this episode, and it has remained a great favourite with him, one he recorded for his 2012 album *Remember*. It has a couple of other pleasing little connections to The Monkees – firstly, John Lennon based the title chant on a TV jingle for Kellogg's, the original sponsors of *The Monkees* TV show, and secondly, like 'Alternate Title', aka 'Randy Scouse Git', it references a BBC sitcom, in this case *Meet The Wife*, which ran from 1963–66 and was concurrent with the original era of Beatlemania.

Back in The Monkees' dormitory, a strange-looking turntable spins and we hear the title phrase from 'Good Morning, Good Morning' repeated three times, acting as an alarm clock, and Micky, Davy, and Mike dispose of their real alarm clocks, all of which say it is six o'clock. Davy and Micky are in pyjamas but Mike is already fully dressed, looking as if he had spent the night as a cat burglar, all in black with shades and extravagant sideburns in full effect. They look for Peter and after much theatrical seeking find him 'frozen' staring at a strange and crudely conceived 'eye' on the television set in their front room which, again, is same-but-different from the friendly place we have grown to know, with the spiral staircase having moved across the room somehow and Micky's bass drum ('that I thought I lost') buried under ragged clothes and clutter. Once they find Peter, initially mistaken by Davy as 'a funny statue sitting in the chair', Micky quickly deduces that 'it looks like that TV has put him in some kind of a trance!' On the DVD commentary, Dolenz notes that the symbol looks a lot like the CBS 'eye'. The 'evil eye' of the television that watches and hypnotises the audience does indeed bear a strong resemblance to the CBS 'walking eye' device, which was very familiar to American TV viewers but also music lovers worldwide via the orange CBS record labels of the 60s. Media manipulation is the show's main theme, but then so is a kind of hybrid of wild childlike imagination and stoner nonsense, all bathed in a strange weak light and bleached colour. Even the neighbour's homes they go into to discover everyone else is hypnotised too are weird, almost like those houses set up in the desert to test the effects of an atomic bomb – still, quiet, simply waiting. It's too weird to be funny – though there are funny moments, such as the Marx Brothers routine in the phone box and the slowly cruising telephone company van Dolenz identifies as 'The Heat!' – and Rip Taylor's villain is more *Chitty Chitty Bang Bang* Childcatcher than Oraculo.

In the end, a talking alien plant – The Frodis – is saved and sent back where it came from in its flying saucer à la *E.T.* by the efforts of all four Monkees once Peter has been awoken. The show is full of tiny little moments – the subliminal cut of Peter's end-title portrait, a freeze frame announced by a caption that says 'Freeze Frame', Bert Schneider on a stretcher – moments that are here and then are gone, in some ways making this more like a disturbing series of dreams than a coherent narrative for a TV show. Even the announcement of a 'Typical Monkee Romp' is misleading – perhaps deliberately so, given the theme of the show – as the strange procession through the streets of LA resembles no other romp across the two series. This is partly due to the way it is filmed – in a kind of slow-motion rather than the high-speed Dick Lester-isms on which the romps were originally predicated – but also due to the music, which is an early version of Bill Chadwick's antiwar closer for *The Birds, The Bees & The Monkees*, 'Zor And Zam'. Adding to this, thanks to the 'evil eye', Peter is catatonic throughout the episode, and here we see his black-clad fellow Monkees having to carry him through the streets. It's near funereal, and the contrast between this action and the familiarity of the LA palm trees and street scenes is unsettling. The fulcrum between 'good times' and 'bad trips' is very keenly balanced.

The final three minutes of the episode (and, as it turned out, the Monkee TV show as a whole) are given over to Tim Buckley's TV debut, and he sits on the bonnet of the car that Frank Zappa took apart in 'Monkees Blow Their Minds', now magically remade. The song he sings would eventually become his most famous, and its renown would go far beyond anything he knew in his lifetime. 'Song To The Siren' was first recorded in '68 but not released until his now-legendary 1970 album *Starsailor*, in a version quite unlike this one. It achieved much wider fame when it became a UK indie cult hit in 1984, recorded by This Mortal Coil. Dolenz filmed Buckley straight, only drifting into double-imaging now and then, or some smooth rolling close-ups. This guest policy – Charlie Smalls appeared sweetly discussing the idea of 'soul' in music with Davy, a sequence rather grubbily skitted in the next episode by Nesmith's stunt with his guest Frank Zappa – could have helped the show develop and probably taken its audience with it, rather than driving them away, which was the consequence of *Head* and *33 1/3*. By the time they'd had a rethink, the show was cancelled, they were a trio, and all the mainstream friendly appearances with Johnny Cash and old friend Glen Campbell, or on *Hollywood Squares*, weren't going to help.

So, in truth, the plot of 'The Frodis Caper' provided the end of the show in more ways than one; story is secondary to the continuous visual effects and the flow of images, which is partly what the episode, written by Dolenz and Jon Anderson with help from Dave Evans, is about. The year 1968 was a long time before the internet, and television was still by far the main source of and for information; as such, those who ran it could more firmly control and mediate how stories were told and what they were allowed to become. And, if one controls the message, one controls the meaning. It's not quite Marshall McLuhan, but it's not far off his idea of mass communication that 'the medium is the message'. We can find later echoes of the same idea in hard-hitting and consciously enlightened tracks like Gil Scott-Heron's 'The Revolution Will Not Be Televised' from the early 70s and Michael Franti's Disposable Heroes

Of Hiphoprisy cut 'Television, Drug Of The Nation' two decades later. Interesting company for The Monkees. So while this observation may seem more commonplace now, it was not in early '68, and especially not on primetime – an insider like Dolenz blowing the whistle on TV's power is a brilliant twist on his own success, and further evidence of how the difference between The Monkees and mainstream entertainment of the era was actually made manifest in their work: they had a different ambition for the opportunities with which their great success had presented them. Timothy Leary had picked up on this, writing in *The Politics Of Ecstasy* in 1968 that 'The Monkees went along with the system but they didn't buy it' in the way the show spoofed the entertainments, concerns, and prejudices of the parents of the young generation who loved the show, and in doing so opened the eyes and minds of the young to new possibilities:

> The Monkees use the new energies to sing the new songs and pass on the new message.
>
> The Monkees' television show, for example. Oh, you thought that was silly teen-age entertainment? Don't be fooled. While it lasted, it was a classic Sufi put-on. An early-Christian electronic satire. A mystic-magic show. A jolly Buddha laugh at hypocrisy.[6]

Leary's text reads archaically now, perhaps, but he was the first to see and advocate what The Monkees and *The Monkees* were actually doing – using the media to liberate the viewer from that self same form, a message made plain by the complex capers of 'Micagojeo'. Leary's ideas and Dolenz's goal for his work are like little fireflies of optimism and enlightenment that had somehow got in among the bright lights of showbiz and, for a while, troubled them enough to cause a stir. The TV series could not have had a more fitting closer.

CHAPTER THREE

MONKEES ON TOUR: THE *LIVENESS* OF THE MONKEES

I was standing at a place we were playing. We were backstage and it's like two minutes before we're supposed to go on. And this guy walks up to me, he's a reporter you know, like that anyway. I'm standing with my guitar over my back, he walks up to me and says, 'Is it true that you don't play your own instruments?' I said, 'Wait a minute! I'm fixin' to walk out there in front of 15,000 people, man. If I don't play my own instruments I'm in a lot of trouble!' MICHAEL NESMITH, JANUARY 1967

The birth of The Monkees as a live performing act is a more complex tale than one might think – one might figure, from the public narrative, that it wasn't until *Headquarters* that they really came into their own as a functioning musical unit. Well, not quite. It shouldn't be forgotten that the possibility of The Monkees creating their own music from the outset was not ruled out at first – once they were recruited and the series green lit, the four spent a goodly while rehearsing and trying out on their own.

In fact, for a band supposedly manufactured to mime along to the backing tracks produced by the cream of LA and New York's session musicians, playing live together was on the agenda almost from the moment the show was cast. Jones recalled how they used to have to steal moments away from the cameras on set in order to try and get some sense of how they'd function as a band:

> For three months we practised our music. When you don't know a thing about music it's a little hard to keep the beat. I had never even picked up an instrument, but Mike, Micky, and Peter were great on guitar. We just played for something to do, and Screen Gems rented the instruments for us. We decided someone would have to play the drums and Micky volunteered, though he couldn't really play them – he couldn't keep rhythm. Peter got to be the bass guitarist because Mike didn't want to play it.[1]

In Davy's description it really is like a play, with cast members learning to get to grips with a role, and the most ambitious ensuring they bag the role they want. In these circumstances it soon became apparent that 'casting' is one thing, and 'being' is another. What's more, the pressures of time were such that they would simply not be able to develop as a group, putting in the dedicated and exclusive hours it takes to build up a real group sound. Had they flown out of the blocks musically in spring '66, perhaps some kind of balance might have been achieved, but the four backgrounds were so different that a musical union proved elusive, and would have to wait a year, until they really did have something in common: being Monkees.

As with any other new band, the early results were mixed. But the truth is it's rare for a band to find their sound right out of the blocks, and if they do it's often the result of years of playing together away from recording studios – think of the early murmurs of R.E.M. – or that the sound they chance upon defines them and they find it difficult to develop beyond it – think of Gang Of Four and their *Entertainment!*. So the quartet had to find moments to play together and – imagine this happening to your first musical efforts – were scrutinised by TV studio executives, music publishers, and hit songwriters.

Unsurprisingly, despite the 'not good but not bad' sound they made (according to Nesmith), pressures of time and deadline led the investors in the show to fall back upon the swifter, safer option of calling in the Brill Building system – hit songs by proven hit songwriters. The difference here was that, as we will see, Boyce & Hart's songs were to some degree the signature sound of the early Monkees tunes – that is, something with obvious teen appeal and, please, extremely good pop songs, which sounded *now* but not like they'd been cut from the cloth to order by a musical tailor in a single morning's labour. So this compromise between song, time, and sound gave The Monkees a musical identity that involved but also overrode the difficulties of mixing four distinct musical identities together very quickly. Micky Dolenz is fond of drawing a comparison between the mixing of identities in the quartet to a chemical reaction that could easily get out of control, and he's not wrong – the songs of Boyce & Hart provided a common musical language all four could speak, and for the time being, the nuclear reaction was kept safe within the confines of the lab. Once the songs were provided for the four to play, the musical identity could grow.

The first public appearance the group made was, it may surprise the reader to learn, playing live. Not only that, but playing live on a train. A competition organised by a Los Angeles radio station, Boss Radio, provided the Monkee project's target audience with their first opportunity to see the foursome, and see them play live. First they met the members of the band on the beach at Del Mar, about 100 miles south of the city, on the way to San Diego. Del Mar had been renamed 'Clarkesville' for the day, with the approval of the town's mayor, who was understandably glad to grab some of the excitement and lustre for his patch. The band arrived by helicopters – no mistaking the 'specialness' or indeed the investment there – and mingled with the 400 or so winners on the beach, then all clambered aboard a train which carried everyone back north to LA. On the way, The Monkees gave their very first live show for their target audience. Some footage of this day survives, incredibly, and can be found on YouTube – originally in colour and with sound but preserved there in silent black-and-white, as if it were 1912, but it is unmistakably the swinging 60s in full flight, the blue touch paper clearly about to be lit for the next stage skyward. Indeed, the event took place the day before the TV show debuted on NBC on September 12 1966. NBC was then pursuing a younger audience as the baby-boomers reached adulthood and was weeding out longstanding shows in favour of smarter, quicker, and more contemporary programming. *The Monkees* fitted right in.

This was the first in the great dazzling succession of events at the time, and three months later, due to the demand caused by the success of the show and the records, they would make their 'real' concert stage debut in Hawaii on December 3 1966, but this curious, charming event did indeed incorporate their first live show – as ever with The Monkees, the music was at the centre of things, right there in the mix, but not the whole story.

We don't have a record of that first show, but we know some facts, and we have a great example of its probable highlights in 'Monkees On Tour'. The show was staged by David Winters, who also directed two episodes of the TV show, one from each series – 'A Coffin Too Frequent' and 'Monkees Blow Their Minds'. He also taught choreography to Teri Garr and Antonia Basilotta, aka Toni Basil, both future contributors to *Head*. The efforts tour designer Winters put into the staging – if not choreography in the girl-group or modern boy-band sense – were clearly paying dividends, and the innovative use of film clips and images to accompany the live performance was not only already in place but also proving itself very effective. An obvious mix for a band made for television, we might now observe, but pioneering stuff in late 1966, and the multimedia dimension of the live show – even the pops of the flashcubes – was a key part of its impact. (This continues up to the most recent Monkee shows in 2016, with Davy able to 'perform' via the screen for the likes of 'Daddy's Song' and 'Daydream Believer'; and, in another amazing twist, Nesmith was able to contribute 'Papa Gene's Blues' to the live set from home via Skype.) The indivisible connection between popular music and the moving image has always been central to the appeal and success of The Monkees and requires us to rethink our whole idea of what live performance is and can be. But the kids in Hawaii didn't care about that – they just wanted to tell the new band how much they loved them.

I asked Bobby Hart what he recalled from his experience of these early shows:

> Well, we were all surprised from the first tour. We went out for about six months or so and it was mind-blowing. We couldn't believe that you could turn an American group into something like The Beatles that fast, but of course with television it was instant. It was fast with The Beatles, too. The show came on in September and we went out on the first tour, I think it was January of '67. It was quick, and there was a hiatus too, since they'd just finished the shooting season so they put them out on the road. It was hard work for everyone, and the pandemonium didn't make it any easier: parking the limo, getting caught in crowds. The energy out there for these four guys was amazing, though, and even though it was the music that got them there I suppose they didn't want to hear the songs, just see their heroes.

You can definitely hear that love in the summer concert recordings. Did you do a little set for The Candy Store Prophets (Boyce & Hart's band) and then come on for the solo spots, I wondered? How did that work?

> We did little spots. They were well received, but people were just waiting for Davy to come out. The supports had 20 minutes. I don't think anybody was really interested. Nobody cared. They wanted to see Davy and Micky. Behind the scenes, I guess the real fans started to look at the labels to see who wrote the music, but I think even today people assume artists write their own songs. They don't even think about the background, who is playing, who is writing or whatever. There's no information that you can read on a download. In those days, with the labels and jackets, the print was big enough for you to see the names.

So, while he was right at the centre of the phenomenon in terms of involvement and being on the road with them, Hart also seemed to feel a distance between himself and the band who were making his songs, if not the writers, very famous indeed. The Candy Store Prophets were the first group to develop the template for these live shows that would last throughout the peak period of The Monkees' success, coming back on mid-set to provide backing for the solo spots. Thus even as The Monkees developed fast as a unit, their individuality was emphasised via the solo spots. As hinted at in 'Monkees On Tour', the four were quite different: Davy's show tunes ('Gonna Build A Mountain' or, occasionally, 'The Joker'); Micky's James Brown R&B shtick built into 'Mary, Mary' (a song that has had a strange and wonderful afterlife as the basis for innumerable hip-hop tracks) was supplemented by his take on Ray Charles's 'I Got A Woman'; Peter shone with his folk banjo playing (usually 'Cripple Creek' but sometimes 'East Virginia Blues' or 'I Wish I Could Shimmy Like My Sister Kate'); and Mike unfailingly delivered 'You Can't Judge A Book By Looking At The Cover', Wille Dixon via Bo Diddley, complete with maracas and stage moves.

So – show tunes, rock'n'roll, folk tunes, and R&B/soul numbers. Four types of American. An unlikely palette from which the teen sensations of 1967 should choose to draw, but that was The Monkees – or at least part of them. With some bands you can say they are more than the sum of their parts, but in The Monkees' case it's harder to tell – like much else in their story, courage and innovation provided the impetus, rather than settled acquaintances with a certain style, sound, or songbook. This template – band work, solo spots, multimedia presentation – was innovative in 1966 and '67, and remains the core of their shows to this day. Their gigs through the spring of '67, both before and after the 'great revolt', stuck close to this model. Then they came to England.

ENGLAND SWINGS

The Monkees were booked to play a run of shows at London's prestigious Empire Pool venue, part of the Wembley complex. Located right next to the legendary Wembley Stadium, it is now gone, with the modern Wembley Arena standing on its site. It was the biggest indoor venue in Britain at that time. The Monkees played five shows in three days there, over a school-age-audience-friendly weekend from Friday June 30 to Sunday July 2, with two shows a day on July 1 and 2. The venue held 10,000 people, and each show was sold right out. The gigs came just under a year after England's footballers had won the FIFA World Cup in the stadium next door, so this was a charmed time for them to arrive in the city. The world was indeed coming to Swinging London. *Sgt Pepper* was just about to be released, The Monkees had taken control of their own musical affairs, summer in the city … and there were the four dinner plates, each with the world generously dished up on them.

It wasn't just the gigs that made this a golden week. 'Alternate Title' was flying up the UK charts, the weather was wonderful; Princess Margaret even sent a telegram to their hotel from nearby Kensington Palace, asking if their fans could keep the noise down. *Monkees Monthly* gave its readers an in-depth review of the shows in its August '67 edition, also reminding us that their press conference on Thursday June 29 at Kensington's Royal Garden Hotel was, amazingly, their first ever:

> **Journalist**: When you prepare for a press conference like this do you anticipate the line of questioning or do you agree on a certain line the answers ought to take?
> **Dolenz**: We've never had a press conference like this. It's the first one ever. It's really neat too.
> **Journalist**: Did you do any preparation for it?
> **Jones**: We had breakfast this morning!
> **Dolenz**: We've been asked the same questions before but not in this kind of circumstance.[2]

That this was their 'first ever' encounter with the press is remarkable enough for a band of their popularity, but it also illustrates how tightly controlled contact had been between press and act up to this point. That's the traditional Hollywood model. The sense of freedom flowered further in this encounter, all of which was witty and good-natured, with even questions about Nesmith's supposedly 'difficult' personality handled humorously.

The magazine's lengthy review of the live show reveals it to be a great development of the show caught by 'Monkees On Tour', responsive to what works and what doesn't and sensitive to current affairs – for example, the slideshow accompanying 'I Wanna Be Free' included a picture of Mick Jagger, who had just been sentenced to three months on drugs charges. (On July 1, William Rees-Mogg published his famous editorial in the *Times*, asking, 'Who Breaks A Butterfly Upon A Wheel?') The show was a kind of white-hot nexus of popular culture. Another splendid little curio is that while Nesmith's 'Sunny Girlfriend' appeared in the set on Sunday the 2nd, it was sung by Dolenz from behind the kit. At Wembley, the role of The Candy Store Prophets as backing band for the solo spots was taken by Dusty Springfield's band Epifocal Phringe, who also traded under the less groovy name The Echoes and here backed Davy, Micky, and Mike on their solo numbers. Support also came from Scottish pop-soul singer Lulu, a real current star in the UK who would become very close to Davy over the next year or so. (She too is still touring as of 2016 and making some great music.)

Back in the high heat of Wembley '67, Jackie Richmond's description of the near-psychedelic climax to 'Steppin' Stone' is a treat in itself:

> They always close with 'Steppin' Stone' accompanied by another burst of colour slides – each one earning a separate cheer and scream. And this is where the stage really bursts into colour and visual excitement. Multi-coloured lights flicker and change. Davy on piano bass, Mike crouched by the amplifiers, producing wailing guitar sounds … the show ends with incredible excitement … they left an exhausted audience, memories of the most staggering pop performance ever. The boys had worked unstintingly for more than seventy minutes. They'd given their all to please their knocked-out fans. I'll never forget it. Never. Those Magnificent Monkees.[3]

When they arrived in London, scuffles at the airport recorded by Pathé News seem to exemplify the stories of over-enthusiastic fans and the group's wariness of them, but there is a curious little tale of their time in England that proves the opposite can be the case. On the morning of Independence Day, Tuesday July 4 1967, Micky was returning from a party in the early hours when, instead of dashing into the Royal Garden Hotel, he walked toward the fans who were camped out in front of it and in Hyde Park. In a 2012 TV documentary, fan Jan Swanton, who was there that day, told the story, alongside comments from Micky:

> **Swanton**: Micky came walking from the hotel and just walked up to us all and said, 'Hello, you're not going to chase me, I'm just going to walk and I'm going to sit on the bandstand.' He sat up there and he just started singing to us.
> **Dolenz**: I started singing Monkee songs and then I said, 'Well, you sing to me,' and all these hundreds of little girls started singing their school songs.
> **Swanton**: He divided us up into groups and got us singing 'Row Row Row Your Boat' and we were all singing that and I was sitting there thinking, 'This is what it's about, this is what life's about. This is what I wanna be about.'
> **Dolenz**: And so we all start singing to each other, we all start crying and the girls are crying and I'm crying and I'm singing and they're singing back and it becomes this ... [voice tries to go hippie-dippy, but he stops short of it] *beautiful*, why can't we all live together and be happy!
> **Swanton**: And then he just walked back to the hotel and it was the most perfect moment ever, it really was. For years afterwards we used to come up on the anniversary, put flowers on the bandstand, and sing 'Row Row Row Your Boat'.[4]

Those girls have never forgotten those few gentle minutes of kindness, connection, and glimpsed possibility. So whenever I see the riot scene in *Head*, I understand it as a narrative construct, but I also think about Hyde Park.

BACK IN THE USA

Once The Monkees were back in the US, they toured throughout the summer of '67, where they were backed by The Sundowners. A number of the shows were recorded for a projected live album, and these tapes were eventually recovered 30 years later and issued on a four-disc boxed set, *Summer 1967: The Complete US Recordings*, being shows at Mobile, Seattle, Portland, and Spokane. At the Spokane show, Dolenz can be heard 'calling Chip' – a semi-ironic call for help from their friend and producer. Semi-ironic, that is, because Chip Douglas was actually in the house, helping supervise the recordings:

> We recorded them live at these three concerts … some things came out good; some things didn't come out so good. The big appeal in a live album is in between the numbers: all the clowning around. The excitement with all the kids screaming is groovy but it's not that great sound-wise.[5]

Hank Cicalo, the other key tech figure behind *Headquarters*, was on the road too:

> We were trying to put together a live album. The problem was there was so much noise on stage and so much noise from the audience. I mean, the screaming started before they got on and just went on and on. So from a technical standpoint the recordings were barely usable. I didn't feel there was anything there performance-wise and there wasn't any new material either. So doing a live album, although we recorded it in a couple of places, was a bit weird. Even though we had a good truck and good equipment and everything else. I mean … boy it was horrendous onstage.[6]

Cicalo and Douglas are right about the 'technical standpoint' – the sound is rough – but in truth that only emphasises the remarkable nature of the event being documented – the roof is only just managing to stay on everything. It has an elemental quality to it which I find cherishable

– one wouldn't listen to it every day, but as a scholar of pop history I welcome the care taken with and commercial release of these recordings: certain rites of pop are observed in full effect here and are recognisable across the decades.

The Monkees didn't tour again until late '68, by which time they were almost through as a quartet; the shows in Japan and Australia were their last as a foursome until 1997. In late September 1968, the band undertook their first trip to Australia, arriving via a stopover in Fiji, and played 14 shows in 11 days (September 18–29), fitting in the main cities of the country's green southeast – Melbourne, Sydney, and Adelaide – as well as skipping up to the Gold Coast to play in Brisbane. They gigged on seven days out of the eleven, playing a matinee and an evening show at each venue. On their days off, *Monkees Monthly* reported, they explored various wildlife parks and game reserves, with Micky and Michael being joined by their wives, Samantha and Phyllis. The venues were similar in scale to the US arenas they were used to playing, with the 11,000-seater Sydney Stadium sold out for six shows. There was clearly no dropping off of enthusiasm among the Australian fans.

After that, they played six gigs in five days in Japan (October 3–8), three in Tokyo, one in Kyoto, and two in Osaka. That audio exists of the gig at the legendary Budokan in Tokyo on Friday October 4 (the third of three shows in two days at the venue) is a stroke of luck. The copy that circulates among collectors appears to be taken from a video of the concert screened on Japanese TV, footage that now seems lost or as yet unearthed; *Monkees Monthly* confirmed the following month that 'one of the concerts was televised for future showing'.

What is perhaps surprising, given the almost complete absence of live gigs between August '67 and this tour, is the great leap forward in stage proficiency. The garage-band disinhibition of the '67 gigs has been replaced by a harder, tighter sound even on the 'lighter' material – the complex harmonies of 'Cuddly Toy''s closing section make themselves heard very nicely, thank you, and 'Salesman' rocks away very chippily indeed. The real musical treat is saved until last – a half-speed, fully measured version of 'Steppin' Stone', in an arrangement I've not heard elsewhere – controlled, malign, Dolenz really relishing the spite in the lyrics, with the song kicking into a higher gear for the frenzied bridges. It's quite something, and the famed freak-out at the close really catches fire. And then it's over – in more ways than one. Despite this final number being among the strongest live performances we have from the original era, within two months of Tork bidding the crowd a respectful 'sayonara', he'd left the band.

THE SIGN OF THREE

Despite the manic reception in Australia and Japan, the brutal truth was that The Monkees' star was falling vertiginously fast back home; *Head* had failed at the box office, and its now highly prized soundtrack album had proved, after an initial flurry of sales to the still-devoted, a similarly hard sell at the record store. The TV special *33 1/3 Revolutions Per Monkee* was, a couple of musical numbers aside, a depressing dud, and a sorry way for Peter Tork to bow out. A rapidly released attempt to stabilise the ship by returning to some of their previously reliable territory, *Instant Replay*, surfaced in February '69 (and in the summer of that year for the UK) and met with a similar fate. The writing may already have been on the wall for the project, but their response was to undertake something that was in its own way as audacious as the '67 rebellion, or *Head* itself: with a tour booked for the Spring of 1969, they took to the road with a soul revue band, Sam & The Goodtimers, about which Micky Dolenz said, in an outtake for the 1997 documentary *Hey Hey We're The Monkees*, 'I'm telling you, that was the most bizarre thing we ever did.'

Sam & The Goodtimers were the real thing, having backed Ike & Tina Turner and spent years on the racially integrated LA R&B club scene, playing lengthy residences at the Soul'd Out club on Sunset Boulevard (which may well be where they were spotted by Nesmith and Dolenz) and later at Willy Roker's Showcase in the Baldwin Hills area of LA. Named for Sam Rhodes, the true leader of the group was revered sax player Clifford Solomon, and they were very highly regarded on the scene; no less a player than Fred Wesley was briefly a member – a period he recalls in his lucid and funny memoir *Hit Me, Fred.*

There are no listenable recordings of that tour, but we do have some evidence of the band's sound as tapes survive of the group's April 24 1969 appearance on ABC's *The Joey Bishop Show*. 'I'm A Believer' slow-burns like something on Stax, so much better than the awful take on the Jack Good TV special; 'Someday Man' sounds robustly like itself; and 'Listen To the Band''s country-funk suggests an early hint of where we got to with Little Feat or The Meters. It sounds pretty good, but the road led nowhere. Once Nesmith left in late '69, Micky and Davy reportedly made a few appearances halfway down fringe festival bills in 1970 – events which must have been a challenge to the pair's professionalism, and manifest evidence of how far their star had fallen, and how swiftly. It would be 1986 – 18 years since the last time they all stood on a stage together, at the Budokan Hall in Tokyo – before a full Monkee reunion took place.

CHAPTER FOUR

LISTEN TO THE BAND: THE MUSIC OF THE MONKEES

The Monkees may have begun life as a made-for-TV project, but as soon as the music began to flow, it quickly became a made-for-radio one; the tales Dolenz and Nesmith tell about turning points in the band's story being dependent on what was played on the radio are particular to them, but once the music was on vinyl and on the air, who could tell that this group was any more or less 'manufactured' than any other record on the playlist or the chart? Bob Mould, leader of noiseniks Hüsker Dü, wrote in his 2013 memoir that as a child The Monkees were as cool to him as any other group, including The Beatles, while acts from Yo La Tengo to The Go-Betweens peppered their early sets with Monkees covers, and in 2016 young bands like The Lemon Twigs and Foxygen cite The Monkees as a strong influence on their sound. So once the music is out there, it is simply heard and enjoyed and works like any other good music does – passing on the influence. The division in their work is fairly clear we might think – the first two albums were built around superior grade manufactured pop; the following half-dozen were self-directed, with diminishing returns commercially and – perhaps – artistically, with 1970's finale, *Changes*, a sorry afterthought to the whole trip, returning to the vocal-only model of the debut but with none of the original charm or energy. There is something in this received version of events but it doesn't tell the whole tale.

In truth the musical legacy extends far beyond oldies or nostalgia; musical innovation was rife throughout the catalogue both before and after the revolution of early '67 – for example, Nesmith's 'Different Drum', a song written before he was a Monkee and briefly bumbled through for comic effect in the episode 'Too Many Girls' propelled Linda Ronstadt into a glamorous solo career; and on the way he also arguably invented the hybrid form country-rock, which was turned into gold in the 70s by Ronstadt and her California cowboy comrades like The Eagles. Perhaps even more surprisingly his 'Mary, Mary' has had an influential afterlife as the sampled root of a host of hip-hop tracks, and his love for bossa nova – pleasingly on show in the birthday wishes he sent to Astrud Gilberto via Facebook in March 2016 – surfaces occasionally too. We also find the common ground of TV and film themes employed as a starting point for a new band learning to play together. Peter Tork's interest in mixing folk, blues, and jazz with pop and rock structures found its way in via his two tunes for *Head*, a series of 'lost songs' such as 'Lady's Baby', and not least through the extraordinary jazz and vocal showcase 'Goin' Down', developed by Peter from a riff in Mose Allison's 'Parchman Farm'. Aside from delivering outstanding vocals on tunes like that one, Micky Dolenz created an array of true, instinctive originals – 'Randy Scouse Git', 'Mommy And Daddy', 'Just A Game' – while Davy Jones forged his 'Broadway rock' style, best heard on tracks like 'Dream World', 'Changes', and the blistering 'You And I'. Meanwhile Rhino's exemplary managing of the tape archive has shed light on a wealth of near-forgotten material, introducing the music to a whole new generation.

For reasons of space, this section is necessarily representative in its selections. We begin with an investigation of the role of the Brill Building school of writing and the invaluable contribution made by Tommy Boyce and Bobby Hart. We move on to a more detailed look at their two 'full band' albums, *Headquarters* and *Pisces, Aquarius, Capricorn & Jones Ltd.*, then pick a number of key tracks from the latter phase of the original era. So if your favourite isn't here I apologise, but wherever you look in the Monkee songbook, there's something unexpected, with a story attached that tells us something about the group and their times. Got your jukebox money? Put the coin in the slot.

THE BRILL BUILDING

Walking through Downtown Manhattan, for anyone who is not, in the words of the song, a native New Yorker, is like walking through a culture's dreamscape or, at least, a kind of living, breathing cultural gazetteer. Look up there: Broadway. Down there: Fifth Avenue. Standing here: Times Square. The very first time I visited New York City, one freezing week between Christmas and New Year nearly 30 years ago, there were two places I especially wanted to visit on my first day. Right atop the crowded list of must-sees were the Radio City Music Hall on the Avenue of the Americas, just a few streets away from Times Square, and the Brill Building, the address of which I knew off by heart: 1619 Broadway, New York, NY 10019, United States of America. Having paid homage to London's 'Tin Pan Alley' on Denmark Street in London W1, it seemed a courtesy and an obligation to go and stand outside the Brill Building. Anyone who is interested in the history of pop music in the modern age owes something to this somewhat monumental Manhattan block.

It was named after the Brill Brothers, who opened a menswear store at street level in 1924 and, as a consequence of the Wall Street Crash of 1929, after the building's completion found they could not be so picky about their tenants for the upstairs offices, so it became home to music publishers such as Southern Music, Mills Music (no relation), and Famous. Come the early 60s – after Elvis, but before life got harder for the publishers with the rise of the singer-songwriter – there were over 150 publishers occupying the building. It was like the music business under one roof – writing rooms, rehearsal rooms, and demo studios co-existed with offices, agents, and accountants. Once you'd made your connections within the building, there were reps from record labels and radio stations that kept offices there too. So it was a way of running a business, almost like a kind of cottage industry that was also the centre of a huge and very lucrative industry, but chiefly it was a *sound*.

It's a sound you know when you hear it. What worked travelled from office to office, from song to song – innovations spread fast – so while it was a business environment, it was also a truly creative one. People like it – it's hard to resist – but they also feel guilty about it; the Brill Building is in some ways the mother lode of that most postmodern of cultural trinkets, the guilty pleasure. This is decently summed up by a book title like David Wild's *How I Learned To Stop Worrying And Love Neil Diamond.*

Regardless of this, it is impossible to knowingly hear the name, let alone stand outside the building, without the echoes of scores of three minute slices of superior pop cake baked within those walls racking up in the jukebox of one's mind. A1 on mine would be 'Be My Baby', Brill-written by Ellie Greenwich and Jeff Barry, alongside input from Phil Spector in early 1963; yours will be a different one. As with any neat mythology, further digging reveals inconsistencies – for example, much of the work was done in another building close by, at 1650 Broadway, but the sensibility and the aim was the same: Write hits! And then write some more. The Monkees story straddles both these eras and in some ways encapsulates the tensions and fractures of this moment of cultural change in the making and the marketing of popular music, dramatizing in its details this shifting landscape. Their direct link with the Brill culture stood about so high and answered to the name Donald Clark Kirshner.

'ONCE, IN THE LAND OF KIRSHNER …' (MICKY DOLENZ, IN EPISODE 23, 'CAPTAIN CROCODILE')

Donnie Kirshner was born in the Bronx on April 17 1934, and by the time he was 25 had established himself as a major young light in music publishing, chiefly through the success of Aldon Music, a company he formed with his friend and business partner Al Nevins. Nevins, born Albert Tepper, did not get to see his partner's subsequent success with The Monkees, passing away in January 1965 at the early age of 49. Aldon's roll call of writers really does read like a *Who Was Who* of the era; try these: Goffin & King, Mann & Weil, Paul Simon (yes! he was a Brill worker), Neil Diamond, Jerry Keller, Phil Spector, Neil Sedaka. Kirshner's methodology was to place writers with each other; he orchestrated some of the great songwriting partnerships of pop history, so everyone who loves pop should tip their hats to him for this alone. As Davy Jones, the Monkee most simpatico with Kirshner's methods, motives, and wider view of the 'entertainment' function of pop, recalled:

> He was the guy who put songs in TV shows and movies, he had the Carole Kings and the Neil Diamonds and Carole Bayer Sagers, the Neil Sedakas, the Nilssons, Barry Mann, Cynthia Weil, Leiber & Stoller, Sears & Roebuck, Neiman & Marcus ... he had them all under contract![1]

Jones's memory serves him well – The Monkees recorded material by every one of the writers here, although in a lovely bit of Mancunian deadpan he also dropped in the names of two department stores. It's funny but also pertinent – the Brill Building culture embodied by Kirshner was about selling.

From there, Kirshner ran labels such as Calendar Records, a name possibly borrowed from Neil Sedaka's beautiful little tune 'Calendar Girl', or perhaps the aim of having a hit on the chart every week of the year, and the hugely successful Dimension, started in 1962, which focussed on a girl-group sound that drew heavily on Goffin & King's output and scored big with Little Eva's recording of 'The Loco-Motion'. Even in the midst of this heated and competitive environment, King was not only a behind-the-scenes-writer; she also sang on her own hit, 'It Might As Well Rain Until September', which charted at the same time as 'The Loco-Motion' in summer 1962. Ads of the time trumpet, 'Nevins-Kirshner Debuts A New King And Her Name Is Carole On ... Dimension Records' and let the reader know that King is 'Top Writer, Top Arranger, And Now Top Artist With The Smash Summer Standard Of 1962'. This was right, but also canny – praising one of his writers was partly a way to spur on the others, as King recalls in her memoir:

> With each of us trying to write the follow-up to an artist's current hit, everyone's song sounded similar to everyone else's. But only

> one would be chosen. Inevitably the insecurity of the writers and the competitive atmosphere fostered by Donnie [Kirshner] spurred each team on to greater effort, which resulted in better songs. It wasn't only about writing a great song; it was about *winning*.[2]

Selling and winning: Kirshner was expert in both. Even when vanquished in the great Monkee revolt of 1967, examined later in this book, he adapted and survived. He revived Calendar Records, which boasted Eydie Gormé's late-60s singles alongside that Monkee nemesis The Archies, and the label saw further success in the 70s with prog-pop bunglers Kansas. Not having been turned against the marketing power of TV in cahoots with pop, he also ran a very successful live music franchise for The Monkees' TV parent, ABC TV, through the 70s. *Don Kirshner's Music Concert* drew the world's most successful acts onto the small screen between 1973 and 1982, starting with The Rolling Stones and ending with Van Halen.

It's important then to note that Kirshner was not some old-school duffer who was in the way; rather, he was a consummate music-industry professional who had a proven track record before and after The Monkees. He characterised himself as 'The Man With The Golden Ear', a justifiable boast in that he was connected with so many hits and so many great writers. Above all, he was a businessman – Dwight Witney of *TV Guide* pegged him as 'a rough-and-tumble musical pragmatist to the lapels of his Sy Devore suit'.[3] This self-assurance meant that he felt, with a great certainty rooted in the balance sheet of his companies, that he knew what made a hit record.

The Brill school delivered some extraordinary and enduring tunes for the group, such as a bundle provided by Goffin & King, whose contributions extended far beyond the changes of '67 right up to 1969's *Instant Replay*. On the debut album, their slice of bright optimism, 'Take A Giant Step', was given a contemporary Eastern/psychedelic frosting by a 'fire and skill' blend of Boyce & Hart's band The Candy Store Prophets and a number of LA studio sessioneers. 'Sometime In

The Morning', on the second album, is an exquisite and diaphanous piece, much loved by Micky Dolenz, who has returned to it several times in his post-Monkees recording career. Less well-known gems like 'I Don't Think You Know Me' and 'I Won't Be The Same Without Her' were caught in this early period too. Meanwhile, Kirshner had had his golden ear caught by Neil Diamond's smash hit 'Cherry Cherry' and wanted some of that flavour for his new project. Diamond was hot, his hit having reached number 6 on the *Billboard* Hot 100 in summer '66. These were the kind of credentials that Kirshner could not resist, and luckily for the young songwriter his breakthrough came at just the right moment to catch the attention of The Monkees' music supervisor, who was in want of sure-fire hits. With Micky's sublime pop-soul vocal on board, 'I'm A Believer' became a pocket Romeo and Juliet and sold a million in advance orders alone.

Kirshner's infamous liner note to *More Of The Monkees* is the most we have from him, at least from this era, on the subject of how the records came to be. He minimises Nesmith's contribution (two songs on each of the first two albums written, produced, and – with the exception of 'Mary, Mary' – sung by him) but does acknowledge two young men who could easily have been contenders for a berth in The Monkees themselves. Instead, their role was to provide the most readily recognisable early musical identity for the group: Tommy Boyce and Bobby Hart.

BOYCE & HART

Bobby Hart's splendid memoir, *Psychedelic Bubble Gum*, was published in 2015 and in it he writes about his childhood and youth in his hometown of Phoenix, Arizona, where he had been born on February 18 1939. His family were devoutly religious, and although he of course responded to this environment, it did not speak to him the way it did to his parents. Music, however, seemed to. A stint in an army reserve unit led to him being involved with the Armed Forces Radio Service, dreaming of Fats Domino tunes while cueing in John Philip Sousa songs. That placement was in San Francisco, which got the Arizona kid to California for the first time. As his book records, despite the to-ing and fro-ing that finding one's way forward demands, he never really left the Golden State again.

Sadly, we will not have the pleasure of reading his musical partner's reflections of life from the wisdom of his older years, but in his 1974 book *How To Write A Hit Song … And Sell It*, Tommy Boyce focussed on the 'how to' element of his title, leaving aside the details of his life that had brought him to the songwriters' table. This is appropriate, as the book is a self-help manual of sorts, but it is frustrating for anyone looking for clues about how and where his talents came from.

Boyce had a strong track record in advance of both his teaming up with Bobby Hart and their mutual link to The Monkees. A little younger than Hart, he was born in Charlottesville, Virginia, on September 29 1939, just as World War II was beginning in Europe. When he and Hart first met in 1959, however, he was resident in Los Angeles, still living with his parents, who had relocated to the city. Indeed, his father, Sid, was his greatest advocate, directly approaching music publishers and record companies advocating his son's music. It worked, because in late 1959 Boyce got his first break, placing a song with Fats Domino, 'Be My Guest', and he did so via the Brill Building method: by hustling. So, despite the apparent schism later on between Boyce & Hart's material for the group and the Brill material, they seem to flow from a common source – the idea that writing pop is a trade, a craft, and a business.

The chapter in Hart's book that discusses their New York period is entitled 'Finally, The Promised Land', which, given their poor material circumstances, is an ironic one, but it also illustrates that New York was still where it was at in the music business. However, things began to change within the American music industry in early 1964, following the arrival of The Beatles, and Boyce & Hart followed the scent once again, this time to Los Angeles, as the music industry began to gravitate to a West Coast offering a freer and more conducive environment, in almost every sense, to that familiar from New York. Hart:

> I was being represented by Lester Sill. He got Tommy first, then he got me. We moved back to LA. It was an East Coast operation

> that had been bought by a West Coast motion picture company, Columbia Pictures. So they opened up a West Coast office and they wanted to send us. The West Coast chief of operations was Lester Sill.

Kirshner, meanwhile, stayed in New York and 'rarely came west':

> Lester had a track record of his work from the past decade, so [Kirshner] called him over. He wasn't second-in-command or anything. We were getting calls from people who wanted to put us on TV and publish the music, lots of calls. And Lester didn't have a lot of staff on the West Coast. In the East, there was a big staff of writers, but over here there were very few people, but we were getting those offers anyway.

This was particularly helpful in the wrangles that went on before Boyce & Hart finally landed the full Monkee commission – Bert Schneider and Lester Sill had made very positive noises about their chances and level of involvement, but many, many Screen Gems writers had pitched songs to the project, and Don Kirshner was not wholly sold on their stewardship of the new show's musical direction, as Hart writes:

> 'Sure you guys have had hits as writers,' he told us as we met with him at the Screen Gems offices, 'but for a project of this magnitude, we need producers that have a proven track record.'[4]

So, for a few tortuous weeks, Boyce and Hart had to wait on the sidelines while Screen Gems tried an array of approaches to name producers such as Snuff Garrett who tried and failed to make something magical happen in the studio. By June 1966, with the show just three months away, nothing had been set. Head hustler Boyce went back to Kirshner and told him to come and see him and Hart set up a few songs with their band The Candy Store Prophets by way of an 'audition' not unlike the screen tests the four Monkees themselves undertook the previous autumn. The short session took place at Rainbow Studios on the corner of LA's music row, Vine Street. They didn't try Donnie's patience, instead performing the three tunes they had written for the commission: 'This Just Doesn't Seem To Be My Day', 'Let's Dance On', and the 'Theme'. Kirshner liked what he heard, and they were in, as writers, players, and producers.

I asked Hart whether he and Boyce felt The Monkees considered them to be on 'their' side or on the management side:

> Now that's a very good question, and I've got a couple of things to say about that. Michael Nesmith has been in books and Monkee records for over 50 years now, and when they interviewed him for a documentary being made about Tommy and myself *[The Guys Who Wrote 'Em*], I was surprised to see and hear him being so cordial and saying such nice things about Boyce & Hart, saying that they were never enemies, that the West Coast guys were 'part of us', meaning The Monkees.
>
> At the time we would only see Nesmith now and then; he was friendly enough, but we would always hear rumblings from Lester Sill that he was unhappy. So occasionally I had to take over. The second thing is we didn't use studio musicians on our sessions with The Monkees. We used our band, The Candy Store Prophets. Maybe Michael didn't care for that, but we knew what we were doing. We were on the scene, the guys and Tommy and I, moonlighting around LA. It didn't sound like the other sessions when we played – we sounded like a real rock band. I think a lot of what came after from The Monkees came back to that sound. Of course it was a little different and mixed with whatever else everyone was doing on the scene. It was a guitar-driven sound and everybody kind of copied that.

The multiple approaches and inputs into the project may have caused some tensions between rival songwriters pitching in to get their songs included, but even at this early stage there were perhaps some feelings of friction between the most musically ambitious Monkee and the people directing the project, which to some degree did indeed include Boyce & Hart. Yet Nesmith knows what's good and what isn't, and he could have heard what the songwriting team brought to the party. And yet Hart indicates that he was not leant on to write in a certain style:

> They didn't give us any direction at all. The Kirshner staff was on the West Coast and not paying any attention to what was going on. The year 1965 we were preparing for the show, they didn't know if it was gonna sell, so they didn't pay any attention to it. He took an interest later on when the big sponsors started coming in but at first not so much. The only instructions I remember came from the TV producers, and they were about certain things for the television show, not the records. They were concerned that this was the first time you'd have a group on TV that wasn't improvised by anybody. Young kids, no authority figures, long hair. They wanted that to be perceived as non-threatening, and you can kind of hear that woven into the theme song. Beyond that, Tommy and I told ourselves we didn't want to sound too Beatle-esque. We just figured we'd write the songs and then the production crew would make them sound good.

Here Hart lets us see the difference between the very early days of the project, just after Lester Sill had made the connection between them and Raybert, and how things tightened up as it got closer to the launch date – moving from 'no direction at all' to specific instruction about how to construct a certain 'non threatening' identity for the act and for the songs: 'You can kind of hear that woven into the theme song.' Asked if he had a particular group in mind that he wanted The Monkees to sound like, he told me, 'We listened to ten, maybe a dozen, other groups and styles and we decided we could have elements of all of them.'

The songs themselves were therefore free to be both complete as they were but also to draw in 'representative' elements from everything that was happening in popular music at the time, be that teen-ballads or something wilder, so that the whole field of popular taste, with all its symbolic associations, could find a place in this music and in the new way of making and presenting pop. The majority of the songs were written specifically for the project:

> We had a few we had stockpiled, like 'I Wanna Be Free', there were two or three versions of 'Words' before we got it with The Monkees. But once we got the project, we started writing specifically, and just tried to make it sound cohesive, and sound direct.

This professional approach connects the role of writing for The Monkees with not only the Brill method – write hits – but also with the idea of the Hollywood score, making music that suggests and illustrates a way of life, character, and situation, and all in a 2:30 pop song rather than across 45 minutes of music spread across a two hour movie. So, I wondered, how did they get the sound and the personalities to meet in the music? Did they write with a particular vocalist or character in mind?

> We didn't want to write 'for a TV show', we just wanted to write hits. But when we got the project and got these two great voices – we knew Micky was basically the lead singer, but we also had Davy with his Manchester accent, which was reminiscent of the British revolution stuff. We definitely utilised him well, and the fact that he was the heartthrob let us give him the romantic ballads and so on.

So the personalities of The Monkees helped shape and directed the personality of the music; in their intuitive understanding of this Boyce & Hart were the ideal writers of Monkee Music and the project was very fortunate to find them and have them. Like much else in this story, the elements just magically seemed to fit together, which would allow the group and show to succeed hard, high, and fast.

The songs they contributed were key to the project's success: '(Theme From) The Monkees' effectively tuned the group into existence, like an image gradually clarifying on a television screen. Based on the swinging rhythm of the current Dave Clark Five hit 'Catch Us If You Can' (itself a movie theme), it works as a song and as a distinctive theme for the show. Whatever the local variation, a good theme always works in the same way – you know it and recognise it whether you are a fan of the show or not. If you are, it's a call sign – come and see! It functions then as an ad or a jingle – all the 'brand values' of the show encapsulated into a minute.

The very unusual thing about Boyce & Hart's '(Theme From) The Monkees' is its acknowledgement of being a theme. They could have called it 'Here We Come', or, as many people grew up thinking it was called, 'Hey Hey We're The Monkees', but the somewhat formal, even utilitarian title it has does the job. It's the theme to a TV show, but also, like the James Bond theme, the theme to a world that you can dream of being part of, a set of people and places and adventures and ways of living accessible only though that little window, swinging open at the sound of that tune. It certainly performed a double function for The Monkees, being a theme tune for a television show but also the annunciation of their arrival in the parallel world of the pop industry.

Their first single, 'Last Train To Clarksville', was evidence of that world beyond the theme – a contemporary-sounding guitar riff ringing out, but it was also wholly distinctive, with its 'steam engine' rhythm rising and falling, all topped by Micky Dolenz's supercool yet emotionally expressive vocal. Yet another classic the pair gave The Monkees was '(I'm Not Your) Steppin' Stone'. Facing off against Neil Diamond's immaculate conception on the other side of the 45, here was a surging, powerful slice of garage-band grind, tougher than leather and twice as supple. Opening with a rapid-fire quartet on the snare, the rhythm falls directly into a relentless, Troggs-like stomp of a beat, but it is not merely a blunt instrument – it has a spring, limber flow and is not to be messed with. Micky's vocal is recognisably Monkee, but there is no mistaking the raw emotion caught in the primal pound of the beat and the aggressive chord progression, a closed circuit of four chords relentlessly pumped out but never achieving release or resolution – this is where the song's sense of building, unrelieved tension has its root. It's little wonder the song was later covered by the Sex Pistols; it was the supposed 'plasticity' of the group that punks loved (as opposed to the dull authenticity of rock's canon), and many of them had watched and loved the show a decade earlier as children.

By the end of 1966, The Monkees had recorded nearly 50 titles, 21 of them Boyce & Hart songs – quite an achievement considering they were in competition with Carole King, Gerry Goffin, and the rest of the Screen Gems stable. The debut Monkee gig in Hawaii on December 3 contained four of their songs, and the final four-piece show of the decade, two years later in Osaka, still contained three Boyce & Hart tunes at its centre. Scrolling forward, the epochal 2011 set contained seven. Every Monkees album up to and after *Head* contained their songs. So if you're looking for the key creators of the Monkee sound you still hear on your radio every day, don't look to the Brill Building – it was crafted via the songs of Tommy Boyce and Bobby Hart.

BREAKOUT: 'THE GIRL I KNEW SOMEWHERE'

The track that provided the key to the door was Nesmith's own 'The Girl I Knew Somewhere', and the presence of it on the B-side of The Monkees' third single and first of 1967 became a make-or-break moment for Nesmith and thereby the group. The band were already recording with Chip Douglas producing by late January 1967, working on Bill Martin's 'All Of Your Toys' and Nesmith's song. Don Kirshner's great mistake was to push ahead with a bit of old school Brill bullishness by issuing a 45 of a Davy-only version of 'She Hangs Out' in Canada while they were on the road. This, combined with the evolving group identity which grew out of them playing gigs live onstage together – becoming a 'real' group – and the *More Of The Monkees* debacle – when they found out that the disc had been issued without their knowledge while out on tour and had to send someone to a record store to buy a copy of their 'own' album – pushed them to the limit and then beyond. Nesmith has spoken of listening out for a much-trailed play of 'a new Monkees' single on LA radio knowing that if it wasn't his song, the great revolt had failed and he was, as he had confessed in his screen test, 'out o' work' and back out on the street.

Chip Douglas, late of The Modern Folk Quartet and more briefly The Gene Clark Group immediately post-Byrds, had been approached by Nesmith to produce the first 'free' Monkees recordings. I asked him how it happened:

> I was in band called The Modern Folk Quartet, which ran out of road, so when that broke up I kind of fell in with Gene Clark, who had just left The Byrds, and that caught the attention of a couple of guys in The Turtles as they were big Byrds fans. So when The Gene Clark Group fizzled out I was asked to join The Turtles as a bassist and made the record 'Happy Together' with them, and *that* caught the attention of Michael Nesmith. He approached me in the Whisky A Go Go … he had been a fan of The Modern Folk Quartet, and Michael asked me to produce. I hadn't really produced before but he liked what I'd done in arrangements for The Turtles I guess.
>
> I was a little hesitant at first … I was fairly happy being in The Turtles and having a good time for a change, and I wasn't sure if this was really gonna happen. Plus I'd never really produced a record and The Monkees were a big group by that time, and being responsible for getting all the music together seem like a lot to take on. But Michael kept assuring me – 'don't worry, I'll teach you everything you need to know, we just need someone we can communicate with in the studio'. So I said all right, and regretfully had to leave The Turtles.

Harold Bronson of Rhino saw a parallel between The Monkees and The Turtles beyond their mutual connection with Chip Douglas:

> Like The Monkees, The Turtles were docked prestige points because sometimes they didn't write their own hits. But I think out of the 60s bands the Turtles records were the very best produced of the time. But they suffered from being on White Whale, had they been on Columbia it had been a different story.

Chip Douglas was of course substantially responsible for that high quality level of production – something Michael Nesmith was no doubt fully aware of. So, having recruited their new producer, the next task was to learn how to work together as a unit in the studio and become the band they felt they already were on the way to being, and they set about the job with some gusto:

> They'd learned to be a band a little bit by playing on stage and they could do their songs just fine! Really Mike's way of looking at it was that he wasn't really getting a chance to express himself in the studio. He really wanted to produce the stuff himself but he couldn't do that while also being a member of the group. So his best deal was to find somebody else who thought like he did, I guess, and see if that would work, plus he knew what I was capable of as an arranger. So he brought me into it on that basis.
>
> The very first thing we did was at Gold Star studios, because I don't think time was available at RCA yet, there was something booked and we wanted to get in there and get started and learn how to work together. So we worked on 'The Girl I Knew Somewhere' there along with a couple of other things.

Nesmith's songs, shoehorned onto the first two albums, had set a kind of style which was ahead of the pop curve in the way it matched country shapes to pop moves and a dash of R&B in the rhythm section. Chip Douglas understood this and what was needed. So hearing 'The Girl I Knew Somewhere' isn't like hearing an unfamiliar, brand new sound, but rather a fuller, freer exposition of a style already inherent in their work – Nesmith's melody, Dolenz's voice, their vocal stylings together and singly, even the harpsichord first heard on 'Take A Giant Step' but now played superbly by Peter, all here, all familiar yet also changed, and resurgent, the sound of the quartet asserting themselves.

Irrefutable evidence of the full realisation and control over their material comes in the form of the gorgeous stop at 1:38, over which the last note of the harpsichord arcs and connects to the restart with the restatement of the opening riff leading to the song's climax; on the way, there's a golden moment when Dolenz and Nesmith trade a couple of lines in the final verse. It's a brilliant effect as their voices suit each other very well, and the reserve demonstrated by only doing it twice shows how in control of the material they were. As a point from which The Monkees could begin, the song holds a very special place in the band's catalogue.

CHIMES OF FREEDOM, OR EVERY LAST STINKIN' LITTLE NOTE: *HEADQUARTERS* (1967)

The Beverly Hills Hotel opened in 1912, just as the cogs of the cinema industry began turning, and it is partly responsible for turning the surrounding area into the fabulous adjunct to the Hollywood Life it became, with its elegance, exclusivity, and rows of bungalows later used by legendary writers or actors or lovers or all three. Reclining in lush, water-sprinkled languor just off Sunset Boulevard, its walls are rightly famous for their easiness on the eye: flamingo pink on the outside, wedding cake iced-white within. I got to visit it one hot August evening at sunset and it was like passing through a portal to paradise; life could be a dream, sweetheart. So closely is it associated with the idea of California and Hollywood in the popular imagination that it became symbolic of that life long before it appeared, looking mysterious and not a little Hispanic, on the sleeve of the 1976 Eagles album *Hotel California*. Yet that image isn't the hotel's only claim to pop music fame; as the taproot of the very idea of Hollywood, it is somehow appropriate that it was at the Beverly Hills Hotel on January 25 1967, at a meeting to decide who controlled the music of The Monkees, Michael Nesmith put his fist through a wall in one of those exclusive bungalows ('$150 a day', according to *TV Guide*'s report of the incident later that year) and began the 'palace revolution' in such palatial surroundings.

Like the moment at his surprise birthday party in *Head* where he tells Micky to ask him 'how does it feel' and answers his own question with 'I don't like it, that's how it feels!', having 'everything' according to the rules of Hollywood felt like something he sorely wanted out of. A contemporary report suggested that after his rage cooled he felt he had behaved badly:

> Later Mike told his 'angel of peace', the ever-conciliatory [Bert] Schneider, 'I blew it. I shouldn't have lost my temper. But it's horrible to be the number one group in the country and not be allowed to play on your own records.' Schneider said, 'Well it's rewarding to see you guys act as a group rather than four egotists who don't pull together.' To which Mike replied, 'It's the first time we've had a wagon to pull.'[5]

His mixed feelings are laudable, his advocacy of the strength of the group remarkable. Once that $150 a day wall was broken through, a special kind of freedom lay on the other side. For The Monkees, in the short term, that meant shutting down the TV show and prioritising the music. So even though they had started to work on their own material in advance of Kirshner's formal dismissal later in the year, that declaration of independence in a cool and moneyed room unlocked a huge store of energy and ideas – to whit, *Headquarters*. It was recorded in a flash of white-hot activity between Micky returning from London on February 23 and the band's next live gig in Winnipeg, Canada, on April Fool's Day.

Chip Douglas recalled the atmosphere surrounding the sessions:

> It was a little rough at first because we had never worked together. As things developed and *Headquarters* evolved there came a kind of camaraderie, and we were all pulling together to make this album that was supposed to be only them playing on it. In fact maybe my best contribution to The Monkees was that I wanted to see them doing *everything* on their records, with nobody in the background who wasn't a Monkee. So if you hear a vocal part, you're gonna hear Micky or Davy or Peter or Mike, and nobody else.

The album is the sound of liberty itself. The count-in at the opening of the first track, 'You Told Me', is a playful nod to the squonky equivalent on *Revolver*'s opener, 'Taxman', but also a gleeful little shout of autonomy, followed by those opening chimes of freedom on a 12-string guitar. Likewise, the reclamation of Nesmith's second number on side one, 'You Just May Be The One', from the 'TV version' is complete, as the track does indeed feature just them – the four Monkees. Chip Douglas handled the bass on some of the tracks to allow Peter to add extra colours on keyboard and guitar but on this tune, already played in on a dozen gigs between New Year and February, it was the quartet alone:

> Peter did play bass on a couple of songs – in fact he played on 'You Just May Be The One', and he really did a great bass part on that too. He played in a little different style to me, playing with a flat pick and I don't. Maybe you can hear that on the record, I don't know.

The album showcases Nesmith's flourishing songwriting styles – pop-folk ('You Just May Be The One'), country-pop ('You Told Me'), a sound greatly assisted by Tork's banjo, and pure '67 pop with a gloss of psychedelia ('Sunny Girlfriend', complete with backward cymbals). It also allowed Peter Tork to expand his musical contributions many fold – playing guitar, banjo, and keyboards, arranging for cello and French horn ('Shades Of Gray') and writing 'For Pete's Sake' (with his flatmate Joey Richards) which became the end-title theme for the second series, signalling the changes in the TV show as well as in the studio. It is a freedom song for the group as well as a claim on the rights of a whole generation. As Tork's lyric declares, 'We gotta be free!', echoing sentiments of the first album's 'I Wanna Be Free' while remaking and expanding it, exchanging the individual wish for the collective assertion. In spring '67, youth culture was on the threshold of the Summer of Love, and this song, with its bluesy guitar picking, washes of organ, and effortlessly soulful vocal from Dolenz, chimes perfectly with that. The Monkees' apparent escape from their gilded cage is a fine metaphor for a cultural transformation and a flight into freedom.

Peter also shared a lead vocal with Davy on the sublime 'Shades Of Gray', a track to which his plaintive folksy vocals were perfectly suited, poised as it is at a crossroads between a melancholy present and the pleasures of memory. Davy got to keep his contributions, too, only better, with the ideally suited chirrup of 'I Can't Get Her Off My Mind' finding a counterpoint in his soulful vocal on Douglas's own 'Forget That Girl' – a song Smokey Robinson would have been happy with – and what is in my view his finest ever vocal performance, on their recording of Diane Hildebrand and Jack Keller's 'Early Morning Blues And Greens'. I asked Chip Douglas about this particular song:

> Actually it was one of Lester Sill's discoveries – he was our boss during that period of time, president of Screen Gems and Colgems Records – and one of his favourite things. To me at the time it was just another song we did … Davy went in and sang the vocal and treated it like he wanted to. The words made him sing it a certain way, with a softer approach, which I always liked. In subsequent years when I worked with him I'd try to get him to sing in a little deeper range. I mean he had quite a range, he sang all kinds of things, from 'Star Collector' to Broadway tunes to this kind of number, but I always especially liked that little aspect of his voice.

Like all the *Headquarters* tunes it is a 'real' Monkee record, with all four on the track, plus Chip Douglas on bass, and Tork taking the keyboard role here, on electric piano and organ. The former brings a rolling, forward momentum to the track which adds a creative tension into play with the stillness described in the lyric, while the organ adds a spectral depth and presence in a solo at the bridge and the closing section to the fade. There's a rattling, metallic echo to the rhythm on this track which fascinates but is also alarming – it is harsh and something of an unknown quantity, although Andrew Hickey is no doubt close to the mark when he identifies it as a mix of organ and reverb'd guitar, the latter being struck rather than 'played'.[6] So the marginal experiment eventually finds its place in the mainstream. Arguably it was The Monkees' lack of studio experience and surfeit of enthusiasm at this particular stage that delivered innovations of this sort.

This fresh approach to working together gave us the album's 'gag tracks'. 'Band 6', which rather beautifully is placed at band four, is a bit of *studio vérité,* and special in its illustrative function. It is a mere 39 seconds long but manages to give us an example of how the group worked together and how they learned from each other. It opens with Mike playing an approximation of the 'Loony Tunes' theme on his pedal steel (if they didn't share a common musical root, they all knew film and TV music and could work from there). This encourages Dolenz to find the beat and pick up on it – it comes and goes, but he kind of misses it most of the time. In the second half of the track after Mike's reinforcingly positive 'I think you got it now Micky' they go at it full tilt and do indeed get through it, Dolenz on the nail every time. Bursting through the tape on the finishing line at the end, as he does on the bridge in *Head*, a riot of rejoicing breaks out in the studio; it's great to hear. Even though it is obviously an edited and collapsed version of events it reveals such a lot about the processes involved in making this album.

'Zilch' is further evidence of what happens when everyone is in the studio and all are working toward a common goal – as the sleeve notes say, 'When four people just go with their thing, what comes out is a whole.' The 'whole what' in this case is demonstrably quartered – four separate recordings of them speaking and repeating their single lines edited by Douglas into a coherent whole and just over a minute of soundplay. It's funny, fresh, and fast and over in a flash – pop art. The track's title is part of the plot too – an American slang word for 'nothing'. Davy liked this new Americanism enough to use it as the name of his shortlived boutique opened in October 1967 at 217 Thompson Street in Greenwich Village. He said at the opening: 'Everything I chose for the store is something I'd wear myself.'[7] And indeed the green round-collared top he wears for much of *Head* was part of the store's range.

Micky's contributions to the album are key. He takes two of the three Boyce & Hart reboots, 'I'll Spend My Life With You' and 'Mr Webster', both improved in having their arrangements reduced, and one unmissable solo composition. Inspired by his February 1967 trip to London, where he met The Beatles and Samantha Juste, whom he would later marry, the lyric to 'Randy Scouse Git', aka 'Alternate Title', is an impressionistic stream-of-consciousness travelogue of that flying visit. It's easy to understand what a head-spinner it must have been for Dolenz, even after six months of Monkee business. Here he was, used to being told what to do on a TV set or what to sing in a studio, suddenly welcomed as an equal by The Beatles into Swinging London. The lyrics have been decoded by Micky over the years in interview. The four kings of EMI are The Beatles, of course; the girl in the yellow dress is Mama Cass; the being known as Wondergirl is Miss Juste; and so on. The verses carry this autobiographical element, while the chorus has a firmer (and unrelated) set of generational challenges: 'Why don't you cut your hair? / Why don't you live up there?' and so on.

It is the overall sound of the track that accounts for its enduring popularity, though. Opening on a dramatic, theatrical kettle drum roll it has a lop-sided piano riff, a clip-clop melody, and a startling transition from the chatty good-naturedly confused verses and the *sturm und drang* of the chorus. The juxtaposition of these elements allows the two distinct lyrical moods to co-exist. The song's mix of the dream-like and the serious is captured beautifully in the Rainbow Room clip which appeared on the TV show. Micky's tablecloth poncho and his near-goofing off during the scat section seem to work with the song's musical dramatics toward a common goal. It's an amazing thing.

The song's double title is another souvenir from Dolenz's visit to London: *Till Death Us Do Part* was a biting satire on British working-class life by screenwriter and jazz aficionado Johnny Speight (who also scripted 1967's dystopian pop-opera, *Privilege*) and ran from 1965 to 1975. It was just about the biggest and easily the most controversial show on British TV at the time, so it's no mystery that Micky saw it. Indeed, it was so successful it was remade as *All In The Family* for American TV. The BBC show starred Warren Mitchell as Alf Garnett, a native of East London who, despite being at the bottom of the heap in British society, was a true blue Conservative party supporter and Royalist. This provided the leverage for Speight's satire. In the show Garnett lived in a small, crowded house in London's East End with his wife, daughter, and son-in-law, whom he despised as a lazy Northern idler. Garnett's ritual abuse of his feckless Liverpudlian son-in-law was to call him a randy scouse git at high volume in a fabulously broad East London accent – you have to hear it for the full impact really – and the phrase surely caught Dolenz's attention for its rough poetry, rhythmic absurdity, and (lest we forget that Dolenz was a skilled actor as well as everything else) its performative appeal.

To clarify, randy scouse git means a perpetually horny slob from Liverpool. That's an open definition, but close enough for jazz. Anyone in England would have understood the phrase, it being as clear there as it was opaque in the US. It would also be directly associated with Alf Garnett. So, if the BBC and wider state censors weren't to be called in, an alternate title was needed. It's credit to Dolenz that he came up with the perfect alternate title which both adheres to and good-humouredly thumbs its nose at the attempted censorship. For British purposes, 'Randy Scouse Git' became 'Alternate Title' and a hit record in the UK, reaching number 2 in the charts as they conquered London in June and July '67. Remarkably, no singles were issued from *Headquarters* in the USA.

The song's unusual structure suggests everything might fall apart at any moment but also equally strongly asserts its internal logic, and it came along just at the right time for The Monkees. Their star was shooting high into the heavens in the UK as elsewhere, and it arrived as the UK gigs of summer '67 were announced. Yet in the wider reaches of popular culture, bastions of conservatism were apparently crumbling, evidenced by shows like *Till Death Us Do Part*, presenting loud and brutish working-class life on TV for the first time, and anti-hero US film hits like *Bonnie & Clyde*, *The Trip*, and, in the UK, *Bedazzled*. Things were changing fast, and 'Alternate Title' freed up a little space for such experimentation to enter the mainstream of pop, sharing some of the freedom the group had suddenly won for themselves.

'YOU'RE UNDER THE SIGN OF THE MONKEES AND EVERYTHING IS FAVOURABLE': *PISCES, AQUARIUS, CAPRICORN & JONES LTD.* (1967)

This album represents the band's high imperial moment, the brief period in which they were utterly unassailable and possessed of such mercurial momentum that even Elvis, Beatles, and Stones could not break their bones. That certainty, that *élan*, runs through the grooves like cognac. They had come so far in so short a time it must have felt as though it would never end. The album, though less organic than *Headquarters* is arguably their most sophisticated group achievement, yet also one that Peter Tork remembered as when 'we went into what I call mixed mode', accommodating a broader blend of group and outside contributions in place of the determination to play 'every stinking little note' on *Headquarters*. This process would eventually undermine the group's musical identity, which, after the TV show was cancelled in summer '68, was all that remained to bind them together. Their fourth album in less than a year, *Pisces* is musically a more measured and sophisticated record than its predecessor. This starts from the first track, 'Salesman', written by Craig Vincent Smith of Nesmith protégés The Penny Arkade. It features not Micky on drums but an old comrade of Chip Douglas, Eddie Hoh. When Peter hears the drum fill toward the song's end during the TV show episode 'The Devil And Peter Tork', he observes wryly, 'Now you know that Micky didn't play that fill!' The song chugs along nicely, rolling steadily on an up-down country-boogie rhythm that provides the ideal vehicle for its Kerouac-meets-Arthur-Miller portrait of a travelling salesman. Quite what he is selling has been a moot point almost since day one, a debate magnified by the song's use in the same episode's still-near-the-knuckle 'damnation' scene. He may even be a pop singer, dragging his songs to the marketplace, here today and gone tomorrow, but with all the 'benefits' that are supposed to go with the job: 'Short life span, but ain't life grand?' The lyric has an inventory of what he's carrying – copper kettles, different kindsa tin – but we also learn that he is 'sailin' high again', and a call-and-response vocal bridge emphasises the word 'high' up to a 'Twist And Shout'-style climax. Nesmith also confides about some unidentified 'secret goods that push while you talk'. His inventory may be a mystery but what's clear is that Nesmith delivers a frank and chatty vocal which, unless my ears deceive me, has been pitched a little so he sounds just that bit brighter.

Next up, and sounding like quite a different band, is 'She Hangs

Out'. This is a song with impeccable finger-poppin' credentials, written by Jeff Barry (who also wrote this album's unalike 'Love Is Only Sleeping' with long-time partner Ellie Greenwich) and is a remake of the song which cost Kirshner his job as Monkees musical supervisor. He promptly sued Screen Gems and received a choice settlement. The song was reimagined and much improved in its *Pisces* version, turning it from a limply churning piece of teenarama into a jalapeno hot soul-pop blast on which Jones delivers another of his career-best performances – listen to that 'wow!' at 2:11 – with the whole performance at an extremely high level of pop-thrill and sheer cheek.

'The Door Into Summer' was written by Douglas and Bill Chadwick. Sandoval records that an early version with Micky on drums was attempted in late May of '67, so this tune was one of the last of the 'every stinking little note' phase, before Micky surrendered the drum stool to Eddie Hoh. It opens on a great keyboard and bass double, matching each other note for note, and a very effective combination of Chip and Peter that lifts the song into its lyrical intro of picked acoustic guitar. The song is not unlike 'Salesman' in that it tells a character's story, but this man is very different from that picaresque figure – he is beguiled or trapped by material things, by money and the need to make more and more of it. Chadwick, sole composer of 1968's antiwar fable 'Zor And Zam,' slips in a reference to the immorality of the pursuit of wealth for its own sake by referring to the protagonist making a killing on the 'market on the war'.

The images of the pennywhistle band and circus performers could be yesterday or the Middle Ages. It stands as a fading but still potent reminder of what life could be like if one breaks free of what William Blake called 'the mind-forg'd manacles' of trade and industry and the worship of money. These are big themes for a pop song but they were in the ether at the time. This tune was recorded just as the Summer of Love was about to break across the Western world and the counter-culture was finding a shape and a voice. Other ways of being, other modes of social organisation were not only considered or proposed, they were lived out – on the streets, on the campuses, even in the private and exclusive dream-houses of wealthy men like Peter Tork. He eventually paid the price for believing too deeply in dreams like these and found himself badly ripped off by the people he opened his home to and whom he thought he could trust.

Despite its decidedly unpoppy style, 'Love Is Only Sleeping' was to be the follow-up to 'Pleasant Valley Sunday'. It was planned as a standalone single, not to be included on the album. Its appearances in three episodes of the TV show shows it was obviously rated. Written by Brill favourites Barry Mann and Cynthia Weil, it is a curious song and would have been an odd single. It has an off-kilter rhythm established by Nesmith's 'Pleasant Valley Sunday'-style opening riff, unsettling little sizzles of percussion, and a chorus that is not the catchiest the co-composers of 'You've Lost That Lovin' Feelin'' ever came up with. The lyric itself has an ambiguous adult theme, appropriate to the Summer of Love in some ways but seeing beyond youth and beauty: 'her sweet young face looked old' or 'once I loved, but love is dead'. Finally, Nesmith's vocal takes on some of the thoughtful shapes he would return to in his more sage-like solo work in the 70s, notably on *And The Hits Just Keep On Comin'* and *Pretty Much Your Standard Ranch Stash*. As a song about trouble with love, it's certainly a long way from the teen dilemma of which-girl-to-choose depicted in 'Look Out (Here Comes Tomorrow)' a mere six months before. Things were moving fast.

Harry Nilsson's 'Cuddly Toy' is next, giving another young songwriter a break and a big payday. Nilsson signed to RCA as a writer in January 1967 and had, through that, come to the attention of Lester Sill. Chip Douglas already knew of him as his group The Modern Folk Quartet had recorded a successful version of the very early Nilsson tune 'This Could Be The Night', produced by Phil Spector. So when Chip was asked by Nesmith to produce The Monkees in the same month Nilsson signed for The Big Victor, it was almost inevitable their paths would cross. Douglas brought Nilsson and the band together, with Mike and Micky keenest on having him write for them. The demos he gave them have circulated as a bootleg for years, including songs like 'Good Times', which would be exhumed for the album of the same name in 2016. 'Cuddly Toy' was on that demo and was chosen for inclusion on *Pisces*. Nilsson apparently bagged a $40,000 cheque for the song but such was his prudence and caution – virtues he later misplaced in a bar somewhere – he didn't give up his job at the bank where he had been working until he had heard the song played over and over again on national radio. So Nilsson was effectively discovered by The Monkees as a writer, and the success and association elevated him to a solo deal with RCA. Micky drums on this tune, for what proved to be the very last time on an original-era Monkees track. Peter noted this in his DVD commentary on 'The Devil And Peter Tork': '"Cuddly Toy" was the last track with the four of us playing music, and after that Micky never played drums again until *Justus* as far as I know.' Davy and Micky co-vocalise for much of the track, although it is seen very much as a Davy number. The piece rocks along sweetly and with real panache.

Piling straight in through a sharp edit from Chip Douglas at the end of 'Cuddly Toy' is 'Words', a Boyce & Hart song that survived from the band's earliest days. It was originally recorded by The Leaves, and two Monkee versions exist: the earlier TV version from July '66, as heard at the close of 'Monkees In Manhattan'; and this *Pisces* remake a year later. This version is much more satisfying, with period experiments like backward tapes and flutes replaced by the cool considered menace of Tork's organ solo and a great shared vocal by Micky and Peter – listen to how he sings 'kicks'.

The musicianship has a lighter touch, too, bringing an airiness to the song's wistful angst which allows atmospheres of indeterminate doubt and urgent certainty to mingle together in the song's haunted search for a way out of its central dilemma. The guitar serves the song purposefully by confining itself to quietly subversive R&B runs, while Tork's Hammond brings a soulful texture. His solo in particular elevates the track – it's one of his very best contributions to the band's catalogue, showing that when he trusted his instincts he was usually right. Dolenz's sureness as a singer has clearly grown between the two versions, reaching more deeply down into the confidentiality of the verses and daring to go further with the emotional expansiveness of the chorus. Also, the backing on the chorus now agrees with rather than cuts across the words Dolenz is singing. The interplay with Tork is more successful, as well, with Peter's folksy tone having acquired a new gloss and poise while sacrificing none of the openness that characterises his voice.

Flip the album.

'Hard To Believe' was the first song Davy had written that did not involve the other four and was not a one-off. It illustrates the point made by Chip Douglas about the four starting to work apart. In the period following *Pisces* and up to *The Birds, The Bees & The Monkees*, Jones wrote a bundle of tunes with other writers: some good, some shaky, but all the products of verve and hard work – 'Dream World', 'The Poster', 'I'm Gonna Try', and notably 'Changes' (a possible try-out for the theme song for their movie under its working title) plus a protest song of sorts, 'War Games'. This represents quite a run of work, indicative of the 'Broadway rock' that he wanted to pursue under the auspices of the Monkee brand and as detailed in the *Hy Lit* interview in support of *Head*. Perhaps the best such number he sang as a Monkee was Harry Nilsson's 'Daddy's Song' for that movie.

Back in the summer of '67, where all things must have seemed possible, this neat and precisely constructed little musical parfait was smooth and shimmery, concealing a nutty kernel in the form of the lyric, telling a story of possible betrayal – 'I try not to hear the things you say about me' – balanced with the chance of redemption for a love – 'And if you feel what I feel, you won't go away'. It's a perfectly executed little match of melody and lyric and benefits from a tidy brass-and-string part complementing its near-Latin swing. Jones is sometimes thought of as the kind of singer my father used to call a belter, meaning a brassy, overdriven, showbiz delivery. Sometimes he did stray into this territory, feeling quite at home with its theatricality, but he was also a highly adept singer, sensitive to meanings as well as the shapes of words and melodies. 'Hard To Believe' gives us one of his best vocal performances, in my view, to be placed alongside 'Early Morning Blues And Greens' and 1969's 'You And I'. All three are fine examples of where he could go and explore with his voice when the song suited him.

'What Am I Doin' Hangin' Round?' takes us South of the Border, too. If the blues had a baby and they called it rock'n'roll, as Muddy Waters taught us, then here the union of pop and country delivers a brand new sound, too, which eventually got to be called country rock. Make no mistake, Nesmith had been driving down this road for a while – 'Papa Gene's Blues', 'You Told Me', 'Different Drum' – but this is arguably the first really widely heard country-rock song, where the two musical vocabularies collide and a new and distinct musical voice tumbles out. The dynamic connection between the two musical languages comes alive. It has the features of a country song – trains, lost loves south of the border, nostalgia, passion – but the verve of a pop song. It was written by Michael Murphey and Owen 'Boomer' Castleman of Colpix act The Lewis & Clark Expedition, but it doesn't sound much like them. Their album was a mix-up of current pop styles, and their impressively vigorous and mop-headed appearance in the teen movie *For Singles Only* revealed a band who dressed like the Buffalo Springfield and could sound like a poppier Seeds. So perhaps this territory was being newly explored by Michael Murphey as well. The banjo on the track, it grieves me to report, was not played by Peter Tork but – here's the good news – by ace player Doug Dillard, scion of the great Missouri musical family and co-conspirator with ex-Byrd Gene Clark in the early country-rock outfit Dillard & Clark, whose first album was recorded for A&M in 1968, a year after he was invited to play on this track. Clearly, this song started something. Tork included the tune in his set for years and always plays banjo and takes lead vocal on it live, so why he wasn't involved here is a mystery, but it is further evidence of how the togetherness of *Headquarters* had started to fragment. The song is a great fan favourite, and the performance tagged on to episodes of the second series is possibly the definitive document of the band in that period, still wearing their powder-blue eight button shirts but making music all of their own.

'Peter Percival Patterson's Pet Pig Porky' is a bit of plosive palaver Peter produced to showcase his comic technique and it fits into the established gag-track tradition of Monkees albums. It's funny, but it's not a joke. It precedes 'Pleasant Valley Sunday' and thanks to a brilliant close edit by Douglas cues in directly after Tork's last word, which is, appropriately, 'popped'.

'Pleasant Valley Sunday' began life as a response by Carole King and Gerry Goffin to their own environment, written about the neighbourhood of Pleasant Valley in West Orange, New Jersey, where they were living before decamping to California. Older than The Monkees, younger than the Screen Gems studio heads, they were well placed to deal with both sides of this apparent generational schism. One sees the appeal of suburban comfort, but one also feels the pull away to somewhere less well ordered, to where things might 'happen' without being planned. Lester Sill got the demo to Chip Douglas, as he recalled:

> That came via Lester again, though obviously Carole and Gerry already had songs with The Monkees. Once I heard their demo of 'Pleasant Valley Sunday', I just sat in my apartment and went through it over and over, just on the rhythm guitar, and figured out how I thought it should sound. The demo had her doing it with a band, I think there's a drummer on there, but it's a little bit more laidback, not as aggressively fast-tempo'd. I guess it just became that way after I'd started playing it over and over. I would hear these songs and kinda get the words as best I could in my head and play them over and over … and I can't remember if the chords are exactly the same as Carole had them. But that's what I came up with, and then I taught it to the boys after I'd figured out how I wanted it to go. When we were in the studio … I can't remember if I played bass, Bill Chadwick played acoustic, Micky played acoustic too. Mike did the lead guitar part live and then again over a rhythm track which we'd recorded earlier and overdubbed those lead parts. Her demo was a little slower, with a great feel to it, but it wasn't quite as up-tempo driving as it became.

The song's central riff owes something to George Harrison's playing on

'I Want To Tell You' and 'Paperback Writer' but by no means everything, according to Douglas:

> I remember doing 'Pleasant Valley Sunday', and we did that all together, except we just had Eddie Hoh on drums. I remember I taught Mike the intro, and we had a couple of Vox amps we used on that and doubled up the guitar part, did it twice, and I think some overdubs might have been added later … but Mike did it all himself. It's a beautiful dry sound on there.

The song's finale is one of the most exciting in their catalogue and arguably in pop history. From 2:33 the song heads for a vanishing point somewhere on the sound-horizon and rather than simply fade on the repetitions of the title, the sound is instead overdriven to the point where, to use Lemmy's famed phrase, everything is louder than everything else. I asked Chip Douglas how this climax came into being:

> We were mixing it down, and Hank Cicalo the engineer said well, what are we gonna do in the ending? Are we gonna just fade it out? We might have made a mix where it faded straight away. But then he said why don't we crank up some echo? We began to add as it faded out until the plate-reverb chambers just became a big mix of all those instruments in there. It's just a case of cranking on the echo and adding more and more echo as you're fading out, adding and adding more chamber. It's the kind of thing that can happen when you're mixing down, and that's why I've never been a fan of automated mixdowns. That's the part where the engineer is kinda like one of the musicians, so each mix is going to be different. With an automated board it'll always be the same. Some mixes are magical and have something that others don't have. This one turned out pretty good.

It certainly did. By pushing the desk, amps, and tape equipment to the limit of what it could do and then perhaps just a little further, Douglas and Cicalo created a stunning sound implosion that keeps a kind of order (you can still discern the vocal and a ghost of the song's riff) while also conjuring up an overdriven mushroom cloud of noise that will still trouble your loudspeakers. What is remarkable about the finale is the control – this isn't some pointless life-denying racket as happens to 'Listen To The Band' in *33 1/3*, nor is it Hendrix setting fire to his guitar, or Townshend splintering a Strat. There's barely any feedback – just the tiniest touch, perhaps – so it isn't that, either. Instead, it's the creation of a new sonic vocabulary for pop, one predicated on the capacities of the equipment itself. It's an idea that would not find its time and place in the currency of pop until the young listeners to The Monkees music got to form their own bands. You can hear this dramatic mix of force and restraint in bands like Hüsker Dü, R.E.M., and early Yo La Tengo, Monkee fans all. Yet it's not just their fans who rate this one. Dolenz routinely announces it onstage as one of his favourite Monkee songs, and in his memoir called it 'one of the best tunes we ever did'.[8]

'Daily Nightly' is generally remembered for two things: its symbolist lyric based on poetry Nesmith wrote in the light of the curfew riots on Sunset Strip in 1966, events that inspired more directly The Mamas & The Papas' 'Safe In My Garden'; and it was the first time a Moog synthesizer was heard on a million-selling mainstream pop record. Micky acquired one of the first Moogs in September '67 (the 20th Moog modular, serial number 1019, if you must know) and the track's famous synth sounds, dubbed on late by Chip Douglas from the recordings he made while Dolenz played around with it, are all the more effective because of the rock-solid band working away underneath them. They hit a groove on what is effectively a three-chord trick and make it sound both sizzling and mysterious.

Beyond the sonic novelty, it proved less useful to Monkee music than might have been expected. After *Pisces*, Micky gradually lost interest in his expensive new gadget. In 2009, he recalled to the *Los Angeles Times* how first-generation synthesizers such as this one had to be manually rewired whenever the player wanted to use a different sound:

> Ahh, my little Moog synthesizer … it was actually a pretty difficult thing to use. I threw a party for John Lennon one night, and he sat there at the Moog for four hours making flying saucer sounds. It was great for flying saucer sounds. I sold it to Bobby Sherman [and] I think he still has it.[9]

'Don't Call On Me' provides a cool breath of summer night air between the troubled dream-visions of 'Daily Nightly' and the culture shock of 'Star Collector' at the end of side two of *Pisces*. It had been around since at least 1963, when it was regularly featured in the folk-club sets Nesmith and his co-writer John London gave as Mike & John around the So.Cal folk scene, occasionally accompanied by Bill Chadwick. You can find a demo of the song from 1964 online, which could very easily have stood up as a 45, perhaps for the Omnibus label with whom he would issue a single in '65 with London and Chadwick as Mike, John & Bill. Here he sings folk-club live, accompanied only by acoustic guitars. It is not wildly different from the version we know from *Pisces*, but the folk roots of the song are more clearly audible as he compresses some of the lines and hurries toward the conclusion of others, leaving more space between them, as on the transition from 'or any other day' to 'OK little girl'. On the demo, the end of the first line almost crashes into the start of the next, where the *Pisces* version has Peter's languid Hammond organ solo to separate them. It's unfair to compare songwriter demos with carefully crafted million-sellers-in-waiting, but it's useful for us to hear how far Nesmith went in three years, and also how far into writing performing and recording he was pre-Monkees. Chip Douglas recalled to me that he always liked hearing Mike & John, highly rating Nesmith's songwriting and the sophistication of his arrangements, even in the folk clubs. This rare demo allows us a little snippet of what Douglas might have been talking about.

The song's appealing mix of roots and Vegas schmaltz is on show here, too, with some of the changes treading a very fine line, taking the good from both sides while never quite belonging to either. It has a haunting melody and is pitched unusually for Nesmith, requiring a little more breathing space around the delivery than some of the more straight-ahead pop and country deliveries that were to come. His vocal on *Pisces* is somehow symbolic of the events of the intervening three years – more assured, and the delivery of an older and more experienced man but also unmistakably the same person, albeit one to whom an extraordinary thing had happened. The way the tune stretches out and revels in its own delicious melancholia is evidence of that. He has time to exhale – in pleasure rather than exasperation – and he inhabits the later performance with more personality and a broader, deeper range of expression. Chip Douglas adds a gag element with some studio/party chatter that brackets the song, allowing Micky to give one of his superb skits on style and form in media announcements and Bob Rafelson his single musical contribution to a Monkees track, tinkling away on piano.

The synth-strewn oompah of 'Star Collector' is not only a conventionally well-made song with wide open verses and all-in chorus, complete with call-and-response backing vocals, but also like a little leak of music from the future. Tradition and innovation wrap around each other in this song. Goffin & King, skilled artificers as they were, were well suited to change and flourish in any set of styles or cultural conditions. Dolenz opens the song by scratching at the mic and trying a silly-serious hum and '*Hello*?' but it is Jones who turns in a brilliant vocal on this track – showy, brash, even swaggering, but delivered from experience. The verses are swinging and energetic, with some stagily scathing tones. Surely no English listener can hear it without raising a smile at the very Northern vowel sounds on the line 'collector of stars', rendered as 'cullek-tehhr uv staaaaahhhzz' in an unmistakably Mancunian tone. The tone of his vocal modifies the contempt in the lyric somewhat, and we sense a touch of fondness for the boldness of this girl, even as he sings, 'It won't take much time before I get her off my mind.' I love the way he sings that last line, atop the seething, thrilling bed of noise before the track gives way to a lengthy instrumental section, gradually overwhelmed by a dramatic organ chord and the synth swirling and chopping around Eddie Hoh's pulse beat. What we hear on *Pisces* is an edit of a longer jam that Chip Douglas, as ever, went to work on and made something much more exciting emerge from the elements. It is long enough to keep the sense of innovation and boldness in the sonic exploration of themes but also concise enough – pop enough – to preclude otiose twiddling. Right at the track's finale, in amongst the organised chaos of Hoh's rising drum rolls and Paul Beaver's Moog breakdown into what we might call off-white noise, Dolenz's voice slowly surfaces, chanting 'bye bye' at first under and gradually over the bedlam. Then suddenly the noise resolves itself and he picks up the beat and skips off into the fade, chanting 'bye bye, bye bye, bye bye … ' while the bass picks up the beat under him. It suggests this song will carry on long after the fade and maybe even become something else again. The song doesn't finish – it's just that we've run out of playing time. It's some way from 'The Day We Fall In Love'. The deliberately mechanistic textures are still startling, and there is a delicious irony in how the synthesizer – the revolutionary instrument that would change our understanding of the 'real' in music – was introduced to mainstream popular song by the first and most famous so-called 'manufactured' and synthetic band in pop history.

HAPPYSAD: THE LIFE OF 'DAYDREAM BELIEVER'

Following 'Pleasant Valley Sunday' into the chart as the band's fifth 45, 'Daydream Believer' was for a while a standalone. It was recorded at the *Pisces* sessions but was held back as a sure-fire hit for the next album. Certainly all four Monkees are on this track, which made it unique for the album on which it did eventually emerge, 1968's *The Birds, The Bees & The Monkees*. The song was first laid down on June 14 1967, the day after they completed 'Pleasant Valley Sunday', showing how well they had hit their stride as a group and how much working under the guidance of Chip Douglas was helping them. It is arguably the group's best-loved hit.

Where did the song come from? It was written by California's own John Stewart who, in summer 1967, was 27 and fresh out of the ranks of the recently dissolved folk-revival stalwarts The Kingston Trio. He was an acquaintance of Chip Douglas from the folk scene, and with the producer-sponsored submission of 'Daydream Believer' to The Monkees, he got life-changingly lucky. Chip Douglas told me how it happened:

> I met with John Stewart, who was the writer and a friend of mine, and he played it for me. The thing that grabbed me about it was the way he sang in the line 'the bluebird as she sings' in a big resonant low note. So we were hanging out, and I recorded him on it and took the cassette in and Davy said [*tries Manchester accent*], 'That'd be good for me, man.' We went in and cut a track and Davy sang it, but I didn't think anything of it, it was just another song that we were working on. I wasn't thinking this is gonna be the biggest hit single or anything. It was Lester Sill who heard it and loved it when it was all done, with the strings and beautiful parts Shorty Rogers came up with for it – that little trumpet line in the middle, that just suits it perfectly. The string parts were kinda my idea and I sang them to [Rogers], he noted them and added them. When it was all done, Lester Sill heard it and said, 'This is it! We're going with this one buddy.' I said, 'Really? Well, I've never thought about it that way, but OK … you're the boss!' Of course he was right, it was a big, big hit.

The song was recorded at the same time as the *Pisces* material:

> The thing they did in those days was to keep the single for the next album … there really wasn't a single from *Headquarters* I guess – 'The Girl I Knew Somewhere' was supposed to be the one but it didn't get very far – but when they did *Pisces*, they were selling plenty of albums and they had the TV show. They didn't need to have a hit single, so they took 'Daydream Believer' out of there for the next album, that was the theory.

Peter Tork's bright piano part is as central to the song's enduring appeal as the lyrics or the vocal. It's a musical smile, which the eardrum returns, and is almost fit for a child's skipping game, such is its sense of energy, simplicity, and optimism. Yet mixed in with this delight is a hint of melancholia. Innocence and experience mingle in the happy-sad mood. Dolenz is on backing vocals and Nesmith contributes the guitar touches that gild the verses. This is no guitar song, but the intuitive sensitivity of the little harmonic chimes (hear 0:19–0:24) gladden the heart and certainly lend the song much of its appeal. In the famous Rainbow Room clip, we see how Nesmith emphasises and enjoys playing these harmonics during the second verse with an uncharacteristic showiness. Harmonics are the pure note, freeing it of upper or lower vibration, and on the track Nesmith plays pinch harmonics, delivering a gentle, ringing tone, rather than the tapped harmonic more closely associated with heavy rock. It's interesting to note that the prime exponent of the pinch harmonic in the past 30 years of pop and rock is The Edge, and in his solo spot on U2's tours he has often performed 'Daydream Believer'. Perhaps the song's influence stretches further we think.

The record starts with the voice of Chip Douglas announcing that this is take 7A and a moment later a distracted Davy asks, attention not entirely focussed, 'What number is this, Chip?' Douglas reiterates with some partly-staged irritation, '7 … A!', and is joined by another voice, that of Hank Cicalo, engineer on the session. Jones reminisced that he was a bit peeved at this session, and we can hear the resentment in his vocal. That may be so, but his comeback is self-deprecating and good-natured: 'Whoah, don't get excited man … it's just because I'm short, I know.' Their exchange is concise, funny and real, and adds something to the song. It's an unusual start to a single that would get four million airplays, for sure, but is consistent with Douglas's endearing tendency to encourage the inclusion of little bonus elements to records. Think of 'Band 6', 'Peter Percival Patterson', or Micky's Moog on 'Daily Nightly'. Douglas recalled that it was just a happy accident:

> In those days we were doing 'take to take' vocals, which meant we would play the track on a recording machine, feed it through the board in the studio and Davy, or whoever was singing, would put their vocal on. This was then printed on another machine, so you'd get a bunch of vocals that were overlaid – you'd have

> take 7, take 7A, 7B, or C, and so on – these were all subsequent vocal takes. So I announce 'it's take 7A' and Davy says 'What number is it, Chip?' and it's me, Lester Sill, and Hank Cicalo all chiming in at the same time – Lester Sill was always leaning over my shoulder making sure things were getting done and nobody was fooling around too much. Anyway, I decided to leave it in there, it's kinda cute, 'Oh, I'm short, I know' and all that. Why not? Just a little extra thing in there.

Davy's vocal is perfectly matched to the song's mood of optimism moving from a confidential yet reassuring tone in the verses to a brassier, head back approach in the unstoppably cheering chorus. Watch the Rainbow Room clip of this song (perhaps the definitive Davy Jones TV performance) and you'll see how easily he catches the beat, red shirt, love beads, straight outta Openshaw and the world's coolest Summer of Love hip cat, feet shuffling just right, hips swaying, hands clapping in contented, unforced accord with the song's rhythm. As he turns his back and heads for the back of the set toward those groovy coloured lines running across and up the back wall, the optimism and magical calm of the song are so strong that you almost believe they stretch to the horizon and that he could walk along them and just keep right on going. That's what pop music is for. Cheer up, Sleepy Jean.

NOW IT'S PART OF YOU: 'TAPIOCA TUNDRA'

What makes 'Tapioca Tundra' so appealing isn't the way the words flow like the sequences in a dream, nor is it the tight playing of Nesmith and Eddie Hoh, or the forward velocity of the song. It's the sum of all these parts making something greater. The rhythm of the words is the speed of the music is the steadiness of the beat is the wildness of its images, a complete whole. On the back cover of *Headquarters* the band's manifesto of a sleeve note counsels us against asking 'a whole what?' in relation to the music, but here I think they might forgive us. 'Tapioca Tundra' is a remarkable sound world, much more concise and effective than the contemporary macro-experiment to do a similar thing, Nesmith's

Wichita Train Whistle project. On that album, the instrumental version of this song is neither here nor there – arranged that way, it loses far more than it gains. 'Tapioca Tundra' is an integral work of art in itself, each feature dependent upon every one of the others. It is a wholly linear ride, too. We don't loop back, so that even though certain motifs are repeated, they are rendered differently. Listen, for example, to how Nesmith sings the chorus phrase, 'Sunshine, ragtime blowing in the breeze', differently each time, employing different emphases and pitching. I doubt he consciously set out to do that, but that's what he did, just like a painter may not formally decide to put orange *here* and yellow *there*, but just do so, because they're an artist. The colours of 'Tapioca Tundra' are evening indigos and deepening purples, in my mind at least. There's something of the twilight time about the song, even though it has a relentless forward-facing energy and for the most part a near-Ramones-style tempo. In fact, one of The Ramones' signature features appears accidentally in the song's intro: the numerical count-in, but with a canny twist. Opening with a sauntering guitar motif accompanied by a wilfully casual whistle, we hear Nesmith's voice, heavily treated to sound as if it were coming from a tinny megaphone or had been recorded on a 78rpm record. He counts from one up to five and then back down to zero in a flat, neutral tone. The combination of the shellac sound of the voice with the robotic countdown brings together the Jazz Age and the Space Age. The brittle sharpness of the sound conjures the early days of records and recording, while the countdown was familiar to any listener in 1968, when the USA was deep into the NASA space programme that would lead to the moon landings of the following year. In the age of Apollo – which was also, coincidentally, the era of The Monkees – the countdown was a sign of modernity, of the present pushing tirelessly on into the future, the proof being the countdown to zero. Nesmith combines these found elements, creating a fascinating juxtaposition of evocation.

So we take off, reach an apogee, then return. That 'zero' is extended and distorted by Nesmith's delivery and also by special effects that overlay, build, and distort the sound of his voice – then a clear space in which Eddie Hoh shows why his nickname was Fast Eddie, the eight beats punched out like rocket engines firing up in sequence until the song has the thrust to take off. Lift-off accomplished, the song reveals itself as a rare creature – a melange of Latinate percussion (maracas throughout and dig those bongos in the last verse!) and stream-of-consciousness poetry, all bound up in a sleek sling of psychedelic country-pop. The on beat is emphasised, in the Latin style, by a beaten cowbell. The opening guitar sounds electric but the one we notice most readily is an acoustic that delivers the hugely foregrounded octet of chords that punctuates the song, separating and connecting sections. The song's forward momentum is such that these splashes of acoustic serve as landmarks and signposts for the listener: we're here again, but it's different this time.

A shadowy world, twilight time – like 'Daily Nightly', a vision from the space between waking and sleeping with all the unstoppable logic of a dream. It's easy to call some of the images Dylan-esque, but they are most likely mined from a common seam rather than a conscious borrowing – 'freshly tattered shoes'. But the touchstone line, and the lyrical equivalent of those big acoustic chords which immediately follow it each time, is: 'It cannot be a part of me for now it's part of you.' To me, that could be about love, dreams, or even the song – it came from one person, and now it belongs to everyone who cares to hear it. So the line isn't a denial of propinquity between singer and song, but rather an acknowledgement that what was once one thing is now another. Nesmith explained this conundrum in a 2013 interview:

> The song itself is about the moment when the performer realizes that the songs he or she sings belong to the people – the fans and the crowds – that love the song, and the performer is only there in service to that relationship. 'It cannot be a part of me – for now it's part of you.'[10]

THERE'S A WAY: 'JUST A GAME'

This little number, issued on 1969's *Instant Replay*, feels as much like a clearly distilled thought rather than a formally constructed song and has a longer history than we might suspect. It was originally written in the band's first phase of freedom in early 1967 and was demoed instrumentally during the sessions for *Headquarters*, released in the *Sessions* boxed set of 2000. While it is only the second song Dolenz ever wrote for the band, he had by this time strongly influenced the songbook by his vocal prowess and his intuitive contributions to other people's songs, most obviously bringing the Moog into the mix on *Pisces Aquarius* on 'Daily Nightly'. Like 'Alternate Title' the strength of this delicate little piece is its apparent fragility and the sense that it could just simply melt away at any moment, like a snowflake caught and scrutinised in a warming palm. Tried first on March 28 1967, it was named 'There's A Way' almost off the cuff by Dolenz.

At the start of the track, the ambient noises from Tork and Jones aren't encouraging – 'What was THAT!?' The demo was recorded directly after 'No Time', where the band would have been on a noisy, collective high, so this probably isn't surprising. Once Dolenz and the song are given a chance, things settle and we hear a little sliver of a song that already resembles the version that made it to *Instant Replay*. Dolenz is cool about the busy bluster in the studio and the initial lack of enthusiasm among his bandmates, saying, 'I'm hip, I know it's a draft … I just wrote it!' Nesmith can't be heard on the session, but Dolenz would later credit him for encouraging his songwriting and to submit songs for possible inclusion. 'It was one of the first songs that I had written … I think I played it for Mike on the guitar once and he encouraged me to record it. That's really when I started recording my own tunes.'[11]

Andrew Hickey is spot-on when he notes that it resembles French chanson, as typified by Georges Brassens or Jacques Brel, and that it would not seem out of place on an early Scott Walker solo album. That is partly down to the restraint and elegant power of the Shorty Rogers arrangement which but also is inherent in the song's innate structure. It has a reflective, melancholic, chamber-music quality, minimalist in practice but ornate, even rococo in effect. It is also a highly disciplined piece, compressing complex emotions and experiences into just over one hundred seconds of music.

Each verse hands the baton to the next – there is no chorus. The required repetition is delivered by the chords that seem almost mechanistic in their progressions while retaining an organic pulse, a blend that reflects and accommodates the mix of rational and emotional deliberation in the lyrics. The last line of each verse becomes the first of the next, lending the lyric a kind of philosophical inevitability – if you say *this* then the consequence must surely be *that*. One thought gives way to its more highly developed successor, leading the narrator to the conclusion that it may all be 'just a game'. So the lyric can be read as the thought process through which one reaches an inescapable and unmanipulated conclusion that is indeed 'all just a game'. The song reserves the right to be proved wrong, however. He is 'afraid' that this is the way it is, not certain. It's that uncertainty which gives scope for the hope and also the anxiety which courses through this remarkably direct and complex lyric. Like many of Micky's songs, it has an ingénue quality, a kind of naive art quality that holds together innocence and experience, intuition and expertise, to create something quite special.

Rogers's slowly building arrangement must take a bow: the arrival of the vocal cues in an answering triplet on a harpsichord, echoing the end of each line. Then it begins to track the vocal line and is joined by a flute that duplicates its steps. At the start of each verse an extra ingredient is added to the ensemble – harpsichord in the first, flute in the second, then strings for the third, additional choppier violins in the fourth, and brass arriving for the fifth. By this time the ensemble has created a kind of pulse effect, which we associate with more modernist or even avant-garde American music, such as the work of Steve Reich or Philip Glass. It's fabulous to hear it on a Monkees tune and, though Shorty Rogers clearly deserves a garland, the structure that made it possible is testament to Micky's remarkable, instinctive creativity. The ensemble falls away as the fifth verse ends and we drop into the final rumination on whether this is all just a game, accompanied by the solo acoustic guitar with which we began. In the final seconds, all that remains is that free-floating flute, representing the wandering thought, freed by the careful and disciplined structure that has brought it forth. It's an amazing miniature, *multum in parvo*.

PETER'S BABIES: THE LOST SONGS OF PETER TORK

Peter Tork's musical contribution to The Monkees is in some ways the hidden strand of the story. Of the four, he is easily the most emotionally engaged with the idea of making music as an individual or as a group. He is also the least represented on the group's original official recordings, taking only two lead vocals ('Your Auntie Grizelda' and 'Long Title: Do I Have To Do This All Over Again?') and two shared ('Shades Of Gray' and 'Words'). His folksy voice was outdone by the styles on offer from the other three in the studio. Lacking the showbiz chops of Micky or Davy and the personal drive and focus of the Mike, Peter's contribution was to some degree sidelined.

A by-product of Rhino's archival project has been to shine a light on what Peter was doing musically after the revolution of '67. Once they stopped working together in the studio as a band – something that disappointed him a good deal – he began working on his own material. We can describe his style as West Coast singer-songwriter, gentle flower-child music with a pop sensibility. He recorded some beauties, such as Jo Mapes's 'Come On In' and his own 'Tear The Top Right Offa My Head', a harmonica-driven folk-pop thrill worthy of John Sebastian at his most optimistic which surfaced in the live set in 2015, and a co-write with Diane Hildebrand, 'Merry-Go-Round'. However, the song that occupied much of his time in this period was 'Lady's Baby', which went through multiple versions.

The earliest version we can hear features Karen Harvey on backing vocals and Stephen Stills on guitar, while Peter brings bass, guitar, and harpsichord to the blend. The shared vocal sections are of their time – somewhere between a Mamas & Papas blend and a live sing-along in Peter's house – but the sound is good. Stills's guitar simply adds to what is already there and Tork's lead vocal is feeling its way into the tune. On the version recorded a month later he is joined by the drums of Dewey Martin, and the song is rendered in a full-band style, packing a decent punch as Peter's vocal explores the melody with much more confidence. The key line in the song seems to be 'Tension puts you in the ground', the kind of phrase which the counterculture traded freely, but also a wise observation. It's the baby who lets him know that life was made for livin' slow. This idea of the innate natural wisdom of the child is another familiar theme from the era and one that bobs up in songs like The Beach Boys' 'Child Is Father Of The Man' and is part of a yearning for lost innocence and a sense of wonder that has somehow been eroded by experience. That is implicit in the music, the simple and appealing melody being child-like rather than childish. The contrast is well expressed when the chorus steps up the pace and then sinks back into the more languid verses, which swing between the busy and the relaxed, the full-on and the laidback, familiar to any parent. The pudding is rather over-egged on the version issued in 1994 when the cooing noises of the song's subject are added to the mix, but we see the connections between structure and realisation. A version featuring Buddy Miles has plenty of space in it, which I like, and Miles is jazz-responsive to where the vocal line is going, but overall the drums are too busy for the song. It needs to just strrrretttch out. What's most remarkable about the song is not on tape – it's that a man could write so generously and tenderly about someone else's child, the father being someone who in other times, other places, would have been thought a rival for the mother's love. In that sense the song is a product of a remarkable cultural moment and an even more remarkably enlightened gentleness and generosity of spirit.

In a different mood altogether – the comedown, perhaps, after the bright ecstasy – is 'Merry-Go-Round'. Here was an opportunity for Peter to work with Diane Hildebrand, who had written the stunning lyrics for 'Goin' Down' and co-written 'Early Morning Blues And Greens' with Jack Keller. Peter had the slow, sweetly sad melody and played it to her. He recalled that she said 'this is what it sounds like' and that she wrote the lyrics.[12] The song was composed quickly and worked on in five sessions in a month over December '67 and January '68. Each featured Peter singing and playing solo, contributing piano, guitar, and bass.

It is a strange, haunting little piece, ideally suited to Tork's folk strengths, with voice, melody, and lyric perfectly matched. It is troubling in some ways, restful in others. In this it sits on the cusp between innocence and experience, looking forward and looking back, ideal for a song recorded over the New Year, maybe, but especially appropriate at this stage in Peter's career as a Monkee when he created this almost-perfect miniature quite alone. Hildebrand's lyrics are so well suited to the melody it again makes me wish they had made the time to work together more, had he been able to climb down from the merry-go-round. The last verse is a memento mori:

Useless merry-go-round
Tomorrow, they'll tear you down
To build a parking lot
If it lives or not
It was just a toy
All it brought was joy.

The Monkees are seen riding a carousel in early publicity shots, and some of these made it into the title sequence and the musical inserts. To me, the merry-go-round is something of a symbol of The Monkees' success: brightly coloured, starting slowly, building to a thrilling speed, and then, gradually but inevitably, winding down until it stops, leaving only the blurry memory of delight. All it brought was joy. The song ends abruptly because there is nowhere else it can go. The ride is over.

CHAPTER FIVE

WHAT IS *HEAD*?: THE ROOTS OF THE POP FILM

What is Head*?* SLOGAN FROM TV, CINEMA, AND PRESS ADVERTISING CAMPAIGN FOR *HEAD*

Well, it's not a remake of Magnificent Obsession. COLUMBIA PICTURES' 'PUBLICITY CHIEF' IN 1968, AS REPORTED BY DICK STRAUB

The next logical step for a successful TV series is a realisation on the cinema screen. These can have mixed fortunes. British sitcoms, for example, have a poor track record. Even all-time greats like *Dad's Army*, *The Likely Lads*, and *Steptoe And Son* found the transition very tricky; what works well for 28 minutes might not survive the transition to 90 or 120. A film is not just three episodes stitched together, nor is it a single one stretched to three or four times its natural length. What other US TV hits were made into movies in the 60s? Surprisingly few – Adam West's *Batman* movie of 1966 was a notable exception – and many of those shows had to wait until their audience had grown up into directors, producers, and nostalgic cinemagoers to have their moment on the big screen, as in the case of *The Addams Family* (1991), *My Favorite Martian*

(1999), or *Bewitched* (2005). So the plan for a Monkee movie owed much to the fact that pop groups making movies had become a standard response to success by the time they broke through. Those movies included *A Hard Day's Night* and *Help!*, for sure, but also less well-remembered pictures such as *Ferry 'Cross The Mersey* (1964) featuring Gerry & The Pacemakers and The Dave Clark Five's *Catch Us If You Can* (1965), the theme of which provided unwitting inspiration for Boyce & Hart's '(Theme From) The Monkees'. The time and the conditions were right and, after all, *The Monkees* was conceived as a television show and was born in a Hollywood studio.

In the summer of 1967, The Monkees were still working at a prodigious rate. Less than a year after the show's launch, they were already on their fourth album, and the TV series was veering off into truly uncharted territory. Consider the speed at which these events had followed on from each other and how it might be possible for anyone to keep up that kind of productivity and sheer hard work. The tours, the recordings, the TV shows, the whole experience – nothing could have prepared anyone involved for what was happening. So when the idea of a Monkee movie was finally mooted – though it will surely have been on the slate since day one, given that the visual vocabulary of the group was based in Dick Lester's Beatle movie – it's likely that the studios thought they were going to get a 90-minute version of the television show. After all, the show had broken the mould of US television, it seemed, and the world had carried on, turning, selling, succeeding, and so they'd had their little revolution now, and it sold, so what could go wrong?

On Boxing Day 1967, The Beatles' TV movie *Magical Mystery Tour* – straying into Monkee territory – was screened on the BBC as part of its Christmas schedule. It was in striking psychedelic colour (though most people saw it in black and white) and benignly plotless. A nation harrumphed; it was considered the group's first stumble, their first wrong step. They had of course very recently undergone great disruption with the death of Brian Epstein in August of that year. They were now obliged to strike out on their own, without the protection of their showbusiness mentor, upon whom they had depended greatly. Where the Beatles had changes forced upon them, The Monkees had actively pursued a revolution in the way they worked. They had sought this 'freedom' through a startling act of self-assertion, where it was forced upon the Beatles – but by late 1967 the two groups were both exploring *terra nova*. Newspaper headlines of the time made the connection clear: 'Beatles Ape Monkees' blared the front page of the *Melody Maker* in August 1967, in response to the news that their new single, 'All You Need Is Love', would be debuted worldwide on television.

Part of the difficulty of *Magical Mystery Tour* was shared with another UK television cult TV favourite, Patrick McGoohan's *The Prisoner*: both efforts featured acts and actors whom a large audience knew and thought they could rely upon. They expected them to deliver a certain type of performance and a certain type of narrative – a variation of what had gone before. McGoohan had been offered the role of James Bond in 1962 and turned it down and in the mid 60s, thanks to his hit series *Danger Man* (*Secret Agent* in the US), was the highest-paid actor on British television. Surely he understood what his huge and loyal audience wanted? Yet in *The Prisoner* he did what The Monkees did with *Head* – approached success differently and, instead of rehashing the same stories over and over, created something wildly, even disturbingly, different which would challenge rather than pacify their audience. Both paid the price – *Head* took only $16,111 at the box office, being released commercially to only six movie theatres in November and December 1968, and McGoohan had to hide out until public anger at the inconclusive conclusion of *The Prisoner* had died back.

It's no coincidence to me either that Patrick McGoohan used 'All You Need Is Love' as diegetic music for a cacophonous machine gun showdown in the final, brilliantly chaotic episode of *The Prisoner*, entitled 'Fallout'. The double meaning is clear – the aftermath of a nuclear explosion, but also what comes after a kind of disappointment or a trusted source behaving differently. Indeed, one can imagine 'Fallout' as a possible title for *Head*. The refusal to acknowledge negative energy proved to be the dark underbelly of the hippie dream, an ideal challenged nightly by newscasts from Vietnam and the corruption of the utopian spirit made manifest in the heinous crimes of the Manson 'family'. *Magical Mystery Tour* was greeted with confusion – where had our Fabs gone? – and Britain's top TV star had, it was said, 'conned' the viewing public by not providing them with a traditional and satisfactory narrative resolution to *The Prisoner.* A change of mind and direction in the established entertainer rarely goes unpunished: the thumbs-down given to these projects was the reward for the disruption of expectation. But maybe the momentum of The Monkees – a project which had not only shaken up but effectively recast the way popular culture could be made, mediated, and sold – maybe that momentum would carry them through the transitions they sought. Maybe people could surf the wave with them. This was The Monkees after all, outselling the world and his brother in 1967.

THE ROOTS OF THE POP FILM

The move for a pop star into movies was by no means a novel idea; indeed, it was arguably film that lit the spark that helped rock'n'roll spread far beyond its original appeal in the 50s. A film like *Blackboard Jungle* (1955) used the new music as a background to images of juvenile delinquency, but within a year the music and its attendant 'lifestyle' was the star: think of *The Girl Can't Help It, Rock Around The Clock*, or Alan Freed's *Rock Rock Rock*, all from the breakout year of 1956. It wasn't until the arrival of Elvis on the soundstage that same year to shoot his first picture, *Loving You*, that the new music truly found an embodiment in Hollywood. This marked a new dynamic between the two industries, with film greeting its younger cousin, pop, as an update of the long-standing and very successful relationship between movies and music. That connection stretches right back to the very first widely seen talkie, which was, indeed, a picture about a singer. *The Jazz Singer* arrived in 1927, showing off the new sound synchronisation technologies that constituted the talkies – scripted, as we have seen, by Samuel Raphelson, uncle of Bob. These Monkee connections go deep. In this movie, Al Jolson played himself and turned his own success story into further career capital, increasing his popularity many fold. Suddenly you didn't have to go to a theatre in

Manhattan or Chicago or Los Angeles to see someone as famous as Jolson – instead, he came to your town and sang for you in the local picture house. This magical formula was the basis of Hollywood's surging success in the 30s, riding on the back of stars like Jolson, or the popularity of the Broadway musicals, or cinematic assemblages of the kind of thing people wanted from musicals, such as the *Gold Diggers* series of anthology movies. All this, and the attendant problems, are beautifully portrayed and frequently sent up in *Singin' In The Rain* (1952). This is arguably the first post-modern movie, a film reflecting upon the history of its own media form. As that form and the related technologies developed, new conventions and advantages became apparent – for example in *Gold Diggers Of 1933* we get wildly intimate close-ups of Ginger Rogers as she sings that satire on the Wall Street Crash, Dubin & Warren's 'We're In The Money'. These were not views available from the upper circle or, indeed, the front stalls of a Broadway theatre, and as such provided an extraordinary intimacy to a performance.

This was the great advantage that cinema had over live performance and it worked particularly well for popular song. The two industries remained distinct but connected. Frank Sinatra was the most obvious crossover success, working on TV with the Tommy Dorsey band and in many movies; indeed it could be argued that film saved Sinatra's career after the initial phase of his success had started to cool. Come the 50s the Hollywood response to the grassroots groundswell of popularity for a new kind of music was initially either to ignore it, mock, it or outdo it in terms of spectacle – as was the case with the extravagant gorgeousness of *High Society*, probably the last ever 'classical' Hollywood musical, released in 1956, the year of Elvis Presley's film debut.

However, the one thing Hollywood can be sure to do is follow the money, and that was, suddenly, hitched much more closely to the tastes of that invention of the post-war age, the teenager. So Elvis, embodying the new music in a highly marketable form, proved irresistible for both Hollywood and audience. The impact of Elvis's movie years upon his music is a matter of some debate, but what we do know for sure is that between 1957 and 1968 he released 25 albums, 17 of which were soundtrack recordings. So during this high period of his popularity, the great majority of the musical output was tied into his movies, album promoting movie, movie promoting album. Which was most important in keeping the kettle boiling? It's hard to say – but the common element was Elvis himself and he could be sold as movie star and pop star. A veritable plethora of copycat pictures was made, trying to tap into the popularity of the new music; but there was something missing, and that was Presley. Notice was taken in the UK too, and the late 50s and early 60s saw the rise of that odd phenomenon, the British pop movie. The top dog here was the UK's own 'Elvis', namely one Harry Webb, aka Cliff Richard. He was schooled in the art of playing to the camera on programmes like *Oh Boy!* by maverick TV producer Jack Good, later to crop up in the Monkees' story. Cliff's early films, like Elvis's, played on the air of danger around the new pop, in films of London youth like 1956's *Serious Charge.* But this soon settled into the benign vivacity of pictures like *Summer Holiday*, which was released in February 1963, just as Beatlemania was gripping the nation. These films were considered in a similar way to the way the pop single was then viewed – something to be heavily promoted, sold very quickly to the large audience, and then, before too long, replaced by a new one – a careful variant on the successful formula – and the process would begin again. It's not for nothing that factory-produced pop was called 'bubblegum' – a quick, intense delight which, once it loses its flavour and its 'pop', can simply be replaced by a new, fresher one, loaded again with the ingredients that delight the palate.

It was in this spirit of catching and cashing in on a passing moment that the first Beatles film was commissioned by United Artists in October 1963, primarily so they would get the rights to a soundtrack album. Unusually for a film company, they had their eye on the music sales, promising the rapid turnover and high volume that always equals a handsome profit. As the film's producer Walter Shenson recalled in the documentary *You Can't Do That: The Making of A Hard Day's Night*, they said, 'We need a film for the express purpose of having a soundtrack album … just make sure there are enough new songs by The Beatles for an album, and don't go over budget.' In this they had clearly seen the business model pursued by Presley's manager 'Colonel' Tom Parker, and decided that this new group from England were next in line for a success of this sort and that they wanted to be there for the financial windfall. The album they received delivered twice as much as they could use in the movie – seven songs, constituting side one of the LP, were duly badged on the record sleeve as being 'From the soundtrack of the United Artists film *A HARD DAY'S NIGHT*'. Six more new songs were on side two, unconnected to the movie, formally at least. Tony Barrow's inimitable sleeve-note-writing skills for Beatle discs served him well here:

> It became apparent that no more than six new songs should be introduced via the soundtrack of the film. To increase this number would have left insufficient screen-time for the action of the plot. … When you listen to the second side of this record you will agree that it would have been a pity to cast aside such a fabulous set of songs solely because they couldn't be fitted into the structure of *A HARD DAY'S NIGHT*. … At the same time it is interesting to remember that the LP … is the first-ever album release to be made up entirely of self-composed and self-performed Beatle compositions.

So this is a 'real' Beatles album, as well as being the soundtrack or souvenir that UA wanted, and in his sign-off Barrow cannily tips the balance toward the band rather than the movie – this is all their own work. They were in a position of financial and pop-cultural strength to insist upon this distinction between what the movie represented and what and who the band actually were and what their primary interest was: the music. This has clear resonance for the case of The Monkees, who did not have this leverage. In fact, they had to work very hard to get away from the sense that they were 'owned' by the studio, partly because, due to the unique circumstances of their conception, they actually *were* owned by Columbia and Screen Gems, whether they were making TV, music, or movies. This even extended to their name, which in later years they had to pay to use, licensing the brand name from Columbia, which of course owned it.

So The Beatles' first connection with the film industry, to which the whole Monkees project owed so much, was a carefully negotiated one, mindful of the injurious impact that the films of Elvis had had on his music. UA got the whole album to sell, but they only got 50 percent of the music on it to badge as theirs. The Beatles held their own in this case, using the promotional opportunity of the film industry as much as Hollywood tapped into their great commercial appeal. The trick was repeated the following year with Dick Lester's second Beatle film *Help!*, a film in which suddenly, à la *The Wizard Of Oz*, the world was transformed into full colour. Again, seven songs were featured on the first side of the album as belonging to the movie, while seven more on side two stood independent of it. In this way the movie's imprint on the music was reduced, and both these albums are considered as completely legitimate parts of the Beatle catalogue rather than side-projects in the way that the jumbled releases surrounding *Magical Mystery Tour* and *Yellow Submarine* are.

In some ways, then, the first two Monkees albums could be considered soundtrack albums – the soundtrack to the success of the first iteration of the television series, 'as heard on TV'. The marketing campaigns for the albums certainly pushed the discs and their accompanying single records to retailers in this way, with a flurry of statistics and the media bombardment that would prove so successful in making the Monkees records irresistible to the target market, rendering resistance futile. Take for example this advertisement from *Billboard*, dated September 17 1966:

> It's here! The Monkees' first fantastic Colgems album, *The Monkees* COM/COS-101, featuring twelve exciting tunes from their new TV series, including 'Last Train To Clarksville' and 'Take A Giant Step' #66-1001. It could be one of the most important new albums of the year.
>
> And this is just the beginning! The action gets rolling tonight with the debut of the Screen Gems TV show *The Monkees*, produced by Bert Schneider and Robert Rafelson – every Monday night on NBC-TV at 7.30 pm. E.D.T. Success story? You *know* it!
>
> 'Last Train To Clarksville' produced by Tommy Boyce and

> Bobby Hart. 'Take A Giant Step' produced by Tommy Boyce, Bobby Hart, and Jack Keller. Music Supervision, Don Kirshner.

As a consequence of the barriers to their contributing to the first two albums, *Headquarters* could be seen as their musical debut, with the album that accompanied *Head* their third soundtrack. Yet paradoxically the *Head* soundtrack stands apart from the movie as a work of art in its own right.

Pop films as a whole don't have a glittering reputation – and it is interesting that the best regarded are the more troublesome ones that failed to deliver the pop thrill in their own day but are later reconsidered. I'm thinking of *Head* of course, but also a film like Peter Watkins's *Privilege* (1967). By contrast the standard pop film, be it *Every Day's A Holiday* (1964) or *Spiceworld* (1997), tends to be a wafer-thin narrative in which the band gets into amusing scrapes and eventually wins out, singing a few songs on the way. This has something in common with episodes of The Monkees' TV series of course, although the quality of the writing, acting, and music in the shows was of such a stellar standard that I'd suggest this is where the resemblance ends.

When it came to an opportunity to make a feature film, one thing they knew they did not want to do was make a '90-minute episode of the TV show'. They had already explored almost every possible variant on the formula and indeed were almost through with it, as Dolenz explained to *Mojo* in 2002:

> I was getting a little bored with doing the same show every week – even after only two years. We'd met The Beatles. We'd been around the world. To come back to doing a half-hour TV show seemed like a bit of a let down. In retrospect, I think we probably should have kept doing the TV show. But the idea came along to do this movie.

As he notes here, their experiences out in the world beyond the studios and soundstages of Hollywood had changed everything – they were real pop stars, who had been welcomed into the company of the greats as equals. How could they, why would they, go back to working for rate on a TV show? In the episode 'Monkees In Paris', first broadcast in February 1968, they had already played out their dissatisfaction with the formula on screen, aided and abetted by director and kindred spirit Jim Frawley. The opening scene unravels as the Monkees contest the point of carrying on making the same show each time, objecting to the predictable 'scare', in which they are menaced by a couple of heavies, and declaring instead that they are going on holiday to Paris.

So by this 54th episode, the familiarity of the visual beats of the show had clearly become as repetitious and formulaic as those in the music that they had thrown aside the previous year. This little intro, rehearsed and agreed as it may be, is effectively a striking out for visual freedom in the way they had sought and gained their own musical identity. The Parisian scenes were filmed just before their shows in London in June and July 1967 and because they were not as well known in France (the TV show was not on air there) they could film in the street with relative anonymity; the chase sequences were staged, whereas in Britain they would have been very much real, as can be seen in the Pathé newsreel of their London visit, when Davy was briefly 'lost' in a bundle of fans.

The idea of making changes was very much in the air. In late '67 they began to plot what their movie might look like. With the help of Bert Schneider, Bob Rafelson, and a few of their hangers-on, such as long-time B-movie actor Jack Nicholson, they set about dreaming up something entirely different.

OJAI

It's unusual that the exact time and location of the genesis of a movie can be specified, but that is the case with *Head*. From the 22nd to the 26th of November 1967, the four Monkees decamped with Bob Rafelson, Bert Schneider, Jack Nicholson, and de facto Monkees manager Brendan Cahill to a resort hotel in Ojai, California, where they spent a long weekend which was both 'lost' in the rock'n'roll sense and extremely productive. What made it doubly unusual is that the sessions and discussions were free form, verbal, and recorded on reel-to-reel tape.

It is a moot point as to who contributed what and how much to the ideas which populate the movie. While the final screen credit for the screenplay went to Rafelson and Nicholson, it is clear that the band were capable of their own freakery: Micky Dolenz would write and direct 'The Frodis Caper' immediately after the Ojai sessions, and it's worth noting that the weekend before this stoned soul picnic Nesmith had supervised his own deliberate mash-up of the familiar into something new, with intense two-day studio sessions for *The Wichita Train Whistle Sings*. His first solo project, this was a startling reimagining of his songs; some were identifiable only by their titles, stripped as they were of both arrangement and vocals and then rebuilt as something rococo and wildly extravagant. In some ways, *Wichita* is a musical manifestation of the same impulse to both subvert and recreate that we find in *Head*; it seems in no way coincidental that both had their genesis in same week. 'Circle Sky' – perhaps the garage-band antithesis of the muso-complexities of *Wichita*'s baroque and sometimes berserk arrangements – was also first demoed at this time, showing Nesmith's range and also his understanding of the musical shapes he was working with.

The brainstorming session for the proposed movie took place at the Ojai Valley Inn golf resort in a fitting combination of the mundane and the surreal. The town of Ojai is beautiful and cultured, with its long-established music and literary festivals. Some in the town call it Shangri-la, an ideal place to work and dream at the same time. While the idea of a creative free-for-all might seem out of kilter with the way a mainstream TV show had to be made, it wasn't completely different either – consider the breakdowns and grabs for reality that characterise elements of both series of the show.

Rhino Films' biopic *Daydream Believers: The Monkees' Story* makes a decent stab at recreating this event, necessarily telescoping and making every idea a winner (or, at least, one we recognise as having been included in the film). It's an intriguing part of the story and rare in Monkee lore in that it did not take place in front of a camera or a studio microphone. The Nicholson character – played with commendable Cheshire cat grinning sleaze by a strangely uncredited actor – proposes that 'You guys … could be like dandruff in somebody's hair!' and the scene fades to a recreation of the scene in the movie where that is precisely what is asked of them. Sober, we see that in this case at least they are obliged to act out someone else's idea and fantasy of themselves, just as much as they did in 'Here Come The Monkees' two years before. The Ojai meeting was a rare behind-closed-doors episode that has gone relatively undocumented, though some film evidence was hinted at in an observation Dolenz made on the commentary track of *Daydream Believers*:

> Hey, I got 16-millimetre film of this actual event out in Ojai, sitting around talking about the movie. What ever happened to those tapes? Hmm.

Snippets of material were included on the Criterion box set Blu-ray version of the movie. Micky also recalled the wider context of the meeting in his *Head* Blu-ray commentary:

> There was just the four of us, plus Bob, Bert, and Jack. We just talked for two days. It seemed to be more about what we didn't want to make. A basic rambling about everything. Jack was trying to get a sense of who we were. Now that I see the movie, it's clear they were looking to make a deconstruction of The Monkees [and] a deconstruction of Hollywood as well.

He omits Brendan Cahill but by other accounts he was the eighth man. Rafelson reflected on the film's genesis too, telling *Mojo*:

> To a degree I was parodying Hollywood. But I was also saying, I'll probably never get the chance to make a movie again, so I'm going to make every movie this time out. Ojai was sort of a group therapy session. But Jack was dumbfounded to think The Monkees would say things like, 'We're better actors than Marlon Brando.' Jack said, 'Jesus, who are these guys? They're out of their

> minds.' I said, 'Just be patient, Jack. They all have their virtues, they'll do everything quite well.'

The baggy nature of this process of collecting ideas hit trouble as soon as they sobered up and got back to the office; it soon transpired that the four Monkees would not be getting a writer's credit on the movie. Caught up in a dispute about who did what, Nesmith acted as 'shop steward' and, backed by his personal manager and lawyer Jerry Perenchio, urged the others to go on strike for a script credit – and, therefore, some guaranteed income and credit. Perenchio knew what he was talking about, having headed up MCA in the late 50s and gone on to run his own agency. In the 70s he effectively introduced Elton John to the American market, and later moved into film and TV and became one of the richest people in the world, being listed as number 240 on 2015's *Forbes* Richest list. He knew a rip-off when he saw one.

So it was that on the first day of shooting, February 15 1968, only Peter showed up on set. Shooting didn't actually begin until the following Monday, the 19th. They didn't get a writing credit in the end, settling instead for points on the movie – a percentage of the take. This would amount to very little indeed. The period of shooting *Head* was more or less the same duration, at more or less the same time of year, as *Headquarters* 12 months earlier. It's an indicator of how fast things had moved and changed. With regard to the ownership of ideas, Tork still saw the group as being secondary to the writers in 1994. 'The four of us, Bert Schneider, Bob, and Jack Nicholson all went to Ojai and talked about what we did and didn't want. We sort of found a common ground. What exactly that was, we wound up leaving to Bob and Jack – the exact script of the movie was basically their idea.'[1]

Lots and lots of stimulants and relaxants were imbibed at the Ojai hotel and that certainly explains some of the wilder elements of this movie – but this isn't to say that such an approach works against it. The tale is told that Nicholson structured the movie along the lines of an acid (LSD) trip. 'We didn't shoot the movie on acid but Jack did structure the movie in his mind on an acid trip,' Rafelson told *Mojo*. He had form in this area, coming to the film off the back of writing the script for Peter Fonda's *The Trip*. The movie clearly does have a kind of trippy dream (or nightmare) quality in part, but not all of it. In some senses *Head* reminds me of an older kind of trip, Lewis Carroll's 19th-century fantasy *Alice In Wonderland,* where one scene or object doesn't simply give way to the next, rather that one moment seems to grow unstoppably from the one before it. 'Always changing inside, what does it become?' asks 'Can You Dig It?', and that is one of the central questions the movie asks – what does it become? No wonder the original title was 'Changes'; that's what is at the heart of the picture – perpetual change.

Within a week of the Ojai session, Nicholson had typed up a substantial first draft of a script for a Monkee movie, even going so far as to provide a logo for it, a spin on the Monkee guitar-shaped logo, with the word 'Changes' in the guitar shape instead of 'Monkees'. Why 'Changes'? The connotations are multiple. There are musical connotations, as in 'what are the changes?' in a piece of music. There are stylistic changes – we used to sound like this, now we sound like this – and this has a special meaning for The Monkees, because 'there's no group sound, there hardly ever was', as Dolenz told *The Hy Lit Show* in 1968, apart from *Headquarters* and the concerts. Changes are difficult for fans too as they can miss the older or original style. This is a challenge for all artists of course – think of how The Beatles changed from *Please Please Me* to *Abbey Road* in both musical style and visual appearance.

Change is also to do with the passage of time – even if we just stand still, time will change us. So changes are inevitable; it's how they are dealt with that makes them more or less influential. There's a theatrical, performative dimension too: within a production there will be any number of costume changes, the putting on and taking off of personae. In a performance one's clothing is a key source of information for a viewer, loaded with the character's 'real' personality in a way it is not in 'real life'. So we see The Monkees in this film dressed individually but characterfully – Mike's suit, Peter's orange Nehru shirt, Davy's green shirt, Micky's jumper (worn, appropriately, as he jumps) – but also colour-coded. The white outfits of the Salt Lake City footage look fabulous, and demonstrate that attention to visual detail is a key part of the impact of live musical performance, whether one is associated with a TV show or not. The colour – or rather absence of it – allows the group to be seen as 'blank canvas' onto which you could project anything you wish. That was certainly the case for the real and wholly delighted audience in Utah. Let me note that the gig took place on May 17 1968, a full six months before The Beatles strove to make a similar point with the plain white cover of their eponymous double album, aka *The White Album*. In the case of the scene in *Head* the plainness of the white clothing becomes a rich and complex set of possible associations and connections, as well as providing an illuminating contrast to the intense kaleidoscope of colours associated with psychedelia – as seen later in Mike's birthday party scene, for example. Thus the 'Changes' are coming thick and fast and from all sides and you had better be ready to deal with them. The title 'Changes' is shared by a Davy Jones/Steve Pitts co-write first recorded in February 1968, so clearly the word had some currency; the song was very probably an effort to create a title song for the film. Nothing so conventional would emerge, and even though the last-gasp Monkees album that just made it into the 70s was optimistically entitled *Changes* – it was effectively a Jones and Dolenz album – the song still did not surface. It eventually emerged more than two decades later, blinking into the digital era via Rhino's pursuit of their *Missing Links* in 1990 and elsewhere since.

The script that has slipped into the public domain reveals much about the movie: what was originally in the Ojai draft, and what was added as they went along. What one notices immediately is that much of what must have been very early material survives into the finished film. Equally one sees scenes that were either lost on the cutting room floor or in all likelihood never made it off the page. Reading them, the scenes seems implausible, almost unrealisable – but perhaps if you had removed, say, another key scene – the boxing match? Desert scene? The factory? – that too would seem, on paper, implausible. It's very difficult to say. Try to explain any of the scenes to someone who hasn't seen the movie. It soon becomes very tricky.

Inevitably, the film has come to be seen – when it is seen at all – as a time capsule of the era, of the moment when the early optimism of the 60s, which flowered through popular culture and found a response in art, music, film, and belatedly TV and radio, started to wither on the vine and go bad. It's no coincidence that the spectre of Charles Manson has touched the Monkees story at one or two points, as it was he who embodied the way the free love hippie dream became a ghastly nightmare. Like the Beatle films, the movie was made admirably quickly, between February and May 1968, the final act being the recording of a live concert, especially staged for the purposes of the movie, on Friday May 17 in the Valley Music Hall, Salt Lake City, Utah, their first visit to the Mormon state. A competition run by local radio station KCPX ensured that the 4,000 tickets reached a very enthusiastic audience, as can be seen in the film and heard on the 2012 *Head* boxed set.

The movie is sometimes characterised as being overtly cynical about the group, their success, the music industry, media manipulation, human nature … and in some ways it is. Yet this cynicism does not flow from the central performances – the band play live in front of real fans who really love them – but is in part a creation of editing and the directorial viewpoint. For example, in this same scene we note how the performance and its implied assertion of the situation's reality is undermined by the device of having the crowd rush the stage, only for the band to be revealed as mannequins; the crowd don't seem too upset, clutching their souvenirs anyway. But the grit in the gloss is Rafelson's. That's fine – it's his movie – but it shows how the dynamics between him and The Monkees differ in almost every imaginable way from those that existed between Richard Lester and The Beatles. For your information, in neither of the Beatle films do we actually hear the band playing live; they are miming to playback throughout. I'll leave that irony with you for a moment.

Rafelson's cynicism upset Tork in particular, but Peter could also understand why he and Schneider tired of them:

I think Bert and Bob had love/hate feelings for us. They liked us

> because we weren't normal characters, and this is a case of taking the bitter with the sweet. You can have Hollywood-trained actors who know how to be quiet and sit still when they're supposed to sit still, and act when they're supposed to act, but you're not going to get crazies like us. I think they eventually got sick of it and didn't want to do it any more.'[2]

Head has some superficial resemblance to other pop movies but its essential purpose is different. Where *A Hard Day's Night* and *Catch Us If You Can* were designed to build a public image and add a seductive visual dimension to an already-successful pop music act, *Head* sets out to undo previous work of this sort and, indeed, to shatter the carefully constructed public image. This may on the surface appear to have something in common with the band's goal when they took over creative control of their own music or when they walked out of their own show (that scene in 'Monkees In Paris'), but its actual goal is not simply to *show* them being put back in the box but to ensure that they *are* put back in the box. Yet if we look at the constituent elements of the movie, many of the set-piece scenes build on or relate to episodes of the incredibly successful TV show: the desert scene links with 'Everywhere A Sheikh Sheikh'; the horror scene echoes the many 'haunted house' riffs such as 'Monkee See Monkee Die' or 'A Coffin Too Frequent'; the Wild West stuff mirrors 'Monkees In A Ghost Town' or even 'It's A Nice Place To Visit'; the science fiction reflects 'Monkees Watch Their Feet' and 'Mijacogeo'; the crooked boxing match reflects 'Monkees In The Ring'. Even the kissing contest with Mimi Jefferson reminds us of the four of them pursuing April Conquest in 'Monkees Get Out More Dirt'. So, on paper, there are no real revelations or wild divergences form the formula of the successful TV show here. So what changed?

What seemed to work very well almost immediately for The Monkees was marketing. As a glance at the contemporary magazines shows, the TV show was extraordinarily heavily marketed: 'Win a Guest Slot on the show!', 'Win a pair of Monkee socks!'. Monkee soft-drink nightclubs were franchised alongside the wide range of clothing and merchandise. All media networks and magazines were schmoozed and on board, and as early as May 31 1966 a feature in the *Washington Post* reported that the 'Synthetic Quartet Will Hit Tube Hard'. Nesmith said in the 1997 documentary that 'what made it succeed was the size of the machine' and he wasn't wrong. By contrast, *Head* seems to have been born under a bad sign. Something that is routinely asserted is that part of the reason for the film's failure was its deliberately opaque marketing scheme: even Nesmith seemed to agree that 'the marketing of it was obscure'.[3] However, it's not quite true to say that *Head* was deliberately un- or even anti-marketed.

The infamous posters featuring John Brockman staring out at the viewer were deliberately obscure in their refusal to promote a movie in the conventional way. Yet this is just the top layer at which certain marketing decisions were made by Rafelson and Nicholson. Both tell the story of going around Manhattan in advance of the premiere promoting the movie by plastering Brockman stickers over everything they could find. That reminds me of what it was like promoting my band's gigs and records, trying to put up posters and stickers in the street without attracting the attention of the local constabulary, rather than a campaign to wake the world to the arrival of the film debut by what was still one of the world's most popular acts. So they were mainstream, major-studio-funded would-be auteurs behaving like student filmmakers. It's a remarkable and probably unique situation.

Yet this idea is very much of its time, too, as the mainstream became flooded with ideas that seemed to come surging in from the margins. The avant-garde suddenly took centre stage through Yoko Ono's work, Andy Warhol's connection of the pop artist and the pop star, and The Who and The Monkees' old support act Jimi Hendrix smashing up their expensive gear every night on stage. So the auto-iconoclasm of *Head* is not a freakish cultural one-off. It's extreme in its unrelenting persecution of its own stars, certainly, but then the phenomenon of The Monkees was in itself one borne of and experienced through extremity. *Head* was part of a wider pattern of challenges to the culture industries and the idea of ownership of creativity, and what creativity could actually mean.

Yet behind Brockman's head and under the Mylar, Columbia did conduct a gamely upbeat marketing campaign of a much more conventional kind. There were press packs, lobby cards, a campaign press book, and a variety of posters, all of which make The Monkees their central design feature. So it is untrue to say the film was not marketed. Instead, Columbia took a two-pronged approach to promoting the movie: 'Two Unique *Head* Campaigns Reach Audiences At Every Level' chirped the press book, hopefully. Campaign A was for the hipsters, while B targeted the more traditional cinemagoer and Monkee fans. The monochrome Brockman was the face of A, and the Van Gogh sunflower-yellow poster of the band falling was B. The former has no mention of the group; the latter has their name right in the centre in fiery red alongside unmistakable images of the four. Variants of both existed and are now much desired by collectors. Highly creative radio film and TV trailers were produced and broadcast, but to little effect – whichever route was tried, audiences A and B (and probably C–Z) were unresponsive. In truth, The Monkees' falling star and the unique nature of *Head* would have foiled any marketing efforts.

Within *Head* there is a great tension between the director's vision of the group and their view of themselves. This places the four Monkees in strange and hitherto unexplored terrain, not unlike the constantly changing environments within the movie itself, colluding in an act of auto-iconoclasm which has been impressed upon them by their increasingly weary makers. The 'Frankenstein' analogy is both obvious and apposite – the maker creates the real from the plastic, is overtaken by the creature, and then looks for a way to rid himself of it. In a cool and clear-sighted estimation of the film, based on a preview screening, John Maloney wrote in *The Hollywood Reporter* about this dynamic:

> The faults of the Raybert production of *Head* are rather neatly symbolized in the title, an insistence on playing it both ways. … Individually The Monkees are a very talented assemblage. Little effort is made to explore or develop their screen characters or styles … box office will depend on the residue of goodwill

> for The Monkees. The film's psychedelic boutique was more commercial when production began.[4]

In this prescient overview of the film and its making, Maloney casts light on the tussle between the director and his subject, and the former's effort to keep control over the latter; to keep them where he wants them, like an old school Hollywood director, but also to accommodate a contemporary (if fading, as Maloney notes) bouquet of freedom and expression. According to Rafelson:

> We called it three different things at three different times. The first title, *Changes*, seemed best because changes meant something at that time – to do with hallucinations and the cliché that the only thing you can rely on is change. And of course the picture was constantly changing throughout. Then we called it *DASturb* for a while. Today everybody misspells words but it was very new at the time. The third title was *Head*. Why? First of all, it took place in somebody's head, in Victor Mature's hair. The Monkees were dandruff. A lot of head imagery …

Davy Jones reflected on this 'dandruff' idea:

> And this would, to me, explain my feelings about Schneider and Rafelson. I – we – were playing dandruff in Victor Mature's hair, OK, in the Monkee movie *Head*. Dandruff, dandruff. I think that's the value they put on us, to tell you the truth, and that would sort of like hold true with some of the things I've said so far about these guys. They were never very helpful to us, other than they gave us the opportunity to do what we did. I guess that was everything.[5]

He is clearly conflicted about what he (and The Monkees) do or do not owe to Rafelson and Schneider and this is part of the great tension in the movie – are they being exploited like never before or are they setting themselves free from that 'factory system' by putting the whole process up there on screen and revealing it for what it is, with themselves by-products of it? It wouldn't be the first time, as Michael Nesmith had effectively said the same thing back in January 1967, in the infamous *Saturday Evening Post* whistle-blowing feature, asking writer Richard Warren Lewis to 'tell the world that we're synthetic, because, damn it, we are. Tell them The Monkees were wholly man-made overnight. Tell the world we don't record our own music.' So that piece of information was already out there and known worldwide, causing a stir wherever it was reported – in the UK the *Melody Maker* (as opposed to the fan mags) ran an interview with Dolenz as a front-page splash entitled 'Monkees Don't Play On Hit! Micky Dolenz Admits'. The 'hit' in question was 'I'm A Believer', their very first in the UK. So the production line nature of their early music was old news by the time *Head* was being planned. The scrutiny in the movie went deeper and in some ways past The Monkees altogether – the narrative surrounding the group and driving the film became a way of shining a light into the heart of the whole entertainment industry itself, into the workings of the machine – into the black box.

Asked whether he and The Monkees were trying to change the perception of the band with *Head*, Bob Rafelson recalled:

> Not to try to change it, no. To try to tell the truth about it. And end the saga gracefully. The whole purpose of *Head* – which, by the way, any number of my friends and my associates tried to argue me out of doing, for my sake. 'What the hell do you want to make a Monkees movie for? You've done this already.' I said, 'Yeah, but we never told the truth.' So let's tell the truth of what it is like to be manipulated by the establishment. What does it mean to me? What does it mean for The Monkees? And do it in a very abstract, but very, I thought, audacious way. So audacious I suppose that nobody went to see the fucking thing.[6]

People say it's a chaotic, structure-less movie but I don't see it that way. I'd concur with Rafelson's term 'audacious', however, as 'telling the truth of what it is like to be manipulated by the establishment' from the very heart of that establishment is indeed bold.

Jack Nicholson's involvement in the movie was actually his big break. He'd been on the fringes of Hollywood for a long time and his luck was to be known to Rafelson at the right time, as Dolenz recalled:

> Nicholson came into the scene, you know, as a friend of Rafelson and Schneider. They'd worked together on projects pre-Monkees and probably didn't get them off the ground, and all of a sudden, they pulled him in, and Jack was much the same as Clint Eastwood. He'd been making sort of like spaghetti westerns and doing small parts here and there. If you looked through his roster of things he did way before he was Jack Nicholson to the world, and you'll see some really funky stuff.[7]

This is true enough, and everybody's where they wanna be, but the fact remains that without the Monkees Nicholson would probably never have climbed beyond the spaghetti western and shlock horrors he had already worn a rut in. Rafelson has expressed surprise at the cultural impact of the movie:

> To this day, I get letters from all kinds of people asking if they can see a print of *Head.* … even Mick Jagger asked me once. I've just been asked to re-release it on DVD, with a director's commentary. Which I doubt I'll do because I've never done it [he didn't, but gave a short interview about the Monkee experience as a whole which was a bonus feature on the Criterion Blu-ray box set of three of his movies]. Through the years this has turned into the anthem movie of rock'n'roll. That's shocking because The Monkees were hardly rock'n'roll anthem bearers. But rock bands identify with it.[8]

What Rafelson fails to see is that much of the appeal of the movie to other working musicians and rock bands is that it lays bare the processes and machinations to which they are exposed and subjected – often by people who hold positions of contractual authority over them in the way that Rafelson did. It's ironic that he was more of an establishment man than the band – it was he who was funded by Columbia, and had his cake and ate it by burning up the studio logo right at the film's finale, not the Monkees themselves.

> They wanted everything. They were kids. They didn't know anything about the movies. Yeah, they wanted writing credit – but, my goodness, Mr Nicholson was dumbfounded as to why. Now, their recollection is probably different because they think they invented themselves. From a certain point of view, as I was inspired to make a movie about The Monkees, they may have thought they deserved it. But there was little I learned in Ojai that I didn't already know.'[9]

Here we see the hand closing the door of the black box, like the scientist, Inspector Shrink, played in the movie by Charles Macaulay. The group could not have contributed anything of substance because, well, how could they when Rafelson and Nicholson were there? Everything the four gave was processed through and therefore 'owned' by those directing and constructing the film. The coup de grace here is Rafelson's incredulity that '*they think they invented themselves*'. This is the dark dilemma at the heart of the Monkees story – ownership. I have had parents introduced to me by their children on graduation day who, semi-jokingly, have claimed their child's academic success as their own – 'she gets it from me', and the like. It's always an awkward moment, as I know how hard the student has worked and how far they have travelled in the three years since they arrived at university – but still, the parents, perhaps uneasy at the child's success, claim it for themselves. This is precisely what Rafelson is doing here – the child has outgrown him and he is trying to undermine that progress, and to put them back in the box. In the movie, it is always someone else, someone of a previous generation who traps them – Inspector Shrink, The Big Victor – but in truth it was, and is, Rafelson; it's his script, it's his film. So far so subtractive; but what is more interesting for us is that he refers to being 'inspired to make a film about', rather than 'featuring', The Monkees, and this is a much more artistically intriguing clue to the film. If it is 'about' The Monkees then surely that changes everything we see in it, so that as an integral piece of creativity, it is metaphoric and allusional rather than documentary or indeed 'authentic' as a representation of the meaning and experience of The Monkees as a cultural phenomenon. Rafelson:

> I can't attribute the failure of the movie to it being 'ahead of its time': it may be partly that but it may also just be not a very good movie. But if it isn't a good movie it's not a conventional enough movie for anyone to come out of it saying what it was about. What it is is certainly not a movie where everyone could come out of the cinema and say what it's about.[10]

To Rafelson, *Head* will perhaps seem an anomaly, juvenilia even, and his view of it is a filmmaker's, not a pop historian's or a fan's. His idea of failure in the cinema is not necessarily indexed by, say, box office returns or indeed cult status. What we can say though is that the movie provided a very central bit of heft into the period characterised as the American new wave, now an established era in film history, as written about multiple times, not least in Peter Biskind's famous book *Easy Riders, Raging Bulls*, which documents the era and how the key directors of the time reshaped US cinema. While Rafelson seems a minor figure on a list containing names such as Spielberg, Scorsese, De Palma, and Coppola, he is important in that story because, without the success of movies such as *Easy Rider* and *Five Easy Pieces*, it is arguable that the doors of Hollywood would never have swung open wide enough to let these characters in, allowing them to work up the cinematic revolution that followed. In the same way that punk allowed and inspired much more commercially successful acts like U2, the mainstream is always commercially refreshed by periodic infusions of new blood that begin by rocking the boat and challenging the mainstream. It had happened in Hollywood with the arrival of sound in 1927, rock'n'roll in the mid 50s, and again with Rafelson and his peers in the American new wave of the late 60s and early 70s. It is also true that without his involvement with The Monkees, Rafelson would most likely never have been in a position to act as a catalyst of this kind; he certainly would not have been bankrolled and granted creative freedom for his debut feature to the extent he was for *Head*.

The film has been good for Rafelson and, despite the way it abuses them, The Monkees. Better this than a banal document that fails to speak of the reality of their experience or of the times: despite the antagonism, they needed each other. As is often the case, Micky Dolenz has the most telling appraisal of the work:

> We all wanted to do something different than a 90-minute version of the show. Which, in retrospect, would have been a lot more commercial. But then again, we wouldn't have this strange little cult movie, which I'm very proud of.[11]

Let's take a look at this 'strange little cult movie'.

CHAPTER SIX

PRODUCTION 8888: *HEAD*, SCRIPT TO SCREEN

Head, assigned Production Number 8888 at the time of its first draft script, made its New York debut on November 7 1968 at The Cinema Studio at 66th and Broadway, opposite the Lincoln Centre. It opened in LA at the Vogue Theatre – The Monkees' star on the Hollywood Walk Of Fame is now right outside it – on November 14, and went on general release on November 20, reaching a meagre six theatres nationwide. The *New Yorker* film critic Pauline Kael, who famously claimed never to have watched a film more than once, walked out of the NYC screening after an hour.

> The movie might have worked for bored kids at kiddie matinees, but the filmmakers got ambitious. The by now standard stuff of girls squealing as pop idols perform is not even convincing when they're squealing for The Monkees, and when this is intercut with documentary footage of the suffering and horror of war, as if to comment on the shallowness of what the filmmakers are manufacturing and packaging and desperately trying to sell, the doubling up of greed and pretentions to depth is enough to make even a pinhead walk out.[1]

I don't know if that makes her a pinhead or not but she clearly did not care for what she saw even as she misunderstood it. She wasn't alone – most reviews liked it lukewarm, some finding fragments to praise, some seeking to damn it.

Columbia Pictures was in deep trouble, and had been reliant on Screen Gems' success in TV and radio – notably that of The Monkees – to keep it afloat since the mid 60s. Indeed on December 23 1968, just weeks after *Head* received its premiere, Screen Gems was fully incorporated into Columbia. If they were depending on *Head* to get this new relationship off to a successful start, they were to face disappointment. Yet in many ways the film repeats many of the tricks of the wildly successful TV show, right down to some of the scenes and locations. How could it fail? Let's see.

OPENING CEREMONY

Head opens with no titles or credits, on a squeal of feedback and a strange, unidentifiable close-up on a field of hot pink. Pulling back, we see that it is a ribbon being held by a policeman at some kind of opening ceremony. There's no dialogue but a murmur of voices, only faintly discernible under the voluminous chugging throb of helicopters and truck horns blowing. We are at the opening ceremony of a bridge, 'played' by the real Gerald Desmond Bridge at Long Beach, south of central LA. The bridge was brand new and unopened when the scenes were shot. The bridge scenes were shot in April 1968, and it did not open to traffic until July 1 of that year. The cop, played by John Dennis, greets a group of bystanders and saunters over to a black car. He leans down to an open window and says: 'Mayor, I think we're ready to go.'

The mayor, a Murry Wilson lookalike, is played by Charles Irving and he handles the curiously weighted scene well. Just about to step to the mic, he is called aside to make an inspection of a Guard of Honour, delivering one of the first of many blink-and-you-miss-it comic moments in the film: the portly white man walks down a line of tall African-American soldiers, and as he passes each one there is the sudden shift and click of arms being presented. There are ten soldiers, with the sixth being the single white man, standing at least a foot shorter than his colleagues.

He is accompanied not by the sound of a rifle being presented but instead we hear a hollow 'ponk' sound, like a tin bucket being kicked. It's a good sound-and-vision gag but it also draws our attention to the ironies of the situation – America depending for its defence, and its prosecution of war, upon a minority it treats badly – and is also a taster of the film's mix of the serious and the ridiculous.

After performing this duty, 'Mayor Feedback' walks over to the mic and tries to begin his speech. There follows a bit of deadpan comic business between the mayor and the cop, a playlet with little echoes of Keaton, Laurel & Hardy, even Samuel Beckett. The officer tests the mic, and it works fine, his 'Testing!' echoing out into the morning. The mayor tries to begin the speech five times, with the cop testing the mic, increasingly tetchily, three times. On the last occasion, he stands tapping the mic hard to show that there is no problem with it and fixing the mayor with a last-chance stare.

Little shards of the incidental and ambient noise in this scene find their way into the first track on the *Head* soundtrack album, appropriately entitled 'Opening Ceremony', as does much of the mayor's speech, though on the album it is echoed, looped, and psychedelicised. The mayor ploughs on, no doubt too fearful of the cop to stop again. The echoes swirl around in a curious vortex of sound which blurs his words so their end seems to overlap with their beginning: 'Ladies and gentlemen, I hereby dedicate this magnificent model of modern architecture … one of the largest suspended arch bridges in the world, to the people of …'

We never find out who will be the honoured beneficiaries of this dedication, because he is brushed aside and away from the mic by Micky Dolenz, who rushes from the top of the shot across the scene and bursts through the ceremonial tape like a sprint winner just as the mayor is about to cut it. His arrival is heralded by a new pitch of noise and ambient clamour, cut by a sharp high sound. He is in turn pursued by the other three Monkees and they sprint into the no man's land of the unopened bridge.

They run together, fast, and Micky keeps ahead and reaches the centre of the bridge well before they do. Who are they running from? Is Micky running from his bandmates, or is he just ahead of them, all running from a common enemy? They all look like the guys people would recognise, but more so – Micky is in a very cool pair of light brown cords, a suede jacket and round-necked white sweater, pre-iconic Adidas trainers on his feet, helping that swift run he is on. Behind him runs Nesmith in his shades, linen trousers, and a smart two tone jacket, Peter runs in a very groovy orange Nehru shirt, round high four button collar all done up right, love beads, and blue jeans. Davy goes like a little rocket in his khaki trousers and green mandarin collar top – which, he later claimed, was bought years later by Michael Jackson in a showbiz memorabilia auction. Once you know the film, these outfits assume a significance that is not apparent from this first scene: they are the outfits they are wearing in the photograph on the back cover of the soundtrack album.

The ambient sound fades away to be replaced by a montage of sirens, klaxons, and horns which float free from their background, melding in an atonal yet rather beautiful conjunction, slowed down as if in a dream, or the instant of an accident. Dolenz throws off the jacket and all sound cuts dead as he stands on the ledge of the bridge and contemplates the fall down into the water below. He decides quickly what he must do, looking behind him – at his bandmates? his pursuers? or are they one and the same? – clambers onto the handrail of the bridge and – ah! – he jumps. As he does so, all sound ceases aside from that of the wind blowing. The scene cuts momentarily back to his stunned bandmates, as they watch him falling the great and surely fatal distance to the harbour waters beneath the bridge. The Gerald Desmond Bridge had a 155 feet (47 metre) clearance above the surface of the Cerritos Channel below. We endure six clear seconds of silence – hearing the windsong – until the first chord of 'Porpoise Song' chimes in as he falls. The opening chords strike up and run for 28 seconds, nearly half of which is occupied by the superb, daring suspension of melodic progression as Micky falls, and we watch. His body spirals in a remarkable montage sequence, twisting, turning, at one stage absolutely faithfully, even movingly shot from above as he reaches back up toward the viewer, in some ways not unlike the money shot of *Titanic*.

The close ups were filmed as he bounced on a trampoline on dry land and, for the long shots, his place was taken by a reasonably lifelike dummy (scholars of the film will note the word, and how many times that idea crops up in the movie). These shots of the mannequin falling were the product of a whole number of takes, and in the one which made it to the final cut the dummy strikes the water at an advantageous angle for the camera – body fully facing, right side of the head impacting the surface first. It's terrifying really. When it immediately cuts to the underwater scene Dolenz enters the water back and feet first, but who cares about a little discontinuity at this stage? Not I, especially when we reflect upon the musical accompaniment to this whole scene.

Before we swim on through this scene we should reflect again on how music is used to help the movie get here. From out of the windblown silence come those first notes. There are an asymmetric seven chords, piano and organ in accord, tubular bell chiming – five years ahead of Mike Oldfield – cello murmuring below, gradually emerging as the water rushes toward us. This sequence runs toward that held, still moment that is both controlled and entirely free, tumbling toward an unknown fate. Under the piano and tubular bell chimes, the cello squirms, negotiating the spaces between these crystalline chords. As the seventh and final note rings out the cello is daringly held for 12 seconds before he hits the water and the song flies free. Like the viewer, the music is holding its breath. The tension finds its release as Dolenz breaks the surface and we are propelled into another realm. The music changes direction and starts to move more freely, picking up a momentum through a repeated chord on the piano, and then a drum ushers in the main body of the piece. The shots of Dolenz slowly twisting and spinning underwater seem as remarkable as the spacewalk shots in Kubrick's contemporaneous *2001: A Space Odyssey* – a human being, out of his element. The reality of filming was, of course, more prosaic than the final effect, as Dolenz recalled:

> It was a bit scary … this is in the Bahamas, just me and Jack … he ran the second unit, we found this little area, shallows, well, it was deep enough to drown. … They put weights on me so

> I'd sink. … The girls were from the Nassau Waterworld show or something; they were room-mates. And I had to hold my breath as long as I could then wave frantically at these two scuba guys, and they'd swim as fast as they could toward me, and I just remember the silver mouthpiece and I'd go 'urghh urghh' and surface and Jack would say 'OK, one more time.'[2]

At first he is alone, and the water is seductively blue, full of bubbles as the precious breath silently flows away from him as his body spirals down; the camera is level with his face, then suddenly deeper, and we see him from below, left arm raised, now the right arm, limbs slowly wheeling away, the light above his head. It's certainly a transcendental image, and is the cue for a change in the way this scene looks to us. It cuts to a long shot of him sinking, sinking, sinking, shot from the point of view of someone beneath him, and, as the soles of his feet approach the camera, the image changes from natural colour to what we would now recognise as a signature psychedelic colour scheme. At first it turns from blue to green – those early morning blues and greens again – and then yellows out into full-on trippy orange for a wondrous shot of Dolenz's head tilted back, air bubbles streaming up from his nose and mouth, ringed in fiery oranges and yellows, ebbing into greens and reds and back again. Nothing stays still, nothing stays the same – a condition of permanent change. In a seemingly endless descent implied by the shots from above him as he keeps going down into the depths, it takes 50 seconds from him entering the water to reach the 'ocean floor'.

Just at this moment, and as the song moves into its first chorus ('the porpoise is waiting …') his salvation appears in the shape of two figures who appear behind him, just as he seems certain to perish on the outcrops of coral that litter the ocean floor. They are mermaids – of course they are! – and the pair swim gracefully past the eye of the lens, one smiling a sweet yet troubling smile (mermaids or sirens? salvation or ruin?) as they gather up the floating figure and bear him away. For over a minute they swim, very fetchingly, along the seabed, with Dolenz impressively inert, limp, and entirely dependent on the two Nassau room-mates who bear him along, one at each side. After a minute or so, they return him to the perpendicular and push him back up toward the surface, floating up toward the light and away from the camera and the perspective of the mermaids.

The startling visual effects in the scene are the result of a process known as solarisation, a way of over-exposing the negatives to light either by accident or design. One often led to another. For example, the artist Man Ray's experiments in this area were kicked off by a 'mistake' in his developing laboratory, and he liked the effect. It's more often seen in photographic printing than in film, as attached to moving images it has a very specific cultural connotation – the rearrangements of the senses associated with psychedelia. Its use in *Head* is one of the lengthiest and most striking examples in cinema. Be the image moving or still, it is a beautiful but faintly disturbing effect; a famous solarised photograph is Minor White's 1955 print 'The Black Sun', a shot showing just that – a black sun. Solarisation renders the familiar detail, place, or feature strange. Here the deep aquamarines of the underwater sequence – peaceful, calm, restful – are made fiery, volatile and near-infernal by the solarisation process. In narrative terms, it shows the viewer that we are entering a world where normal rules do not apply and reality may well have its rules disturbed.

All this is harmonious with the overall ambition of the movie, of course. It shows us the wild instabilities that lie just beneath the surfaces of the known and the familiar. The scratchy, echoey quality of the guitar on the track – it's almost a percussive element – contrasts so powerfully with the tannic richness of the cellos that it provides a musical parallel to the sharpness of the corals and the smoothness of the seabed, the struggle of the falling body which then gives way to a kind of willing abandonment of that struggle and an admission of a kind of rapture in the deep. It's just at the moment that Dolenz seems to stop fighting the water that his salvation arrives and he is sent back up to a new surface, a new reality. The song complements the visuals in a manner so effectively that it really does need to be seen and heard to be believed; the solarisation somehow reproduces elements of the action and art and emotional impact of listening to the song, attaching images to the music not in the manner of an advert or a music video but by opening the viewer's eyes and ears to the possibilities of music and moving images working together – this is a theme close to the core of The Monkees' success in the first place.

In the script, the opening musical sequence is less open-ended than the beauty we see in the movie, with a host of ambient sounds and random visual detail. For example:

> We hear a distant pulsing sound of some huge generator, then the word 'Kundali' whispered and elongated. This word signals the start of MUSICAL NUMBER ONE. ... We hear, elongated almost like a Gregorian chant, 'We want The Monkees', added to the growing soundtrack, which by now should probably include the beginnings of some sub-oceanic musical sounds.[3]

What we can establish right from the outset is that in this film the sounds are going to make as important a contribution to the way the story unfolds as the moving images. Indeed, they are two aspects of the same thing: 'As each high, crystal clear note sounds, we change colour filter moving into even deeper tones.' This kind of active synaesthesia is a central motif of the film's ambition and, even though this detail was not in the final version, the ambition is embedded within what we do have. Looking at the 'Porpoise Song' sequence, the solarised swirls of colour move and flow into each other like musical notes and progressions, revealing the images and the moving bodies in them as being absorbed into the colour field as aspects of a unified expression of feeling: music, colour, movement – sound and vision – but transformed. It's this transformation of the everyday – the person we see in the mirror, the world we see through our eyes or via a screen – that *Head* seeks to explore, and the head-spinning extremity of these opening shots let us know immediately what is coming. There are abandoned visual details in the script too, including a list of symbolic (or perhaps random) objects that are listed as 'drifting by camera':

> Ticking clocks, musical instruments, mannequins and parts of mannequins, TV dinners, a cat, a baby doll attached to some

> balloons, drifts up, a boxing glove (referee's shirt), streamers of bright silk, newspapers, records.[4]

The song comes to a halt as it does on the soundtrack album version, on the four drum beats which haul us back and up and out of the water. By way of one of the film's many visual non sequiturs the water in the ocean seems to become the water in a fish tank at The Monkees' pad, through which we see Dolenz (fine, safe, and dry) engaged in a very adult kiss with a girl, who could possibly be a landlubber incarnation of the mermaids, and this kiss is a mouth-to-mouth resuscitation … or maybe not. Either way, she makes her way round all four Monkees, soul-kissing each. The girl is Mimi Machu (also known as I.J. Jefferson), who was a girlfriend of Jack Nicholson at the time and who had been a go-go dancer on the US TV pop show *Shindig!*, made by ABC between 1964 and 1966. *Shindig!* provided three female characters for *Head*, Mimi, Teri Garr, and June Wilson, also known as June Fairchild; the choreographer on the show was Toni Basil, who also appears in the movie.

The men are passive, sitting down, and Mimi leans into them very sensuously and gives each a long, lingering kiss. This never happened in *Help!*. The exception is her kiss with Davy, which – skitting his role as starry eyed charmer in the TV series – makes the windows open wide, admitting momentary bright sunshine, a host of lovey-doves, and a romantic orchestral flourish from Ken Thorne. A more workaday walking bassline accompanies her as she picks up her coat, slings it casually over her bare shoulder, and makes for the door – but Mike is keen to hear her verdict. 'Well?' She looks unimpressed and, giving the international sign for 'so-so' with her right hand, decides that it's 'even'. As opening dialogue in a movie goes, it's plain stuff. Stagily blocking her exit by the pad's door, he whispers in her ear: 'Why don't you come back later when the guys aren't here?' Her response is a real takedown: 'Are you kidding?' She opens the door and, looking back, gives a little hiccup of laughter, which crops up again in a key point of the film and the soundtrack album. Mike quickly comes to – this isn't supposed to happen to pop stars, they get what they want – he fixes and straightens his tie, looks into the full length mirror by the door, and declares: 'Hey now, wait a minute, wait just a minute!' The soul-kissing and mirror shots were the earliest work done for the film, on the first full day of filming, February 19 1968.

WAR CHANT

In the movie this cues in the startling 'Ditty Diego/War Chant' sequence, but the original script of *Head* shows that there was a short sequence of mini-scenes planned for here that may well have been screened as part of the original 110-minute cut, the one that fared so poorly at test screenings in the run-up to the film's release. According to the script I have seen, each Monkee stands before the full-length mirror and admires himself, the reflection showing them in some kind of symbolic outfit – Peter as a sad Pierrot clown, in full make up; Micky as a satyr complete with cloven hooves and pan pipes; Mike as a Marlboro man, a look he carries off with considerable ease; and Davy as a *Desert Song*-type matinee idol, no doubt borrowing from Peter O'Toole's look in *Lawrence Of Arabia*. Tantalising glimpses can be seen in the so-called 'NY Action' trailer easily found online. Warning: it moves with such speed that it is really difficult to watch, and some of the editing is so sharp and fast it amounts to subliminal cutting. Stills of the four in character were published in fan magazines as the build up to the film began through the stormy summer and early autumn of 1968.

In the movie we cut to the dramatic 16-screen shot that accompanies the performance of 'Ditty Diego'. This is in some ways a huge spoiler, giving us a kind of advance notice of key scenes – or, perhaps, just scenes – in the film we are about to see. I've always thought it would be a perfect 'chapters' screen for a DVD . The early ones are already history – we've seen them – and we speed through the movie in a series of organised fragments. This concludes with the final rectangular screen in the bottom right hand corner, which suddenly becomes the image in every screen we can see – it is the infamous moment in which South Vietnam's chief of National Police, Nguyen Ngoc Loan, executed handcuffed prisoner Nguyen Van Lem, a suspected Viet Cong member. The film, and its accompanying photograph, was taken on February 1

1968 by a cameraman for NBC, and Eddie Adams, an Associated Press photographer. The photo (captioned 'General Nguyen Ngoc Loan executing a Viet Cong prisoner in Saigon') and film would become infamous images in American photo-journalism. *Head* began filming on the 19th of the same month, less than three weeks later. This was so contemporary as to be virtually taken from the evening news.

The war in Vietnam provides a kind of parallel text to *Head*, footage and references cropping up several times during the movie and also 'felt' as a cultural tension throughout. Between the dates of filming and entering post-production, things happened and things stayed the same. In February, Walter Cronkite (Dylan's 'Old Cronkite on the 7 o'clock news' in 'Black Diamond Bay') returned to the US from Saigon and told his millions of viewers that 'the bloody experience of Vietnam is certain to end in a stalemate' and when filming ended in mid May it was around the time of the Battle of Dai Do, across the DMZ, which costs 2,000 lives. The day after *Head* debuted in New York, on Thursday November 7 1968, Richard Nixon was elected 37th President of the United States, an administration that would end in ignominy, impeachment, and disgrace. These were troubled times.

The footage of the shooting of Nguyen Van Lem is truly hideous, and has lost absolutely none of its power to shock, appal, and nauseate. Quite a thing to include in what had to be considered a pop film – or any film – and every year as I show the movie to my students they gasp or shriek at the sight. As the shot rings out, 19 of the 20 screens are filled with the monochrome image of Lem's murder, except the screen at far lower right, the one it originally appears in. This becomes a slow-mo shot of a blonde girl holding her hands to her face in what at first appears to be horror at what she has just seen – the kind of gesture my students make when they first see this moment – but then blows up to be a single full-screen shot of her, when it becomes clear she is seated amongst a throng of other young girls behaving in the same way. Rafelson may well crush a butterfly on a wheel here, but the point is made – is the girl screaming at the hideous inhumanity of what we have just seen, or is this her intense emotional response to what she is about to see? One of the film's serious purposes surfaces here – addressing the inundation of images through the media, and how popular culture is employed to satiate, distract, and pacify human response and potential resistance to the world that moves around us. The film does not revile or mock the young girl – it wants to wake her up. But it didn't necessarily work – you can plant the idea but you cannot control how people receive it. Micky:

> Well, the guy being executed in Vietnam had already been on the news a million times, it wasn't news to anybody, but still a little bit shocking to our fans … one girl caught me in the street and asked how could we glorify war like that. I couldn't believe what she was saying to me.[5]

Davy reflected on this moment and its consequences for the movie and the wider tale of The Monkees:

> That's why this film couldn't go to a general audience, because they wouldn't take it out. That one little scene. I always thought The Monkees would make a film like the show, lots of fun … like the Sandra Dee, Bobby Rydell thing … but no, we took the events of the time which we'd been asked not to talk about … and then suddenly the top comes off the bottle and all this comes out. [6]

His remark here about why the film 'couldn't go to a general audience' is a puzzle, as all the posters, literature, and trailers I have seen and heard refer to it as being suitable for 'General Audiences'. This is an amusing paradox in itself – was there ever a movie less built for a 'general audience' than *Head*?

'Ditty Diego' is in itself a kind of grotesque graffiti across the early Monkee image, the one which was indeed built to appeal to a general audience: it is a studied and very deliberately iconoclastic deconstruction of Boyce & Hart's original '(Theme From) The Monkees'. That theme had been something of a punchbag in the show's second and final season

– see the close of the infamous 'Fairy Tale' episode for an example – and to my knowledge it has never been performed live with the lyrics intact. It functions simply as the 'theme' it was designed to be as they come and go, on and off stage. 'Ditty Diego', on the other hand, *has* been performed live, in the 80s and 90s as a dubious 'rap'. The words were written not by musicians or lyricists but by Rafelson and Nicholson. It is the most blatant aspect of the overall schema to subvert and redefine the meaning of The Monkees, allowing them to pull the rug out from under themselves. We don't see the four chanting the lyric, we just hear the chatter and clatter above the steady stacking of images on screen. Each succeeding image gets two seconds of liveness in the montage before it is frozen and replaced by the next, in a neat little image of the industrial nature of the narrative: a moment in the foreground, and then replaced. Which moments make it to this 'map' of the movie? In order – Nesmith looking in the mirror, where the montage starts, followed by the war scene, the desert scene, the harem dance number, the 'barbed savage's arrow' moment, the boxing scene, the 'As We Go Along' interlude, the factory scene, inside the vacuum cleaner, 'Daddy's Song', Micky riding the scree, harassment by the police, chained to the dungeon wall – 'now here's my plan' – solarised Mike in the hallway before the party, the groovy dance scene for 'Do I Have To Do This All Over Again', back in the box in white suits, escape from the box, the box being choppered over the desert sands, the final run onto the bridge, and finally, lower right, the execution of Nguyen Van Lem. There's your score of mapped moments. If we're looking for a sense of 'beats' in the film, a series of steppin' stones to take us through, then this is as good as we've got. The vocals follow the switches between the images and the final line 'we're here to give you…' is truncated as the shot rings out.

Suddenly we are among a real Monkees audience – the crowd seems to have almost as many boys as girls – awaiting their idols' arrival, and we hear them chanting 'We Want The Monkees!'. Cut very sharply into the shots of the crowd, with their sweetly sensible outfits and fan banners, are glinting glimpses of the foursome getting ready to take the stage. The editing here is so busy – pow, pow, pow – that it hasn't really been possible before video and DVD to really discern what's here. The band seem to be getting ready in the Monkee pad and then exit together via the door of the pad once clad in their stage gear. Almost impossibly brief shots of the four self-consciously allude to, or even recreate, elements of the shots used over the closing titles of the TV show (check Peter's 'scream face', just as seen in the TV sequence), but a strange moment where all four of them kneel and hail some unseen deity before the stained glass window in the pad adds some uncertainty to these familiar elements.

The four are seen running, in a line, facing forward down a long, darkened corridor and then out into sunlight, all suddenly sporting white sweaters with the letters W (Davy), A (Peter), and R (Micky), alongside an exclamation mark on Michael's sweater. The Monkees cry like cheerleaders 'Give me a W!' 'Give me an A!' 'Give me an R!' and Mike asks the crowd, pointing at the camera, 'What does it spell?' and they cry back, 'WAR!' This sequence was filmed at the Rose Bowl in Pasadena, alongside the 'card raising' which spells 'WAR!' on the bleachers, but the *Head* boxed set of 2012 revealed that the war chant itself was caught at the live show in Salt Lake City that we are about to see. The word flashes up on the terrace and cuts to real footage of carpet bombings and rocket launchers in Vietnam, any of which could again have come from that evening's news broadcasts – this was happening, *now*. In the script, the explosion at the end of the 'War Chant' is an atomic one, speaking of the 'beautiful roaring angles of this fiery mushroom as it burgeons ghost-like through the atmosphere'.[7] It's early in the movie to go nuclear, and this reads better than it would have looked; in a film which reflects upon the impact of the mediated image on the experience of the everyday, the Vietnam footage chosen instead is far more effective. Furthermore, Jack Good got to push the button down at the end of *33 1/3* later in 1968, to very little effect.

The Vietnam footage proves to be a set-up for the film's first major 'acting' sequence, with the four Monkees cast as serving soldiers, entrenched in the middle of a dirty looking battlefield – Mike is the sergeant, attentive yet indifferent to the battle, while Davy, Micky, and

Peter loll about in the trench, similarly relaxed. It opens with Mike blithely blowing a bubble in his gum – a reference to the band's public image, perhaps – followed by a joke at Davy's expense, the kind we have heard a dozen times in the TV show, but never quite like this. He complains that he cannot see over the rim of the trench as it is 'too deep – I gotta have a boost or something'. This leads to Micky offering Davy his helmet to stand on, like his infamous on-set 'manmaker' (a box the five-foot-two Jones would stand on to make him seem closer to the same height as the other three, six-footers all). But Peter admonishes him – 'you really oughta wear your helmet' – just before a shell lands right by the trench and throws Davy backwards across the trench, across the eyeline of the camera. He staggers and reels, and ends up on his back spitting dirt out of his mouth, but instead of sympathy he earns only 'him again' glances between Micky and Peter.

Peter offers his helmet to Micky, who scorns the idea and then, in a little bit of darkly comic business, nuts himself on the underside of the trench overhang. In this scene we are reminded that Micky is an actor of some coolness and ease – detailing how shots might very easily come in from any direction, and 'blow off the right side of my chest'. Ringo was not required to do this kind of stuff. Another close call with a shell cues a wildly physical and deliberately overacted 'death scene' as he flings himself about the trench as if mortally wounded. It's both silly and disturbing, not unlike its parent picture. His comrades remain unmoved. When he's had enough, the Stan Laurel smile returns to his face and Peter drily notes, off-camera, 'Well I'm wearing mine.' 'That's cool,' grants Micky. Sgt Mike pipes up that they need a volunteer as they are out of ammo – Peter's offers to go is met with an icy 'See that you do' from Nesmith.

Peter hurries out into a misty no-man's land of gunfire, blazing wreckage, barbed wire, and blockades until suddenly from out of the murk comes an old-school photographer, with embedded-press jacket, hard hat, and popping flash gun in tow. Placing himself right in Peter's path, he says 'Hold it – this is for *Life*!' Immediately he takes the shot, the scene cuts to a quickly spinning mock-up of a front page of *Life* magazine with the picture supposedly taken filling the front page, appended only by the famous magazine masthead and the text, top right, 'So War Goes On'. Tork recalled:

> Bert tried to get *Life* magazine to OK me being on the cover … *Life* said no, but Bert said do it anyway … a great example of his audacious style of business.[8]

Cutting back to the battlefield, Peter arrives at the ammo dump only to find – guess – an American Football player, yelling and pawing the ground, calling out 'We're number one! We're number one!' Is he talking about America's global ranking? The pop charts? Or simply the number '1' he has on the front of his shirt? In his yellow pants, green shirt, and golden helmet he looks like some kind of forgotten mythological warrior. He charges at Peter, crashing him to the ground and driving him into the mud wall of the trench over and over again. He is clearly some kind of symbolic figure, asserting and over-asserting American importance and dominance to a sociopathic degree. But his impact on Peter is anything but symbolic as he charges at him and, for real, throws him to the ground and piledrives into him.

Ray Nitschke, a famous name in American sport but unknown to a British audience, was clearly a man for whom it was best to step aside should he come running at you full tilt. Billed as Private One in the movie credits, in real life he was a player for the Green Bay Packers, fulfilling a lifelong dream to be a professional American footballer. Known for his preternatural toughness, he was five years away from retirement when he appeared in *Head* so was still somewhere near his prime. Here his shirt bears the single digit '1', but rather marvellously his usual number was '66', the year of The Monkees' arrival. A coincidence, no doubt, but a good one. This scene, along with the war sequence of which it forms part, is the first of many assaults on The Monkees, individually and collectively, in the film. In fact we can declare it as a theme of the film: being under attack. So this bizarre little sequence, almost impossible to grasp in a single viewing, and a notable narrative disjunction in a film full of them, shows the embattled state in which the group found themselves.

Back in the trench, Sgt Nesmith chews on and drawls, in a deadpan and slyly comic tone, 'He'll never make it through this in-*tense* bom-*bardment* ... *nobody* could.' On the Blu-ray Micky delighted in this line: 'I love how Mike plays this ... really cool, my favourite line in the movie ... [laughs]. This was in the world famous Bronson Canyon, where I had already filmed about 20 times in *Circus Boy*.'[9] Micky is right, and as the scene pulls out we see the four still dressed as soldiers, crossing a grassy landscape – real now, as opposed to the set we have seen before – throwing 'grenades' toward the mouth of a cave as Ken Thorne's strident military music plays. If the gaping cave mouth looks familiar it's because it was also used as the entrance and exit to the Batcave in the ABC television series of *Batman*, produced between January 1966 and March 1968, roughly the same period of production as *The Monkees*. The show was blessed with a similarly enduring popularity, and proved almost as difficult for its stars to shake off.

In they go, Micky wearing Nitschke's gold helmet, carried back across the battlefield by Peter – and directly we are back in the tunnel, the band seemingly passing through flames and running away from the camera toward the source of a great rising wave of noise; we are back in that 'tunnel' that all the Monkees spoke about their lives being confined to. And then they emerge into that pool of light. Unusually this time they come through the audience, down the aisle from the back of the auditorium. This live show was filmed on Friday May 17 1968, the very last day of filming for the movie, at a special show at the Valley Music Hall in Salt Lake City, Utah – Mormon Central in the popular imagination, mainly thanks to the Osmonds, though only around 40 per cent of the city's population are actually members of the Church. The band arrived in Salt Lake City the day before and 'took over' (as was their wont) the local radio station, KCPX. No recordings of this session have surfaced, but pictures show that all four were indeed crowded into a small radio studio; furthermore, between the 16th and 17th Peter lost an impressive moustache. As they run through the crowd, the fans are genuinely thrilled at their arrival, and some gentle manhandling goes on – all four look pleased to be there.

CIRCLE SKY

The fans may well be screaming loud enough to drown out the music but they have to work hard on this occasion, because 'Circle Sky' starts loud and gets louder. In many ways it is one of the most remarkable performances by a rock band ever caught live on film, from their stage entrance, to their garb, to the way it is filmed, to the sheer ear-bleeding roar of the glorious din they make. The four wave and seem absolutely sincere as they do so. While we see that a point is being made about the relationship between stars and audiences, wildly distant from each other even as they share the same space, we should also note how that point is being made in the editing suite. In Salt Lake City, there were no ambiguities: the fans loved them and the band were happy to play for them. If ever a song was written in order to give this expensive garage band something to hammer out together, 'Circle Sky' is it. It somehow sounds like heavy metal, punk, grunge, and a protest song all at once and rocks righteously but deftly too – listen for Peter's wandering bassline in the mid-section. The song listed in the script for the 'Circle Sky' sequence is 'It's Only War, That's All, So I'll See You Again Some Time', which suffers both from being an over-literal interpretation of the moment and sounding like it could have been the product of some early software to generate protest-song titles. Nesmith:

> It's an interesting piece of footage … because by this time we had really coalesced into a *band*. When you're looking at that footage, you're watching The Monkees in concert, and that's probably the only three minutes of us playing … up to that point we were just fighting our way along. We were a garage band except we were filling up these stadiums! It was hard … we couldn't hear, nobody wanted to rehearse, so it was very tough … we were hiding behind the fans and the screams … but with 'Circle Sky' we had to do it over and over and over, because we were live and

> filming. Somebody, maybe Bob, said 'No, this has got to be live, this has got to be the real thing.' So that's what happened, and we were good enough to play exactly what you heard. Now, in the annals of rock does 'Circle Sky' belong in the pantheon? It's just a crash burn rock'n'roll song, informed by its time.[10]

This gives us an insight into the realities of being in a group successful in the way they were. It also shows how the music had to fight its way through to the top of the list of priorities for everyone involved. Nesmith is also right in that it is the only piece we have, after 'Monkees On Tour', of the original band playing live. The group are all dressed head to toe in white clothes, and even Nesmith's Gibson guitar is in on the colour scheme. Why white? Innocence, purity, a blank canvas on to which an audience can project anything? All of these, none of these. But it looks superb. Add into this Dolenz's double-kick-drum kit with the legend 'DRUM' emblazoned across the front of the drumheads, a beautiful art-pop idea, and we have a performance which is also a performance of a performance. A curiously calm shot from above shows the stage as a circular pool of blue light in the darkness of the theatre, their white garb making a striking contrast, somehow more effective than if they had gone for a classic 'two tone' black and white effect.

We don't only see the band's performance: the accompanying footage of scenes from Vietnam edited into the live sequence were, and remain, shocking. It's powerfully troubling to be listening to loud rock music while seeing images of real human beings fleeing for their lives, or cowering from the blasts of military hardware, or making appeals to the common humanity of a soldier, or, infamously, being executed on camera. The black and white news footage edited into the lush colour images of the band on stage make clear the point: at the same instant we are entertaining ourselves, others are suffering and dying. Their shock value is undeniably exploited by Rafelson, in a very direct way. Some – Pauline Kael being but the first – have suggested he does so in a morally ambiguous manner, but in truth he is saying: 'This is going on. Now.' The juxtaposition with a pop phenomenon in full flight is stunningly powerful; it would be hard for anyone to say they unambiguously enjoy watching the 'Circle Sky' sequence, for all its technical virtues, but equally I cannot see how anyone could watch it and not be changed by it.

Under the images of the band are slowed-down clips of fans' reactions to the performance. I always find the shots of the fans in the concert sequence of *A Hard Day's Night* very moving, and so it is here – the beauty and mystery of pop music, captured truthfully. This footage is therefore quite anthropological; aside from the deliberately jarring juxtapositions with the scenes from Vietnam, it records at least *how* if not *why* pop is such a powerful cultural force on its audience. Through precisely chosen edits and effects, the two discourses speak to each other – as Nesmith sings the first line of the song, a girl in the audience holds her hands to her head as she screams and bumps up and down in rapture, and the film cuts to a Vietnamese family cowering by a wall in fear of some kind of attack, their tiny daughter putting her hands to her head in just the same way as her American cousin – the very same gesture for very different reasons.

Like much else in this movie, once you look beneath the apparently chaotic surfaces, there is careful, fine detail crafted into it. By virtue of the technique of 'ghosting' two sets of images together, we get to see the performance and the reaction to it at the same time. This doubling and mirroring gives the whole episode a dreamlike quality that is appropriate to the high emotional level of both the audience and the 'real world' juxtapositions. With the exception of some pretty neat maraca moves by Davy, the band's performance is studied and non-demonstrative. They are concentrating on their playing, and this again provides a contrast with the heightened level of what is going on around them; they are almost a neutral, still point around which everything else seems to whirl and revolve. The neutrality of the white dress code suggests this too, alongside peace and non-alignment – white is the colour of surrender, sure, but allied to the fiery fierceness of the music it is lent a kind of militancy. It's a uniform, like they were wearing as soldiers in the preceding clip, but here they seem like soldiers of peace. The mirroring may seem like a stock in trade psychedelicisation of the moving image –

and I suppose it is – but in 1968 this was something cinemagoers were not used to seeing and added much to the deliberately disorientating aspect of the sequence. Are we supposed to enjoy this performance or not? It's like a popsicle that suddenly turns out to have unexpected extra ingredients. When Nesmith is bracketed by the same image of a screaming girl with her hands over her face (roughly from where he sings 'Telling more, than before' to the self-consciously referential close of the vocal, 'Yes it looks like we made it to the end') it's as if he is being quoted by her, his position defined by her visual contextualisation. This may well be accidental, you say, and you may well be right, but that's what it says to me.

And as soon as Dolenz, Tork, and Nesmith drop that last *BLEERRRRR* on the song's final note, the film slips back into a more stagey style. As we have seen, the concert section is heavily edited and manipulated to tell a certain story; but we shouldn't forget that the music itself (no matter how roughly hewn it may be) provides a free space in the movie where the uncontrollable truth can flourish for a few moments before the auteur resumes control, delivering a more scripted, weighted version of events. This is particularly interesting here because the beautifully managed concert sequence suddenly breaks down into a kind of chaos; during the number the audience stayed put, remaining in their seats despite the apparent hysteria, yet once the last note rings out they rush the stage. This breakdown of the 'fourth wall' is alarming anyway – crowds rushing, crushing, people potentially getting hurt – and the camera picks out alarm and confusion on the four Monkees' faces, especially Nesmith's, chewing gum with apparent insouciance yet registering the imminent assault from the stalls. It's Tork the fans reach first and a very smart edit convinces us that the mop-headed figure they bring down is him. To a first time viewer – spoiler – it is a few moments before we can feel sure that the four Monkees are not really being ripped to shreds by their fans. A shot of a girl cradling the head of Davy Jones in mannequin form allows us to sigh in relief but then focus on what actually is happening before our eyes. It's a riotous display of possession, the endgame of proprietorial desire for a hysterical fan, gaining ownership of the entire being of the object of their desire, not merely their image or recordings. The trophies of head (that word again), body parts, and shreds of clothing are fought over and exalted in once acquired. This was not exaggerated for effect; it was a distinct possibility. Nesmith spoke of his experiences as a Monkee, which have made him cagey about fan interaction to this day: 'They didn't just want a little bit of you, they wanted all of you, and they didn't care which parts they got!'[11] It was by no means unique to The Monkees, of course, and has a wider cultural resonance about the behaviour of the crowd and how the object of desire is perceived, whether on stage or on screen.

CHANNEL SURFING AND NO MONKEES IN JAPAN

On page 15 of the script is the sole instruction 'OMIT: REMOVE PAGES 16 THRU 29.' Unfortunately the first page of the next scene has been removed from the copy I have, so it's not clear how we get from the concert sequence – no riot planned – to being in Japan, but that is the leap we make. The Monkees are indeed in Japan, and are talking with a girl called Toshiko who wishes to be reunited with her father. She speaks no English and Peter demonstrates a hitherto unknown skill by translating. In a style that recognisably belongs to the film, they are hunted down by legions of Samurai, and the script self-consciously speaks of using '100 sight gags in parody of Japanese battle sequence'.[12] It also employs that most Japanese of cinematic characters, Godzilla. There's a happy ending – including a droll scene where Davy, drunk on sake, wanders dangerously at large in Godzilla's court – but the scene is very long and, even if it were filmed and turns up as a collector's item somewhere down the line, I'm glad it was expunged from the movie. It reads more like a short-ish episode of the TV show, 'Monkees in Japan'. At its close we are back in more familiar territory with a close-up of a hand changing channels in rapid succession on a TV with a remote control.

Though the first TV remote had been marketed in the mid 50s, the technology was still high-end in 1968 in the US, and may as well have been in 007's gadget rack or on the props shelf of *Star Trek*, so fantastical would it have seemed in Britain. Rafelson uses the remote's potential for finding and creating startling juxtapositions, delivering a quickfire sequence that could easily stop anywhere. What does our channel hopper find? We find legendary Hungarian actor Bela Lugosi, best known for his portrayals of Dracula, in a scene from *The Black Cat*, a Universal picture from 1941. Then a shot of someone's left hand, squeezing the up and down channel-changer buttons with his thumb, watch around the wrist. Time is passing, but being filled. The face of TV gossip columnist Rona Barrett appears, and she peddles some then-topical gossip which now sounds merely arcane, even nostalgic. It concerns the story about life with actress Barbara Stanwyck that her son intends to sell to an unnamed buyer. Coincidentally or deliberately – you can choose – Stanwyck starred in the film *Golden Boy* (1939), which the later boxing-and-violin-playing scene parodies. This cuts to an ad for Ford cars featuring Ralph Williams. These ads were a mainstay of late-night 1960s Los Angeles television and soon became regarded as a running joke, with Williams's awkward screen manner embodying the second-hand/second-rate ambience of the used car, later caught perfectly by Bruce Springsteen's 'Used Cars' from his extraordinary 1982 album *Nebraska*. The presence of the Williams ads was a hipster in-joke at the time but also speaks to a bridling against a key part of the American Dream.

We cut back to a report from the riot at the Monkees show, with a few previously unseen moments of further carnage amongst the mannequins. The unseen viewer quickly switches over again, to a moment of Charles Laughton at his most imperious as Herod in the 1953 movie *Salome*, addressing Alan Badel as John the Baptist – 'but YOU are the Messiah!' – following a line which suggests treason, 'He acknowledges a King higher than you.' We switch again and see Ronald Reagan, in 1968 the Governor of the State of California, being interviewed through a car window, clearly for television, and saying 'Our ship better be sailing out of that harbour on its way home within 24 hours or we're coming in after it.' This was Reagan's style, of course, the steel under the folksy charm that would carry him all the way to the Capitol; the movie's choice once again proved to be farsighted, as within a year Reagan had sent the National Guard on to the University of Berkeley campus to quell disquiet there, leading to at least two deaths on May 15 1969, which became known as Bloody Tuesday. He was unrepentant, saying on April 7 1970 at a meeting of the Council of California Growers, 'If it takes a bloodbath, let's get it over with. No more appeasement.' There's a clear link between this and what we hear in *Head*. The apparently random element becomes the prescient detail.

Further 'clicks' prove the inescapability of advertising and Ralph Williams in particular – he pops up three more times, in quickening succession, and in the third appearance the faintly troubling price '666' appears in the windscreen of one of the cars – would this have been a kind of in-joke too? Maybe they just liked the visual precision of the price … or maybe not. Hard on the heels of the Number of the Beast comes … Dracula. In a second clip from the same scene in *The Black Cat* we see and hear Bela Lugosi once again. This clip joined its predecessor in making the soundtrack album – indeed having a track to itself. 'Superstitious' – track one, side two of the vinyl – consists of the voices of actors David Manners and Bela Lugosi, in that order:

> **Manners**: Sounds like a lot of supernatural baloney to me!
> **Lugosi**: Supernatural, perhaps – baloney, perhaps not...

Next up on the matte TV screen is a figure rolling down a sand dune. We don't know, on this first time of seeing, that it is Micky Dolenz. What we do notice is that, unlike everything else seen on the small screen in this sequence, it is in colour. The image stutters and distorts, a creative use of faults and interference, a kind of visual equivalent to feedback, which had entered pop's lexicon via the success of The Monkees' old support act, Jimi Hendrix, or perhaps Micky's experiments with his Moog. The incorporation of uncontrolled effects such as these is a technique harmonious with the rest of the film, for accommodating and incorporating accidental or found material is what this sequence is all about. This approach brings *Head* closer to the uncontrollable rough edges of reality, paradoxically, than a glamorous and shiny Hollywood version of the real, where everything is in its place and a satisfying resolution is always reached. 'Who can remember how and what the fuck comes next in that movie?' mused Rafelson on the structure of the film. One could say the same about one's daily life.

Two clips from vox pop interviews with faintly dazed and confused sounding young men make a marked contrast to the aggressive certainty of Reagan's soundbite, with their lack of interest in what is actually happening in the world illustrating how the professed counter-culture may well have smoked away its potential to force social change: 'I don't read papers, I don't listen to the radio, and I haven't seen a television in years.' Hurtling into view comes another found film clip, from a 1944 Columbia film, *Jam Session*, in which Ann Miller takes the role of the energetic hoofer to the limit. She gives a whirligig impromptu audition to 'studio heads' George Eldredge and Eddie Kane (as Berkeley Bell and Lloyd Marley respectively) with a blazing, kinetic, and faintly absurd avalanche of tap dancing in order to break into movies: 'You make motion pictures, don't you? You're always looking for new talent – well watch this!'

This system is of course still in place, be it in Hollywood back rooms or live on Saturday night TV talent shows like *X Factor* or *American Idol*. This clip is the one in this sequence most obviously connected to the Monkee project itself – auditions, showbiz, the dream of getting that lucky break, that moment of access that changes everything. You have that model of showbiz nutshelled into these few frantic moments. In immediate succession comes the second dazed hippy who asks 'What happened?', a clip well-chosen to illustrate the speed at which things are happening – almost too quick for comprehension. Appropriately this clip is gone almost as soon as it arrives and we cut again to a Ralph Williams ad, and the sequence now starts to ping-pong between Williams and shots of the figure in the desert. Given the luxury of a DVD we can pause, we see the detail. Having previously rolled down a dune, he is next seen from behind climbing again, and in loose fitting military clothing – cut to Ralph – then standing atop a dune, draining what seems to be the last of his water from a flask. One final appeal from Ralph Williams Ford and we are into the next scene, with the figure revealed as a now-shirtless

Dolenz. The shot pulls out so the screen is filled with the image of him padding exhaustedly toward the camera.

DOLENZ OF ARABIA

We hear Micky's voice: 'My canteen is empty, where once it was full …' At first it is a classic non-diegetic voiceover, heard only by the viewer and not the character: 'I felt I couldn't go on … But something, something kept telling me I must.' But then we hear the voice address Micky: 'You MUST!' Suddenly we see that Micky hears the voice too – the non-diegetic sound becomes diegetic, heard by the character within the film world, and that the dialogue is all taking place in Micky's head. What is this other voice? His conscience? The angel/devil on the shoulder trick we are familiar with from cartoons?

This dialogue is also by way of prelude to the scene's first great visual joke, and one of the best in the movie, where the technique of the startling non sequitur is truly effective. Continuing toward the camera, Dolenz staggers up a dune, leans in toward the camera and – what? – inserts a coin. The coin rattles and shakes and as it does so his expression changes from weary anticipation to painfully vexed frustration, screwing up his eyes and letting fly with a tantrummy 'OhhhhhNOOOO!' as he slams his right hand against something. As he does this, the shot changes and we see him from behind, grappling with a mid-60s Coca-Cola vending machine. As visual surprises go it's a pretty good one. It also looks exquisite, the machine's red and white colours standing inert and idiotic on the crest of a sandy dune ridge, the brilliant blue sky behind it, Dolenz stripped to the waist in khaki trousers.

This sequence again provides Micky with the chance to show off his physical acting skills – cruelly denied, he attacks the machine, scrambling up its racked side, punching it, shaking it, kicking it, flinging himself against the rocks. He rages and grunts and howls in frustration while the machine stands inert, enigmatic and motionless, as indifferent to the assault by a Monkee as the obelisk in *2001: A Space Odyssey* when attacked by the apes. The impotence of his rage and frantic scrabbling is coolly confirmed over and over again as the EMPTY sign fills the screen four, now five times, before reaching an almost subliminal flash-speed of editing.

At this frantic moment, a real Coke jingle strikes up – which may be a little comment on the band's track record in corporate sponsorships, or it may simply have been added to lighten the mood as the scene is intense. The last beat of the song is provided by his final kick against the foot of the machine. Coca-Cola was not happy about the use of its product and livery in this way and, it is said, tried to serve an injunction on the movie. By the time the movie started to be seen more widely via cable, videotape, and disc, Columbia Pictures had actually been bought up by the Coca-Cola corporation and the issue, if it was noticed at all, was set aside. Micky:

> Oh, the coke machine. This is a genuine part of me, Jack might even have seen me do this, where I bang my head on a cabinet or a wooden worktop, something happened to me with a mechanical object … I've been known to smash telephones with sledgehammers because they wouldn't dial … you have to teach these mechanical objects a lesson, you can't let them get away with it or they'll come after you every time. This was in the desert near Palm Springs, and just behind the camera was a housing development, and gradually sand dunes built up around the houses and everyone moved out.[13]

So the fantastical is based in part on the real: the two states connected by a common element, Dolenz himself. Back in the Coke-dry dunes, Micky falls back on the sand, exhausted, the few moments of windblown silence broken as he is taunted further by his 'other voice' as their dialogue strikes up again: 'PATHETIC! It's pitiful!' Micky tells his tormentor to 'Shut up!' The dispute rages between the voices, telling each other to shut up, until Micky loses his cool and manically yells 'You-you-you-you-you-shutup-shutup-shutup-you!!' To which comes the capricious reply, 'OK … I *will.*' A look of infantile, even silent-movie delight crosses Micky's face, soon turning to confusion, fear, and dread as he holds his hands to his head: 'I … I can't hear it, I'm deaf … Come back!' He whimpers and falls back into the supplicatory position before the Coke machine. Suddenly the isolation in the desert takes on a symbolic value, evidence of some form of existential crisis. Pushing away his only companion he is truly alone in the emptiness. A helicopter shot (you may just see the scattering sand in the right-hand portion of the frame on your DVD) shows him and the machine, still and isolated in the sea of sand. As the shot climbs, in comes a new voice, slow, deep, sonorous, and with a genuine streak of malice: 'Quiet, isn't it? George. Michael. Dolenz. I said … quiet, isn't it? GEORGE. MICHAEL. DOLENZ.' The use of his real name, in full, makes his plight seem punitive: highly particular and acutely personal. In an interview with the *New Musical Express* ahead of a British release for the movie, which never came, Davy revealed that this device was repeated later in the film:

> There is another sequence with Mike dying of thirst in the desert and a voice from above says, 'Thirsty, aren't you, Michael Robert Blessing Nesmith?' That's God. And a coke machine appears. Mike takes a coke and empties it into the sand – defying God. People do that – people are like that.[14]

Whoever this voice belongs to – and in the script the scene featuring a suffering Nesmith does indeed credit the voice as belonging to God – he clearly has power over this rather puny figure of Dolenz, a speck in the sand. What boundary has he crossed, what transgression has he effected? We don't find out any more as Ken Thorne's dramatic 'desert epic' music announces itself and prepares the way for a horseman, rapidly approaching Micky from the north-east. It's strongly evocative of the Academy Award-winning music by Maurice Jarre for the 1962 film *Lawrence Of Arabia*, which had its soundtrack issued on Colpix. The whole scene is an extraordinary piece of physical work by Dolenz.

> This obviously for me was a very dramatic scene, and I was a little bit nervous about it. I hadn't done any 'drama' like that, maybe

> a bit as a child. Bob worked on that with me for a while to make it as real as possible, not too over the top. These characters are based on our real personalities as opposed to the 'wacky Monkee' characters ... it was probably the toughest sequence for me to do as an actor. But now I'm very proud of it.[15]

Dolenz spends the rest of the scene in a state of passive confusion as a sequence of strange events simply happen to him, appearing out of the blankness of the desert; from such an empty canvas, anything might appear. His first encounter is a close-up one, with the 'Arabian' horseman played by William Bagdad, who had already taken on a similar role in the TV series, in the episode 'Everywhere A Sheikh Sheikh'. The film was in many ways drawn from the same well as the TV show, although it may at first feel wildly different. The script gives the direction:

> In a LONG TELEPHOTO ANGLE we watch a black garbed Arabian HORSEMAN drive his steed across the expanse of dunes to a halt, directly in front of Micky. (There is no Coke machine.)[16]

What's interesting is that Micky is now standing and facing the direction from which the horseman is approaching, as if he knew something was coming over that hill but didn't know quite what. As the horseman pulls up alongside, Dolenz wipes the sweat from his eyes, almost as though he can't believe what he's seeing, but also in anticipation of the spit in the eye he is about to receive. The horseman pulls his veil aside, leans down from his horse, and emits an aggressively confidential 'Psst!' Dolenz leans closer in and the horseman, more forcefully this time, spits 'Psst!' again. The in-joke is that on the second 'Psst!', the word appears on screen in the form of a subtitle, as if we were watching a movie by Jean-Luc Godard or Michelangelo Antonioni. Nesmith claimed to Harold Bronson that he 'wrote' this little moment for the film.[17] In the script, 'Pst' is spelt with only one 's'.

With this important information imparted, the Horseman is off, racing away again up and over the dune ridge and out of sight, swallowed up by a swirling cloud of sand, from which comes, a moment later, the unmistakable sound of a hardworking engine. It proves to be a tank, painted in a khaki tone for desert combat but clearly marked with a large Italian tricolour directly in the camera's eyeline. Shots cut between this spectacle and Dolenz's perplexed, powerless expression – at this point, he is as clueless as the viewer – so character and audience are in the same place. The tank crests the ridge and snaps to a halt on the downward slope. The lid flips open and out pops a natty little Italian soldier, played by Vito Scotti. He was another actor familiar on Monkee sets, having appeared in 'The Case Of The Missing Monkee' as the wicked Dr. Marcovitch. If we look long and hard at the credits, we see his character listed as I Vitteloni, Rafelson's cineaste's nod to Federico Fellini's 1953 film, *I Vitelloni*, a semi-autobiographical comic drama. The title translates roughly as *The Young Calves*, a Roman euphemism for the good-looking, pleasure-seeking youth of the city: an English equivalent would be young bucks. Scotti's soldier calls out to Micky from the security of the tank, in a fantastically caustic Italian street-bawl: 'Americano? Americano, eh?' Micky acknowledges: 'Si, Americano.' The soldier clambers down – 'Ecco, aspetto un minuto, eh? Aspetta!'('Here … wait a minute, eh? Wait!') – and on reaching Micky gives him the Latin-European greeting, kissing him on each cheek. There's no Judas kiss here – he hands over his pistol, putting it into Micky's limp right palm, being careful to turn the direction of the barrel away from him, but toward the audience. As he says, 'Aha – eh, boom boom!'

There's something of a lost joke in all this. The end of World War II was only 23 years behind when *Head* was made, and was within the lifetimes of the four Monkees and certainly of their elders who made and produced the film. Likewise, the image of the Italians as either cowardly or simply uninterested in 'the fight' still stuck to them, often via Hollywood representations of them in World War II movies such as *Anzio* (1968), in production at the same time as *Head*. A truer depiction can be found in Roberto Rossellini's neo-realist classic *Rome: Open City*, filmed in the streets of Rome in the dying days of the war in 1945.

So while the deeper meaning of this little interlude may be lost on a contemporary audience, the point isn't – and lest we miss it, a slice of faux-Italianate opera sings out over the scene until the last soldier lopes by. Dolenz watches them disappear over the ridge and is alone again. Dropping the pistol, he stands amidst the detritus of a battle that never was – perhaps Zor and Zam's war, the one to which nobody came. He clambers aboard the empty, stationary tank and begins to carefully and deliberately rotate the turret. In this scene, the tank is seen from the side, from ground level, and from eye level too – one of the cameras is mounted, it seems, on the barrel of the tank's gun, looking back toward Dolenz and his dreamy but determined expression as the turret cranks round, the footprints of the disappeared Italians pit-pattered across the dune tops. It's a strangely peaceful moment. The turning turret clanks to a halt. Shot from slightly below the barrel, we see Micky dip down into the turret to haul on a lever. He bobs back up, and a single shot fires from the muzzle. We cut to a long shot of the malign Coke machine being blasted into pieces. We cut back to Micky's expression of satisfaction, a stage smile which stays on his lips as we fade to him sitting in a desert tent. As the dream-like juxtapositions of the film go, this is quite a rational one, and we find ourselves in a crowded, exotically furnished tent interior at the start of the harem scene. Proof positive is that Dolenz is now sporting the classic Hollywood signifier of the Arab at this time, the head-dress with the ornamental cord known as the agal, a look which would also have been familiar to a mainstream audience from *Lawrence Of Arabia*.

The 'supplicio' or surrender scene is exactly as described in the script, and is all the more impressive for that: well written, well executed, superbly acted. Watching *Head* reminds us that Micky Dolenz is a highly accomplished actor, mostly but not exclusively comic. My students, seeing the scene for the first time, never quite know what to do as he suffers in this scene: is he going to goof off any minute? Is this 'serious'? Dolenz keeps it this side of the line and delivers a superb psychologically complex performance which still retains much of the physical comedy at which he excelled in the show.

As the harem scene begins, up flow the appropriately exotic-sounding opening notes of the movie's third musical setting, of Peter Tork's 'Can You Dig It?' which has an appropriately North African feel in its tone and percussion. The mix of this musical exotica and the harem scene creates a sense of sensory abandon, and quite an adult one too. The soul-kissing with Mimi Jefferson in the earlier scene develops here with the unabashed sensuality of the dancing girls: smooth bellies are shaken, diaphanous gauzy veils are slinked aside, juicy fruit is slipped between young men's lips. Nesmith takes it in his stride onscreen, at one point humorously crunching into an Edenic apple while peering over his shades the better to inspect the belly and thighs of a girl who presents herself to him. But he recalled how tricky this was as a professional engagement: 'I was so consumed with passion and … lust for these girls. I think I tried to date them all, but struck out!'[18] Micky, perhaps more used to adult-pretend, recalled the how and who a little more clearly:

> This was a beautiful set – the same stage we used for the show. We just sat there while the girls did all the dancing and we just wallowed. I don't know who envisioned these music videos … they're full blown music videos … must have been Jack, and Bob. That girl Helena [the dark-haired dancer who leads the troupe of girls] was a friend of Jack's and she opened a nightclub in LA in the 70s or 80s, became a very hot spot. Nothing in the hookah pipe: it was just a prop. The layering, the special effects … took a long time.[19]

The layering and mirroring in the scene resembles techniques used in the 'Circle Sky' sequence but all the more so here; the mix of the ambience and atmospherics suggests – perhaps even encourages or recreates – the derangement of the senses associated with intense pleasure. It's brilliantly realised and very effective. There's also a little diegetic addition to the track we hear on the soundtrack album; in the song's instrumental interlude, we hear the sharp slap of the girls clapping in unison on the offbeat. This will have been a technique familiar to the 'girl Helena' to whom Dolenz refers. She is Helena Kallianiotes, a dancer at The Intersection, a Greek restaurant in North Hollywood that Nicholson loved. Through this start she ended up playing non-dancing roles in a number of movies in the early 70s, including *Five Easy Pieces* alongside fellow *Head*-dancer Toni Basil. She is also the girl with Art Garfunkel on the front cover of his biggest selling solo album, *Breakaway* (1975), sitting to his right and accepting a light for her cigarette.

If all this abandonment of reason were not enough, it is also the first time we see June Fairchild. As Paul McCartney says in 'Helter Skelter', she may be a lover but she ain't no dancer – but who cares about that? I see June but, appropriate to the scene's representation of the clouded experience of pleasure, it's hard to tell how many dancers there are – there might be eight, there might be fifty – it's deliberately unclear. The whole scene is presented as if through gauze, playing with the senses, drawing the viewer in. What are we seeing? Is it simply part of a dream? Passing from the outer thirsty emptiness of the desert into this inner, warm enclave of plenty and of sensual overload is both a reference to the desert epic genre and a nod to the promise of life itself, from the famine to the feast in the blink of an eye, or perhaps going from pot-washing or being a self-declared failure to being part of the world's biggest band in a few months. The song is one of The Monkees' very best, and makes the script's original suggested title, 'I'm Sorry Bubbles But It Is Only A Sheik Who Offers You His Heart', seem as lame and silly as it actually is.

The scene and song reach a shaking climax together, on the brink of breaking down in a frenzy of acoustic guitar notes, somehow more powerful than the boosted sounds of an electric. Just as we think the whole moment is certain to fly apart, we are directed to the mouthpiece of the hookah Dolenz has been enjoying, what the script refers to as 'the water pipe of many visions'. He initially cocks it toward the viewer on the first 'Heh!' of the song's finale and then presents it for our contemplation as the whirling circles of the song eventually settle back to Earth.

BOB, I'M THROUGH

The camera focuses in on the mouthpiece and it transmutes via cross-fade into … an extended index finger. We pull back just a little and it is revealed as belonging to Teri Garr, who is at the lower right of the frame, looking up at Dolenz, who is staring at the finger and its owner.

She asks him, in a tone not entirely devoid of sexual intent, 'Quick … suck it before the venom reaches my heart.' This line was striking enough for the first part of it to be included in the sound collage of 'Opening Ceremony'. The camera moves back to show her bloodied but beautifully manicured fingertip and Dolenz in profile, thinking about it. Before he has the chance to decide, stagey noises of gunfire and riot distract him. Forgetting the damsel in distress, he wanders over to Nesmith, who is slumped against a fake tree in a Western set, in full Daniel Boone attire, coon-skin cap and all. Dolenz is wearing a very natty Civil War outfit (Union, or the North), deep blue shirt and pants, with his hat tipped back in *Bonanza* style (he once told *Rolling Stone* that he was 'no more a Monkee than Lorne Greene is a Cartwright'[20] – and perhaps he was wrong). A quick insert of stock Cowboys 'n' Indians footage slyly flags up what's coming: a revolt against the bogus, the playacting, the fakery. Nesmith asks him, with considerable precision, to 'help me by pulling this painfully barbed savage's arrow, by snipping the head off in the back and pulling it from the front quickly so it doesn't hurt me'. Micky asks after Davy and Peter, and Mike tells him that they have 'gone to Fort Bridger for reinforcements', and in one of the film's many little treasures we get a fast Monkee-cut to the pair back in the harem tent being fed grapes by the dancers. This seems to me to balance the disdain with which Peter's efforts in the war scene were treated – here's his reward! Having removed the arrow, Micky goes over to the prone and still-acting Teri Garr and, in an ungentlemanly way, starts pushing her with his right foot, telling her to quit pretending: eventually she comes out of character, asking 'what is this?' in an incredulous tone. Finally Micky breaks:

> Ahh, I don't wanna do this anymore man, all the fake arrows and all this junk and the fake trees, Bob, I'm through! It stinks, man! [He walks off away from the camera tearing through the 'Wild West' backdrop.]

Teri Garr's question is the right one – what is this? The emphasis on being done with the 'fake' and the 'junk' and, indeed, 'acting' lays bare the dilemma between the real and the manufactured that encircled The Monkees from the very start. The moment Micky rips and walks through the backdrop is the turning point of the movie; everything that happens thereafter is a consequence of this gesture. In the original script, this runs into a scene where a nun is caught kissing a Native American (presumably two actors from different productions), again asking us to question what lies beneath the surface details of what we are seeing. The scene includes a bit of verbal interplay about who is, or should be, 'ashamed' of what they have done. This ties into the movie's theme of The Monkees being persecuted for simply existing.

The script catches up with the finished film as we find Davy on the steps of a New York brownstone set. He mimes along to a recording of violin playing in a beautifully recreated 30s Lower East Side street scene, while Annette Funicello sits adoringly on the steps listening to him play. It's lovely, and a small admiring crowd is gathered around, but it is soon revealed to be part of the fakery Micky has lost faith with. As Micky and Mike enter from the viewer's right they stomp past Davy and Annette up the steps. The audience's point of view draws back to reveal camera and playback technologies focused on Jones; it's a pleasing if curious feeling to watch this, like Russian dolls revealing layer within layer, or, more viscerally, the guts and wires and ugly parts that go to make something that persuades us of its beauty and truth. For added comic value and to drive home the point, the disc on which the violin music is recorded gets stuck. A dog, equally disturbed by the ructions – and not acting – barks and barks, the repetitions echoing those of the scratched record. (Davy later revealed that this was his own dog, Susie.) Once up the steps they are gone, but in the script more is made of this scene – it is a windy day and a piece of paper blowin' in the wind lands upon Davy's face. It is a picture of John Lennon and 'It stays in a mask-like effect' and Davy's next few lines are listed as 'Davy (as John)'. Such overt reference to well-worn themes in the Monkees tale must have been tempting at first, but the right decision was taken to lose this kind of obvious symbolism; ironically, given its reputation for obscurity, the film would have been reduced by including such straightforward material.

The trio swing free of the street scene and bump into the man the script calls Dernsie and the final film credits as Lord High 'n' Low. Dernsie suggests that the part was originally created for Nicholson's friend and his co-star in *Psych-Out* (1968), Bruce Dern: his actress daughter Laura would later become a favourite of David Lynch, another outsider who somehow broke into Hollywood through movies even weirder than *Head*. Played in the movie by legendary Hollywood wildman Timothy Carey, Lord High 'n' Low is several steps freakier than the kind of villain played in the TV show by Monte Landis (a serial bad guy, with swindlers, wicked hypnotists, and even Satan burnishing his Monkees CV). As Dick Straub said in a 1968 radio piece to promote the movie, 'Timothy Carey has been what Hollywood calls a 'heavy' for years.' In fact he is way beyond 'heavy' here and into a whole other order of strange. It is hard to discern what he is saying even if you are familiar with the film, which is a shame because it's a neat if lurid denunciation of the way a successful pop act is exploited via marketing far beyond its music and image. This kind of slipstream success is satirised (albeit barely comprehensibly) by Carey's character, and his mock-heroic soliloquy is worth reproducing in full: 'Anyway the idea is this – by-products! Imagine the tie-ins! Blonde wigs for kids! Swords! The whole phallic thing is happening! I mean why don't we use classic things? Millions! I'm telling you, millions!'

It sounds as though it emerged directly from his alarming personality and possibly deranged mind, but actually this speech is in the *Head* script, word for word. This seems appropriate in that it illustrates how the apparently free and spontaneous thought is actually a planned and strategic one – like the launch of a new pop band, perhaps – and it is clearly deliberate that the man who elucidates a marketing campaign targeting kids is a maniac. Carey certainly embodied the element of wildness the film was looking to portray, the madness at the heart of the system:

> **Nesmith**: Tim Carey was all over the place, a huge, large character, not just physically but spiritually. He just sort of took the place over.

> **Dolenz**: I think Timothy Carey represented merchandising, distribution, the whole marketing of The Monkees ... representing greed. And he is, if you notice it or not, discussing selling Monkee ... bodily fluids and other disgusting things as merchandise.[21]

Mike is disgusted and he, Micky, and Davy turn and go on their way, leaving Carey's character to shout at their retreating backs: 'Hey! Nobody walks out on me ... not even myself!' The scene is completed by an excellent sight gag as his Spaghetti Western style poncho swirls around him, perfectly wrapping him up and ensuring our final thought of him is as absurd rather than frightening. The script puts this at page 39E, noting that it was added on January 24 1968, the printed first draft date being December 19 1967. In this we see how quickly the film followed on not only from the Ojai summit but also from the success of the records and TV show.

The beats of the following scenes are more easily watched than described but are effectively a set of signals passed around the studio lot that, as the original 1966 ad for the show put it, 'The Monkees is coming!' The cry is 'They're coming! They're coming!' and this is the cue for a mass exodus on the lot and, in particular, from the canteen toward which they are heading. What follows crosses the Marx Brothers with the telephone box scene from the 'Mijacogeo' episode as they try to squeeze into the canteen at the same time everyone else (the script optimistically suggests '9,000 people') is pushing to get out, 'in a full panic'. The canteen scene in the script and on the screen are virtually identical; either way, it's hard on The Monkees. Once inside, they are confronted by famous female impersonator T. (Thomas) C. (Craig) Jones, whose character is dubbed Waitress in the script and 'Mr and Mrs Ace' in the movie. Whatever you call her, she's openly, sardonically critical of the group personally and professionally. The opening salvo is beautifully enunciated by Mrs Ace for maximum impact, and to let us know that they are in for it: 'Well, if it isn't God's gift to the eight year old. Changing your image, darling? While you're at it, why not have 'em write you some talent?'[22]

The Monkees' response – defence – is a faintly nauseating surrealism, adding a Dali-esque touch to the scene. Mike orders 'a finger sandwich and hold the mould' and, more famously, Davy requests 'a glass of cold gravy with a hair in it please'; that one-liner made it to the soundtrack album, but the track doesn't include the zinging comeback: 'One of your own?' The waitress has a particular insult for Micky, sitting on a bar stool, still in his Civil War blues: 'Still paying ['sending' in the script] tribute to Ringo Starr?' When he puts in his anti-delicious food order, '12 Boff crackers and a cup of mushrooms, crisp', with a mock-flourish, back comes an insult disguised as an in-joke: 'Yes … and I'll throw in a side of mouthwash, on the house.' Dolenz apparently had a reputation for halitosis on set. By the time Davy subverts his own role as wooer of girls in the show by telling Mrs Ace not to move because he wants 'to forget you exactly as you are' and that he'd love the pair of them to 'go to some place where we won't bump into each other again' it seems that the verbal punches are getting nastier and nastier, somewhere between the end of a marriage, a Hollywood royalty 'comedy roast', and a scene from a perverse sitcom. The symbolic violence of the verbal fisticuffs is suddenly itself outdone. A movement by Mrs Ace to slap Davy is transformed via a brutal, shocking cut to Davy being punched right in his famously pretty face, which is suddenly bloodied and disfigured.

MANCHESTER COWBOY IN THE RING

The camera pulls out to reveal we are in the midst of a wildly mismatched bout between Davy and – yes – Sonny Liston. He was heavyweight champion of the world from 1962–64, when he was defeated (twice) by Cassius Clay, later Muhammad Ali. Where Ali was nimble, quick, and witty with his mouth and his fists, Liston was seen as a slow slogger who had nothing but the ability to hit hard and direct. Ali's first round win on November 13 1964 was seen as a changing of the guard in the sport, a moment encapsulated by Neil Leifer's famous photograph of Ali standing over the stricken Liston as he lay on the canvas. Furthermore, Liston had been involved with racketeering in his home city of Philadelphia in the 50s and had served time for assaulting a police officer. His symbolic value to the movie may have been that while he was undeniably very successful and a champion, he was not respected or admired. Here this man mountain (six foot and 218 pounds of heavyweight) is in the ring with Davy Jones (five-foot-two and weight feathery). Liston tickles Davy's chin with his red-gloved fists, and the Englishman even manages to lay a couple on him. This scene is cast-iron proof of Jones's professionalism and his willingness to do what it took to get the work done. Can you name another pop star in a movie who allowed himself to be treated like this and have his pin-up countenance effectively pulped on-camera? Certainly not one of The Beatles, nor latter-day self-styled tough-guys such as 50 Cent or Eminem. It's an amazing, upsetting, brilliantly realised scene, end to end.

Mike and Micky are in the crowd, Micky yelling at Davy to 'stay down!' in an echo of the corruption and match-fixing that Liston couldn't shake off and which still haunts boxing. This idea of a deliberate mismatch, a fixed fight that one side couldn't win, again taps back into the Monkees narrative. Nesmith has often complained that their battle for their right to exist could not be won as far as some of the tastemakers and countercultural figures of the time were concerned. Then and even today some are telling The Monkees to 'stay down!'

Mike is dressed as a gangster, gnashing on his cheroot and impatiently adjusting his Al Capone hat – he took tips from Nicholson on how to connote menace in a gesture or two – and sitting next to him is his date, played by Carol Doda, the San Francisco stripper and topless dancer at the city's Condor Club who was famous, certainly, but not necessarily in the way a Monkee fan's parents would like. Her cameo is welcome – she looks fantastic – but it also moves the ground under the film's feet once more, for she is a problematic presence, even if one appropriate to the sleazy glamour of the scene. As Davy stares out at a concussed image of Nesmith and Dolenz, the scene cross-fades into a heartfelt flashback talk between Jones and Annette Funicello, the former Mouseketeer, whom we previously saw in the violin-playing scene. In a faithfully 30s movie style she tearfully implores him not to return to boxing, pleading with him to follow a musical career instead, but he vows to see the boxing racket through.

This little exchange is punctuated with one of *Head*'s key 'spoiler' moments – we see a spot of glycerine being delicately applied to Funicello's right eye to make her cry, the moment of application being awarded a sparkly little glockenspiel note. It's a crummy, nakedly cynical point – look, these emotions are fake – but it is made effectively, and is consistent with the rest of the film's import. These spoiler moments are a series of small, niggling jokes that the movie plays on its audience, its cast and on itself. As Mike will later say: 'Well, who needs it?' A good question – but the stripping away and exposing of the fake is central to *Head*'s thesis. So the stripper with silicone breasts sat next to Nesmith might be there for more than decorative reasons. Scene in the can, Jones suddenly brightens and becomes Monkee Davy again, cocky, loquacious, walking away from Annette Funicello without so much as a backward glance. He trots up a backstage metal staircase and walks along an identity parade of seven 'fighters' (four black, three white: the script notes '15 fighters') according to Rafelson, who goes with him. Jones picks Liston and invites him to try and lay a punch on him. Liston very gently moves to touch his bare knuckled fist on Davy's offered-up chin; at the moment of contact we are thrown back into the fight scene, just as Davy is thrown back onto the canvas for the nth time. It's a superb, awful, visceral effect.

Davy keeps getting up, much to the displeasure of Mike and Micky. When the former calls the latter a 'dummy' for not fixing the fight 'properly' Dolenz goes into a frenzy and rushes into the ring, lashing out at everyone, taking out Jones, the referee, Nesmith, even Liston. He then claims the fur-clad Carol Doda as his prize, parading her around the ring until – it's still shocking to see – she is punched out too and Dolenz, brown-suited and Adidas-trainered, launches into an extraordinary bout of physical acting, trying to shake off and take down anyone who comes near him. It takes five uniformed policemen to hold him, and a photographer (not necessarily for *Life*) pops a bunch of bulbs trying to capture the scandalous scene. Dolenz refuses to be calmed until from off screen we hear Peter Tork call his name and remind him of their respective roles in this world: 'I'm the dummy … I'm always the dummy.' Peter is pictured alone and distinct from the riotous assembly in the ring, the ropes behind him, dry ice mist swirling around him; he's there but he's not part of what's going on. Micky, now kneeling and in no need of further restraint, suddenly agrees: 'You're right Pete … you're always the dummy. I forgot … sorry.'

The original script has Micky seeing Peter beside the ring and then calling out to him; the finished film's moment of calm works better for the narrative, and connects more closely with what Dolenz called *Head*'s depiction of their 'real characters' rather than the wacky Monkee personae. I also like how he calls him Pete, which, speaking as a Peter, implies a degree of empathy, friendship and – Nesmith's word again – propinquity. Peter's reminding his friend and bandmate that he is 'always the dummy' both condemns him to and frees him from the restrictions and conditions of that role. As we saw as far back as 'Monkee vs Machine', in the show Peter could play the Harpo Marx dummy (two types of dumb there, we note) very well but the intensity and unique nature of the show's success somehow left the four individuals well and truly cast in those roles. An ephemeral fragment from *16* magazine seems relevant here:

> Dear Peter,
> You always play the dumb one on the show. One of my girlfriends says that that's the way you are in real life, but I don't believe that. You look intelligent to me.
> Vera Klause
> Raleigh, N.C.
>
> Dear Vera,
> Thank you, thank you, thank you! It's hard for me to toot my own horn, as you know – so I'll simply say that I play my Monkee role purely for comedy and that certain characteristics that you see there are truly mine, and that in my private life, there is a serious and studious side to me that doesn't show on *The Monkees*.
> PETER[23]

His acknowledgement to his young correspondent's sweet and smart question – are you reading this, Vera? – is that while part of Monkee Peter is 'truly' his character, there is also a lot of him that isn't on screen. This is an unusual clarification for an actor to have to make – no-one assumes Daniel Craig really is a British spy. The difference for The Monkees was the music, the magical and transformative element that locked the characters into the black box. Part of Micky's frantic response to being called a dummy in the boxing scene of *Head* is a reflection back onto those roles and how, in order for the balance to be maintained, they had to stay within them – and so, Peter is always the dummy. By finally acknowledging that on camera, Tork is allowed to put some distance between himself and Monkee Peter.

With his voice repeating 'I'm always the dummy' over and over, we fade back to the scene we had forgotten we ever left, back in the studio canteen, with Peter staring at a stickily melted ice cream cone. Mrs Ace speaks comfortingly to him and Peter asks her how she feels. After the reply 'Comme ci, comme ça', Peter's response is to send her sprawling with a punch. Mrs Ace lands in an adjacent chair, a voice off calls for the shot to be printed, and a bell goes for a break. The camera becomes hand held, documentary style, and lingers on Mrs Ace long enough to show her slowly slide off a wig to reveal that 'she' is a bald man in drag. So although Tork has been entirely absent from the staged violence of the boxing scene, the final punch of this part of the movie is thrown by pacifist Peter and he doesn't like it – worrying that the fake violence might affect the image of the real man. This is the 'serious and studious' side he referred to in his reply to the fan letter in *16* magazine.

The actual content of this little scene is often overlooked because of a focus on star-spotting – not only does Rafelson make a rare appearance in front of the camera but so do Jack Nicholson and, more briefly, Dennis Hopper. The scene is broadly as scripted, and therefore not quite the piece of handheld reality we're encouraged to think of it as, but it gives rise to a number of valid points. Peter objects to hitting a woman, claiming it runs counter to both his public image and private views. Rafelson says the punch can be cut, but Peter complains that such promises are never delivered upon. Then he asks Davy what he thought, and Davy tells him it was 'great, great, terrific!'

Peter is right to be concerned – two women have been punched in the last five minutes – but in neither case were things as they seemed. Micky didn't actually hit Carol Doda and Peter didn't actually hit T.C. Jones, but once Rafelson shouts 'cut and print!' then the scenes become 'real' in some way that marginalises the make-believe. The difficulties of Peter's personal situation here is made manifest by the way the entourage of hippies and hangers on who are loafing around the set move away from him as he leaves the canteen, casting him reproachful looks. Like Little Jack Horner, he goes to sit alone in a corner and, locating the scene in the fantastical once again, 'snow' begins to fall on him and him alone.

INTERLUDE

The fake flakes become heavier and heavier and as they do so we hear the first chords of 'As We Go Along'; the snow clears and as the image clarifies we see Peter walking across a snowfield in the mountains. The scene was filmed in Alaska and is the opener in a montage that presents The Monkees as belonging together but also as entirely distinct. In a way it's the visual equivalent of their idea for a double album version of *The Monkees Present*, with each individual presenting a side of material under the single banner of The Monkees. The directions in the script for this segment read:

> MUSICAL #4 We do a simple pastoral ballad beginning in a snow setting and working through the four seasons.[24]

As good as their word, we find Peter taking a walk out to winter in the deeply snow-clad mountains, followed by Micky seen from afar picking his way through a verdant, vine-tangled spring woodland, full of running fresh water streams. This in turn fades into a summer garden bursting with bright, brilliant flowers which Davy strolls through; finally we see Mike dressed in autumnal shades walking on a beautiful beach as the sun sets over the sea. Each Monkee gets two slots of equal duration. The 'simple pastoral ballad' is Carole King and Toni Stern's 'As We Go Along' and is a perfect fit for the scene and its ambitions. The song was written specifically for the movie, perhaps even with sight of this scene – Davy told the 'Open End Radio Special' promo album issued to promote the film (commercially issued with the 2012 box set of the *Head* soundtrack) 'the songs were written to the movie, for the movie' and while that's perhaps not completely true we can see how well the commissioning of project-specific material works here.

Rafelson intended this part of the movie to be an interlude, allowing the audience a breather, and it performs very well as such. The film was shot between February and May 1968 so the representations of the seasons are more symbolic than calendar-accurate. The whole point here is about atmosphere and instinct. It's almost like the hole in the centre of a record – without it, the rest of it wouldn't work. The scene surrenders gently to the movie's more frantic pace by the camera eye focusing on and then blurrily passing through a – dare I say it – vulvic aperture in a rocky outcrop on the autumnal beach, through which the setting sun can be seen. Once through the breach we find the mellow mood of this section undermined and overtaken by an accelerating series of images of prohibition ('WARNING. Underground Cable Crossing') and billboard advertising for Marlboro, American Airlines, and the Marines, to name but three, cut together super-fast to make the newly woken dreamer's head spin. The song's closing section is an accelerating pulsebeat of rising scales as pressure builds and the narrative speeds up again; as the song fades behind these images, an industrial rhythm rises.

MARCUSE, THE MONKEES, AND THE BLACK BOX: INSPECTOR SHRINK'S FACTORY

This boom-boom beat ushers in the factory scene, where we see the foursome being give a tour of an industrial institution by a man identified as Mr Hugh Grevich in the script but on the film credits as Inspector Shrink. He is played by Charles Macaulay, a mainstay of US TV series from the early 60s right into the 90s. Raybert had the financial means and the industry clout to call on good people for these kind of cameo roles. Macaulay's voice can be heard on the 'Opening Ceremony' and 'Dandruff?' sound collages on the *Head* soundtrack album. The scene was filmed, as Dolenz recalled, 'down at the sewage treatment plant at Playa del Rey – very appropriate'.[25] All Monkees are wearing zipped-up-to-the-neck boiler suits, once again all in white as in the 'Circle Sky' sequence. As they move through the process in the factory, Macaulay's industrialist explains everything to them in a voice both weary and zealous (what the script describes as 'disarmingly routine in tone'). It's through Davy that we notice that the head falls off a mannequin sitting behind a typewriter, workers drink foul-looking discoloured liquid from rank taps and fall unnoticed from gantries, while huge boxes tumble from great heights and no-one bats an eyelid. The others shuffle through, mildly interested in everything and nothing.

This shows us workers dissociated from the products of their labours, certainly, but is also a reference to earlier representations of this kind of concern, notably Chaplin's *Modern Times*, man (as well as Monkee) vs machine. It is also a clear reference to the industrial production of culture that mediating technologies have delivered into the marketplace – film, photography, publishing, recording – all the forms that helped 'create' The Monkees. Indirectly, it connects this part of the film's thesis to the ideas of the Frankfurt School of cultural theory, notably works like Max Horkheimer and Theodor Adorno's *The Dialectic Of Enlightenment* (1944), Adorno's own 'On Popular Music' (1941), and Herbert Marcuse's pop-era *One Dimensional Man* (1964). Each work addresses the connections between culture and consumerism and the influence of mass-production on the idea of art and the notion of an 'original' piece of work or creativity. Clearly when we are thinking about The Monkees in general, and *Head* in particular, we can see how such ideas might be relevant. These works are full of observations about what Marcuse calls the creation of 'false needs' through advertising and the notion that happiness is related to the consumption of material goods.

> People recognize themselves in their commodities; they find their soul in their automobile, hi-fi set, split-level home, kitchen

> equipment. The very mechanism which ties the individual to his society has changed, and social control is anchored in the new needs which it has produced.[26]

The factory is producing goods for consumption and the man who seems to be in charge of it speaks as if reciting from Horkheimer or Marcuse:

> Change one tape, the whole process is re-geared. Leisure! The inevitable by-product of our civilisation. A New World, whose only preoccupation will be … how to amuse itself. The tragedy of your times, my young friends, is that you might get exactly what you want.

This is a remarkably prescient piece of writing, owing something to the Marxist cultural theory so central to the Frankfurt School, but also factoring in the new pop age, where what we might now call the Baby Boomer generation were encouraged to think of themselves as consumers and to position themselves culturally and socially according to their tastes and preferred modes of consumption: there's enough food and drink, there's shelter, there's material well-being – so now we need entertaining. Where might that freedom of choice – or, as Marcuse would say, that illusion of the freedom of choice – lead the young? The idea that getting exactly what we want may equal a tragedy is food for thought – what might be the consequences of such perpetual and unrelieved gratification? If nothing else it would require an industry to feed that need – a cultural industry, a factory which manufactures entertainment and sensation by the black box-load. The thoughts may have been abstracted and European – both Horkheimer and Adorno were German Jewish exiles fleeing to the US to escape the Nazi terror – but the context was very American: from 1940, the two exiles lived and wrote in the Pacific Palisades district of LA, not a million miles away from Hollywood or The Monkees' fictional pad in Malibu.

The manufactured products of the factory seem to be cardboard boxes of various shapes and sizes, all marked with the image of a rectangular black box. It is both a corporate logo and a warning of what is to come. The whole scene and set up suggests the lair of a Bond villain (Macaulay's Inspector Shrink has something of the manner and bearing of Joseph Wiseman's Dr No) and this is made obvious toward the film's close when they fight their way out and the disposable jumpsuited goons are disposed of. Here, however, at the end of their tour the four are directed by their guide into what is later revealed to be the movie's central and most enigmatic symbol, the black box.

THE BLACK BOX

Guys, you got to listen to me or you'll end up back in the box!
PETER TORK, *HEAD*

The black box has a real and a fantastical aspect, much like the Monkees experience in itself. In the movie it is clearly used for its symbolic value, which we can explore, but it was based on a very real physical model. Due to their developing a tendency to wander off from their dressing rooms or make noises which disturbed the filming, by the opening of the second television series a large 'box' replaced their individual dressing room spaces; it had a meat cooler door and was a made of foot-thick metal, completely soundproof. The large (but shared) enclosed space was designed so the production team would know where they were at all times and so whenever one or more of the group was required on set, they could be quickly located and alerted, individual lights letting them know who was wanted. So in some ways this was a gilded cage: a comfortable, agreeable prison. What it also reveals is that by the time of the second series The Monkees were well past the stage of doing what they were told. It sounds unlikely, certainly by today's standards. Would they put the cast of *Friends* or *The Big Bang Theory* in a box? Yet it lent itself to interpretation as an idea and an image – control and confinement, certainly, but also packaging, branding, and mass production: when we first see the cardboard boxes in the movie, in the factory scene, they are all alike and all bear the black box logo. So the image of the product is also the instrument of their confinement; it's clear why it was a useful symbol in the movie. Part of the purpose of the real black box on the set was to keep them where they belonged, to keep them under control, and that is a key theme in the film too – this is why despite all of their efforts they always end up 'back in the box'. All the Monkees had their own view of what it represented, which are consistent with their personalities as Monkees and as private individuals:

> **Dolenz**: So here we are, back in the box. What the box always represented to me was not so much that we were trapped or imprisoned, but rather that we'd live from one black box to the next.
> **Tork**: We were trying to get out of the karmic box. There was a black box on the set of the TV show where we used to have lunch or behave in ways slightly less than … licit.
> **Jones**: I think the point was made, you know, let's see each of us try to get out of the box and me being naive to the whole cosmic side of the idea of the 60s and Hare Krishna and waterbeds and brown rice [a description of the scene in general and Peter in particular that Davy used many times] I never really went for any of that.[27]

Though he didn't comment on the matter here, I'm certain Nesmith's later fable *The Prison* has its roots in the ideas of freedom and containment that *Head* investigates, and that his retrospective interpretation of it would have been a philosopher's one. However on the 'Open End' interview Davy refers to Nesmith as 'conning' his way out of the box, so maybe future archival finds will clear this one up for us.

The box is a moveable feast too, making it much harder for them to run from; we recall the dramatic scenes of a real helicopter flying a real black box over Palm Springs. As Davy says on the Blu-ray, with marvel in his voice, 'They actually flew the black box. Actually flying!' Rafelson decided against a scripted touch to put the faces of The Monkees on the outside four walls of the box in this scene, and he was right: the blank and neutral tone is much more useful to the film than such an overt illustration of meaning. Clearly, the box has the power to transport as well as trap them – to move them where the film wants them to go. It is an image of their powerlessness, to an extent, like them being Victor Mature's dandruff, yet it is also evidence of their non-compliance: they're on the run from it.

The black box, to me at least, also suggests television – what's on the box? – and the fact that they were born on the small screen, magically transported to millions of front rooms worldwide via the black box in the corner. The only problem is, being so closely associated with the fake world of television, how do you then escape the box, as the lyrics to 'Porpoise Song' ask, 'to know what is real?' What are the consequences of making that effort, as they did? Will you ever be truly able to escape the box? *Head*'s final grim joke on the group suggests not, but that has in one way possibly turned out to be a good thing – it is through the constant rediscovery of the TV show by succeeding generations of kids 'on the box' that interest in The Monkees has kept being renewed, keeping the name alive, whether the four wanted it or not. This is in itself unusual for pop, in that if you wanted a Monkees reunion you didn't have to wait until old resentments had died down and quarrels patched up, as with other bands: you could just turn on the TV and there they were. Likewise in the early concerts, the band would burst onstage out of four black boxes dressed to look like giant amplifiers made by one of their sponsors, Vox. So the black box stood for mass production, confinement, control, means of distribution and exhibition, karma, the cosmos ... like the monolith in the contemporary *2001: A Space Odyssey* it is the object's lack of precise definition that allows its meaning to shift and keep changing while it remains in itself eternally unchanged. What was the original title of the movie again? Oh, yes: *Changes*.

After Inspector Shrink guides them into the box for the first time, they enter what at first seems to be a pitch black space, which after a few moments of a blacked out screen is flooded with a blinding light – the audience are as baffled as The Monkees themselves. The contrast between their all-white boiler suits and the deep pitch of their surroundings makes for an impressively stark contrast – it's a black and white image in full colour. Rafelson in voiceover bids them to come forward and instructs them to clamber into what looks like a great congregation of industrial brush-hair, shiny, coarse and anthracite black. It also looks like four enormous Beatle-wigs, referring back not only to the band's origins in the black-and-white world of *A Hard Day's Night* but also to Lord High 'n' Low's marketing manifesto and his vision of 'blonde wigs for kids' earlier in the film. Doing as they're told, the four climb into these black wigs for giants and as instructed jump up and down, 'being' dandruff. On cue a jingle plays back, a bogus yet remarkably authentic-sounding one, recreating with unnerving accuracy the advertising methods of the 50s and early 60s *Mad Men* era, turned groovy with a post-psychedelic Warholian gloss: 'Dandruff! Dandruff! We know it can be tough!' Bizarre as it is, the sight of the four of them wrestling with the synthetic hair is one of the few visual gags in the movie that could have featured in an episode of the TV show, a bit of slapstick that any kid would find silly and funny. As the jingle wraps, the camera pulls back and we see that the hair now somehow belongs to Victor Mature. He is first seen in profile like a Roman Emperor on the obverse of a coin and then his chair is turned to face the camera full on. He seems very relaxed even when a young woman starts to vacuum his hair, but our attention is drawn by the four tiny white-clad stick-like figures drawn up out of the shiny black mane into the nozzle of the vacuum. The poster promised some 'sci-fi' in the movie and here it comes.

EVERYBODY'S WHERE THEY WANNA BE

The debt this section most obviously owes is to Richard Fleischer's *Fantastic Voyage*, a story of four scientists shrunk to microscopic size to pilot a kind of submarine around the body of an injured colleague in order to try and repair damage to his brain caused by a head injury. The film won two Oscars in 1966 and would almost certainly have been on Rafelson's mind as a model for this portion of the movie. The ABC sci-fi series *The Time Tunnel* (1966–67) also contributed something to the look, I'd say, with the section showing The Monkees being drawn down the vacuum tube being quite similar to the time-travelling sequences in that show. The movie goes to town on the sound effects in the first half of this scene with electronic squeaks, bloops, and squawks getting us used to the sci-fi idea nice and fast. Of course, Monkee fans familiar with the debut of the Moog synthesizer on 'Star Collector' and, especially, 'Daily Nightly' the year before had already heard the sound of the future in this way.

The filming of this portion of the movie was fraught, not least because it involved the four Monkees being suspended on wires for nearly four hours with not a chance of stand-ins. Carol Deck, the reporter sent to the set by *Flip* magazine, reported the day's events as being full of danger and ill-humour. She felt a palpable tension on the set, writing of the vacuum-tube scene: 'I have to say that I found the whole thing rather frightening, but the director seemed intent on making the guys do it themselves … all four do all their own stunt work in the movie … the shot, which took over four hours … will probably be less than a minute in the finished movie!'[28]

In the scripted pandemonium, Davy becomes separated from the other three by catching hold of the side of the tubing while they are sucked right down into the belly of the whale, landing with a real method-acting bump at journey's end: 'The Monkees had to climb to the top of a tall scaffold and fall down … onto a kind of trampoline so they wouldn't get hurt. But the fall was not far short of ten feet! It was pure luck that they managed to get the scene right the first time as Mike sprained his ankle.'[29]

Despite the arduous nature of the day's work the film gives us a witty, even cartoonish scene as the trio splutter in the dust and then poke around amongst the random debris – a huge stamp bearing an image of George Washington's head, a sword-length pin, two oversized drawing pins and an equally elephantine paperclip, a yard-wide white button (leading Peter to announce 'Mother of pearl!' in an impressed tone), and a large roll-up cigarette end, which has clearly been ground out in an ashtray before ending up in here. This of course becomes the focus of some mildly daring allusions to what kind of smoke it might have been:

Nesmith: Hehe-he … this is not one of your standard brands!

> **Dolenz**: Oh! An El Zumo! [*spears the cigarette end with the sword-sized pin*]
> **Tork**: Imagine having to smoke *that* whole thing.
> **Nesmith** [*lobbing the cigarette end away as carelessly as if it were normal size*]: *Smoking* may be hazardous to your health.

Nesmith's opening line has become a site of mixed and contentious memories, with differing versions of what happened and which tone to strike. As Carol Deck wrote in August '68's *Flip*, they were clearly uncertain how to put this to her young audience: 'This line turned out to be quite a problem as they argue over how to deliver the line – should it be obvious what they're talking about or subtle?'[30]

Much later, in *Shindig* magazine, Dolenz recalled: 'That one line shut down the entire set for three hours trying to decide what we would call that. I remember there were enormous discussions. Back then it was still pretty much a no-no.'[31]

Just how well art can conceal what's really going on is evidenced here, in that the scene is coy and funny in the way it deals with this problem of the no-no of mentioning marijuana. It does so with more sly invention than a previous flirtation with forbidden words and ideas in 'The Devil and Peter Tork'. The word in that case was hell, and Micky capped off a censor-baiting scene by saying 'You know what's really scary? That you can't say [cuckoo sound] on television.'

Banter over, they realise Jones is not with them and they attempt to look for him, clambering up out of what Peter, in a nice little hipster joke which is in the script but not the movie, decides 'must be the bag we're in'. There's a nice clutch of lines here, bouncing off each other, notably Peter's 'Everybody's where they wanna be', a piece of new-agey sounding cod-philosophy (and a favourite of Jack Nicholson's, according to Rafelson) swiftly swatted by Micky's earthier approach: 'That's a particularly inept thing to say, Peter, considering that we are in a vacuum cleaner.' The script gives Mike a line after Micky's, 'And in as much as it poses as a truth, it is also a lie', which was either scrapped on set or the victim of a post-production edit; either way it reads more like an epigram from one of his early-to-mid-70s album sleeves than the right line for this context. The three call back up to Davy, their shouts echoing up and down the empty orange tubes.

DADDY'S SONG

We cut to see a small white figure drop back out of the nozzle and make his own tough landing, this time on a hard soundstage floor: Davy is once again in white against the darkness. Ever the trouper, he wipes his mouth, gets up and, in contrast to the sound-effects-laden section just gone, we enter 30 seconds of a kind of loudly ambient silence as he walks nervously toward a spookily illuminated doorway at the rear-centre of the stage. Holding his hand to his eyes to shut out the suddenly brightening spotlight, he approaches the doorway and passes through it. None of this is in the script, which specifies instead that Davy is 'silhouetted against a light high above him as he climbs toward it'. The finished movie's realisation of this moment is much more satisfactory, giving us a pleasing sense of directness and tangibility even in the midst of all this fantastical stuff.

The moment Davy passes from sight, a bright and brassy fanfare goes up: the opening of 'Daddy's Song', which would become the second Harry Nilsson song that Davy would make famous. But, as with much else regarding *Head*, there were disputes and last minute changes of tack; the script notes 'Davy makes his way into the light and sings "Magnolia Simms".' That is a Nesmith tune which ended up on the fifth Monkee album, *The Birds, The Bees & The Monkees*, issued in April 1968. It's a kind of McCartneyesque pastiche of songs from the early days of recording in the 20s and 30s. Indeed, it goes so far as to concoct snaps, crackles, and pops as part of a deliberately lo-fi recording to make it sound as if you are listening to a well-loved 78rpm shellac record on a vintage wind-up gramophone. Nesmith originally wanted to do this song-and-dance routine to his own song. It is the only song in the version of the script I've seen that is actually identified for inclusion by its title – recorded on December 2 1967, it was already in the can by the time Nicholson was typing up the script. Yet not only was it dropped but Nesmith's own recording of 'Daddy's Song' – which features a vintage vocal effect à la 'Magnolia Simms' and 'Tapioca Tundra' and appears on the various *Head* reissue sets – was also set aside, giving the song and staging to Davy. On the DVD commentary Nesmith recalled that it was Nilsson who insisted that Jones get the gig:

> I wanted to do the dance to 'Daddy's Song' but Nilsson said no, Davy is the song-and-dance man. For me it was an aspiration; for him it was a vocation. When Davy did the song it put the song into a different space, a Broadway space. They could have made things much more hard-edged but toned it down as our audience was 9–14 year olds. Though these were pretty hip 9–14 year olds, let me tell you.[32]

Nesmith is not wrong, and while he may have huffed at the time, the intervening years have made things clear: 'For me it was an aspiration; for him it was a vocation.' The two men had their individual strengths, as did Micky and Peter, and the Monkees project was at its best when it adhered to them. It's intriguing to speculate what Mike's hoofing to either his own or Nilsson's song would have been like, but you'd need to make a very, very good case if you wished to argue that the wrong decision was made, because Davy's performance of the song and its accompanying choreography is one of the visual and musical highlights of the evening.

Jones walks out into a bright white spot on the same darkened stage area, now frock-coated but still dressed in white against the black, this time incorporating the drama of the visual contrast into his own outfit – white jacket and trousers, black shirt. He gets to centre front just before the vocal, points a smart little index finger at the camera, and – pow! – we are suddenly on a brightly lit set, Davy now in black jacket and white ruffle-fronted tuxedo shirt. This reversal of polarities in the colour scheme runs throughout the next 2:42 so we never quite know what we are going to see. Rafelson deftly edits across between the black-on-white performance and its foil the white-on-black performance, and it is utterly seamless in execution; this is also testament to the skill of Jones in giving his director identical performances with which to cross-cut and experiment. Rafelson said that it was because of this scene in particular, and the amount of work all the cutting generated, that when he made movies thereafter he deliberately cultivated long single takes and kept editing to a minimum. That's understandable, but as an experiment in form and technique, the staging and visualising of 'Daddy's Song' is undoubtedly worth that Herculean labour. Jones wrote, or endorsed, a sweet little piece about the session for *16* magazine's August 1968 edition, full of fan-friendly confidences but also fascinating technical detail about the routine filmed on 'a tense and thrilling day in mid-June':

> Today was probably the most important day in my entire show-business career. Today was the day we began to film the big musical production number I perform in The Monkees' new movie. I had chosen the song called 'Daddy's Song', not because it's sentimental (in fact, it's quite the contrary, so don't misinterpret it when you hear the lyrics), but because it's such a good tune that I feel it will be an instant hit.
>
> All last week, The Monkees costumier Gene Ashman and I had worked together designing two groovy outfits for me to wear in this sequence. One is a black tuxedo with a long flared jacket, and the other is a white tuxedo styled exactly the same way. With the black tuxedo, I wear a white shirt – and with the white tuxedo, I wear a black shirt. The two shirts are exactly the same design, ruffled at the neck, cuff and down the front. They're almost a line-for-line copy of the beautiful yellow batiste shirt Gloria Stavers had made for me and gave to me a little over a year ago. That shirt, by the way, is still one of my favourites. I only wear it on special occasions.[33]

The excitement is real, if possibly overstated, but the routine is undeniably Davy's 'moment' in the movie, making the best use of the palette of skills his very successful pre-Monkee career. In the moves we see a rare blend of his 'Monkee dance' (the little knee-to-head body wiggle as the feet are planted flat on the floor, later lifted by Axl Rose of Guns N' Roses) and his more traditional musical theatre chops. In keeping with the theme of *Head*, these characteristics are being satirised at the very moment they are being displayed – from his extravagant reach-the-back-row bodily movements and facial gestures to the very Northern English way he pronounces 'up' as 'oop' in the first verse. Davy is right to warn his young listeners not to misinterpret the song when they hear it, because, despite the energy and vigour of the routine and the blousy jollity of the sound, the song is actually a story of child-neglect drawn from Nilsson's own experience: he was the illegitimate child of a Swedish sailor who rarely saw his father. We also learn that Gene Ashman – namechecked in the earlier canteen/boxing scene – was closely involved in designing Davy's two outfits, identical in all but tone. Davy very smartly nods to the relationship between the teen mags – in this case *16* – and The Monkees by dropping the name of that magazine's editor Gloria Stavers, encouraging a feeling of involvement and ownership among its staff and its readers. In this tiny detail we see how well the importance of the circuit of supportive connections was understood by the Monkee organisation.

> While I was in the dressing room getting ready, choreographer Toni Basil came in to greet me. We had been rehearsing together for two weeks and now she explained to me that she thought it would take us (Toni appears in the movie in my big song-and-dance number with me) about two and a half days to shoot the 'Daddy's Song' sequence. Those two weeks with Toni were real educational, let me tell you! I found out that it requires more effort to get into perfect physical shape to do a dance routine than it does for a jockey to get into shape to ride in races! Mr Fred Astaire has my profound respect.[34]

Davy's candour is winning, tying the learning of a dance routine into terms the young reader could identify with – learning, working hard, and practice makes perfect – with classic Hollywood tradition, through the reference to Fred Astaire, 'Mr', no less. Add in the biographical facts that any true fan would have known – his long-standing interest in horse-riding – and the circle is complete.

The piece also suggests that originally the song was arranged with a slow opening section and the second half upbeat and that the contrasting outfits were similarly kept separate:

> Our sets were designed in a very stark and unusual manner. During the first half of the song, I'm in black – so we dance on white tiles with totally white backdrops. During the second half, I switch to my white tuxedo – and then the tiles and backdrops turn black ... I sing this song slow at first, and the only prop that enters is an umbrella which flashes on when I have one line, *'It was such a rainy day...'* After I have sung the song slowly, Toni dances onto the set and we do our big duet together. I hope you like it, my little sunshines, 'cos your boy Davy lost *ten* pounds learning to get it all down just right for you!! After the dance sequence, I suddenly appear in a white outfit and do the tune up-beat – and do a fast dance with it for the grand finale.

It's no wonder he lost nearly a stone in the preparation for this scene; just look at how he jumps about, sending up his own theatricality whilst simultaneously demonstrating it quite brilliantly. The camera has to stay in long-shot much of the time because his performance is so kinetic, coming in close especially to allow Davy's deliberate over-performance to be clear, for instance on the line 'he was his Daddy's pride and joy', which also allows the promised white umbrella to be sneaked into his right hand from behind the camera. There's a bit of Gene Kelly business with it as a prop, a little tribute to the other great screen dancer to balance his nod to Fred Astaire. The umbrella is tossed aside as he falls and a fast cut takes us back to white set/black suit, and Toni Basil is already walking in from screen left. She too is observing the dress code, in a black pantaloon suit with a ruffled white blouse, exactly matching Davy's outfit in shade and style. At first we think she is offering her hand to help him up, but no – she wags her right index finger at his outstretched hand, turns on her kitten heels and walks away from him. The line immediately following this is 'trying to take away the pain', and the elongated word 'pain' is visualised by violently fast cutting between the black/white and white/black scenes. This really *is* a song about child neglect. The routine between Jones and Basil begins as a kind of battle of wills, pushing toward and away from each other, keeping each other literally at arm's length. On the word 'man', both put their hands to their heads and move sideways toward the camera and then embrace each other and begin to dance together, Fred and Ginger style, he spot on the mark, she doing everything he does but backwards and in heels.

Basil, the choreographer of the whole scene, is only onstage for 30 seconds of the routine but makes a huge impression with her lightness of gesture, her nimble grace, and the intelligent expression of movement; it's clear why she went on to have such a successful career in professional choreography at the highest level in theatre and film. The last section of the routine sees Davy sing live to camera; this is straight out of his musical theatre textbook: no musicians, no trickery, and alive, alive-o. Some notes go awry but that's what happens when things are live, as anyone who has been on stage will tell you. Things are perfect only in playback and then something more valuable is lost from the moment. As the lyric's last words fall away, the heartbreaking hope for his future son's happiness ('let the sadness pass him by'), we have a moment of silence that allows not only reflection but a final reiteration of the unsettling, near subliminal black/white editing. This technique crops up three times during the routine with the visually unnerving effects becoming more and more emotionally charged, so that by the time we reach this final moment, applied to a moment of highly eloquent silence, the reinforcing visual impact is at its most intense. As the music starts up again, restating the original blare of the song's opening, Davy wheels away from the camera and toward the back of the stage whence he came, passing back through the door at the precise moment that the song closes with a theatrical if muted stroke on a little bell cymbal: that's all folks.

As lights slowly go up on the stage we see a bunch of hangers-on who start applauding, slowly and ironically, and Davy has magically changed into the mandarin-collared green shirt so closely associated with this movie. As he emerges from the gloom into the light of the lot, who should appear from the shadows but The Critic, Frank Zappa. In the script there are three figures who speak to Davy in this scene, described simply as 'Musician 1, 2, and 3'. The first notes 'Funny song' (funny ha-ha or funny peculiar is not made clear); the second says 'Nice, Davy'; and the third, 'I think you got another Winchester', to which Jones replies, 'Oh, I hope not.' This refers to the 1966 novelty hit 'Winchester Cathedral', by the British outfit The New Vaudeville Band. That band didn't really exist, being a bunch of session musicians put together specifically to record the tune, yet the song's great success put pressure on them to cash in by becoming a 'real' group, recording follow-ups and touring. Sound familiar? Further to this, 'Winchester Cathedral' had been an American number one hit, outdoing The Monkees to win a Grammy for Best Contemporary Song in 1967. This was an irony because, like Nesmith's 'Magnolia Simms', it was designed to sound like a 30s recording. So the contemporary reference in the script was certainly pertinent, and more than a music business in-joke, but broke one of The Monkees' rules – keep topical material to the absolute minimum. It also gave us that rare thing – one of The Monkees being sniffy about *someone else's music*, as it was usually the case that they were on the receiving end. The finished movie restores the status quo, of course, with Zappa fulfilling his title by smirking his way through a bit of sparring with Davy:

Zappa: That song was pretty white.
Jones: Well so am I, what can I tell you?
Zappa: You've been working on your dancing though.
Jones: Yeah well, I've been rehearsing it … glad you noticed that.
Zappa: But it doesn't leave much time for your music. You should spend more time on it, because the youth of America depends on you to show the way.
Jones: Yeah?
Zappa: Yeah …

I like how Davy takes Zappa down with a bit of Mancunian logic – 'So am I, what can I tell you?' – and the reference to his dancing is a roundabout nod to the strength of what we've just seen, even if the movie can't quite bring itself to acknowledge it, hence the double-edged 'slow handclap'. Zappa's observation about the youth of America is clearly snide but such significance seems to come as news to Davy. His 'Yeah?' is a great 'fuck you'. The scene is rounded off by the bull which Frank is leading – did I say he had a bull? – appearing to say 'Monkees is the cwaziest people!', a borrowed phrase from radio comic and *Loony Tunes* voiceover star Lew Lehr. 'Monkies Is The Cwaziest People' was the title of a ten-minute film from 1939 in which chimps are let loose to perform with human gear – cameras, bicycles, dining tables and so on – while Lehr narrates over the pictures. His famous pseudo-Germanic phrasing was funny in itself – though possibly less so between 1939 and 1945 – and the temptation to use this phrase must have been too hard for Rafelson to resist. Davy shakes his head and goes off in search of his fellow Monkees to see how 'cwazy' they currently are.

On the Blu-ray commentary, all he had to say of the scene was 'The only thing I'd change is I'd take the lifts out of my shoes – I'm dancing like Jimmy Cagney half the time', which isn't much, but testament to its near-perfect execution – and, of course, before he became typecast as a gangster, Cagney loved to dance in movies. More revealing is that fact that Jones took care to recreate this routine onstage over the decades to come, performing it within feet of me at Sheffield, England, in 2011. He did it brilliantly, and the fact that he was no longer 22 made it all the more remarkable, testament to his professionalism. Further showing the fondness he had for this routine, his wife Jessica Pacheco took the Toni Basil role on that fabulous UK tour. Many of the audience may have been unfamiliar with the song, routine, even the movie, but it brought the house down nevertheless.

LOST IN THE JOHN – I MEAN, COMFORT ROOM

It's from here that the movie starts to lose its way in terms of having a detectable plot or direction, partly through a failure of nerve. As

XTC's Andy Partridge commented to me, 'It's a psychedelic mess that isn't psychedelic enough!'[35] The black box begins to dominate, and this should provide a totemic device to focus the action around. This it does, to a degree, but the centrality and power of this image gets lost in all the ambient noise. For example, in the first scene after 'Daddy's Song' we see the box rise slowly and mechanically up from underground on the lot. In the script, we are still in the vacuum bag but the net result is the same – the hatch of the box is pushed off and the trio emerge to be greeted by the censorious presence of a policeman, played by Logan Ramsey. In the exchange that follows certain lines are recognisable from the album track 'Dandruff?', but these are spread out across the actual movie dialogue and are presented in a compressed collage-form on the album. Their asynchronous nature is in keeping with the spirit of the movie overall. Despite being on their best behaviour, the cop interrogates them:

> **Cop**: OK, *weirdoes*, just what were you doing in there? And this better be straight. [*Points to Micky*] You! Fuzzy wuzzy!
> **Dolenz**: Er … in the black thing, right? What were we doing in there?

Despite it all this is a very funny scene, as the three try to recall the order of events that has led them here; effectively the cop is acting in the role of a paying audience member, seeking a coherent explanation. *Head* of course is everything but straight. Micky, Peter, and Mike recall fragments of the film we've seen so far, trying to make sense of events and attempting to explain:

> **Dolenz**: Well first we were in a factory.
> **Tork**: And then there was a commercial thing!
> **Nesmith**: No, no it was a vacuum cleaner.
> **Tork/Dolenz**: Yeah, a vacuum cleaner, that's right!
> **Cop**: OK boys … let's go downtown.

It is, after all, hard to explain. Yet in the social ferment of 1968, that absence of a logical explanation, surely, is part of the point and part of what the film actively pursues. Ramsey's cop is just the latest authority figure seeking to trap, persecute, or punish The Monkees in this film. They only escape him by dint of a strangely contrived sequence in which a squadron of soldiers conducts a kind of exhibition-level rifle drill, spinning the bayoneted rifles around startlingly close to the boys, with Tork especially not having to work too hard to feign alarm at their proximity. As they escort the cop away – by means that remain opaque – Mike unexpectedly empathises with him (and, by extension, the viewer): 'That cop must have thought we were totally crazy!' Meanwhile Peter chews his lip and slips in a remark worthy of a pacifist protestor on the turn: 'If he'd laid a *hand* on me … '

Davy slips away to the bathroom, ushered on by Mike bowing low and remarking 'Au contraire'. It has no relevance to the action at all, other than it is indeed contrary to what we might expect him to say. Mike had also used this self-same line, delivered in the self-same way, in episode 40, 'Monkees Marooned'. Davy enters the white-tiled john and, after washing his hands, looks into the mirrored door of the medicine cabinet above the sink, messing with his hair. He swings open the door and is confronted by a huge bloodshot eye staring out at him, the sight of which is accompanied by a sudden, shrill organ chord, horror-movie style. He slams the door, stares into the mirror – which is where the camera is also looking, so we see his face full-on – and then reels back in shock against the bathroom wall. Peter strides in, whistling what turns out to be a little snatch of 'Strawberry Fields Forever'. Looking in the same mirror he pops a pimple and mutters 'talk about police brutality' to himself. He is at first oblivious to Davy, and then spots him in the mirror; we can see both their heads in the reflection, so although we are behind them we see them both from the front and back.

He spots Davy and says casually, 'Hi mate – what's happening? Are you all right?' Davy's terrified wide-eyed mime directs him to the mirrored medicine cabinet and he goes to open it – Ken Thorne's incidental music rises to a little crisis as Davy calls out 'Peter, don't!' Peter does, revealing an unexceptional interior, empty but for a medicinally green glass bottle.

Both men's heads are seen throughout this little vignette in the mirror's frame, and that is where our eye is directed by the camera. It's like a TV screen, a portrait frame, or the Mylar cover of the soundtrack album: look into it, and see yourself. If you don't, who is staring back? In this film The Monkees are continually questioned, scrutinised, and observed – by their fans, by the police, by the camera. That's what a made-for-TV group is built for, to be looked at. The eye behind the mirror is just another manifestation of that perpetual scrutiny.

Closing the cupboard door and putting the mirror back in the room, Peter is unperturbed, having not yet seen the eye ('I get it. The old mirror routine, right?') and exits, drily quipping one of the film's best known lines: 'Well, let me tell you one thing son, nobody ever lends money to a man with a sense of humour.'

As he walks to the door, the shot is cut by full-screen captions, with huge white upper-case letters on black (back to 'Daddy's Song') spelling out the last dozen words. In another example of the very fine high-speed cutting that so exhausted Rafelson, these edits go by so quickly it is almost impossible at normal speed to discern their nature. Again these are borderline subliminal cuts, the kind that were banned from advertising (though not from overall use in film or TV). Rafelson is definitely flirting with the margins of what could and should be done with media technologies within film. Thanks to the miracle of DVD slow-mo we can see that each word caption is cut into, rather than over, the succession of images of Peter walking to the door, wagging his right index finger as he speaks. Some words are repeated – 'NOBODY', 'LENDS', and 'HUMOR' are shown twice in a row – while 'TO' and 'A' and 'WITH' and 'A' are cut together without a shot of Peter dividing them. Most brilliantly, 'MONEY' looks like it is going to be repeated but its 'mirror' caption is left blank – a blank cheque? The line is famous because of its starring role in 'Poll' on the soundtrack album, but its mix of faux-wisdom and mischievous cynicism is a highlight anyway, catching some of the spirit of the movie in a highly repeatable epigram. No doubt this is why it was picked out for the album by Nicholson in the first place, but the captioning effect, though sub-subliminal, is really effective in the way it burns the phrase into the viewer's memory of the movie. In a 2014 radio interview, the English broadcaster Iain Lee quoted the line at Tork and he responded, with a good-natured weariness, 'I've been told that.'

Alone again, Davy returns to the mirrored cabinet, plucks up the courage, and swipes open the door – the one green bottle accidentally falls. He looks askance, vexed, at the debris in the sink and closes the door again. Instead of the scene resolving itself by Davy following Peter back out onto the lot, the nightmarish scene has now filled the mirror – 'the old mirror routine' – and suddenly Davy finds himself transported to a haunted-house/schlocky-horror movie set, complete with huge tapestry wall hangings, suits of armour, skeletons, cobwebs, and zinging electronic sound effects. The TV shows featured several visits to spooky mansions and castles but this is another order of stage-creepy. At the end of the corridor there is a door not unlike the one he was drawn to prior to 'Daddy's Song', this time illuminated by pulsating red light. The script says: 'A long Gothic vestibule room, theromins [sic] in behind him … the camera pans over the looming shapes of baroque furnishings, conveying mystery, horror and commercial success'. In the script, Davy speaks as he walks down the corridor, 'Hope I didn't disturb anyone,' making use of another of the film's projected titles, *Das-turb,* but in the film he doesn't speak – we hear a cacophony of sound and maniacal cackling.

At the corridor's end Davy slowly squeezes open the door to reveal, fears realised, a huge, hideous insect of the type familiar from 50s science fiction movies. These movies expressed primal fears but also Cold War anxieties – *Invaders From Mars* (1953) and *Them!* (1954), which gave Van Morrison's Belfast rhythm & blues band its name – and these are the sort of films Rafelson would have seen in his early adulthood; he understood their techniques and their dynamics. Here, the extreme close-up of a real insect is pretty ghastly, made all the more so by the awful squawking, squonking noise that accompanies the shot. Yet no sooner are we pushed back into our seats by this spectacle than we move on to a close encounter of a second kind – Dolenz's face magnified through a glass as he scrutinises us down the camera. Dressed in preposterous pith helmet and colonial hunter gear, he declaims in shock: 'The Lancashire

Midget Greenie!!' This is a three-pronged trident of a poke at Jones: Manchester was in Lancashire; his stature was a staple joke in the TV show and indeed in this film ('I can't see! It's too deep!' in the war scene); and he wore a green shirt in the movie. In surprise Dolenz falls backward and is shown tumbling down a scree slope. It is orchestrated literally and figuratively, in that Ken Thorne's music accompanies his ride and the images are edited and mirrored. Dolenz did the fall himself in Bronson Canyon and how he didn't hurt himself remains a mystery.

Reaching the bottom of the slope, he is instantly grabbed by a group of distinctly un-PC straw-skirted 'tribesmen' who lead him off and chain him to a wall where Peter and Mike already hang. When the camera dollies along to reach Nesmith at screen right he turns his head and confides 'Now, *here's my plan*', at which exact moment the wall revolves and we are back in the bathroom, this time with the cop interrogating them once more about what they think they are doing: the script sneakily links these wildly disparate scenes by using the same term to describe the still-missing Jones. Peter and Micky try to be ever so polite ('Sir', 'Good officer, Sir') and he lets them go. This comfort room seems to exert a good deal of power over the characters and their actions, despite being utterly featureless, banal, and liminal – no-one 'owns' a public bathroom – and so it proves here. Alone in this strange space, the cop checks the cubicles and then does a strange waddle of a dance to Vegas-sleazy stripper music. Peter thought this a minor theme worthy of a mention on the DVD: 'Look at this cop, PC Faye Lapid! And T.C. Jones was the other sexually ambivalent figure in the movie. Two of them, isn't that interesting?' In both cases we are asked to not take them at face value or at least are shown what might happen if we do – what lies beneath? It's an idea not unrelated to the thesis of the movie and the Monkees story as a whole. The magic mirror in the bathroom delivers again as after his dance, the Cop looks into it and calls out 'Victor Mature!' Mature is seen standing, grinning, and tipping his cigarette in the Gothic vestibule that claimed Davy. No sooner do the words fall from his lips than he collapses into a dead faint. It's interesting that Mature is namechecked: the only example in the movie. While it is not the first time we have seen him –

remember the dandruff? – it is possible that it was in his contract to be formally introduced in this way. The screen swirls like a cross between a psychedelic piece of Murano glass and a spot painting, and we are drawn into a sequence announced by a caption as 'The Cop's Dream'.

MYLAR AND A '38 DODGE

Mike sits bolt upright in his bed – has he just woken up from a nightmare that occupied the last 30 minutes or so, or have we gone deeper into the realm of the imagination? Rising unseen behind him is a silver 'balloon pillow'. He has been 'das-turbed' by the insistent buzzing of a doorbell. We recognise as he stumbles in his pyjamas across the room that we are back in the Monkee pad, and as he opens the door we see Peter and Micky sitting on a sofa with acoustic guitars, concentrating on their strumming and seemingly oblivious to the angry-bee buzzer which still persists. Peter, surprised by Mike's irritation, says he'll get it and puts down his guitar. Mike shuffles back into his room muttering 'Well I'm happy to bring it to your attention.' Peter opens the door, as he had done so many times in the TV show in order to welcome a new plotline, and there stands a small telegram delivery man, chained to a much taller and much younger girl. Listed in the cast as The Heraldic Messenger, he is played by vaudeville act and 50s movie star Percy Helton. He announces that 'I got a wire for Monkee' as he hands over the note. Peter thanks him, the man says 'It's nothing', and Peter delivers another of the movie's more gnomic lines, 'Oh I wouldn't say that. We all have loved ones, you know.' Unfurling the note he reads, stops and, suddenly agitated, crumples the paper.

The scene cuts to Mike's room and a door slams. Immediately the Gothic vestibule theme starts up once again, Thorne's horror score serving the film well by connecting the scenes in a way dialogue simply could not. Impatiently, Mike puts on a somewhat incongruous white silk scarf and then a kind of pale blue housecoat. Micky is still on the sofa clutching his guitar doing a very good 'what, me?' face as Mike goes to the door, opens it, and calls after Peter. We then cut to Peter running down the Gothic vestibule to the illuminated door. Just as he reaches for its handle we hear the command 'STOP' and cut back to the telegram he discarded now being read by Mike. At the top it has the Monkees pad address (1334 North Beechwood Drive) but its message says simply 'STOP', a word said twice by Mike, once in voiceover and once on camera in the scene. 'STOP' is familiar from telegrams but also an unambiguous command – as in 'quit!' or 'why keep fighting?' Calling to Dolenz he sees that he, too, has disappeared. Suspecting a prank, Mike quickly loses his patience. Up to this point the script and the movie are effectively identical; in Mike's speech to the empty room we find substantive differences.

> Mick? Come on. This isn't funny. Is this supposed to be funny? I'll melt all your guitar picks, fellas … tell your right ages … tell everybody how we do it. You guys think I'm a sap? Is that it fellas? One thing I have never been accused of is a sense of humor. Which equips me for being more … terrified than your average eight year old.[36]

This is the script's second castigation of the eight-year-old. In the movie we get:

> Hey Micky? All right now come on! What are you guys doin'? … Mick? … [*long pause*] Hey, this isn't funny … [*long pause, punctuated by chimes of a clock striking 11*]. OK, you think they call us plastic now babe but you wait till I get through telling 'em how we do it, huh?

In this spiel is a clear reference to Nesmith's infamous *Saturday Evening Post* 'outing' of The Monkees a year earlier: 'Tell the world we're synthetic, because, damn it, we are.'[37] So when Nesmith shouts out to Dolenz that the STOP message was 'as much for you as it was for me' he means it: it's for all of them. And, just to help the film prove the point, as he opens the door of the cupboard in which he supposes his tormentors are hiding, a lifesize waxwork of Dolenz falls out and smashes its nose on the floor. This is the second time in the movie that effigies of the band have been abused – think back to the post-concert 'riot'. In the script this point was made even more intensely – or in a more laboured way, according to your view – as it specifies that 'three wax images of The Monkees fall head down on him'. To add a soupçon of the gruesome, some hot candle wax is accidently spilt on the models: 'We HEAR A SHRIEK. The hot wax has burned into Davy's eye.' This rightly stayed off the screen; the borderline sadism of this is merely gratuitous.

Mike's transit from pad to the haunted house is freaky on screen and freaky on paper, though quite different in effect; in the script he suffers far more, passing through 'mist and glutinous textures … moist walls', suggesting some kind of unsought physical intimacy. As he moves in a slow motion kind of trance-state 'the SOUND transports him … as if he were on a moving platform only able to control his movement from the legs up'. In the movie he lurches in slow motion out of the pad pulled by some unseen force through his room, full now of the silver Mylar pillows which we had seen behind him at the start of the scene. To a foreboding electronic soundtrack he wheels and staggers on, and Rafelson polarises the moving image into negative so he looks like his own ghost. This effect, in combination with the unnatural movements of the pillows and the addition of a highly amplified heartbeat to the soundtrack, is most unsettling. You can hear much of this section at the close of 'Poll', mixed with the maniacal laughter that greeted Davy's arrival. It's meant to be disturbing, of course, but that doesn't help us swerve the nerves. Nesmith recalled that he had first seen Mylar used in this way at an exhibition at the Art Institute in Chicago and that Rafelson was similarly impressed:

> When I came in to see the Monkees pad remade in Bob's pop art image, one of the things that stood out was that Rafelson wanted to use the contemporary art scene – that was more striking to me than any film references.[38]

Mylar was, and is, the brand name for a type of stretched polyester film which has been used in the extraordinary (the Apollo lunar modules had a type of it on their framework), the task-specific (the shiny metallic blankets given to those in shock or after a marathon, say), and the everyday (the helium filled balloons that an child might buy at a fair or a circus). Wherever it's used it is noticed because it is so incredibly shiny and reflective. Perfect, perhaps, for a film concerned with reflections and mirrors and *looking*. The pillows perform well in the spooky slow motion and look good in negative too. Mylar appealed to conceptual pop artists of the mid-to-late 60s for this very quality, as an expressive medium with which to work. Hence its controversial use on the original soundtrack album cover; the cover is itself a work of art, but not everyone thought it was a good idea. Lester Sill recalled with undisguised irritation his feelings about what he saw as wastefulness and frippery:

> I didn't pick it. I didn't want it. I fought against it. That was Bert Schneider's idea. Mylar … the problems that arose from packaging that thing were horrendous. They almost had to hand-wrap those things, it was monstrous. The record company, Victor, just fought against it. I had nothing to do with the concept; that was Bert … when you looked you saw your head, that was the idea.[39]

We can appreciate the difficulties and they were very real. The usual packaging machines at RCA's factory could not cope with this material without ripping it, so the original run of albums did indeed have to be virtually hand-wrapped, just like original artworks. Nevertheless the appearance of the Mylar pillows in the movie and the use of the material on the album packaging is a neat conceptual link, and it has proven to be a smart move in the (very) long run. Modern reissues have recreated the shiny mirrored effect while using much more stable material; had they given up on the idea, and issued it in the plain white cover that everywhere outside the US got in 1968, we would have lost this extra dimension to *Head* as a whole.

As Mike makes it to the door at the end of the vestibule through which we have seen Davy and Peter (but not Micky) pass, the negative very slowly returns to the positive and the camera tilts up slowly, even slightly jerkily, to become fully naturalised as Nesmith's face reaches the centre of the frame. As we'd expect from Nesmith, there's no fear in his countenance: caution and curiosity but no fear. There is no insect to terrify him, just a long darkened chamber at the end of which are three cowled figures, heads bowed, candles held out ahead of them, tips of the flames held at chin height. Distant monastic-style chanting is heard and it grows louder as Nesmith moves toward the figures. The camera tracks in, keeping the trio in the centre of the frame for the big reveal. They throw back the hoods and it is Davy, Micky, and Peter – hey hey they're the Monks – and they begin singing 'Happy Birthday'. Lights start to go on all around the previously dark room and reveal dozens of people, a DJ's double turntable console, and all manner of fittings and furnishings, too much for him (and us) to take in so quickly. The boys get to the end of their song, the beautiful people mob Mike, and with a little tumble of bass notes we are off into one of the film's musical and visual highlights, Mike's birthday party hooked up to Peter's 'Long Title: Do I Have To Do This All Over Again?'

The room is immediately full of frantic, vibrant movement, writhing dancers and the grooviest of light shows. Everything is in continuous flux: colours, faces, bodies. In the melee, we see Tork, Dolenz, and Jones dancing like crazy in the throng and Rafelson wandering about, filming with a handheld. Just before the vocals come in, June Fairchild delivers a look of love, made from just an icy stare, right down the camera: a superb moment. The only still figure in this scene is Nesmith himself, who, despite being at the centre, sees everything revolve around him without actually involving him. He looks mildly amused, good naturedly nonplussed, and even a little impressed sometimes – with good reason. It's a visual bonanza, with the rich, fiery colours licking up the sides of the room and the psychedelic lightshow still stunning. Rafelson pulls out all the stops – silhouettes, projections of colour on people's faces and bodies, liquid lenses giving us those archetypal psychedelic shapes on the wall, and great lovin' spoonfuls of solarisation. Nesmith recalled something of the scene:

> I remember Bob trying to explain the process of solarisation to me, trying to visualise it in my mind; then I saw it and got it. But of course that was the sort of thing you saw at every single light

> show at every single rock'n'roll psychedelic club in the country. So it was right where it needed to be.[40]

This isn't the first time we'd seen solarisation of course – the mermaids sequence during the opening 'Porpoise Song' makes startling use of it – but here it seemed more in its natural habitat. As part of the universal heat and thrill of the nightclub it looks and feels unique but it was also a key part of the scene at the time. It looks and feels *out there* but it was also commonplace; the counterculture functioned distinctly from the mainstream in a way that would be very difficult to sustain in the age of social media, but the mainstream positively welcomed the latest underground trend rather than demonising it. According to Micky:

> This was a crazy day of filming, a great party. Most of this work here [the dance scene] is done in editing ... You see me doing some dancing, Davy, Peter ... and Bob Rafelson and his camera, breaking that fourth wall, which these days is not unusual but then it was. They did a master of probably two or three cameras of the whole crowd, and then they would stop, do a close up of me, there's one of Mike, and then they had us behind some screens. There was a lot of wild footage. But it was always to playback.[41]

Dolenz reflects that while it looks wholly organic it was nevertheless staged just as much as a party scene might have been in a classical Hollywood musical like *High Society*. Evidence of the careful matching of image to sound comes as Rafelson pairs eight solarised stills of dancers' heads with eight notes from Stephen Stills, whose lead electric guitar work we hear on this track. The effect is all the more striking because of the contrast with the frantic movement everywhere else in this sequence and the assault on the senses it represents. We are able to look at Nesmith, June Fairchild, and six other heads and study how the colour lies on their skin and changes our sense of where and who they are. It may well be trippy (I couldn't tell you) but it is beautiful and mind-expanding all on its own.

As with the first verse, cued in by June Fairchild's arresting look down the camera, the song has a visual cue to fall back into the verse from the instrumental interlude as Nesmith cocks an eyebrow. As he does so the screen changes completely, and where we had wild and riotous colour we suddenly see in black and white again: not the stylised 'Daddy's Song' type this time but authentic Pathé newsreel footage of a Broadway dance troupe, captioned 'Music Hall Rockettes Paris Bound'. The dance troupe were and are based at the Radio City Music Hall in New York – they were formed in 1925 and still perform at the RCMH every day the theatre is open. In 1936 they flew to Paris to perform, and it is this trip that features in the clip. The girls, dancing in perfect unison, are of course extraordinarily graceful and impressive, and their gymnastic discipline is quite different from the dancing we've just been watching. Whether the director is enjoying presenting the contrast in styles or has some other agenda you can decide, but it is certainly a startling change from psychedelic colour to cool monochrome, from wild self-expression to collective endeavour. It's also a cool experiment into what happens if you underscore any music with any images – you will often end up feeling some kind of concordance between the music and the moving image. Thus the Rockettes look like they're dancing to the Monkees song – or at least your brain tells you they do. This is the root of the kind of mischievous urban myth-making that has seen people claim, for example, that Pink Floyd's *Dark Side Of The Moon* is designed to correspond with the first part of *The Wizard Of Oz*.[42] Similarly, when we see The Monkees playing their instruments in episodes from the first series we are happy to believe that they really were.

Rafelson's cutting and editing in this sequence is so rapid it becomes less a narrative and more a chain of flashing images that not only expresses or alludes to a feeling but somehow *is* that feeling; it pours out at such a speed the images are not simply illustrative of the music and the moment, they are an equal part of it, just as the lighting scheme has the same fiery ocean colours as Peter's shirt.

There's a beautiful hidden detail in this scene: we glimpse it in close-up early on (right after the mirror ball flashes) and I'd have missed it but for Micky's DVD comment: 'That's the Kienholz car! I don't know how they got that!' The Kienholz car is an artwork by the American installation and assemblage artist Edward Kienholz. Born in 1927, he was an established artist in his early 40s at the time *Head* was made. The work featured is called *Back Seat Dodge '38* and was made in 1964. Kienholz often dealt with themes of voyeurism in his work, and it caused a great deal of controversy when first exhibited at the Los Angeles County Museum of Art in 1966, being called awful and even pornographic. It is the rear portion of a 1938 Dodge car that Kienholz refashioned; its door is ajar and there are two figures made from chicken wire but dressed as a man and a woman embracing. As the back seat has been pushed forward by it only being half a car, the erotically entwined figures are the main features of the piece. In the original artwork there are beer bottles and items of clothing strewn around on a piece of Astroturf that don't seem to have made it onto the set of *Head*. Kienholz used a '38 Dodge because his father had owned one and the artist recalled having an experience like this in the back of that car. Hence it was an autobiographical piece, but the anonymous nature of the figures lent a kind of universal feel to the depiction. Peter also spots the car:

> *'38 Dodge* by Edward Kienholz was a very dramatic off-colour work of art that kicked up a fuss when it was first installed, with a lot of objections to the raciness of it ... The couple were apparently partly nude, and there was apparently some overt sexuality to the nudity which was, ah [*in a resigned tone*] asking too much.[43]

It was withdrawn from general exhibition but became a cause celebre; it was later returned to display, but guarded, with the door closed. Access to it was by request, so each viewer would have to open up and peer inside at the two figures, adding an extra layer to the voyeuristic experience. This idea of the forbidden gaze upon the sensual (remember the belly-dancers in the desert scene), coupled with the piece's controversial reputation, clearly made it of interest to Rafelson, who will have used his contacts to import the artwork into this scene. It is glimpsed so briefly and dimly as to be almost invisible, but is a truly fascinating little indulgence by the director, like a tiny detail hidden in a Renaissance painting, obscure until one really *looks*. That's highly appropriate for a work which plays with ideas of voyeurism and why the Kienholz car suits the themes of *Head* very well indeed.

Cutting back to the party we see Nesmith, still shuddering in a solarised shimmer, preparing to usher in the next scene. As the playback dies down – the Monkees having danced with great enthusiasm to their own song – Davy, Micky, and Peter crowd round Mike, joshing and hailing him. Mike sits on a throne, and it's one that keen Monkee watchers have seen before: it's The Usurper from the very first broadcast episode, 'Royal Flush'. That must have felt like much further back than two years. Over the noise of the party we see Peter play-punch the air and speak to the enthroned Mike: 'Mike you old son of a gun, a millionaire at 25!' The young millionaire beckons to Micky and asks him to set up his next line: 'Ask me, how does it feel?' Micky mis-hears and he repeats the instruction, louder. Micky asks the question and, suitably cued, Mike stands up and declares: 'I don't like it, that's how it feels!' He complains that he doesn't like surprises and that if the gang wanted him to come to a birthday party they should have asked him, not tricked him; the throng, Monkees included, look sheepish, not quite knowing how to take this monologue. This is, surely, breaking all the rules – one is supposed to be delighted when good things come one's way, and good fortune should be appreciated. The links between this little scene and The Monkees' complex responses to their own success seem to me very clear – a millionaire at 25, sitting on a throne supplied by the organisation (and TV show) which has made him a star, and yet still he is ungrateful! I'm reminded of Don Kirshner's incredulous account of handing each Monkee a cheque for $250,000 at the Beverly Hills Hotel and then being relieved of his duties moments later.

> Mike had given me a lot of heat that he didn't like the records. He wanted to do it his way. I was a little disconcerted because we were so successful. I handed each boy – Mike, Davy, Peter, and

> Micky – a cheque. If they had problems with the records I'd have respected them if they hadn't taken the money. They all took the money and Mike proceeded to put his hand through the walls at the Beverly Hills Hotel, which amazed me because I thought they were pretty solid walls.[44]

In terms of the changes from the initial Monkee method, Nesmith was the man perceived to have driven them – Kirshner certainly thought so, as did Lester Sill, who commented that 'I still think that Mike was the catalyst for destroying the group.'[45] In this scene Mike is indeed cast in the role of malcontent, dissatisfied with the trappings of success, but instead of being a petulant showbiz brat or indeed a catalyst for the group's demise, he is a free-thinker, someone who thinks outside the box – a skill which in terms of this movie is particularly useful. It's a nod to his originality of thought and willingness to go against the grain, which is, at the very least, part of an artist's duty. It's funny, too. Having so-whatted the rituals of a surprise birthday party he lays into the other great annual bonanza of commodification: 'And I'll tell you somethin' else too – the same thing goes for *Christmas!*' Despite being hipsters and groovy cats, all the crowd take a step back in shock and a sharp collective intake of breath. Arms folded in satisfaction that his dart has pierced the armour, he smugly notes 'Now how about *them* apples?' This rootsy phrase – meaning 'How do like *that*?' – floats in the air for a moment and there is a quizzical silence, until a girl's nerve breaks and she screams and the crowd mob him once again, without the violence of the Salt Lake City riot but with the same warmth that greeted his arrival. Nesmith is incredulous. It seems even if Monkee Mike denounces birthdays and Christmas he still can't get the crowd off his case. The script makes this clearer – the crowd fear 'the wrath of the master' and as they mob him they cry 'Attaboy! That took a lotta guts! You bet!' So – what to do with that kind of power? What responsibilities does it bring?

As if in response to these unspoken questions the crowd parts to allow the wheelchair-bound Timothy Carey, still in the guise of Lord High 'n' Low, to propel himself slowly into the middle of the scene, a most incongruous sight in the midst of all this youth and vigour and success. The script identifies this character as Bruce Dern, the original choice for the role, for the first time – in the previous encounter the character had been listed simply as Dernsie with no reference to the actor who would be playing him. As he gets up out of the chair, a noose is seen around his neck. The condemned man, but is he on his way to meet his fate or has he just cheated the gallows? Salvation or damnation? Again, the theme of punishment and survival – and which is worse – arises. The script picks up the 'Attaboy, Mike' riff from the crowd scene and runs with it, having this intruder repeat it over and over again, becoming more and more grotesque with each repetition. The direction reads:

> Repeated over and over as he goes through changes with the line, bored, hostile, silly but eventually winding up a slobbering hump-backed adenoidal monster, moaning the lines through his cleft pallet.[46]

If you have seen the movie you'll know how accurately realised this description is by the scene. As Micky says on the Blu-ray, voice tinged with alarmed wonder, 'Timothy Carey was a character, I can tell you that. He did a lot of strange movies.' He was certainly well-chosen for his role in *this* strange movie and it's hard to imagine Bruce Dern bringing this horrible vision to life as vividly. The Monkees slowly back off and clamber back up to the raised platform where the Usurper sits, now empty. Stoned and dethroned, the four are seemingly mesmerised by the spectacle of Carey and, as the direction reads, 'All four recoil in fear and disgust.' As Carey finally reaches the climax of his monstrous monologue, the four Monkees start to collapse into laughter: not smirking or 'good joke there' laughter but 'so hard they could burst' laughter, building to hysteria. The script gives the laughter a motive – 'From fear or out of it they now turn to laughter' – but the juxtaposition of Carey's performance and this mirthless laughter makes for a very disturbing little moment.

A gunshot rings out, momentarily making one fear the worst, but as the guffawing comes to an abrupt halt we see Carey on the set of a

Wild West town. Standing in front of a posse of other toughs, he waves a rifle about, hitches it, and points it dead ahead (a sight which no-one could truly be at ease with seeing). Then he announces, in his best slow psychocowboy drawl, 'Boyyyzzz … don't never … but never … make fun of no cripples.' The script gives us further context omitted from the shot: 'Dernsie now "The Foreman of the All White Southern Mississippi Courthouse Steps Jury".' Indeed, his crew are behind him, posed on what could be some courthouse steps. But all eyes are on the gun. What would be the consequences of breaking the rules as defined by this jury of native justice? One can guess, and images and ideas of law, punishment, and the rifle are immediately picked up in the next scene. As so often in *Head*, apparently unconnected non sequitur scenes are revealed to be subtly connected if we take the time to look and reflect: there's that mirror theme again.

ARE YOU TELLING ME YOU DON'T SEE THE CONNECTION BETWEEN GOVERNMENT AND LAUGHING AT PEOPLE?

That reflective notion also comes to the fore with the next sequence, two minutes of real vox pop interviews on the street with citizens. On the soundtrack album this sequence supplied much of the track 'Poll'. The faces we see answering often unheard questions are real people, not actors – after all that's what we want, right? Real people, not actors – and, Micky reveals, they are being interviewed by Mal Sharpe.

> The interviews were done by the original man-in-the-street interviewer Mal Sharpe, a street prankster and put-on artist. They asked him to go out in the street and ask the questions and these are real answers from real people; that's very clever.[47]

Sharpe and his partner James P. Coyle were indeed early 60s pranksters who also understood very well the conventions that had arisen around the man-in-the-street mode of television interviewing. They satirised those conventions and also the notion that the man in the street was inherently more truthful or in possession of a wisdom that more specialised analysis lacked – before the era of blogs, social media, and below-the-line comments on newspaper websites, there were few outlets for the ordinary person to have a say, no matter how fanciful or uninformed those views might be. It's clear why a put-on artist would fit well into the remit of this film. More than once The Monkees themselves had been accused of being precisely that – think right back to 'Monkees On Tour' where Mike talks on radio station KRUX to a very sweet and composed young girl fan and has a question or two of his own:

> **Nesmith**: Well, since we took over the radio station, we thought we'd find us the prettiest little 18-year-old girl that we could and bring her into the station and talk to her. And we're on the air now: be cool. Let me ask you, if you really found out that none of us could play a *note* and couldn't carry a tune in a bucket, would you hate us?
> **Girl**: [*sweetly*]: No!
> **Nesmith**: No? Why, why is that?
> **Girl**: Well, because you're puttin' people on pretty good if you don't.
> **Nesmith** [*laughs loudly and sincerely*]: That's great! OK, well, for those sceptics out there who still don't believe we don't play our own instruments, come down and tell 'em you know me, and I'll get you in free.

So this idea of the put-on – the ruse within the accepted conventions and structures of showbusiness and/or journalism – is in the air. It was there in part because the first generation to have grown up with electronic media integrated into the home and the conventions of presentation and representation within them – record players, TV, radio – were reaching adulthood and so those techniques, those methods of conveying information, ideas, or entertainment (popular music thrived via all three) were so well known and understood by everybody that they were ripe for satire. Sharpe and Coyle had stopped working together by 1967, so Sharpe alone was involved with *Head*. He usually worked in

San Francisco, so we might suppose that's where we are. It's him we see ask a question familiar from the album – 'Are you telling me that you don't see the connection between government and laughing at people?' – but otherwise don't hear the questions. Sharpe's tone is deadpan and that ensures the answers are too, adding to the surreal ambience. Some responses are just bizarre:

> I think they should be with fish … and that way they could only prey on fish … they might even jeopardise the fish … not halibut!

Some are unpleasant:

> I would take my belt off and – WHAM!

And some are would-be philosophical:

> Skunk bait, that's what the world is full of. That's what it's based on. That's what this *economy* is based on.

We can guess the themes of the questions from the nature of these answers, concerned as they are with the fear of mockery as well as the types and severity of punishment for slights and wrongdoing. For example, a rather dainty looking lady reveals that 'he back-talks me and I slap him across the face' and, in a kind of modal round of social psychosis, we hear an array of possible ways to deal with miscreants: 'possibly fines', 'exile', 'mental institutions', 'correction places', 'I'd use a baseball bat on 'em'. The scene accelerates so we eventually get single-word contributions stitched together – 'contamination', 'the nuthouse', 'Alcatraz', 'jail' – and concludes with a cut back to Carey on the Wild West set blowing a slow, contemptuous and even slightly disappointed raspberry. What does he think of the courthouse steps jury now? This material is all judiciously edited for effect, of course, but it still manages to create a brilliant and alarming collage of that holy grail, the voice of the people, who are supposed to represent the steady middle ground of patriotic American society – this is a 'Poll', after all – as opposed to the fearful freaks and hippies at the lunatic fringe who need reining in with their music and clothes and drugs and hair. Here we are asked to really listen to what that voice is saying. So who are the freaks?

After Carey's dismissive rasp the film does what it has not done up to this point – it fades to black without attempting to connect juxtaposed scenes via symbols, key words, or images. Yet when the next scene fades up we are in a jail cell and Dolenz is hissing 'Guilty!' in voiceover and clearly connecting where we are to where we were – the last word of the previous scene was 'jail' and the last image of Carey was on the steps of the courthouse, passing judgement. The themes of confinement, punishment, and persecution are thus well established by now and this very brief interscene adds to that. It features Jones, Nesmith, and Dolenz as prisoners sharing a cell, names on their overalls and 22 chalkmarks on the wall – days or weeks, months or years? Well, when filming on *Head* began in February 1968 Jones was 22 years old and he is the only one to move in this brief scene. Woken by the jail-cell door scraping open for a moment, he hauls himself up at the barred window and peers into a steam-filled room.

SWAMI PLUS STEAM

From out of the steam comes the voice of Abraham Sofaer in the character the script calls Hari Govinda, but in the film credits is listed as Swami. His monologue is reproduced in full on the album's final track, 'Swami – Plus Strings', there slowly incorporated into a collage of sounds and musical snippets from the movie, providing a bookend to 'Opening Ceremony'. The character is very obviously based on the current fashion for the gurus of Eastern philosophy, most notably the Maharishi Mahesh Yogi, with whom The Beatles had first studied in Wales in August 1967, a visit cut short by the death of Brian Epstein. They had also been to visit him in the Hindu shrine-city of Rishikesh in Northern India around the time *Head* started filming in February 1968. So this was contemporary material, and as a consequence the film doesn't quite know whether to satirise or praise it – undoubtedly a fashion trend but certainly possessed of some real substance. That finely balanced status between being a disposable fad and having long-lasting significance made it perfect material for *Head.* If you listen to the speech on the album it is perhaps more effective as it is more easily replayed and has the contextualising material from the rest of the movie come swirling in to condense meaning. In the movie we have only the steam. It's a remarkable chain of ideas, neither exaggerated for satirical effect, or even particularly 'Eastern' in the conventional sense. It is instead a treatise on the differences and distinctions between the real and the vividly imagined experience and how media technologies can dupe the brain into conflating and confusing the two. I've copied it out in full for you.

> **Swami**: We were speaking of belief; beliefs and conditioning. All belief possibly could be said to be the result of some conditioning, thus the study of history is simply the study of one system of beliefs deposing another, and so on, and so on, and so on. A psychologically tested belief of our time is that the central nervous system which feeds its impulses directly to the brain, the conscious, and subconscious, is unable to discern between the real and the vividly imagined experience – if there is a difference, and most of us believe there is. Am I being clear? For to examine these concepts requires tremendous energy and discipline. To experience the now without preconception of belief, to allow the unknown to occur and to occur requires clarity. For where there is clarity there is no choice, and where there is choice, there is misery. But then why should anyone listen to me? Why should I speak? Since I know nothing ... [*chuckles*]
> **Sonny Liston**: Howsabout some more steam?

Transpose this to a Transcendental Meditation text or a new-age philosophy pamphlet and it would fit right in, yet it is explicitly about the effect electronic media has on our perceptions of what is real. In this film we see real mothers and children hiding from bombs and mortar attacks, we see one man murder another man on camera; unbelievable, but all real. We also see four men sucked into a giant vacuum cleaner and encounter a talking cow; unbelievable, and all fake. Yet they're all there, side by side, up on the screen, as real as the person sitting next to you, or the person staring back at you from your mirror. The question we are being asked to consider is how do we learn to distinguish between the real and the fake, between the real and the vividly imagined experience. These are big questions for any film, let alone one based around a pop group, but they are central to the purpose of *Head* because they are – by accident rather than design – central to the story of The Monkees and the whole debate over what is real or authentic in culture and what is fake or manufactured. The challenge to conventional wisdom represented by The Monkees is that the fake could actually reveal more about truth and reality than the real does – if, as the Swami says, we believe there is a difference to be discerned in the first place. He's right too that it requires tremendous energy and discipline to think for long about these ideas, and one can't just jump to it – *Head* gives us an 86-minute run-up. Peter is a good pupil, sitting at the teacher's feet and clearly focussing very intently on the Swami's words. From what we know of him at the time he would undoubtedly have been conversant with some of the ideas already – in the mainly dire *33 1/3* special filmed in November 1968 he is presented as a kind of yogi figure, swathed in orange and sitting cross-legged on an elevated platform. Micky Dolenz reflected on this as being faithful to who Peter was, and why he couldn't quite embrace these new ideas in the same way, despite being the man who so famously sang 'I'm A Believer'. Like John Lennon's little revelation that 'the Walrus was Paul' in the Rishikesh-era song 'Glass Onion', here we find out that it was in fact Peter who was the believer:

> **Dolenz**: About this time Peter had gotten into some meditation and some transcendental philosophies and stuff. I hadn't, I was always a science geek. I still am. I once experimented with ESP but as a scientist almost. But that was part of Peter's personality, you know.[48]

As the Swami finishes with a lightly-borne disavowal of his own insight we don't get a question immediately from Peter. Instead we suddenly cut to Sonny Liston, who has sat unseen in what is now clearly a sauna-style steam room, and who now speaks his only line in the picture, supposedly Jack Nicholson's favourite and beautifully deadpanned: 'Howsabout some more steam?' He tugs a cord, white clouds billow across the room, and – presto! – the Swami is gone. Too late, Peter calls to him and, finding him gone, exits to the lot. He is still dressed for his consultation, in a large white sheet so cuts a curious and contrasting figure with the busy riot of colour outside. This is the third time in the film white clothing has been used to signify difference but also a moment of possibility and potential change. The script has him saying 'I got it! I got it!' but he doesn't speak in the film. In this moment of reaching for enlightenment he runs into the unedifying spectacle of a crowd semi-interestedly looking up at a young woman – June Fairchild once again – who is threatening to throw herself off the top of one of the buildings on the lot: you can hear her 'I'm gonna DO IT!' in 'Opening Ceremony' on the album. The crowd mill about as Peter looks for Micky and Mike; when he finds them, they pointedly ignore him, dispassionately discussing whether or not she will jump. Peter asks 'Where's Davy?' and receives no reply before commenting that he knows anyway. After a couple of beats Mike turns to Micky and asks, with a mildest gloss of interest, 'What do you suppose he meant by that?' Dolenz shrugs and keeps watching the girl.

> **Tork**: It's June Fairchild, standing on top of the building. Saw her recently, she is still mightily attractive. She was one of the dancers in the Arab scene too. Something awful about those two deciding betting 10 bucks if she's going to jump or not, and here I am, just trying to be of service, providing the answer as I have just received it at the feet of the guru.[49]

In this comment we can see something of the clash of cultures within the group itself, with Peter 'just trying to be of service' while the tougher nuts show that they have some work to do on distinguishing between the real and the vividly imagined experience. Davy is discovered in the bathroom staring into the medicine cabinet where he saw the eye, but where he was once terrified is now belligerent, especially when Peter tries his TM-speak on him, but like Ringo Starr reporting that Rishikesh was 'just like Butlins' – the British holiday-camp chain – the Manchester Cowboy isn't buying it:

> **Tork**: I came to tell you … nothing's wrong.
> **Jones**: Nothing's wrong, huh? You know what I saw in there? An eye, man, this big blood-red … it was as clear as the nose on your face! It was looking at me.
> **Tork** [*raises hand in beneficent gesture*]: Peace, Davy, I know.
> **Jones** [*slams cupboard door*]: You tell me nothing's wrong? What's wrong with you? You got a sheet on, you look weird. I'm gonna find out what's going on here.
> **Tork** [*chasing him out*]: Who's to say what's normal?
> **Jones**: I'm telling you there was an eye in there!

It may be weird, but something is indeed going on, and while Mr Jones may not know what it is, he is determined to find out. This is the moment the tide turns in this picture and The Monkees start to move from being a passive group to whom things happen – attacked by fans, forced to be dandruff, sucked into a vacuum cleaner – to a more active presence, making things happen. This may well be ultimately frustrated but it is nonetheless worthwhile. In a darkly comic moment we see June Fairchild being carried by Nesmith as Dolenz counts out ten one-dollar bills, stuffing them into his hand as he holds her. Clearly she *did* jump – Nesmith winning the bet – and Nesmith caught her. He hands her over in a most ungentlemanly way to Peter, who tries to keep up with the other three while carrying her as they march off up the lot. A bit of audio-visual trickery carries her off ('A fork lift truck goes between Peter and The Monkees making a sound transition'[50]) and we are suddenly back in the factory and then immediately, despite Peter's frantic warnings, back in the box. First time they were led into the dandruff ad; this time there's no escape.

They struggle to find a match, and when they do Peter lights a tall, tall candle. Wearing a look somewhere between hip-priest and 'I told you so', Peter then takes the opportunity to put Mike and Micky back in their boxes over their attitude to him in the previous scene. As they quarrel, the script calls Davy a 'turncoat' when he asks Mike to lay off Peter, while Tork's direction as he says 'Thank you, David' is to be 'smug'. These tensions were undoubtedly real; Nesmith called this 'a pontifical sequence' in the *Hy Lit* interview of October 1968, earning himself a stare from the bearded, speeding Peter. Yet if the purpose of the scene is to get Peter set up for a fall, and to show him just as the puppet of the Swami, then it is only partly successful: Peter does indeed repeat much of what he remembers hearing from the steam room, and sometimes paraphrasing for a softly self-mocking effect ('the human mind … or brain … or *whatever*'). Yet he also develops upon and adds to the material given to him by the Swami, and his monologue is full of insight and ideas which are actually very useful in reality. The way he speaks about specific media forms anchors the idea to technologies everybody is familiar with, so much so that we barely notice the effect they have on us any more. The whole point is that we become aware, and awake. This is why the little moment where Micky, who is dozing off, suddenly jerks back to full intentness when Peter says we need to 'pay tremendous attention' to the process, is so funny: an exquisite, telling little detail.

The composition of the image is worthy of note here, too. Whenever we see Peter speaking, he is in close up, his face (or head) occupying the right-hand half of the screen. Filling the left side is an unfocused image of the candle flame, lending a gently powerful aura to the scene, feeling both mystical and scholarly. Looking and listening become the same thing. In this the audience are as one with the other three men: we are all in the black box together. Interestingly it is Peter's cover version of the Swami's sign off that loses his listeners, the one who stood up for him being most disappointed of all:

Tork: But then, why should I speak, since I know nothing.
Jones [*incredulous*]: Nothing? You know *nothing*?

> **Tork**: That's right.
> **Jones**: You mean to say we've been sitting here listening to you and you know nothing?

The philosophy may be useful in regard to life and how to live it but not for the situation they are in:

> **Jones**: Now we're stuck in a room. We're stuck in this Big. Black. Box. Now you're telling me to take it easy, and he's saying he don't know nothing. Now what is this?
> **Tork**: Don't you see, David? It doesn't matter whether we're in the box or not.
> **Jones**: Not important, huh? Well let me tell you something, it's important to me. You wanna get out of this box? I'll show you how to get out of this box. [*Davy kicks down the door and they are back in the factory*]

The original concept of the movie was that they would escape from the box four times, each Monkee doing it his own way – in the finished movie we get only two ways. First we had Peter's, which negates the power of the box by denying it is there (early shades of Nesmith's book-with-a-soundtrack *The Prison*) and then we have Davy's 'route one' approach which he describes on the 1968 radio interview disc as 'using violence'. One might not go that far but in its physical directness is certainly a contrast to Peter's use of the mind to effect an escape. All of this tallies with the film's central thesis of confinement and modes of escape – how best to break out? Building on Davy's growing sense of resentment at their situation the revolt is in full flight now – the fight back has well and truly begun. It's interesting too that Davy is shown as the group's leader in this rebellion when – according to Kirshner – he was the least keen on rocking the boat in the 'real' revolution of early 1967.

'EAT YOUR HEART OUT, TOM CRUISE!'

As soon as they emerge, the white overalls are shed and the iconic *Head* outfits are visible once more. The film embraces a lengthy James Bond-style action sequence, letting rip with some crash bang wallop film-making for the first time. Inspector Shrink is head-butted, and various Bond-lair goons are rudely despatched, and in short order. This is all handled by Davy, using that promised violence, while the other three stand by wondering how to help. Peter Tork loved this on the Blu-ray, commenting on Davy's single-handed demolition of the enemy: 'Eat your heart out, Tom Cruise!' It's part-comical of course – Davy Jones as action hero, racing up and down the factory gantries taking out all-comers – but, frankly, with the look on his face who would take him on? Anyway, he had already fought Sonny Liston, you know. Finally Peter, Micky, and Mike get to contribute as they deliver a beautifully synchronised chinning to three goons whom Davy had already pushed off a high platform. Newly confident, the quartet go on, despatching an Oddjob-style security guard played by Lee Kolima, graduate of 'The Spy Who Came In From The Cool', with a single karate chop. And with that they are free – back on the lot. The script note for this section reads:

> The entire segment is conceived as if it were all one camera move. It's a march and even when it slows down it's always moving forward.[51]

The conception is capably realised as there is a mixture of menace and comic power about the segment which does precisely this, reinforcing vigour, physical action, and movement where we had previously been dealing in a kind of disturbed stillness.

Mojo regained, they burst back through the (newly mended) Wild West backdrop, symbolically re-entering the way they left earlier in the movie, and although they are only there a moment Davy somewhat gratuitously knocks a 'Red Indian' off his horse. Now – the big challenge – they are on the set of the Wild West town where Timothy Carey is clearly The Law; what the script calls 'the classic confrontation' will develop. It's the only part of this segment that features any dialogue and it is indeed of the 'classic' kind, as Carey and his cronies stand at their end of the one-horse town's street and The Monkees at the other.

> **Carey**: Where you boys headin'?
> **Jones**: Just passin' through ...

There's a great bit of ensemble comedy as the other three approach Davy, fretfully suggesting he does not take them on – he raises both hands and they humbly retreat, nodding deferential assent. The stage direction is not a stage direction, more of an in-joke to anyone who read the script: 'Davy is as cool as Alan Ladd any day of the week. Taller, too.' There's no plot or visual justification for this; it's just a little joke, if inaccurate. Alan Ladd, famously short for a cowboy, was at 5ft 6ins still taller than the Mancunian Monkee. There's a great bit of see-saw sing-song wordplay for Carey, Nicholson giving him his best lines in the picture, ('unless I don't know what goes on up and down this block and I do') before the posse raise and cock their rifles (50 according to the script, 19 on screen) for the inevitable shoot-out. Cut back to the foursome, and in a rare bit of TV show-style 'wish and it's there' Monkee Magic, Davy has produced a cannon that blasts the posse into oblivion, giving Carey a chance to die like Rasputin – at length and not conclusively. This scene was filmed at the Columbia Ranch, featured in 'A Nice Place To Visit' and hundreds of westerns and TV shows. Rafelson was able to suggest all those representations of the Old West that people already knew by using the same sets audiences had already seen on screen, and that has to be a great advantage to someone wishing to suggest and manipulate conventions within a genre or style.

THE BIG VICTOR

Suddenly, Victor Mature as The Big Victor appears in his Jolly Green Giant mode, a name used for a competing band in the episode 'Find The Monkees' and an appropriate title in the circumstances here. The character is clearly named after RCA Victor, The Monkees' parent company for music. That Mature's forename actually was Victor would have been a happy coincidence and perhaps put the idea into Rafelson and Nicholson's heads to cast him. The Big Victor towers over the Columbia Ranch set, his laughter clearly the same as heard in the horror sequence. He claps his hands like a genie, perhaps a nod to Rex Ingram in Rafelson's beloved 1940 Alexander Korda production of *The Thief Of Bagdad*. Lo and behold, they are back in the box.

Reading the script shows that between the 'classic confrontation' and the airlift there are eight pages of dialogue and direction that are missing from the finished film. Whether or not they were ever filmed, or were part of the lost 20 minutes cut after the disastrous screen-test, is known only to Bob Rafelson – and possibly Rhino. It's clear what the missing scenes were doing. They are short, episodic (of course), and revisit places and characters from earlier in the film, drawing all the disparate narrative stands together to direct the film toward some kind of conclusion. Thus we reprise our acquaintance with Vito Scotti and the Italian army, Sonny Liston and the boxing ring, the cop, Inspector Shrink and the factory, the unstoppable Timothy Carey character, and the Arab horseman. A brief return to the desert/Coke machine scene contains an intriguing nugget echoing an earlier key moment with the same voiceover that taunted Micky turns on Mike, using his early-days pseudonym: 'Thirsty, aren't you, Michael … Blessing … Nesmith.' The final part of the missing section sees them back in the box yet again, and it's Micky's turn to try and find a way out. His solution is togetherness and positive thinking:

> Now I'm telling you – all we got to do is groove together and we'll make it. That's the way it's always been. Right? Right? OK. Here we go. Monkees! A group! The best! Hands together.[52]

This kind of cheerleading/team coach approach rallies the troops and is rare in that it mentions the name of the group – aside from 'Ditty Diego' and the fans' chant we do not hear the name in the film. The use of it here is therefore potent, and a declaration that they should not apologise for existing. Positive self-assertion is at a premium in the finished movie, which may be why this scene did not make it.

As they bond over this idea, the black box starts to become unsteady, throwing the four Monkees about – something has started to come undone, and the instability they introduced is starting to shake the system. It's here we reconnect to the finished movie. The box is suddenly airlifted up, delivering superb shots of the black box being carried beneath a helicopter, swinging on four wires, one connected to each corner. Below are the sands and dunes of the desert at Palm Springs that are so important to the film, the San Jacinto mountains briefly visible beyond – a stunning shot. As it is carried above the desert through the bright sky, we are able to see the black box for the first time. It is visible, and no longer just an idea or indeed what Micky is seen later describing as a 'composite universe'. What we see is ... well, it's black and it's a box. It has a segmented rather than a smooth surface and is to scale, perfectly capable of holding four people comfortably captive. It's real. The script reveals that the original plan was to customise this box like the Monkeemobile or the Monkee-branded Lear Jet they travelled in for their 1967 US tours.

> INTERCUT – REACTIONS OF CITIZENS
> Those who behold this curious phenomenon of a large square box, its four walls plastered with huge portraits of the Monkees.[53]

This is another layer of self-satire – everyone on the ground would know who was on board but also that they were prisoners, being transported like property or against their will. It's an interesting idea, but it works against the enigmatic identity of the black box that adds so much to the movie; the right editorial choice was made to keep it plain. As the box is released it falls like a stone, almost gracefully, and lands hard if safely on the dunes. It reminds me, if no-one else, of the shots of the 60s Gemini and Apollo capsules returning to Earth, carefully managed landings in difficult circumstances at the end of remarkable adventures. Whereas American astronauts always splashed down in the ocean, The Monkees are more like the Soviet cosmonauts who were obliged to make a harder landing in the desert steppes.

In the script there is another debate between the four as to whether they should just stay put once they thud back to the ground, but in the film they are given no time. The box immediately and methodically falls open, walls collapsing back in sequence, leaving them dazzled and exposed to the bright light. Yet again, an amazing sight awaits them as they see all the characters from the movie – their foes – lined up on the ridges of the dunes surrounding the dip in the dunes into which they have been dropped. The long, slow shot pans along the line of figures as they shimmer in the heat making them seem hyperreal and somehow changed. In some ways it's an absurd grab-bag of types – Inspector Shrink and his goons, I. Vitteloni and the Italian soldiers, The Big Victor in his director's chair, Arabs on horseback, even the Coke machine, supposedly vanquished but somehow resurrected – but the film has thrown them all together and now, at the climax, everyone's common purpose has brought them to the same place at the same time. That common purpose is the persecution and extinction of The Monkees. This scene is described by the script as 'the final battlefield' and that is precisely what it proves to be.

THE FINAL BATTLEFIELD

After a moment allowing us to regard the spectacle, and some brilliant psycho-acoustics that are felt as much as heard, the dream-like atmosphere is shattered by a war-cry and all the characters begin to charge down the hill and 'ride like hell straight at The Monkees'.[54] Looking at the scene it's clear that no stuntmen are involved here – it's Dolenz, Jones, Tork, and Nesmith in the midst of all that hurly-burly and those speeding, very strong horses. So when they raise their arms to protect themselves they are not following direction but reacting with a basic instinct of self-preservation. This also has an echo of the Ray Nitschke scene, where he really does barge into Peter in the ammo dump and near-pulverise him, and the scene with Davy in a ring with Sonny Liston. It's clear that Rafelson did go the extra mile to torment the stars of his film, to whom he owed a great deal.

The stunt riders pelt past the foursome as they try to dodge the onslaught, and while Davy gets most fully among the horses, all four are in the firing line. No sooner do the Arabs disappear than the Italian tank crests a dune ridge, no longer minded to surrender, and is instead keen to go boom-boom in their direction. We see the fleeing Monkees from the driver's point of view, and there is a brilliant 360-degree roll of the camera just before the muzzle lets fly. Instead of taking out the band, this blows up the Coke machine for the second time in the film. The Arabs sitting close by are miraculously unscathed and rejoice in the unlimited free cold drinks that have been liberated. Cola wars indeed. The Big Victor swings his golf club – he's in Palm Springs, after all – and his ball whacks into the four, rendered dandruff-sized again in comparison, and they are propelled through the air in the second of the movie's flying sequences. For good measure, a line of Native American extras fire off arrows at them, some of which hit but are brushed off. They land not back in the vacuum cleaner but in the lot, cueing a rapid-fire summary of movie styles as yet unexploited by the film. First, a bit of slapstick as they land – Davy on a bed not unlike the one being pushed through the streets in the title sequence of the TV show, Mike in a trash can, Peter astride Zappa's steer, and Micky on a boom arm which swings around. All of this is done at double speed for comic effect but also to ramp up the pace of the next few shots, revisiting scenes: Peter canters into the canteen on the steer to silly sped-up music, scattering the make-up girls, soldiers, and hardhats sitting at the tables, getting a custard pie in the chops from his old adversary T.C. Jones as The Waitress, aka Mrs Ace (who yells 'Out! OUT!!'), and Nesmith just escapes the crush as people flee the scene.

The four, now chased by a new set of militant extras, try to escape through a studio door and find themselves in the steam room, which leads them – mercy – back into the factory where the seemingly indestructible Inspector Shrink and his cronies capture them. Peter tarries in the steam room, and suddenly we hear the voice of the Swami – 'Well, my son, what is it you have learned?' Before he can reply we cut back to the channel changer and we have Rita Hayworth in a moment from her 1946 film noir *Gilda* (strapline, 'There NEVER was a girl like Gilda') to supply the answer: 'Make hay while the sun shines.' This cues in another short sequence of channel shifting, which offers us little glimpses of Micky talking earnestly in the black box from an unused discussion – 'This box is right now a composite universe' – and this is all we get before the viewer decides that's enough and changes channel. Next up, more real footage from Vietnam, of an American plane dropping fire and destruction onto the ground, a cowering family, child wide-eyed with fear, and the dread sight of the execution seen during 'Circle Sky', this time in slow motion. The film stops short of showing the moment in full, partly to spare us and partly because we have already seen it – the image must be burned into our memories already. It is substituted by a cartoon image of a rifle blasting seen three times and placed aside footage of an elderly Vietnamese woman running for her life. A cartoon depiction of a Jekyll and Hyde transformation is followed by the promised transformation of the self in a Playtex advert: 'It's not me, it's my Playtex cross your heart bra.' This then cuts to the famous shot of John Brockman's face – head – which 'graced' the advertising campaign for the movie; it is in a rich monochrome, and he is seen from the neck up staring straight down the camera. There is nothing to read in his expression apart from a benign ambience and a small half-smile, which is just forming as the channel changes. He is on screen for two seconds. Back to Micky, still expounding in the box: 'Our universe is only stuck inside of our head and can go out in all different directions, in any direction to infinity.' Another shot of Rita Hayworth separates Micky from Lord High 'n' Low who sweeps his cape and hollers 'Mother! I'm coming!' before we get another dose of Rita being embraced and about to submit to passion: 'I think I'm going to die from it.' None of the collage segments is listed in the script, which suggests they were added in lieu of the lengthy reprise segments that were not included.

Suddenly the TV matte disappears and, back in film mode the Monkees are shown in peril, strapped to a conveyor belt in the factory leading to a machine bristling with knives, which quickly changes to silent-movie mode, double-speed images in black and white with generic piano music. Peter battles the machine operator and reverses the direction of the belt. They are free! He then goes to the belt and, instead of his bandmates, it seems he has saved a girl who jumps into his arms. Cut to the happy couple outside the factory and a little burst of Mendelssohn's 'Wedding March' on the sped-up piano lets us know they have married. As they drive away from the factory it is suddenly clear that the bride is a man in drag. The couple drive off in black and white, but coming round the next corner we have the four back together in full deluxe colour in a dune buggy, Peter driving, Davy by him, Micky and Mike riding behind. They hurtle down the street at the Columbia Ranch, scattering the cowboys and smashing through a gallows erected in the middle of the street, upending Timothy Carey for the third time and leaving him swinging (by his hands) from the prepared noose. Then back to the lot and some slapstick as they drive under a platform, knocking away one of the supports but, like the cartoon character who does not fall until he notices he has run off the cliff edge, the workman doesn't tumble until he gazes down. It looks real, but cartoon rules apply. Swerving to avoid a giant telephone they burst through a backdrop and find themselves back in the desert where The Big Victor, finally driven to outright frustration and rage by their unwillingness to quit, tries to stamp on them, his great Gulliverian shoes looking to grind the Lilliputian figures into the sand. Cutting between Victor Mature watching the scene on TV and The Big Victor trying to 'Stamp Out The Monkees', the movie adds a satisfying distance. His stagey yawn is a splendid moment, as is his growing frustration and boredom leading him to kick in the television set. While this is not quite Elvis shooting out his tube because he hated the shows, it's a bit of Jones-style direct action that makes the movie shoot off in one of its different directions, in this case back to its beginning.

The impact sends The Monkees tumbling out of the buggy and rolling down a dune; we can just hear the voice of Mayor Feedback declaring that this is 'one of the largest suspended arch bridges in the world'. They run, pursued by their legion of antagonists, making the bridge at the same moment as they do at the film's opening sequence, so the mayor still doesn't get to finish his speech. It seems the entire cast are now in pursuit of the four, desperate to deliver retribution. Reaching the centre of the bridge, Micky jumps first this time with little hesitation; the other three all stand on the precipice together before Davy loses his balance and falls, while Peter and Mike consciously choose to jump, realising that there is no alternative. As soon as Micky jumps, 'Porpoise Song' fades up and accompanies their slow-motion fall as it does in the beginning; the footage of Micky is the same as earlier and we also see Davy, Peter, and Mike twisting and falling and entering the water in the order in which they jumped. There are no mermaids this time but as soon as they enter the water they are bathed in solarised colour and swim off together looking to make their escape. Surely this time they are free, for how could anyone follow them down there? As the song reaches its aching and exquisite finale – the drums making those four steps to a finish – the solarised colour drains away and we return to natural light. It is revealed that they are in a water tank, on the back of a truck, being driven off the set. Sitting looking pleased at the rear of the truck is The Big Victor, who lights and tips his cigarette and gives the camera one last old-school Hollywood grin. In the many years between finding the soundtrack album and seeing the movie, I wondered what that motorised noise was just before Ken Thorne's orchestral music starts. It turns out it's the sound of defeat, cast as the engine of the lorry as it drives the props off the lot at the end of the movie. But this is not The End. As the script notes in its last line, this is 'The Beginning!'[55]

CREDIT WHERE IT'S DUE

The title of the movie is seen for the first time, coming toward us as the truck drives away; the studio doors start to close, very slowly. Credits come up, Rafelson's directorial credit first, then the writing credit to him and Nicholson. Third come the names of the four individual Monkees, not 'The Monkees'. The word, logo, or any kind of visual representation of the group name is entirely absent from the movie. The four are not listed alphabetically but thus: Peter Tork, David Jones, Micky Dolenz, Michael Nesmith. Some kind of hierarchy is established amongst the guest stars, as there are two captions before we get an 'Introducing' list, headed by Sonny Liston (boldly billed as 'Extra'), and we learn what these character's names were – Carol Doda as Sally Silicone, Teri Garr as the equally alliterative Testy True, and so on. This is followed by Victor

Mature who gets his own caption ('and VICTOR MATURE as The Big Victor'), the only actor to do so. The songs are listed in order of appearance and with their compositional credits, Ken Thorne is credited for his Incidental Music, and Michel Hugo for his role as Director of Photography. Twelve technical staff are listed, including Toni Basil as Choreographer, but she gets no credit for her on-screen appearance. Up next is the infamous caption in which the names and credits are not only reversed but also mirrored, so I can't give you an example – you'll have to see it for yourself. If you were wondering what had happened to the 'bert part of Raybert, well here he comes – a bold solo caption declares Executive Producer Bert Schneider and that ends the formal sequence. We get a yellow on black strapline, A Raybert Production, which then fades to the logo of the Schneider family firm, Columbia Pictures, which, in one final thumbed nose and visual treat, gets caught in the gate. The logo skips, jumps, and then overheats and burns out, the celluloid itself melting down in front of our eyes. The device burned up is not the actual logo of the company at the time, more a variant of it, but it *does* say Columbia Pictures. It's a final, daring little gesture, one which was made from a position of security in some senses – the Schneiders were important to Columbia – but was also very bold. Who else would even dare to think of destroying the device of the company who paid their wages and funded their productions, right there on the screen? The last thing the film gives us, to a dark and blank screen, is sound – Mimi Jefferson's laugh, the one heard as she disappears through the door of the pad right at the film's beginning.

> **Tork**: And at the end, I think we have I.M. Jefferson – little Mimi's ha-ha? Good.[56]

The script shows a variant on this ending:

> Micky is already under water as the other three guys plunge down through the surface. As they do the water begins to turn black. The Monkees press up against the glass side of the tank in an

> effort to get out as the CREDITS roll. A MUSICAL NUMBER begins. The number should recap the film, the box, how to get in and out, and also <u>review</u> the film.
>
> The CAMERA PULLS BACK to reveal that the tank is on a movie set and then that it is sitting on the back of a flat-bed truck. As the truck kicks over and pulls away, the CAMERA HOLDS, revealing Victor Mature in a trench coat and hat as he walks off into four spotlights, waving as he goes.
>
> <u>THE BEGINNING!</u>[57]

The juxtapositions in this closing sequence are in some ways irresponsible and morally duplicitous, but I'd argue that they are justified, being all the more startling and sobering for the mix of the trivial and the gravely serious. There is more information in the last ten minutes of this movie than most others pack into two hours. *Head* simply does not behave like any other movie you've ever seen. A countercultural movie made with Hollywood resources, it was rejected by both the margins and the mainstream, yet it continues to fascinate and give up new secrets each time we're bold enough to really look into its mysterious, reflective surfaces.

CHAPTER SEVEN

CAN YOU DIG IT? THE *HEAD* SOUNDTRACK

When at the age of 14 I first found a copy of the Monkees album *Head*, I was puzzled. I was looking for a copy of *Headquarters*, and at first I thought that there was a misprint on the sleeve, but no, there it was, 'HEAD', in red print on a (slightly grubby, second-hand) white field, with the word 'Monkees' (no definite article) around all four edges of the square in an unbroken line of spindly black text. The front cover provides nothing more, but there is a glut of information on the back, where we learn that this is the 'Original Motion Picture Soundtrack' to '*HEAD*, A Columbia Picture', with the capitalised credit, 'Album Produced By The Monkees'.

I knew a bit about the group at this stage but I'd had no idea they'd made a film. What was it like? Where could I see it? It would be nearly ten years before I got to watch the film, but, thanks to the album, when I did I was already deeply familiar with the songs and the strange fragmentary bursts of sounds and dialogue that flow between them. The album and film clearly shared the same darkly surreal sense of mischief but the record also seemed boldly independent of the movie.

On the back cover we find a black-and-white shot of the group, not unlike the picture on the rear of *Revolver*. The stylistic unity of that particular image isn't simply echoed here though. It looks at first glance as if they are in conversation, but on closer inspection all four are occupied by seemingly different activities: Davy Jones is pulling on some boots, Michael Nesmith adjusts a pendant hanging from around his neck, Peter Tork in his high-collared Nehru shirt is caught animatedly in mid-movement, while Micky Dolenz, far right, is seemingly in the midst of a passionate speech to his colleagues. All four together, yet quite separate and distinct. The image appears to be just on a black field, but once you see the movie you'll recognise that they are in the Black Box, a recurring image in the film, an empty space that is full of meaning – but which is the true one? This picture feels key to the enigma of the album, film, and the whole Monkees project itself.

By the time the album and film came out, the TV series had been cancelled and the band's commercial fortunes were in steep decline. Though now very well regarded, the *Head* album, like the film, proved to be commercial poison in 1968, reaching only number 45 on the *Billboard* Hot 100. The fact of course remains that while the musical invention of their records improved, the sales diminished – it was only with 1967's *Headquarters*, the first album on which they were allowed to make their own mistakes, that there was concord between their own musical efforts and great commercial success.

The *Head* album, ironically, does not feature the group playing as a foursome. This policy had been abandoned after their late '67 album *Pisces, Aquarius, Capricorn & Jones Ltd.*, and although the film shows the band playing 'Circle Sky' live in Salt Lake City, this thunderous version was unaccountably dropped from the album and replaced by a studio take featuring Nesmith and session musicians, which as such is the album's one major error of editorial judgment.

Head contains 14 tracks, listed on the sleeve as Band A–G on both sides, but of these only six are full songs credited to The Monkees. Two are written by Peter Tork ('Can You Dig It?' and 'Long Title: Do I Have To Do This All Over Again?'), one by Michael Nesmith ('Circle Sky'), one by Harry Nilsson ('Daddy's Song'), and the other two by Carole King, in collaboration with Gerry Goffin ('Porpoise Song') and Toni Stern ('As We Go Along'). As an indicator of how well regarded the movie and these songs became further down the line, four of the six became regulars in the reformed group's sets in the late 90s, and all were restored from the 2011 tour onward. The rest are excerpts of film sound and/or dialogue chosen or constructed by Jack Nicholson. These snippets and collages are not unprecedented in the band's recordings: 'Zilch' and 'Band 6' from *Headquarters*, for example, show a willingness to break the rules of what should go on a 'pop' album, and these gags and rough improvisatory edges fit well with the deconstructive ambition behind *Head* as a whole. Nicholson delivered two major sound collages ('Opening Ceremony' and the closing 'Swami – Plus Strings'); a brutal satire on their own musical calling-card, '(Theme From) The Monkees', entitled 'Ditty Diego'; and a handful of shards of dialogue, included isolated one-liners ('Supplicio', 'Gravy', 'Superstitious'), or the products of editing for humorous and/or satirical effect ('Dandruff?', 'Poll'). The sequence of the album follows that of the movie in the order of songs, sound effects, and snippets of dialogue.

We open, appropriately, with 'Opening Ceremony'. It fades up quickly on some dialogue from the film's opening scene, over which we hear Tork, Jones, and Dolenz flatly intoning, 'Coming … soon … *Head*' (a clip taken from a radio promo spot that Nicholson placed right on the frontline of the product itself). The track acts as a kind of abstract of the whole album, featuring mashed fragments of all the songs, clips of dialogue, and sound effects that crop up elsewhere on the record. Nicholson made smart editorial choices, showing an understanding of the strange logic (or, perhaps, anti-logic) of the film's narrative and these musical slivers act as a kind of subliminal cutting so that when we hear the songs in full we both recognise them and experience them as stranger, more avant-garde than they might have otherwise sounded.

The segue from 'Opening Ceremony' into Carole King and Gerry Goffin's 'Porpoise Song' is sublime, drifting gently toward resolution and punctuated by lazy sounding sirens – if we might imagine such a thing – and kept gently buoyant on a gorgeous string arrangement by Jack Nitzsche. A single cello note is daringly held from 0:06–0:17, weightlessly suspending the track in a dream like state, which then modulates up to a piano and drum intro, Dolenz's vocal arriving at 0:24. It has a slow, colossal elegance, both supple and monumental. This is a song of rare and diaphanous beauty, elegiac and fitted to its task in the movie, because despite the lyric being allusive rather than specific it provides a kind of second 'theme' for the group, a lament for what might have been and the passing of their moment. It is august and dignified, intimate and cavernous, its guitars opaque and percussive, the ensemble blending into a single, breathtaking musical voice.

The song bookends both album and film, accompanying the two bridge-jumping scenes and, like the slow-motion solarized visuals, there is a kind of colour-saturated stateliness to its unfolding. The song was written to order and to the images by Goffin and King, who was characteristically unboastful in her reflections on how the song met the film, unexpectedly evoking the name of an old friend:

> I'd like to believe 'The Porpoise Song', written by Gerry and me, was chosen for the opening of *Head* solely because it complemented the images over which it was used, but it probably didn't hurt that Donnie [Kirshner] was in a position to advocate for its use in a Columbia picture.[1]

Oh, Carole! The match of music and pictures is beyond complementary for its audience, but her level-headedness and willingness to acknowledge the role of business in making the work a success makes for a powerful combination of art and industry. Some of her favourite musicians are on the track, including her old friend and former Fug Danny Kortchmar with members of his Los Angeles psychedelic pop band Clear Light, who recorded one album for Elektra. Their keyboard-driven, epic feel serves the song well – the interplay between the organ and the drums clearly reveals the musical familiarity of the players, especially at the gorgeous and unexpectedly abrupt climax, which in the film is matched with the narrative's final twist. Only Dolenz and Jones appear on the track, but the former delivers one of his finest vocal performances, following the mercurial, melancholic melody line way up into the higher registers and following it down into the trickier, more scattered lyric of the second verse. On a historical note, you will perhaps, like me, find it incredible that Micky Dolenz recorded the vocals to 'Porpoise Song' and 'D.W. Washburn' on the same day, April 3 1968.

The bespoke nature of the song becomes clear through a closer look at the lyric; in some senses it bears the mark of its time, with the slow throb of being stoned on life itself, full of metaphysical allusions that seem fantastical ('the clock in the sky') but which can be chased down to specific references to the group and their story.

We feel the urgency of the moment as time slips away – as they sang way back on *Headquarters*, there's no time – yet this is matched with a slow-limbed heedfulness, aware of everything that is going on; this notion of two speeds running in parallel is in itself an idea pitched between Buddhist philosophy and the all-seeing eye of the acid trip. The third and fourth lines are a clear reference to a striving for the real, be that specific to The Monkees' story or the wider field of manipulated media sounds and images of the kind Peter and the Swami mention in the film. Picking on the 'face' and 'voice' seems to target pop music but again has resonance across wider cultures of mediation – politics, film, TV.

Goffin & King wrote the opening lines specifically for Micky Dolenz, 'Riding the backs of giraffes for laughs was all right for a while' calling Circus Boy back into the ring; the second couplet, with its 'castles and kings and things', nods to the extraordinary level of the group's success and the life that it granted to them, if only 'for a while'. Those material goods don't hold the answer, and you better not lean on them too much, lest they disappear – as The Monkees would find out for themselves all too soon. The two bridges connect these fantastical images to a yearning for resolution and understanding: a desire 'to be', 'to hear', 'to see'.

This plea for some kind of enlightenment seeks one which is actually not divine – it's located in the human senses, hinging on those rhymes of 'be' and 'see', 'feel' and 'real'. They are registering dissatisfaction with what has been presented as reality and the discovery that 'living is … a lie'. Rather than offer a pragmatic response to all these earnest questions, we have instead a poet's answer, an artist's answer: 'The porpoise is waiting, goodbye, goodbye', the 'i' rhymes linking the two bridges, and each bridge to the chorus itself. This delivers a feeling of internal harmony and of a kind of natural logic that is appropriate to the song's mood and also its practical function as the 'Theme From Head', as its subtitle would have it. Counting heads we find that eighteen musicians contributed to this track, including luminaries such as Jerry Scheff and Leon Russell alongside Kortchmar and Clear Light, but in my view the best work is done by the four cello players – Gregory Bemko, David Filerman, Jan Kelley, and, most commendably, Jacqueline Lustgarten, who we hear on that extraordinary 12-second note at the song's opening. The texture that the cellos deliver is a key part of the song's identity, appeal and, well, specialness – suggesting vintage, something organic, and natural.

I've puzzled over why Goffin & King chose the porpoise as the central image in their song – it's an image of freedom, certainly, and awareness of the complex innate intelligence of cetaceans was growing in the age of Aquarius; there's a visual fit in the movie, too, as the song accompanies underwater sequences, and the track goes as far as to include audio of actual porpoise song, the 'clicks' they use for communication and echo-location rendered musical by their context. Furthermore, they are natural, and they are *real* – they are certainly not made in a factory. Yet it still remains enigmatic to me – it has something to do with movement and liberty, a way of being that requires a revolution of the mind to comprehend. That is the appeal and the demand the song is making to and of its listener. Yet we can also just lie back and let the mermaids carry us away, such is the celestial beauty of the track.

The sense of elegy and lost opportunity mingle in an extraordinary 2:57 of music – all the more so in that it came within three years of the Monkee project's inception. It wouldn't be the only tune issued under the name of The Monkees to address these autobiographical issues – Davy Jones's song 'You And I', which tackles the subject far more directly and acerbically would emerge on *Instant Replay*, the band's first album as a trio after Tork left in early 1969, immediately after *Head* – but it is almost alone in the Monkees catalogue in its emotional depth and resonance.

The dream is over, indeed, and to make the point, here comes 'Ditty Diego'. This twisted nursery rhyme, chanted by all four, mercilessly deconstructs Boyce & Hart's '(Theme From) The Monkees' into a kind of self-flagellation. Listening to the try-out and rehearsal tapes on the various reissues, the track seems innocuous enough, but once swirled into the sound world of this album by Jack Nicholson it becomes, to use the vernacular, something else. As Nesmith once noted:

> If there is a magic trick inside *Head*, it's Jack Nicholson … he was the guy who sped up 'Ditty Diego' … he was so creative and had such great ideas.[2]

Nicholson's greatest contribution to the project certainly was the album, which more closely achieves the dreamlike flowering of one moment into another that the film strived for, and 'Ditty Diego' is probably the track that bears his fingerprints most obviously. There are nine verses, with the first and last explicitly referencing The Monkees; the seven in between are shared by the group, and in this the track is a rare show of unity, with all four contributing equally in the studio. This hadn't happened since certain cuts on *Pisces*, and it wouldn't happen again until 1997's *Justus*. That togetherness was necessary because in the track they are feeling the heat from all sides, not least from their makers, and, thereby, themselves. Has there ever been a self-critique like this on a pop record, before or since? I doubt it. No wonder it segues into a 'War Chant': they are under attack, a 'manufactured image with no philosophies'.

For the most part, the song is a brutal restatement of their original 'confession' to the *Saturday Evening Post* and many more thereafter; one that was supposed to set them free but, it would seem, didn't quite. The 'no philosophies' refers to the unambiguous nature of the project's original aim – money – but also bites hard on the music as, for example, much of Nesmith's work has an openly philosophical bent – even a great pop love song like 'You Just May Be The One' has the caution of wisdom at its elbow in its qualification that its subject '*just may*' be the one. He voices the second verse, which nods to the 'four-in-one' identity of the group, and the episodic nature of the audience's original encounters with them, week by week – a different story every time, yet one which was always more or less the same. This hinges on the punning use of 'one': we can take it there isn't just one, there are four, or that there is no story at all, just the product standing in for a story.

The third verse – Peter's first – again calls down the world of the TV show but also the links between commodification and popular culture – it's a bargain struck between producer and consumer; the producer creates a need, the audience responds with a desire for it – 'We want The Monkees!' – and then the industry meets that need. In the pleasure of this exchange – leisure for money – we overlook the process and the machinery – something *Head* is careful to show us, onstage and in the factory: 'Let's all lose our minds!'

The fourth verse, voiced by Micky, acknowledges that deal – 'What you came to see is what we'd love to give you' – and offers a simple counting game by way of example. These elements, we have learned, follow each other naturally and inevitably. Yet *Head* is deliberately constructed to vex such pre-digested notions of order and sense and linearity, which Davy's first verse picks up on, throwing numbers about as if they were splats of paint from an action painter's brush – or, if I may be permitted an English note, a child's hopscotch game chalked on a flagstone pavement, with the numbers all out of order, which is the point of the game. *Head* has something of this in it: the child's rearrangement of the linear into something else that makes a different kind of sense.

The next verse, Mike's second, is for us who look for meanings. Nice and upfront, he strongly recommends that we do not take him at his word because what might be true in one moment could prove to be a lie in the next – again, we have the blurring of what we rely on to be fixed navigation points, namely what's the truth and what's a lie. It is simpatico with the questions asked by the 'Porpoise Song' in this, wanting to know what is real. To tug the rug from under such certainties is mischievous but also a kind of liberation, especially for a creative person – the root of the Monkees enigma was that the act became real, so this is absolutely pertinent to their story. What is given can be taken back.

Micky takes the seventh verse, which warms to this theme, and the mention of a 'box' sets the bells ringing for *Head* scholars, as the lyric details ways of taking something back – a reclaimed gift, falling behind in a race – delivered with a brilliant Dolenz crescendo: 'But back in time and space!' This image has multiple implications: in 1968 the Apollo programme was well on the way to meeting John F. Kennedy's stated aim of putting a man on the moon by the end of the decade, so issues of time and space, once the prospect of science fiction pulp, movies, and television – including Dolenz's own favoured comparative, *Star Trek* – were on the front pages of the dailies, jostling with images from Vietnam. It is also redolent of the instant nostalgia that characterises aspects of pop culture – looking for ways to clamber back through time to a happier or younger day through the artefacts of that previous time, which are patently unchanged by the passage of time in the way that we ourselves most certainly are. The audiences are transported back with the artist by their common bond of experience and memory. It's a kind of nostalgia, but isn't as simple or as banal as that. The mediation of sound and image introduces something else to the relationship. This thought struck me while watching the screens at gigs: film and images of the artist in their youth are shown while the real and much older person performs beneath these images of themselves. It must be a curious experience, and one I'd have liked to ask Micky and Peter about.

Davy's Northern English pragmatism is by far the best way to deliver the penultimate verse, and so he does: a shrug, an acknowledgement of the position they're in, and that the ultimate arbiter of what happens is the audience – they are part of the leisure culture which is predicated on choice; you can take it, or you can leave it: 'You say we're manufactured / To that we all agree / So make your choice and we'll rejoice / In never being free.'

This isn't a fuck-you but more of a business-like shrug. Peter's Swami suggests in the film that 'where there is choice, there is misery', but the way it's put here make the stakes seem not so high – they are stuck with themselves whatever the outcome. It also acknowledges that the mask will never come unstuck, whatever they do. This has proven to be the case, and Jones would often curse 'this face!' as the unchangeable architect of his undoing, but it was also of course the making of him in the first place.

He was already a star before he became a Monkee, had his own fan club, recording contract, and the rest.

In another echo of the 'Porpoise Song' ('an image cannot rejoice'), Jones says that 'we'll rejoice in never being free', the band resigned to their fate as they cannot do anything about it. Yet they go down fighting, even as they trash their own most closely associated badges, flags, and emblems in the final verse, giving their theme and catchphrase ('Hey hey') one final kicking – 'We've said it all before' – and a still-shocking last lash of self-flagellation: 'The money's in, we're made of tin, we're here to give you more.' This couplet has the distinction of being the only lyric in the song to be repeated – here at the climax of the performance it is made all the more startling by the repetition; we lose the last 'more' so it also sets up the coming 'War Chant' by suggesting but not supplying a rhyme for 'war!' Instead, on the album, we have a crash and a girl's scream – paired with something that I could not believe when I first saw the film.

A manic Keystone Cops-style piano plays behind them as they chant the lyrics, and the track and vocal are heavily varispeed'd to 'freak' the performance – rather like the snippets on 'Opening Ceremony' changing the way we hear the subsequent tracks – so the familiar voices are wildly manipulated, rendering them by turns both absurd and alarming. In this it darkly mirrors the visual trickery of speed and movement familiar from the TV series, and in combination with the startlingly vicious self-appraisal in the lyrics it both mocks and liberates the group from their public image.

After the girl's blood-curdling scream – is she screaming at the band or something terrifying beyond words? – the track moves on, as it does in the film, to the 'War Chant'. This is a bitter parody of a pop-concert staple, the call-and-response routine, except this time the word is not 'love' but 'war'. Immediately following this we have the sound of bombs dropping and exploding – the film at this point shows (contemporary, don't forget) footage of attacks on Vietnamese villages, and those appalling noises are included here as sound effects which are also 'real' documentary detail. The *Head* boxed set of 2012 reveals the source of the 'W', 'A', 'R' chant – the MC at the band's Salt Lake City show got the young crowd to chant 'We want the Monkees' before they came on, which we hear on album and also see in the film, and after the opening 'You Just May Be The One' (a bit shaky but still pretty good) Davy put them in the picture as to what the show was all about: 'We are kinda *using* you a little here … but as long as we let you know, right?'

Peter then steps up to give an example of what that 'using' might involve:

> In the movie we have this one section where we come out and we cheerlead you … into saying … as if we were cheerleading in a high school called war. It's like, Gimme a *W*! and you'll go … [silence] … ah, come on, pick up guys, the name of this game is pick-up! GIMME A *W*! [Crowd hollers back 'W!'] GIMME AN *A*! [Crowd roars back 'A!'] GIMME AN *R*! [Crowd roars back 'R!'] Whaddya got! ['WAR!']

It must have seemed like weird fun for those innocent fans on the day, but hearing this makes me like it less than I did before, feeling as it does more like a kind of trickery, albeit one apologised for in advance by Davy. Part of the price for letting light in on magic, perhaps. Some might say that all pop music is a trick pulled on the young by their elders, and there may be something in that, but I still don't care for it. Nicholson pulled what he wanted from the crowd recordings, matched it with a shout from each Monkee when they filmed the cheerleader sequence at the Rose Bowl in Pasadena, and that's what we hear on the original vinyl album.

As it does in the film, Nesmith's 'Circle Sky' follows, cued by a two-note lead-in that also somehow connects this tune to the bedlam at the close of the previous track. This tune is something of a riddle – in the movie the band play it live in real power-trio style: the abrasive attack of Nesmith's guitar, Tork's supple, wandering bass line, and Micky Dolenz's ragged powerhouse drumming combine to show that The Monkees could make a real garage noise when they allowed themselves to. The song has been described as a Vietnam protest song, but that assumption seems to be based on its use in the film, where the already dazzling performance footage is accompanied by desperately upsetting images (again, possibly from that evening's news, lest we forget) of attacks upon Vietnamese civilians and, most infamously, the execution or murder of Nguyen Van Lem by Nguyen Ngoc Loan on February 1 1968 in Saigon. This clip is matched to the line 'but what you have seen you must believe, if you can'. It's horrible, and Nesmith had great concerns over the use of these images with his song, but it is also one of the most powerful matches of popular music and the moving image that you will find anywhere.

The song kicks hard but lyrically is a freewheeling, free-associating thing, vaguely psychedelic but sometimes just banal. Nesmith later recalled the line 'Hamilton, smiling down' as coming from a quick search for inspiration when writing the tune, and seeing a Hamilton music stand in the studio – 'I just wanted a simple direct song that we could all play easily together'[3] – and the song's last line is a confirmation of that – we got through it. The studio version rocks but lacks the primal drive of the Salt Lake City version, not least because Nesmith's vocal is buried fathoms deep in the mix, swamped by the arrangement and incongruously foregrounded percussion. The inclusion of this studio take over the pile-driving live one – a choice Nesmith later unconvincingly claimed to be in the dark about – is the album's one wrong move. It closes on a tweak of feedback, leading us into another track.

'Supplicio' – the Italian word for supplication or surrender, and a reference to Vito Scotti and the Italian Army's appearance, although they are unheard on the track – is genuinely spooky, ushered in via a bold orchestral sweep, borrowed from Ken Thorne's pseudo-*Lawrence Of Arabia* music for the movie's desert scene, followed by a phased sound effect of a wild lonely wind, broken by the solemnly intoned single line: 'Quiet, isn't it, George Michael Dolenz … I said.' This cuts straight into Peter Tork's 'Can You Dig It?', the tune that plays during the extraordinary harem tent/belly-dancing sequence. The exotic feel of this track, accentuated by the brisk discipline of an insistent bongo rhythm, derives from the unusual (even for 1968) Eastern-sounding scales it uses, subtly and sensually suggesting atmospheres of mystery and exoticism rather than, say, bolting on a sitar. The song's mix of wildness and restraint is very pleasing indeed and makes you wish Tork had been freer to spread his wings as a writer for the band. The lyrics are of their time to some degree but once again give the lie to the idea that the group themselves had 'no philosophies'. The song uses an on-trend expression to deliver some ancient-sounding insights, heavily influenced by Tork's recent readings of the *Tao Te Ching*, a sixth-century Chinese philosophical work, whose title translates approximately to *The Virtues Of The Way*. We're a long way from the front parlour of Auntie Grizelda.

'Can You Dig It?' is a good example of a brand of hippie philosophy, adapting an ancient idea to a contemporary mode and in doing so creating a mix of starry-eyed stuff and something tougher – 'those who scorn it die'. I also like that it connects singing to understanding: that's the truth there, brother. In the spirit of the movie, it asks something of the listener rather than just offering up an entertainment – the chorus is all question.

The idea of living in a world of heightened senses is certainly one that was having its time in the late 60s but it also connects to the 'wanting to feel' of Goffin & King's 'Porpoise Song', and how that leads on to a sense of what's real. Paradoxically that feeling comes through the intangible – music and the soul. The last line – 'I sing the praise of never change with every single breath' – is stunning, not only in its compression of a complex insight into 11 words but also in how the sound of those words run together in that order makes the impact of that insight real – and, as we know, *Head* is partly about the order of things. Tork's lyric resists the 'changes' even as it welcomes the endlessly renewing nature of existence. In this the duality of the *Tao* finds a contemporary expression and musical context that does not shame it. Plus, we can watch June Fairchild dance to it. That's body and soul working together.

So, a great Peter Tork song on a Monkees album at last. Why doesn't he sing it?

> It was Bert's decision. Because it fell into place in the movie right after Micky's desert scene, they wanted him to be the lead singer on the song, so I put him on it – no big thing. That's the way we did it. The first song Mike ever produced he had Micky sing lead on ['Mary, Mary'], because Micky was the lead singer. Neither Mike

> then, nor I later, thought twice about it. It wasn't until later on that we thought, 'We should do this ourselves, because it's our song.' We didn't have any of that proprietary interest until afterwards.[4]

Micky sings it with his by now customary craft, skill, and sensitivity – listen to where he takes 'die' and 'fly' in the second verse or how he responds to the hidden rhythm in 'I sing the praise of never change': it's superb. Peter's band – Lance Wakely and Dewey Martin – are on the track, with Wakely being responsible for the acoustic pyrotechnics toward the song's climax, and Micky sang over the cut as recorded with the composer's vocals on board. That original take is available to hear on various reissues now thanks once again to Rhino's archival work and, though I love the tone of Peter's voice, I'd miss the way Micky sings it. Bert Schneider's decision to let Dolenz sing this track was a non-musical one, but as Peter noted, it proved to be in the service of the song, and he has the good grace to acknowledge that, taking the chance to note that this is how it should be. That vision is surely part of what drove the song in the first place.

The first side ends with that rare thing, a genuine one liner. 'Gravy' is a snatch of dialogue taken from the cafeteria scene where the band and transvestite waitress try to outdo each other with bon mots of withering contempt: Davy Jones asks, bright and polite, 'And … er … I'd like a glass of cold gravy with a hair in it, please.' The track ends with Mimi Jefferson's lightly mocking, coquettish laugh from the soul-kissing sequence that follows 'Porpoise Song' at the movie's opening.

The second vinyl side opens with yet another one liner, and 'Superstitious' features the voice of Bela Lugosi in a clip from Edgar G. Ulmer's *The Black Cat* (1934), a horror film that is briefly seen on the television screen during the channel-surfing sequence: we hear co-star David Manners ('sounds like a lot of … supernatural baloney to me!') and then Lugosi's darkly European brogue: 'Supernatural, perhaps … baloney, perhaps not.' Somehow he makes even the rather ridiculous word 'baloney' seem portentous. It's a fitting sound bite for this movie – almost beyond belief but also very close to the truth. At my 2014 screening of the movie, a lady from the audience bounced up to me at the end and said, 'I didn't know Bela Lugosi was in it!' When I told her he had made it to the soundtrack album, she vowed to go straight online and buy the album.

'Superstitious' shares the honours with 'Gravy' as the shortest cut on a Monkees album – both breast the tape at eight seconds. If you listen to your vinyl or CD you'll hear Manners's bright yet uneasy line mixed to the left and Lugosi's quietly sinister reply to the right. We are, as the old song says, stuck in the middle. On digital reissues of the album, the rhetorical ploy of having one of these spoken word excerpts close one side and open the other is lost, and hearing them cheek by jowl in short order is kind of weird, and not in the way much else about the album is weird. Somehow their brevity – a virtue when they stand alone – works against the desired effect when they are placed right next to each other. Only one solution – hit pause, wait a minute, then restart. Or listen on vinyl!

Out of the Transylvanian shade and into the light as Carole King's second contribution to the album follows, in the shape of a truly exquisite number co-written with Toni Stern, 'As We Go Along'. The pair had met up on the Laurel Canyon scene after King separated from Gerry Goffin, leaving their pleasant valley suburbia and moving to California. They wrote a handful of songs together, the most famous probably being 'It's Too Late' from King's 1971 album *Tapestry*. King credited Stern with helping her through a very difficult period, documented on her early solo records as she reinvented herself, in the spirit of the age, as an emotionally articulate singer-songwriter, under the influence of peers like James Taylor. 'Toni was wonderful help with the transition from writing with Gerry to writing songs on my own,' she told the *Telegraph* in 2016. 'I didn't have the courage initially.'

That yearning for freedom is woven into the lyric of this song – a sudden opening up of possibility and the chance of growing as a person in experience and understanding. There is a desire for settlement, and certainty negotiating with a restlessness, or what Joni Mitchell called 'an urge for going'. This seems pure Laurel Canyon stuff now, but that was there and that was then – what else should it be?

Like Chip Douglas's description of 'Forget That Girl' as his message to himself, this song is King and Stern talking a state of mind into being.

This degree of self-possession was still unusual for a female act, which the industry still tended to direct toward the girl group or chanteuse categories, with some rare exceptions like Joni, Linda Ronstadt, and Janis Joplin just coming through. Each faced in their own way difficulties in being treated seriously, and King's personal urge for going became, by 1971, a generational one.

Given that *Head* contains generous measures of cynicism, pragmatic brutality, and, occasionally, plain old cruelty, Rafelson was right to suggest that this song provides an interlude – a breathing space for the viewer. This role is clearer in the cinema than on vinyl, but it nevertheless delivers a beautiful, restful spot on the album. The second verse – 'Why think about who's gonna win out?' – connects the song straight into the ethos of the movie, as an invitation to set aside previous concerns of outdoing the competition and 'winning the race' and instead offering an image of freedom via the absence of such imperatives – 'we'll make up our story as we go along'.

The song's title stands as a kind of bridge between fantasy and reality – the film's unusual structure has the feel of a story being made up as it goes along, and it also harks back to the good-natured subversions of conventional narrative on the TV show, and the idea of living according to this philosophy – just allowing things to happen – is also familiar from Peter's Swami speech. Clearly, both film and TV shows are scripted, but, lest we forget, they are not real, and another of the film's quests is to 'know what is real'. Perhaps the way to make such a discovery is just to live and let the story develop that way. The future is unwritten. So this little tune does a lot of work for the film and how we understand the 'story' as it goes along. It's also a sublime four minutes of music; the song counsels *carpe diem* but is in itself poised and unhurried. Micky recalled the recording:

> Again a Carole King tune, written with Toni Stern, on guitar Ry Cooder and Neil Young … and I probably got the song the day before, and it's in 5/4 time, and I'd never sung anything like that before! Only thing I'd ever heard in 5/4 was Dave Brubeck's

> 'Take Five'; Carole spent a bit of time with me getting me to sing it in in 5/4 time. I was grateful to her for that.[5]

As here, the tune is often discussed in the light of Neil Young and Ry Cooder being on the session, as two of five guitar players, Carole King being a third. The sweet pulse of the acoustic is an image of promise and freedom in itself. The light skip of the flute part deserves a mention too, but the details of the session player seem to have been lost, which seems unjust given how much it brings to the track. (A similar fate befell the flute player who contributed to Van Morrison's *Astral Weeks*, recorded the same year, so, flautists, be sure to have your names written down at the sessions. You never know.) While the musicianship is impressive and the track is certainly beautifully played, perhaps most impressive is Micky Dolenz's vocal – a superb, weighted performance that adds substantially to the song's bittersweet gravity. Though it was, in his words, 'a bitch to sing', you'd never know from hearing the soaring, sweeping range of his delivery. The folk-rock arrangement serves the lyric's wistful optimism well, a mood which the movie is careful to subvert by accompanying the closing section's gorgeous rising scales with quick-fire images of signs displaying slogans of advertising, restriction, and prohibition.

That attention to the processes of selling pops up again in the next cut, 'Dandruff?', a clip featuring dialogue from sections in which The Monkees are nearly arrested and then required to 'be' dandruff in Victor Mature's hair, representing their status as an easily removed minor irritant to the Hollywood machine. Nicholson's immaculate editorialising manages to make the sound of a giant vacuum cleaner feel like the perfect link into Davy Jones's version of Harry Nilsson's 'Daddy's Song'. This is an apparently bright and breezy tune, loud with cheerful brass, yet one that tells of childhood abandonment and emotional deprivation. It's an extraordinary trick, and a very Nilsson one, analogous to the fabulous monochrome-in-full-colour dance routine that Jones and choreographer Toni Basil hoof through for this number in the film, a kind of subversively hyper-real Hollywood homage. In the movie, the final verse is sung live to camera by Davy and slowed down for an emotional impact that, typically for the film, is both movingly real and equally obviously stylised; on the album, it is taken at the same rate and with the same arrangement as the previous two. The 'secret pain' of the song is less obvious on vinyl, and it wasn't until I learned more about Nilsson's early years that I joined the dots – it has much in common with a song like 'Gotta Get Up' from his 1972 breakthrough *Nilsson Schmilsson*, which Dolenz and Jones grafted onto their roles in the London stage production of *The Point* in 1976. Mike Nesmith's version of this is good to hear but less effective; it needs Davy's sense of performed emotion rather than a sense of stylistic pastiche, which Mike was right to save up for his 'Magnolia Simms', which you can hear on *The Birds, The Bees & The Monkees*.

'Poll' is perhaps the album's most creative audio mash-up and showcases Jack Nicholson's impish mischief very well, featuring an array of choice lines and vox pops, sound effects, and musical chunks drawn from all over the film. It also includes the soundtrack album's best joke when Nicholson recreates the Zappa/Nesmith tag-team by splicing two one liners together:

> **Zappa**: That song was pretty white …
> **Nesmith**: And I'll tell you sumthin' else too – the same thing goes for Christmas! [*A sharp intake of breath is heard.*]

The lines are 25 minutes apart in the movie; while the soundtrack is pretty straight in its chronology, Nicholson breaks the rules of linear storytelling one more time here, and even a Jack doubter like me has to admit it's funny. He was obviously pleased with it, too, as he crash edits into a few seconds of the 'Circle Sky' intro, drops in Davy's 'He's crazy!' from the start of the bathroom scene, and then adds a wild guffaw of laughter before we hear a gunshot, which, as in the film, silences all else, and up comes Timothy Carey and his advice, delivered on the court steps in the Wild West town. The cumulative effect is to create something compellingly disorientating to listen to rather than just a straight clip from a movie – it's a kind of analogue sampling, the audio version of the fast cutting Rafelson spent such effort on in the movie visuals.

Interestingly, Peter Tork noted on the Blu-ray that 'Bob was a little taken aback that Jack played around with the soundtrack but I thought he did a fabulous job', which suggests to me – if Rafelson was in fact 'taken aback' – that there is indeed some linearity to the narrative which he hesitated to see disturbed.

This extraordinary collage of film audio leads us to a few of the vox pops caught by prankster Mal Sharpe – including Shape himself asking, in Chris Morris deadpan, 'Are you telling me that you don't see the connection between government and laughing at people?' Then comes possibly the film's most quotable line, Peter's 'Well let me tell you one thing, son, nobody ever lends money to a man with a sense of humour.' This couldn't possibly be topped by any other sound bites, so in a great touch, Nicholson borrows the heartbeat from the 'Mike in negative' scene as he falls horribly toward the camera en route to what proves to be his birthday party, matches it with Victor Mature's macabre laughter to evoke the horror movie scenes, and then tees up the next track with a classic horror-movie effect: the creak of a slowly opening door.

Beyond that door in the film we hear the Gregorian chant and the crowd-sung version of 'Happy Birthday'; here, possibly for reasons of copyright or reasons of art (or both), we lean on the open door and tumble right into the album's final proper song, Peter Tork's paint-scorchingly powerful whirlwind, 'Long Title: Do I Have To Do This All Over Again?' Leaving aside the little wobble of nerve under that self-conscious prefix, this song blasts out of the traps and doesn't let up until it finally fades. A model of controlled rage, the lyric paints an image of Sisyphean endeavour and hints at what it must have been like to be at the heart of the Monkee machine. It bites back at the processes associated with being a Monkee but also in one's wider experience – how many times do we need to start over until we get it right? This tallies with Tork's interest in the *Tao* and the pursuit of 'the way'. As Van Morrison wrote in a more reflective mood about the same idea, in 'Here Comes The Knight', 'If you get it right this time, you won't have to come back again.' This idea has found its way into mainstream popular culture, too, with films like *Groundhog Day* (1991) reaching a kind of cult status, the title passing into common parlance for the feeling of déjà vu all over again. As for this song, it clearly has an application to his experience of being at the centre of this machine and also indicates why it would soon end – once you start asking these kinds of questions out loud, the clock is ticking. The second verse hooks up to one of the main themes of the movie – the search for what's really real. This pursuit functions in opposition to being bought and sold like a manufactured commodity – one that now wants a will of its own. Time is here, too – how much is there? What if it runs backward, à la 'Ditty Diego', or has to be grasped right now, à la 'As We Go Along', or experienced as a long continuous now, à la 'Porpoise Song'? All these themes intersect in this blistering hot shakedown of a song.

It's such a joy to hear how well it is sung – Tork's vocal is on the button, wholly assertive, and stands comparison with the best performances by the other three. For a host of reasons, Tork rarely got the chance to contribute compositions to the Monkees, being less business-like than Nesmith, and even those that made it were sung by Dolenz (see 'For Pete's Sake' from *Headquarters* and 'Can You Dig It?' here). His voice could be folksy and plaintive, but it fits this tune like a peacenik fist in a loving glove. The track features Davy Jones on backing vocals, marking a very late collaboration between the two and unusual in a period where all four tended to work entirely separately. In this it's a pleasing mix of Monkees with Peter's band of Wakley and Martin, and sitting in with them was Tork's old flatmate Stephen Stills – the man who put him onto The Monkees' original auditions back in September '65 – and he contributes the upper-fret searing yet impressively clean and precise guitar solo so memorably visualised in the movie. Given the quality of tune, vocal, and lyric of this solo composition, it's a shame Tork never got his post-Monkees band Release past the vague demo/rehearsal stage – had they broken out, they could have stormed it.

The album's finale 'Swami – Plus Strings, Etc.' is another epic sound collage, linking back to the record's opening track in the same way that the movie's conclusion sends the viewer back to the beginning; it opens with the voice of actor Abraham Sofaer, who plays the Swami in the film, a guru clearly fashioned by Rafelson and Nicholson after the Maharishi

Mahesh Yogi, with whom The Beatles had met and studied in 1967–68. The character is presented as wise but also possibly a charlatan, which is not far off the mark, as subsequent revelations showed. The monologue reproduced here is heard in the movie in attentive silence by Peter Tork, and later repeated near-verbatim by him to the other three in the Black Box sequence. Extracts now recognisable from 'Opening Ceremony' slowly fade up behind his voice; 'Porpoise Song' eventually overtakes both, and the track's abrupt conclusion is followed by the flatulent phutt of a truck engine (which carries the band away to be filed as props on a studio backlot) and two minutes of Ken Thorne's curiously bright and busy string quartet music, which skates over the movie's closing titles.

This grand ending is undercut by two more splinters of manipulated and juxtaposed dialogue: Teri Garr's plea to Dolenz in the breakdown scene to 'Suck it before the venom reaches my heart' and Micky's 'inner voice' saying bye-bye in the desert scene after the 'real' Micky has commanded the voice to 'shutupshutupshutupYOU': 'OK … I will!' There's a sexual tone to this, of course – the film's title having a connotation all of its own – and it plays fast and loose with what actually happens in the movie. Indeed it's Micky's refusal to play along and suck Testry True's finger (or pull the arrow from Mike's shoulder in the recommended manner) that triggers the off-piste core of the film, as he bursts through the scenery and out of the linear story, rejecting 'all the fake and the junk'. Miss Pleasure concludes the whole album with one last return of that incredulous, girlish laugh.

On this album, then, the songs are only part of the story, as they were with The Monkees project as a whole: signals, sounds, and ideas interfere with each other throughout. Then there is the correspondence with and distortions of the movie itself, television, Vietnam, The Beatles, the new counterculture – all must be taken into account. The movie is bluesy in its circularity, as is the *Head* album – both finish where they began. For album and film, separate yet intimately connected entities, the circularity is both a freedom and a trap. 'The porpoise is waiting, goodbye, goodbye.' Like the spiral scratch of a record, the ending leads back to the start; the needle lifts, drops, and it all begins again.

CHAPTER EIGHT

AFTERMATH

Nothing had prepared me for the aftermath of something like the Monkees experience, and there really wasn't anything that could. Maybe I intuitively knew that the fall was going to come, and I was trying like hell to avoid it. But you can't avoid it. You mustn't avoid it. If you have the nerve, you should actually use the downward momentum to gather up speed, like a roller coaster, in order to get back on top. MICKY DOLENZ

In this chapter we look at what happened to the four Monkees after *Head*: a TV special followed by the slow and gradual dissolution of the group – reduced to a trio when Peter Tork left in December 1968, then further to a duo of Dolenz and Jones when Michael Nesmith left the group a year later. A new decade lay ahead.

ABSOLUTE BLOODY SHAMBLES, OR, IS IT ME OR IS THIS REALLY BORING?

The *33 1/3 Revolutions Per Monkee* TV special, filmed after *Head*'s opening in November 1968 and originally broadcast by NBC on April 14 1969, is one of the less revisited spots of the band's initial career – it should be celebrated as being the final contribution they made as a four-piece, with Peter Tork telling the others he was quitting part way through the production, but it is almost ignored. Its reputation has not been even partly rehabilitated by the passage of time, as has that of *Head*, and it damaged the standing of its director Jack Good. Good was undoubtedly an innovator in the way pop was introduced to and shown by television (*6.5 Special*, *Oh Boy!*, *Shindig!*) so was on paper at least a good match with The Monkees. Indeed he had already appeared in an episode of the TV show, 'Monkees Mind Their Manor', delivering a droll turn as English lush Lance Kibbee.

The truth is that where *Head* was by turns acerbic, witty, dazzling, boring, cruel, and beautiful, *33 1/3* is simply bad. And, as Bob Seger put it, sometimes bad is bad. Even the musical elements we might have looked at to redeem it are weak. They also demonstrate how far from each other the four were by this twilight stage. Davy's two contributions showcase what he called his 'Broadway Rock' sound, with both 'Goldilocks Sometimes' and 'String For My Kite' being exemplars of the form in style and staging. Peter sang the many-times demoed 'I Prithee (Do Not Ask For Love)' and quietly demonstrated his skills as a harpsichord player by a confident run through Carl Philip Emanuel Bach's 'Solfeggio', which roughly translates as 'Exercise', and as such provides the ideal way to both test and exhibit accomplishment and technique. The choice of a piece by the son of Johann Sebastian rather than by his more famous father also seems significant somehow – less well-discovered corners can hold treasures, if we look. Michael's 'Naked Persimmon' is routinely and probably correctly cited as the best of these solo performances; it is certainly evidence of how he was willing and able to experiment with the visualisation of music.

The duality of his experience of being a Monkee played out via a feat of trick filming by Good, resulting in a Nudie Suited and a *Head*-style cream-cloth-suited Nesmith singing with and at one another, both sitting in front of a Wild West-style Wanted poster reading 'Wanted for Fraud, $25,000 reward'. Nesmith is shown in full-face and profile sketches on the poster below the text. This is typical of the tone of the show's near-pathological self-loathing that the band were obliged to co-operate with, and while *33 1/3* shares some of the auto-iconoclasm of *Head* it is humourless and discouragingly heartless.

Having said that, the song, cued in by Julie Driscoll turning away from the camera and firing off Smith & Wessons at Cowboy Mike (who ducks convincingly) is pretty good, and the musical highlight of the show. Like the image on the screen, the song has a divided soul – half the time it scampers along like a good-natured cross between Elvis's 'A Little Less Conversation' and Dylan's 'Subterranean Homesick Blues', lyrics rattled out, obliging the listener to either pay very close attention or just go with the rhythm of it. The rest of the time, it drops to a slow country strum not unlike something from Nesmith's early-70s solo work. If we do cock an ear to the words we note it is all about the reality of The Monkees, while never mentioning the group by name. It is the only song in the show to directly address 'the gold record situation', and it makes some bold observations about the music industry; if there was anyone qualified and entitled to say these things in late '68, it was most likely Michael Nesmith, who goes so far as to attribute sulphurous intent to a musical supervisor of his acquaintance:

> Well, the devil incarnate running music supervision
> Put me into a state of cataleptic euphemism

Had anyone been able to catch the lyric on TV back then they might have rushed to their dictionaries and been astounded at what this all means. The extremity of the band's situation becomes clear; they were trying to assert themselves musically while simultaneously being required to continually apologise for existing to their critics who by now were legion in both Hollywood and in the counterculture. The irony is of course that those countercultural figures would end up as the new Hollywood establishment, and Monkee money would in part fund that transition. The song concludes with Suited Mike nipping off before Driscoll gets her man, shooting Cowboy Mike, who rolls over and plays dead. It's a restatement of some of the points made in the crowd riot scene of *Head* but with little of the wit and none of the understanding of the complexity of the issues at stake.

Despite Rafelson's mixed feelings about the Monkees project, even his most acerbic visual treatments of them retained some affection for and understanding of them as people he worked with. *33 1/3* was the first TV or film production they had done which did not come through Raybert, and it shows – even Gene Ashman was sidelined, the many clothing changes being the work of Ray Aghayan. Visually, and at best, it duplicates the 'absolute bloody shambles' it seems to suggest is the inevitable outcome of allowing creative people the freedom to develop as they see fit. Jack Good, despite his excellent contact book and impressive CV, proved to be a very bad choice. He failed to understand The Monkees in almost every possible way; his appraisal of how pop music is made, how it works, and what it is for is both brutal and stupid, and his efforts to make them seem small reflects badly only on him and his show. Quite what Brian Auger and Julie Driscoll were drafted in for when – one might guess – he had the pick of American actors for the mad professor and his assistant is another question we might ask. Like their acting, and outside a few exceptions, the execution of the whole programme is execrable, as is its reductive conceit. As Micky Dolenz says on the DVD commentary, sotto voce, 'Is it me or is this really boring?'

The show is notable for one thing: it was during this production in late November '68 that Peter Tork told the others he was quitting. The news leaked out and was broken gently to the band's fans in the teen magazines. 'It is believed that the TV Spectacular will be the last appearance that Peter Tork will make with the Monkees,' reported *Monkees Monthly* in January 1969. Peter's final act as a Monkee cues in the show's finale and also one of the show's few treasurable moments; as he leaves off – or is it abandons – his performance of the C.P.E. Bach piece on the electric keyboard, he is joined by his bandmates on the set, surrounded by *Citizen Kane*-style packing cases for the finale of 'Listen To The Band'. Micky and Mike arrive together, and the trio fiddle and tune up; Micky sets himself at the kit, Mike gets his guitar in tune, Peter changes his keyboard setting for the next tune. You know, like a real band would. Nesmith taps his mic – it's live – and starts, gently and quietly, to strum.

I've savaged this TV special because I find it so brutal and so far off the mark in every sense that I think it richly deserves to be harshly critiqued, but it is equally true that the first couple of minutes of this performance are among my favourite moments in their visual career. Imagine if the producers, writers, and directors had been courageous enough to allow the four to helm a show foregrounding what they were rather than what they were not. So it makes me very happy to hear the music played straight, with no agenda, and to see Mike's genuine smile of greeting as Davy arrives off camera, but it also makes me sad as it was this performance which effectively broke the back of the original group. That's my view, but it is also a fact that the four would not be on a stage together for another 18 years. At least at the outset it is a fabulous performance, restrained and minimal but also somehow very strong. It's also the only evidence we have of Peter playing on a version of 'Listen To The Band' in the group's original iteration, handling the brass part on the keyboard in a fine and quietly funky manner. Live footage of the band is rare indeed and these first couple of minutes are perhaps the best we have – no special effects or manipulative contexts, just four musicians playing music.

After a minute or so, stage-hippies wander in; unlike during Mike's birthday party in *Head*, where it somehow looked like the real deal, this scene tries the same trick – even down to the psychedelic camera effects – but doesn't quite make it. The invaders – supposedly real hippies recruited from Sunset Strip but ironically looking baffled and bogus – don't seem to really know what they are doing there or what their role is and the musicians by and large ignore them. Davy MCs a little, welcoming them with a smile, but Micky is superbly focussed on his drumming and betrays not a glimmer of interest in colluding with them to mach schau. The propinquity of the extras seems to push Mike on a bit, and his last verse is sung in a higher key than on the recording, gutsy and strong, really driving home the point – *listen to the band!*

Good and director Art Fisher should have taken note, for they are very rapidly drowned out by a cacophonous collective featuring old Monkee collaborator Buddy Miles and his band alongside a return from Brian Auger and his group The Trinity Express. I like a riotous finale – rock'n'roll performance has always depended on them – but this is all noise and no centre, created by someone who, in the end, has misunderstood their subject. It grows and grows, occupying the last seven of the section's nine minutes before the camera pans out and the screen becomes a panel in a leather-bound illustrated book. The 'screen' is covered by a butterfly symbol, and the lower half of the page carries the phrase 'Chaos is come again', a quote from *Othello*, where The Moor is reflecting on how he loves Desdemona so much that it puts his own soul at risk:

> Excellent wretch! Perdition catch my soul
> But I do love thee! And when I love thee not
> Chaos is come again.[1]

Quite what the significance is of this to *33 1/3*'s premise is unclear, but Good is clearly interested in exploring the chaos that lies beyond a moment of abandonment – remember earlier on how Brian Auger's character had scornfully predicted 'absolute bloody shambles' should freedom and creativity hold sway. Just when we have something that suggests an interesting idea or a little cultural depth, the book is slammed shut by someone in an ape suit. The cover of the book is marked 'The Beginning Of The End'. Under the scrolling titles is psychedelically colourised film of the dancers we saw earlier, as a voice intones, 'The End … The END' in the rising tone of a hammy mad professor accompanied by what we could now call Darth Vader-esque heavy breathing. The final minute of the programme gives us Peter Tork trilling a few bars of a freaked version of Al Jolson's 'California Here I Come', the lyric changed to *here it comes*: the 'it', we must assume, being the mushroom cloud apocalypse we see on the screen, or perhaps the Big One, the earthquake where the San Andreas fault would finally yawn open wide and swallow California's cities, sending them, like a modern-day Atlantis, sliding into the sea. So Good's thesis involves castigating the band, their fans, and predicting pop's role in ushering in Armageddon. Who could have guessed a show like this would fail?

Sensibly, there was never a soundtrack album of this show, nor, as far as I have been able to discern, even plans for one. Instead the three-piece Monkees snapped back into action with a swiftly arranged night-photo session with Henry Diltz in Las Vegas, in which they look hale and hearty and optimistic about the future. The two albums they issued in 1969, February's *Instant Replay* and October's *The Monkees Present*, are better than you might expect, and less alike than first seems the case – the former has some barrel scrapings of reheated material from 1966 (the dispiriting 'Tear Drop City', the wonderful 'I Won't Be The Same Without Her') but also some of their finest late material, notably Davy Jones's co-write with Bill Chadwick, the acid 'You And I', often noted for its scorching guitar work courtesy of Neil Young but more notable for its extraordinary lyric and Micky Dolenz's pulsing piece of near-chanson 'Just A Game' (studied in depth in chapter four).

Present is the remnant of the proposed double album where the four Monkees would have a side each to express themselves. Instead, the remaining trio get four tunes from twelve each. That idea of four different directions at once seemed unworkable, perhaps, but has since been successfully pursued and not so long afterward – what else were Crosby Stills Nash & Young's albums and live shows but precisely this model? It's implicit in the title of their album *Four Way Street*. Fleetwood Mac did OK with a similar approach, with the songs of Christine McVie, Stevie Nicks, and Lindsey Buckingham locking together to make the palette on which the band drew. So The Monkees didn't get to do it, but others took that idea on and succeeded with it. *The Monkees Present* has, as promised, four of Davy's 'Broadway Rock' numbers, four of Michael's country tunes, and a quart of Micky's own category-defying creativity. It's a promisingly strong album – hear 'Listen To The Band', 'Mommy And Daddy', and 'French Song' for the best of each – but in truth time was up. The album sold 150,000 copies and was not issued outside the US; just three years before, their debut had sold five million in the US alone. No one was listening to the band. In December 1969, as the new decade hurtled toward them, Nesmith bought out his contract.

The final throw of the dice for The Monkees was an album in which they were barely involved. *Changes*, issued in June 1970, was effectively the work of their old producer/writer Jeff Barry and a younger Canadian named Andy Kim. The pair had written The Archies' 'Sugar Sugar', and it is Kim's voice on that record. The album went back while trying to go forward by including tracks recorded in '66 (Boyce & Hart's 'I Never Thought It Peculiar') and '67 (Barry's own Merseybeat pastiche '99 Pounds', sung brilliantly by Jones), and this is a ploy used to greater effect on 2016's *Good Times!* Here it feels somewhat last gasp. Dolenz takes the lion's share of the vocals, including his own 'Midnight Train', which had been first tried out in the sessions for *Headquarters*. The single 'Oh My My' is possessed of a sensual menace and has a slowly funky feel, showing that the ghost hadn't quite been given up. A promo clip was made for the single and has survived to be seen online. Davy turns in a couple of vocals like the professional he was, but it's clear his heart wasn't in it. The album is not terrible, but was an inauspicious way to go – compare it with the finale The Beatles composed for themselves on side two of *Abbey Road*. Precisely because of its commercial failure, *Changes* remains the rarest of the original Monkee albums in its original impression on Colgems; I'd never even seen a copy until I picked up the Rhino reissue in New York in '87. A final single, 'Do It In The Name Of Love', came out on Bell – the reimagined Colgems – in 1971, credited to Mickey [sic] Dolenz & Davy Jones, and that was that. As Ray Nitschke says in *Head*, 'Guess it's game over.'

So in the immediate aftermath of the group's dissolution, being an ex-Monkee was not a particularly strong suit in the marketplace. Each of the four experienced struggles and difficulties in working outside of the extraordinary environment that had permitted and encouraged as well as stifled and directed their endeavours. Outside of that machinery, life was different.

SOLO

It's true to say that the early 70s were something of a fallow period for ex-Monkees. Only Michael Nesmith had any commercial or artistic traction in this period; ever the professional, Davy Jones undertook a series of theatrical roles with some TV thrown in, and eventually he moved back to the UK to focus on his horses and took roles in a touring production of Peter Nichol's play *Forget-Me-Not Lane* and that great seasonal stand-by of British theatre, pantomime. Micky Dolenz, cushioned by the sound investments his mother had made in the high era, was able to live a kind of high-low life with Hollywood friends including Alice Cooper, Keith Moon, Harry Nilsson, and John Lennon, and, when he wasn't drinking, made some interesting solo sides both released and archived, many of which were gathered together by Iain Lee in the debut release from his own 7A Records in 2015, *The MGM Singles Collection*.

Peter Tork fell furthest, failing to realise the potential of his post-Monkee project, a band called Release, who at one point numbered a young Lowell George in its line-up. Unlike Micky, he had, in a hippie dream, given most of his worldly goods away and simply spent up – under-represented on Monkee records his residual royalties amounted to little. This disillusionment led him far from Laurel Canyon (his legendary house there, where scores of hangers-on had helped themselves to his largesse, was sold to his old friend Stephen Stills), and when he was arrested in 1971 for crossing the border into Mexico with a stash of marijuana and sentenced to two months imprisonment, his fall was complete.

Michael Nesmith, always the most driven and business-like of the four, developed what he'd begun on *The Wichita Train Whistle Sings* and carved out a solo career that began in the shadow cast by The Monkees' guitar-shaped logo but quite soon overcame the prejudice that was rife in the burgeoning rock press by the virtue of being undeniably stunning music. His early red, white, and blue trilogy of *Magnetic South* (1970), *Loose Salute* (1970), and *Nevada Fighter* (1971) are now routinely cited as formative documents in the development of country-rock. Nesmith had been mining this seam for a few years already – 'Papa Gene's Blues', 'You Told Me', and the Nashville sessions that produced 'Listen To The Band' and 'Good Clean Fun', among others – but now he was free to explore his interest in this deeply American music full-on. With a formidable line up of O.J. 'Red' Rhodes on pedal steel, his old comrade John London on bass, and John Ware on drums, Michael Nesmith & The First National Band made a righteous noise and made it clear, quick, and cleanly.

Nesmith has made a whole range of daring and innovative albums, right up to the last, 2006's *Rays*, but none of them achieved the sense of integrity and natural shape of these three albums. It's not true to say that he was an outcast in the industry. On the contrary, RCA worked very hard to promote the albums and coined the phrase 'Michael Nesmith: A Cowboy For Today's America' to describe him to the target audience, those hungrily scooping up James Taylor, Carly Simon, and Carole King albums. It's possible that these records were three or four years early, as by the mid 70s country-rock was the highest currency in American pop music, with the California cowboys of Asylum records conquering the world.

It was the mid 70s before the first stirrings of a comeback were felt. Dolenz and Jones teamed up with Bobby Hart and Tommy Boyce to go out on tour as Dolenz, Jones, Boyce & Hart, playing an unapologetically nostalgic show to their original fans, many of whom were now married with kids and looking for a taste of the good old days. What they also noticed was that the audience contained many who were too young to have been there in '67, and had hooked up to the band via old records and, most vitally, the TV show, which has been so instrumental in keeping the name of the Monkees culturally current. They toured for a glorious year, including a July 4 gig at Anaheim Disneyland, where they were joined onstage by a long-haired and bearded Peter Tork. The four made an album for Capitol, *Dolenz, Jones, Boyce & Hart*. The record is a controlled and classy bit of mid-70s retro-pop – the kind of thing bands like The Raspberries had been exploring, and which acts like The Soft Boys and The Knack would later delve into. The music is less frantic than that makes it sound, and it has a Californian coolness that is very agreeable, but the roots of the sound are still back in LA's streets, corner cafes, and beaches. One might expect, given the act's billing (The Guys Who Wrote 'Em And The Guys Who Sang 'Em), that it would be Boyce & Hart songs all the way; it's not. Instead, we have a very lively mix of songs written by a variety of names and combinations of same. Musical highlights include the leadoff single 'I Remember The Feeling', the nice blend of nostalgia and urgency in the title being reflected in the power-pop of the performance, alongside the one and only Dolenz–Boyce co-write, 'It Always Hurts More In The Morning'. However, the key track on the album is Jones and Dolenz's autobiographical 'You And I', which would be re-recorded two decades later for *Justus*. Chip Douglas told me that he 'always used to look at Davy and Micky like Bing Crosby and Bob Hope – not that Bob Hope was a singer, but, you know, one's the crooner, the other is the comedian.' This song is fuel to that particular fire – it is a song about their friendship and enduring relationship. We know now that there were still many chapters to come after 1976, but the song's pertinence and softly affirmative melody both then and now is touching and sincere.

The year 1977 saw Dolenz and Jones together again, working on a stage version of Harry Nilsson's *The Point* at the Mermaid Theatre in London; the soundtrack album emerged on MCA, and is not at all bad, as the pair share leads with other cast members as a proper theatrical ensemble should. A sweet clip of them promoting the show on a British kid's television show survives online.

As a consequence of being in London for this show, Dolenz fell into theatrical and TV production, directing for the BBC and ITV and also smartly investing in as well as starring in a very successful stage version of *Bugsy Malone.* Davy meanwhile tested the theorem that the road goes on forever by playing hundreds of gigs with various pickup bands and his own group, Toast, whose exploits warrant a whole chapter of their own in his 1987 memoir. I saw them, sneaking in underage, in a grotty club in Leeds one hot summer Sunday in 1980, and based on that, his memories ring true. Peter Tork emerged from his exile to play a virtually unannounced show at New York's CBGB's in July 1977, and a recording of it, incredibly, can be found if you go looking for it.

Meanwhile, Nesmith was forging ahead with his solo career, having delivered a series of increasingly sage-like albums to close his account with RCA and immediately invented what he called a medium without a name – a book with a soundtrack – in 1975, with the expensively presented boxed set *The Prison*, one of the first products from his own new imprint Pacific Arts. His bespoke label Countryside Records, set up with the encouragement of Elektra boss Jac Holzman, only released two albums before folding, yet Nesmith was only just getting started in multimedia terms; the second half of the 70s saw his music change and get determinedly more modern and cinematic, resulting in a charming hit single in the UK, 'Rio', in 1977. It was the accompanying promotional clip that proved key to the song's success and also to Nesmith's next step, as he embraced the audio-visual age with great energy and verve. He didn't claim this matching of music and the moving image was a new discovery, as the 30s-musical-inspired promo clip for 'Rio' made plain, but what was new was the sharp focus it delivered to the way contemporary popular music was made, depicted, and enjoyed.

Nesmith was learning all those days on the set of *The Monkees* about how to put music and pictures together in a way that made both halves into a whole. The first step was an idea for a 24-hour pop cable channel called Popclips, which ran via Nickelodeon in 1980–81 and was produced by his old friend Holzman. Sony initially wanted to buy the name as well as the idea but in the end called its new music-video dedicated channel MTV. It is somehow fitting that one of The Monkees – cursed and blessed by their genesis on television – was instrumental in the arrival of MTV. Nesmith also branched out into the new field of sell-through home video with the surreal stoner humour of *Elephant Parts* (1981) and a subsequent TV follow-up, *TV Parts* (1985). His Pacific Arts firm moved into film production in the 80s, too, producing cult favourites such as *Repo Man* (1984) and *Tapeheads* (1988).

While all this was going on, Nesmith was too busy to fully participate in the mid-80s Monkees revival that had been driven by – appropriately – the MTV Monkee Marathon, which showed 46 (of 58) episodes over a single day, starting at midnight on Saturday, February 22 1986 and concluding at 22:30 on Sunday the 23rd. It became known as the Pleasant Valley Sunday. This drove demand for Rhino's newly acquired back catalogue of the albums, which, incredibly, pushed virtually all of them back into the *Billboard* Hot 100, even giving a chart debut to the unloved *Changes*. Out of this flowed demand for new music, and once Micky had been persuaded to set aside his behind-the-camera role in the UK for a while they duly obliged, delivering a handful of 'new' tracks to an Arista hits compilation (Rhino having not yet secured the rights to the full catalogue to do with as it wished) and then a whole new album,

1987's *Pool It!* Produced by the estimable Roger Bechirian (drawing on his expertise in British new wave such as Elvis Costello, Graham Parker, The Undertones, and Squeeze), it promised much but was nobbled by a tinny sound and middling material. 'Heart And Soul' provided something like a hit, and there are excellent moments, but pickings are slim – and I'd have loved to hear Wreckless Eric's 'Whole Wide World', a song built to be sung in a Northern English accent, taken on by Davy Jones, as was the original plan. The main event was the touring, and once back in the saddle, Jones and Dolenz proved themselves the professionals they are by going out and delivering night after night right up to the early 90s, touring sometimes as a duo, sometimes with Tork, and twice even welcoming Nesmith to the stage, in '86 and '89.

After *Pool It!*, Tork managed to balance Monkee business with his own musical interests, and 1994 saw the release of what was, incredibly, the first ever Peter Tork solo album, *Stranger Things Have Happened*. It contained 11 tracks, including his slowed, folky version of 'Take A Giant Step', and cameos from Dolenz and Nesmith as well as Timothy B. Schmit from Poco and The Eagles. The album has some of the date stamps of the era in which it was made but also features some great songs, such as the aquamarine 'Sea Change', which, in its evocation of the ocean's siren call, puts me in mind of the mermaids sequence in *Head*. 'MGB-GT' and 'Gettin' In' are familiar from *Pool It!* but are improved here, the former less frantic and the latter, appropriately, more hypnotic. The opening minute or so of the album closer 'Higher And Higher' is bliss – Peter and banjo – and although this crystalline mood is unseated when the band steam in, it is still an innovative re-imagining of the song. It was a modest success critically and commercially but its very existence was good news.

Post-*Justus*, Tork's musical interests have swung back to the blues, with bands called The Peter Tork Project and, most enduringly and productively, Shoe Suede Blues, with whom he has released three albums. He has also issued three folk-blues albums with James Lee Stanley and played countless solo shows worldwide – including one in humble little Otley, just down the road from me. The handful of albums that came from these team-ups are low-key delights, their relaxed charm irresistible.

It's music made the way he wanted it to be made, and his happiness and enjoyment is a real pleasure to hear.

In the midst of all this Monkee business, Micky Dolenz did not quite neglect his own recording career either. His albums of this period are few but contain some excellent performances, while going under the radar of all but the diehard few. The mischievously titled *Micky Dolenz Puts You To Sleep* (1991) reimagines classic singer-songwriter tunes such Neil Young's 'Sugar Mountain', McCartney's 'Fool On The Hill', and The Monkees' own 'Porpoise Song' as lullabies; 1994's *Broadway Micky* sees him straying just a little into Davy's territory with a dozen songs from musical film and theatre, comprised largely of more obviously kid-oriented choices such as 'Supercalifragilisticexpialidocious' from *Mary Poppins* and 'Talk To The Animals' from *Dr. Dolittle*. He still found room for his old comrade Harry Nilsson's favourite from *The Point*, 'Me And My Arrow', and Charlie Smalls's hit from *The Wiz*, 'Ease On Down The Road'. Both albums were released originally by Kid Rhino, the parent label's child-friendly imprint, and have since been very nicely reissued on a single disc by Friday Music.

Dolenz's 2008 tribute to Carole King, *King For A Day* on Gigatone, was a move back toward pop and rock music and contains an excellent range of her songs, from the bright Brill era up to the barefoot Laurel Canyon songstress of *Tapestry*. The only Monkee tune is one of his favourites, 'Sometime In The Morning', a song by which he seems haunted. This led on to the very best Micky Dolenz solo record, *Remember* (2012), a self-consciously reflective collection, its songs chosen for their significance to him – so we find 'Sugar Sugar' and 'Randy Scouse Git'/'Alternate Tile' cheek by jowl, alongside another version of that elusive butterfly of a song, 'Sometime In The Morning'. The title track, another Nilsson song, is stunningly performed and arranged (outdoing the version on *Puts You To Sleep*), but the laurels go to the opener, 'Good Morning, Good Morning'. A long-time favourite since he sat in on the recording sessions at Abbey Road back in February '67, he got permission to use it in 'The Frodis Caper' – the only time a Beatle song has ever been used that way to this very day – so it clearly has a very special place in his heart. It may be a heresy, but I prefer his slow breeze of a take on the tune to the rambunctious clamour of the original.

Nesmith's later albums were well spaced, so 1992's *... Tropical Campfires ...* (home of his wonderful tribute to Western artist Charles M. Russell, 'Laugh Kills Lonesome') didn't see a proper follow-up until 2006's *Rays*, a mixed bag adorned by a self-referential cartoon cover by Drew Friedman. Jones continued to sell live shows and interesting parts of his musical and theatrical past, primarily via his website, until his passing.

Back on the road, various configurations of Dolenz, Jones, and Tork drifted together and apart up to 1996, when a lengthy trio tour led up to a special event at Billboard Live in Los Angeles on November 20, where the quartet debuted material from their new album, *Justus*. Just in time for that 30th anniversary, Rhino was able to announce that all four would contribute not only to a new album but – what felt even less likely – a new TV special.

Justus was recorded for and released by Rhino, finally cementing what was already clear – The Monkees and Rhino depended heavily upon each other. Despite being written, played, and produced by all four Monkees – the first and only time since *Headquarters* – the album struggled with the same problem as *Pool It!*: what does a modern Monkees record sound like? Improbably, *Justus* strongly features a rather metallic rock sound, occasionally brutalist in texture, and makes no concession to the remembered perception of what The Monkees sounded like – although 'Pirates', from Peter Tork's 1994 *Stranger Things Have Happened*, isn't a million miles from this sound. I like it for that reason – they made the record they wanted to make, not the one they thought they should – but I wouldn't ever listen to it again if it weren't a Monkees record. The album's two remakes, 'You and I' and 'Circle Sky', stand at opposite ends of the musical range of the album – the crushing garage-bandery of the live performance in *Head* is crossed with a kind of Pearl Jam gene to make music which is tough enough but lacks the light and shade that can often be mistaken for evidence of inconsequence.

Sometimes lighter is much better, and somehow also deeper – I give you 'Daydream Believer' and 'Writing Wrongs', smooth cheek by whiskery jowl all those years ago. Which song has done more for you, and for that matter for the world? You know the answer. So, by neglecting that aspect of music – and of their music – *Justus* misses the point somewhat while re-asserting their rights over the name and to make whatever kind of noise suits them. The accompanying TV special, *Hey Hey It's The Monkees*, written and directed by Nesmith, worked from the premise of the band having stayed in their house since 1968, working their way through hundreds of 'episodes' no one saw. The idea is a good one, but the realisation is hit and miss, caught between the urges of nostalgia and self-satire. It featured the album's two remade tracks, 'Circle Sky' and 'You And I', alongside a reboot of the 'Theme' which as far as I am aware has not yet popped up on any reissues. A triumphant sold-right-out UK tour in the spring of '97 covered all four countries and the Irish Republic and culminated in two nights at the location of their moment of giddy success in 1967 at Wembley Arena, built on the site of the old Empire Pool venue. Nesmith bailed out of the American tour that was to follow in the summer of '97, though, meaning that the *Billboard* gig of November '96 was the last time all four played together in the USA.

Things came and went after '97, and as the furore around *Justus* faded back it would be 2011 before another major reunion tour was mounted. Badged as the 45th anniversary tour it was unarguably a new kind of live show, curated by connoisseurial consumers – fans – who had also found themselves in the position of working directly with the object of their interest. The visuals and staging were directed by the erudite and witty Rachel Lichtman, who was also involved in the Boyce & Hart documentary *The Guys Who Wrote 'Em*, and she did a fantastic job. Not for the first time, The Monkees ushered in a new kind of retrospective show – as pop grew older along with those who made it and those who grew up listening to it, the emphasis on youth which marked the early days of the form didn't become embarrassing or difficult to negotiate with. Instead it somehow became more and more focussed on the music, an access point to feelings and memories of youth and directly accessible through the combination of music and images that constituted the package. This is one aspect of the power of music to move, energise, and effectively function as a kind of time-travel. Seeing Davy at 66 performing his routine to 'Daddy's Song' onstage a few yards in front of me while the dance sequence from *Head* plays on the screen above him was a very strange experience – it could have invited an unflattering contrast, or a sense of sadness, but actually was intensely positive and life-affirming, delivering a feeling of continuity and completeness. Likewise – and he may have done this every night for all I know – at the start of 'Porpoise Song', Micky turned his back on the hall and looked up at the screen showing his slow motion fall from the Gerald Desmond Bridge at the opening of *Head*. It seemed like a very private little moment in a very public space. As his figure hit the water, the song broke into its slowly increasing piano intro, just as it does on the album. This sense of a deep understanding of the meaning of these conjunctions between music, moving pictures, and live performance was not only very impressive as a piece of theatrical organisation, but it was also evidence that finally a staging of a Monkees live show had arrived which was sensitive to these key moments and nuances of meaning – technology had finally caught up with the pioneering mix of music and the moving image which the Monkees not only represented but in many ways began. We could be in the moment, the 'now', but also in the 'then'. Each song was accompanied by the corresponding scene from the movie, not played straight but in a kind of bespoke edit, giving us further evidence of the forensic attention and care paid to the staging.

I'd argue that the 2011 dates in the UK were the best and most artistically successful run of shows the band had done since the reunion era began, beating out even the nights Nesmith showed. The set comprised 40 tunes, immaculately played and with barely a breathing space between the numbers. Not quite Ramones or early R.E.M. whirlwind pace, but not far off it. It was a tour that foregrounded the music rather than the theatricals or comedy routines, boldly and unapologetically making a case for The Monkees back catalogue as a rich resource for some of the best popular music of the pop era. No doubt the team at Rhino had a hand in curating the set, but my understanding is that Davy Jones was also key in sifting and choosing the material.

For we *Head* nuts, one especially marvellous piece of news was that all the songs from the movie were to be played in a 'suite within a set', and sure enough they were – though not in the familiar sequence. The *Head* material opened the second half of the evening, after the intermission – one cued in, we should say, by a rare outing for 'We'll Be Back In A Minute', a nice touch that has Rhino written all over it. A pile-driving 'Circle Sky' came first, out of the traps like a rocket from a bottle, with Jones, Dolenz, and Tork all playing guitar thrash-fast and up at their mics, singing together in a formidable front line. The sheets of noise must have had the casual fans checking their tickets to see if this really was The Monkees. Next up was 'Can You Dig It?', which composer Peter Tork sang, having his moment front and centre, with the harem tent scene onscreen, ushering June Fairchild and Helena Kallianiotes into the house. 'As We Go Along' was sung beautifully by Micky and handled very well by the backing band, sensitive to its subtle changes and the rise and fall of its melody, Micky going back behind the kit for the climactic upward climb through the scales that's so visually effective in the movie, so musically effective when you listen. This then tumbled into Peter's 'Long Title: Do I Have To Do This All Over Again?', accompanied by the super-groovy footage of the birthday party sequence. This is such an extraordinarily powerful song, one made all the more so by the way it combines wildness and restraint, and the performance I saw – and others that you can dig on YouTube – was faithful to that. In fact, it was this song that caused the set's biggest stir in my little patch of the venue, around five rows back, just to the left of stage centre. A girl just down from us, who couldn't have been older than 25, was standing up in her seat and *screaming* with excitement – not teen-mania screaming (I've been next to that, too) but a kind of ecstatic howl you might let out when something is just so great it's almost unbearable. *That* kind of scream. And she wasn't mistaken. It was beyond brilliant.

Just when it couldn't get higher: 'Porpoise Song'. This is when Micky looked up at himself onscreen, down a time tunnel of 43 years, and here's that idea I'd have liked to have asked him about. The song's mix of music and visuals is especially effective in the film, and so it was live onstage: very moving and possessed of a colossal yet gentle power. The live performance featured the 'coda' missing from the album version but familiar from the 45 and various reissues and best-ofs to have used the single version; this is a particularly evocative few bars of rolling, tumbling, oceanic music, made all the more stunning by Micky going back to his famous 'DRUM' kit and playing alongside the estimable Felipe Torres, the house drummer on the 2011 tour.

Last up, and the biggest production number, was 'Daddy's Song'. In a white suit (and staying in a white suit) Davy was remarkably faithful to the original 1968 dance routine while singing live; his energy and appetite for performing and for life was an unforgettable pleasure to see and to be close to. He was joined at the Toni Basil moment ('How the mama would explain') by his wife, Jessica Pachecho, who, dressed just as Ms Basil was dressed in the film, partnered Davy in the routine as choreographed for the movie. It's the number best suited to a smooth landing back into a long Monkees set being itself a kind of pastiche of an older sort of song particularly familiar from English music hall repertoires.

This dovetailed well, after a slight pause in proceedings, into the first song after the *Head* suite, 'For Pete's Sake', a tune that is both grounded in Monkee lore (closing titles for the second series) and a song that stands for itself. The set's other distinctive characteristic is what the publicity material around these tours now tends to call the deep cut – another way of saying fan favourite. Songs that were not hits, perhaps album tracks or, in The Monkees' case, not even released in the original era. The set I saw had a handful of these, songs I never ever expected to hear sung and played by them: 'All Of Your Toys' and 'I Don't Think You Know Me' in the unreleased camp, 'Hard To Believe' and 'Someday Man' in the released-but-obscure. Thus the set rewarded the dedicated follower but also allowed the band to reclaim these lost or obscure pieces of evidence for their hidden musical contributions, innovation, and plain old brilliance. Best of all, it opened up these seldom heard treasures to anyone who cared to buy a ticket and come along, undoubtedly with mixed levels of interest – some who just remembered loving the TV show and having a single or LP or two, and others who had scooped up every bootleg, boxed set, and bargain going. All were brought back under one tent by the triple love-punch of the final trio, 'Last Train To Clarksville', 'Pleasant Valley Sunday', and the communal singing of 'Daydream Believer'. A very broad church, all of whom left very aware of what the band's musical achievements were.

Nesmith joined them on the road after the shock of Davy's passing on February 29 2012, and *Headquarters* and *Pisces*-heavy sets in 2013 and '14 were very well received. In 2015, Micky and Peter continued to tour as a duo and, ever the innovator, Nesmith contributed 'Papa Gene's Blues' via Skype at a show in New York in June 2016 as part of the promotion for that year's *Good Times!*, an album willed into being by their label, Rhino Records.

RHINO

The name 'The Monkees' is a Registered Trademark of Rhino Entertainment, Inc. CAPTION FROM THE CREDITS OF THE *HEY HEY IT'S THE MONKEES!* TV SPECIAL, 1997

When Rafelson, Schneider, and Steve Blauner wanted to put together a special edition of *Easy Rider*, they discovered that Columbia Pictures had lost and/or disposed of a great amount of the material and footage relating to the film. Angered by this, BBS (their company) sued Columbia and won, and were awarded ownership of all Monkee audio and visual works – that is, the TV shows, *Head*, and all the music. This they then sold on to keen-as-mustard Rhino, so by 1994 the poacher truly had become the gamekeeper and the still-rolling reissue programme began.

It is impossible to talk about the resurgence and consolidation of The Monkees' reputation and legacy without talking about Rhino Records. Like several key UK indies – Rough Trade and Beggars Banquet, and, lest we forget, Virgin among them – Rhino began as a retail premises, selling new and used vinyl and providing a meeting place for like-minded record collectors. Its first shop was opened in February 1973 on Westwood Boulevard in Los Angeles, adjacent to the UCLA campus, and was both owned and run by Richard Foos and his friend, music journalist Harold Bronson. Foos, Bronson recalled in his 2013 memoir, had first made inroads into record retail with Mojo Records, an attempted door-to-door mail order service which – if you didn't know – is exactly how an English Richard, Mr Branson, began his Virgin empire around the same time, selling prog and krautrock by mail order via weekly ads in the *Melody Maker*. Branson scored an unlikely hit with his fledgling label's first LP, *Tubular Bells* by teenage prodigy Mike Oldfield, and never looked back. Mojo was less successful, but Foos went on working on the innovative fringes of record retail, and he first encountered Bronson when the then-journalist began taking his promo albums in for cash or part exchange to Foos's record concession at Apollo Electronics in Santa Monica. The pair hit it off, and once Foos opened the first Rhino in Westwood, Bronson started recommending his new friend's business to his readers and fellow writers. Bronson soon joined Foos in running the store, and they became the long-term driving forces of the company. Their urbane, pop-culture-literate humour and silly yet savvy marketing campaigns soon saw the Rhino name become a key part of the LA music scene.

Rhino took a little longer than Virgin to make the move into releasing as well as selling records, but by 1975 the label had issued its first single, albeit a shamelessly self-promotional novelty 45 by Frank Zappa's street-find Wild Man Fischer entitled 'Go To Rhino Records'. This set the tone for much of Rhino's early catalogue, which featured an array of comedy records, from mainstream to stoner humour. By 1978, the label was part of a distribution network key to the independent music labels not only of the US but globally, so someone in LA could buy the new Wreckless Eric single on the original British Stiff label, or The Special AKA's 2-tone ska, which led to oddities such as The Untouchables and later No Doubt starting out as curious US ska-aficionado outfits. The label quickly became an outlet for American rock and punk that was too mercurial for Sire or Elektra but reflected intense local popularity, notably in the case of LA neighbourhood heroes The Twisters.[2]

Harold Bronson has the distinction of being the first music writer to suggest that the received critical wisdom about The Monkees may have been wrong and fit for recalibration – he interviewed Dolenz and Nesmith for his piece 'Instant Replay', published in September 1971, a mere 15 months after *Changes* sank without trace and only seven months after the death rattle that was 'Do It In The Name Of Love'. In it, Bronson observed:

> One has to admit that Monkee albums are rather enjoyable. The group was the recipient of great material and was aided by knowledgeable producers, unlimited studio time, and the best facilities and backup instrumentalists available.[3]

It's curious now to think that this was a bold and even controversial claim at the time, not least because in 1971 the group's reputation was at its lowest ebb, reviled by the counterculture and abandoned by their legions of fans from a mere four years earlier. Bronson:

> Although record sales are at a minimum, the TV series is still shown on Saturday afternoons, and the foursome receive something like 1,000 fan letters a week (down from the 5,000 a day at the height of their success, but still substantial for a re-run series). The last Monkees single, 'Oh My My', was released last year and featured only Micky and Davy. Although there are still some 60 tracks in the can, Dolenz doubts whether there will be any more Monkee music.

The transformation of The Monkees from mainstream megastars to cult favourites was one they began themselves, their original audience quickly colluding, and the transformation has been fully realised by Rhino, with the stack of boxed sets and bespoke products designed to appeal to the die-hard connoisseur and collector – that is, the kind of music fan who used to walk through the door at 1716 Westwood Boulevard.

In his memoir, Bronson recalls the 'God Save The Kinks' marketing campaign, which was designed to reanimate the band's moribund reputation and sales – their back catalogue was already a mess, as a result of contractual and label swaps resulting in poor deals, and it must be said it would get a whole lot worse. However, the campaign was successful in itself as the band became more popular in the US than in the UK despite (or perhaps because of) their oft-remarked-upon 'Englishness', as hinted at in that promotional slogan, borrowing as it does from the British national anthem, later usurped and subverted by the Sex Pistols. His memory is of a sense of mission in the company:

> 'Rhino Saves The Monkees' in spirit if not in name could describe the company-wide commitment in mining the group's catalogue and helping to resurrect their career. It was as if watching the TV show had caused a gene to mutate, making Gary Stewart, Bill Inglot, Andrew Sandoval, and me lifelong fans.[4]

While 'Rhino Saves The Monkees' was never a slogan used in any campaign, there is indeed something evangelical about how Rhino has opened up the band's secret history. A major label would never have taken this project anywhere; only a fan – with or without the mutated gene – would find this stuff interesting, right? To prove the point, when Rhino first approached Arista with a view to licensing some Monkee recordings, the only material commercially available was a standard greatest hits compilation: eleven cuts on a single long player. It was actually a 1976 repackaged version of an older LP called *Refocus*, which had first been issued in 1972 on Bell Records. In the early 80s, the band had cut a deal with Clive Davis's Arista, the label that had succeeded Bell and so held the rights to the Monkees recordings.

To illustrate the licensing hash that Rhino had to navigate, some of the tracks had appeared before, randomly scattered across cheaply produced compilations. The real benchmark was, however, the Australia and New Zealand-only *Monkeemania*, an Arista double album from 1980, with a first rate track selection by the Aussie Monkee fan-in-chief Glenn A. Baker, its back cover adorned with pictures of the four from the mid 70s. Baker's book of the same title was one of the first to try to gather all the loose ends of their story together. This insider-knowledge approach extended to the packaging, with the inner bags bearing excerpts from original Monkees cartoons, an array of memorabilia, and an excellent essay by Baker. The album's groundbreaking mix of the hits and the deep cuts and contextual notes provided a signpost for Rhino – it can be done. Harold Bronson told me of how he found the major labels treated their back catalogue, and how what he had learned from working in the Rhino store helped in establishing the Rhino brand with the right people:

> The major labels, especially at the time we're talking about, the early/mid 80s, were focussed on the big-selling artists – Springsteen, Madonna, Prince, U2, and so on – so why would they put time into promoting or repackaging old music? That was their way of thinking, anyway. Pop music has always been of its moment and it wasn't necessarily thought that it was going to last, and that it has isn't anything anyone could have anticipated.

I wondered, too, whether they had an idea of who the ideal audience was for a Rhino product, or if they just went with their own instincts that this music was important in a way that had not yet been acknowledged.

> We assumed there were enough people who felt like we did, but prior to that we had the store, and we'd speak to people and see what they bought and what they liked about the packaging and the like, so there was some awareness based on that experience.

The Rhino team, in retrospect, had the advantage of being the right people in the right place at the right time, but they still had to do it. Proving the point about majors having little interest in the connoisseurial end of music collecting – it was about what's hot now and finding the next star before the other guys do – at first Rhino didn't take on a Monkee hits collection but instead an array of less well known tunes or even variant versions of those tunes, giving the collectors something to get their teeth into. They were therefore also showing a side to the band's recordings that may have passed the more casual listener by. So in 1982 Rhino released their first Monkee product, a picture disc LP entitled *Monkee Business*. Even the title – borrowed from a 1931 Marx Brothers movie, perhaps, but a common enough phrase in itself – has an ideal weighting balanced between fan-enthusiasm and an acknowledgment of the business realities of marketing music. *Monkee Business* sold reasonably well – though it was out of my price range at the time – and begat another similarly eclectic disc in 1984 entitled *Monkee Flips*. In his memoir, Bronson reports that by the end of the 80s these two original releases had sold around 50,000 copies each – not a *Billboard* botherer, but enough to keep everyone afloat.

When Bert Schneider approached Rhino about taking stewardship of the Monkee archives, the roles suddenly changed about. I asked Bronson how it felt to move from fan to business partner of the group:

> Well, the first emotion was excitement – from having been a lifelong fan of The Monkees, suddenly to be linked with them, even if it's not the original creation. Then the second step, and what we tried to do, was the reissues. Most of the reissuing in the United States was not done with quality in mind, it was, 'OK, well how can we get extra money out of these old hits?' For us, the music was more important than that, so it was, well, how can we improve it from other reissues, whether that be packaging, the sound, or liner notes? It wasn't let's just put this out and make money from it; we're moving the listener experience.

In our era of online auctions and digital downloads it's easy to forget how hard to find, how rare and obscure these records were in the 70s and 80s. I'd been fortunate to find many of them but only because browsing in a second-hand record shop was where I was happiest as a kid (and maybe still am, sadly). But copies of *Present* and *Changes* evaded me right until Rhino delivered the goods when I found them in a record shop in Greenwich Village in very early January 1987 at the end of my first very thrilling visit to New York. Even these reissues weren't easy to find in the UK at that time, so I was bursting with delight – I also took pleasure from not needing to buy all the others, my mono UK RCA copies safe at home.

Couple this with the first digital release of the back catalogue in 1994, with the then-innovative extensive sleeve notes and careful annotations of track details – where they were recorded, when, and by whom – and you have a new model for marketing old music. This was all brand new information and not at all how oldies were usually presented; the standard was just to treat them as a cash cow and bash 'em out every few years in a more contemporary looking jacket. Rhino's Monkees series was a whole other notion, treating the music and the listener with respect. It's my contention that, alongside the excellent work done on the Beach Boys archive around the same time, Rhino's Monkees reissues effectively invented the heritage model on which the industry now leans so heavily. The early-90s reissues predate the *Beatles Anthology* series, for example, and it's a little ironic twist that the Fab Four took their archival cue from their American counterparts, The Beach Boys and The Monkees. That the supposed 'prefab four' should be jostling for position with such stellar members of the critical canon is food for thought in itself.

Rhino had been quietly reinventing the way the music industry should treat its own past for nearly ten years by this stage, and it's hard to think of another company that is so closely associated with a single act while not actually being owned by that act – à la Apple or Brother Records, to keep with our examples – and this was demonstrated further when Rhino took ownership of the TV shows, movie, and music in the *Easy Rider* payoff deal with BBS. Bronson tells us that at one point he nearly struck a deal with Michael Nesmith to co-purchase the rights (set at $4m by Schneider and Rafelson), with Rhino handling the audio, Pacific Arts the video, but it fell through. Eventually, a deal to have exclusive North American rights while Warner Music took a third of the rest of the world was signed, and Rhino moved into visuals as well as audio. The TV series has subsequently been issued and reissued on VHS and DVD in boxed sets both ordinary and deluxe and as single tapes and discs, each time with exclusive/bonus content to lure in the completist, certainly, but also adding to the sum of knowledge around the group. A Blu-ray box set of the group's complete audio-visual work across TV and film was issued in July 2016 to commemorate the band's 50th anniversary.

Archival work, though more labour intensive, is in some ways easier than creating something new, especially with a unit the internal dynamics of which were as volatile as those at work in The Monkees. The real work began to bear fruit in July 1987, the *Summer 1967: The Complete Recordings* four-CD boxed set emerged, as did a one-disc 'highlights' set, *Live! 1967*, on LP, cassette, and CD. Right behind these came the first *Missing Links* compilation. All of this in the same summer as *Pool It!* was being recorded. Each one of these multiple releases was of interest to different layers of Monkee fan – are you satisfied with the one-disc live album, or do you need to hear all four? Or are you uninterested in 20-year-old live roughs and instead want to hear the polished, unreleased studio recordings? Or do you want to ride the new wave of Monkeemania with a contemporary sounding reunion album?

It is the deep well of unissued Monkee music that has sustained the marketing of product for Rhino, drawing heavily on the indefatigable loyalty of the band's fan base, as made clear in the notes accompanying *Missing Links Vol. III*:

> A two-year archival dig resulted in 1987's *Missing Links* ... another compilation followed in January 1990 (*ML Vol II*) this time concentrating on the TV rarities from their series. Finally with Rhino's purchase of The Monkees' entire recorded legacy in January 1994 an unprecedented master search yielded a second series of enhanced CD reissues as well as this final collection of 'lost music'.

Several compilation boxed sets followed in the wake of the full access granted, such as *Listen To The Band* and *Music Box*, alongside the legendary *Headquarters Sessions* set, which as of today is still to see a second release. Single albums were reissued with extra tracks and copious sleeve notes, then again ten years later in double deluxe editions; the current phase sees super-luxuriant 'black boxes' of three CDs, an exclusive 45rpm single, and, often, extras like badges or reproductions of inserts. Special mention must be made here of the black boxes that house *The Birds, The Bees & The Monkees* (2010) and *Head* (2012), exemplary models of archival work leading to a unique product that is both musically justifiable and historically significant – untold stories made public. That these sets are derived from albums which originally lasted about 35 minutes or so illustrates just how deep is that archive. What really interests me at this point is how Rhino tuned in to the idea – or the *fact* – that there was an entirely different Monkees story to be told – not the one found on the hits albums, not the one seen in the TV show, or the one told in *Head*, or even the one being told by Dolenz and Jones onstage in the various line-ups. Instead, it was one purely about music – music either rarely heard or never heard at all, sometimes entirely forgotten by those who made it: a remarkable musical archive slowly ageing in the vault, quietly heading for oblivion.

The real deep mining of the archive that began in the early 90s has had its most detailed manifestation in the series of boxed sets that Rhino has produced, based around, to date, six of the nine original Monkee albums. A key figure in the archival and detective work for these projects was Bill Inglot. I discussed the projects in a long and involved conversation with him. (The full interview forms appendix two of this book.)

> Rhino were initially licensing the material from their business successors; they licensed the *Monkee Business* picture-disc from them. Possibly 1982. That began on Rhino's end with initial interest that I had suggested. We began an official licensing in Monkees albums in 1985 and it happened fortuitously before the explosion of the 1986 Monkees revival. Rhino was in a very good spot because we had already licensed the records. We had LP and cassette rights but initially licensors wouldn't grant CD rights in the CD era. So the first CD was *Missing Links*, I think, since the others didn't come until Rhino actually acquired the catalogue. We put all the items out eventually over the course. A few did come out prior to the '86 tour but the others came out during, because that was a time when The Monkees were on the charts. In the States they were massive; they were literally everywhere. I saw a show in Philadelphia and they filled the house with thousands of people. They were doing two shows a day at an outdoor venue. It was an explosion, unprecedented and unexpected by everybody.

As Inglot observes, Rhino was indeed in a very good spot, but that was by choice more than luck – they already knew the value of this 'product' and were in a way waiting for everybody else to catch up with them. When those huge audiences of 1986–89 did finally show up, Rhino had the goods they were after. Anyone who has embarked upon an archival project of any sort, be it family history or the forgotten recordings of a pop band, know that the first key task is to track down your resources, and that might involve not quite knowing where to look first, since the material was stored in 'all sorts of different places':

> It was distributed by RCA Records in the States. The tapes themselves, well some of them, were still in the RCA vault, because of the licensing agreement; some of them ended up with the publishers because it was kind of an all-in deal. It was a division of Columbia Pictures. We found some things in the publisher's office, so to speak, and the RCA vault once the deal ended, that were transferred over to Bell Records, which was the successor to Colgems.

The ensuing detective work involved, at the outset, a lot of phone calls:

> We had an advantage because the material owners – we had a lot of co-operation from people in their offices. We went to publishers, we went to RCA; we had to make sure they knew we weren't just people off the street calling in, we wanted to do business with them. That continues to this day; most of the music catalogue is owned by the Warner Music Group, which now owns Rhino. We're still finding materials, because The Monkees had a lot of unissued material from that time. One of the strengths of not always being the band that was playing in the record was that tons of stuff was cut. You could argue that The Monkees had one of the deepest wells in terms of unissued material, with what Rhino did and what Rhino Handmade did. We put out three discs of unreleased material, a live record, and other bits and pieces as the

> reissue program went along. The majority of the material from The Monkees era was recorded on tape for the most part, and then in late '67 they moved over to eight-track on the one-inch. The Monkees had their demise as an entity at the beginning of what would be the two-inch sixteen-track, there were very few Monkees recordings on that. Most studios were getting two-inch machines around 1970, and The Monkees weren't such a force by then.

Inglot's memory of the gumshoe work in finding the tapes and identifying them is testament to both the obscurity of much of this material – forgotten in publisher's archives for decades – and also the sheer volume of it.

> The Monkees were an anomaly because initially they were recording tracks recorded by others, then they became more involved with their own records, then they became insolvent, and then they became *individually* involved; you had Mike Nesmith recording songs but there wasn't another Monkee within 1500 miles of him. So you had these things kind of splitting off in different directions; a number on a box could represent either the group version of a song or a solo version without the other Monkees.

This abundance and mystery is what an archivist – and for that matter, a fan – dreams of in relation to projects like this, and stands to reason in some ways. There were four musicians with more or less unlimited studio time, so after they took over their own musical production from the fast-working sessioneers of LA and NYC the work rate actually quadrupled rather than diminished. Rhino's careful management of the archive has gradually let light in on this hidden period of pop's development in the late 60s. I wondered how Inglot saw the relationship between Rhino and The Monkees being set:

> Certainly, we had a year that was phenomenal in terms of sales and

> profile. We had seven or nine spots in the Top 200 at the time. Rhino helped raise The Monkees' profile and their acceptability in the precincts of the non-believers. But Rhino was a company who had an incredible amount of good luck around that catalogue; it was a very fortuitous decision to license the rights to it. For us to sell 100,000 copies of an album back then was great, we would break out the party hats, and The Monkees did that for us. It was a priority because it grew the company and enabled Rhino to license things from other companies. We lived or died on licensing. So Arista were doing us a solid deal by not pulling away the licensing rights once it was successful again, or because they got a big record out of it. Everybody came out pretty good by the end of the deal. I don't think there were any losers. Unusually. But eventually the success of the label was spotted by the industry and things started to change for the label, if not for the Monkees output.

As Inglot notes, Rhino was eventually absorbed into the mainstream when its success became irresistible to the majors, and the imprint became part of the Warner Music Group stable in 1999 – with, as Bronson reports in his book, the man who started the company finding himself ushered out of the frame. The label had certainly come in from the cold, but at a cost to its soul.

As far as The Monkees went, it was to some degree Monkee business as usual, because there had rarely been a year since 1965 where the band's identity, soul, or legacy had not been scrapped over by lawyers and copyright holders. The 2006/7 Digipak doubles were the first output under the new regime and Andrew Sandoval, advantaged in the takeover by not being so closely involved with the labels' original identity, was firmly in charge; a safe pair of hands for the parent corporation, Monkee fans, and the band. In many ways it was good news for the diehards – a group like WMG can absorb losses on bespoke products like the Handmade boxed sets, facilitating their release – but the requirement to keep the product coming, quite different from Bronson's own playful idea of keeping the kettle boiling by 'creating Monkee events' every few months, has put the pressure on the archival team and risked saturating even the collector's market.

The story of Rhino in some ways echoes that of The Monkees themselves; entered into with a light heart and a passion for the work, soon encountering the monolithic realities of the culture industries, and needing to find a method of negotiating a passage through, with one's original vision intact, to avoid being absorbed to the point of disappearing.

A question that has played across my mind while writing this book seems at first a straightforward one: how much has Rhino done for The Monkees, and how much have The Monkees done for Rhino? It is a relationship between act and label that is most unusual, perhaps even unique. It's certainly one that has only become possible with the passage of time, so that a label can acquire the rights to – that is, own – the works of an act en bloc. It also required a shift in fortunes for that act – acquired relatively affordably, and later accruing in value.

That was Rhino's good fortune. The Monkees were, in turn, fortunate indeed to have their back catalogue – indeed their entire history – taken up and treated with such respect by Rhino, when no other company in the business seemed to be interested. Given the elevation of the Rhino brand from Bill Stout's original Rocker Rhino to a pseudonym for Warner Strategic Marketing, it's clear that few indies have undergone such a transformative success, and it's equally so that The Monkees have made a huge contribution to that success. Like The Monkees themselves, the relationship is a one-off, forged from the unique circumstances that seem to surround the group at every turn. In their own way, Harold Bronson, Richard Foos, Bill Inglot, and Andrew Sandoval are as important to the story of The Monkees as Bob Rafelson, Bert Schneider, Don Kirshner, and Ward Sylvester, for without their contributions, the story would have turned out very differently. God Save Rhino!

CONCLUSION

THERE'S A GOOD TIME COMIN' ON

In this concluding section we look at The Monkees' most recent returns to the TV and recording studios – the two worlds into which they were born, but never quite fully belonged to – with a consideration of 2016's *Good Times!* album and, first, their final piece of television.

> Who knows what would have happened if Peter hadn't quit on that day, if we had kept recording, kept on filming, kept on Monkeeing around? It's a moot point. Maybe, somewhere in a parallel universe, there are four other versions of us, still living in that funky beach house, married overweight, balding, bringing up teenage children who wear Reeboks and are into rap.

When Micky wrote this in his 1993 memoir, he couldn't have guessed that within four years he would be working with the original group once again on a reprise of the television show that resembles his idea here quite closely. They are not married and bringing up kids, but they are middle aged, some are balding, their weight in check, and all still living in that funky beach house – trying to adjust to the changed circumstances while remaining the same. The 1997 television special *Hey Hey It's The Monkees* was written and directed by Nesmith, and it bears the marks of *Elephant Parts* almost as much as it does the original show. We discover the band still in their original house, still playing and trying to get gigs but explicitly conscious that they are in a television show, with frequent references to plotlines they had already used. The show aspires to swerve a plot but delivers one not unlike that of 'Here Come The Monkees', which we might take to be deliberate. It also functions as a long ad for their new album, including a very funny spoof of cable shopping stations where Peter plugs his range of psychic makeup while guest Davy mercilessly plugs *Justus* and Micky poses as Martha Stewart. There are some rewards for expert Monkee spotters, such as John Brockman coming to the door as a lawyer and Bill Martin playing a guide in a tour of their refrigerator. The doorbell chimes play the Monkees theme.

As for the music, there is an as far as I know unreleased re-recording of the 'Theme', and we hear a nicely jazz-funk'd-up little arrangement of 'For Pete's Sake' as Tork and Nesmith reprise the 'running to the sea and running away again' gag from the original series. Featured songs to get their own standalone videos are 'You And I', 'Circle Sky', and 'Regional Girl'; the first is on ice, the second is festooned with television sets of various vintages, and the last sees the four incongruously placed among moody Gap-ad-style models. None of them are particularly good. The last part of the show is a medley of greatest hits at the party they'd been booked to play, and this is what they'd been begged to do by the host and his 'princess' daughter. It is the real group really playing, and it sounds good, even for a medley.

The Monkeemobile is souped up as a low rider of the sort seen in *Yo! MTV Raps*-style videos of the time (though it looks exactly the same) and has the added bonus of a car radio able to 'switch between dimensions'. The fifth dimension on the car radio is 'the 60s dimension', and that's surely not accidental, being the title of an album by The Byrds, a band with whom The Monkees shared a producer and session musicians. In that little clip, parts of the *Head* 'Circle Sky' scene and the Monkeemobile feature prominently.

There are lots of little treats for the keen of ear. Davy drops the album title in to a discussion about revising the stage act – 'You don't really think we need a gimmick, do we, after all these years of being just us?' – and a child who weeps on the beach has a pet pig who in all likelihood is called Porky. To cheer him up, Davy sings 'Gonna Build A Mountain', his solo spot number from the '67 tours, and the kid cries harder. These are all deliberate little nods, but there is some spontaneity, too. As they sit on a beach discussing plans for the gig, Micky looks at the plastic crab he is holding and starts to wail, 'He's dead, he's dead!' and puts his head on Mike's shoulder. It's funnier than it sounds. Nesmith smiles at someone off camera, and Tork looks at Micky and slowly begins to laugh out loud in what is clearly an unscripted moment that shows some of the real improv spirit that helped the show catch fire in the early days. The repeated 'lizard sunning itself on a rock' is a dig at the non sequiturs and also the way the audition and interview segments were used on the original shows to bring them up to the required running time. It's also a hefty *Elephant Part*, as is the 'Antarctica' sequence and the goofing around with the laugh track. The pad is the same but different, retaining the spiral staircase (which Peter is seen coming down in the opening shot); there is the raised platform where they rehearse; the door is still to the left of the screen, and posters and found road signs adorn the wall.

Next to a cartoonish moose head on the wall are two framed pictures, one approximating Rene Magritte's *La Trahison Des Images* (*The Treachery Of Images*) from 1928–29. A picture of a tobacco pipe above the text 'Ceci n'est pas une pipe' ('This is not a pipe'), it's probably the Belgian surrealist's most famous work. What's interesting is that Nesmith has created a mash-up of the pipe and text from this painting and placed them on the background of another Magritte work, *Le Faux Miroir* (*The False Mirror*, 1928), which shows blue skies and clouds in the shape of an eye looking straight out of the painting. This has obvious connotations for The Monkees – made for TV, to be looked at – but also for the viewer. The artwork is looking at you. It also puts us in mind of the evil eye that hypnotises from the television screens of 'The Frodis Caper'.

Right next to this is another picture with the same blue-sky-and-clouds background; on it are pictures of The Monkees, the four face shots from the end titles of the TV show, with the text 'this is not a band'. It's only on screen for a moment, just shown to us and then left without comment or over-emphasis, but it's a provocative and erudite touch. The titles of the paintings do as much work in making the point as the images themselves. Despite what we are encouraged to think in 'Circle Sky', what we see we should not always believe, for images can be treacherous. The false mirror also connects us to the television and the use of the untrustworthy reflected images in *Head* and the Mylar sleeve of the film's soundtrack album.

Though I like very much the juxtaposition and the proposition set up by this little moment, I also take issue with part of it. It will depend on your view of the artwork, but to my eye The Monkees *are* a band, and the evidence is all around us, but I also understand the point made here – they are not 'more' or 'less' than a 'real' band. They are something else altogether. Like a work of art in the age of mechanical reproduction, they are entirely unique yet were also infamously 'manufactured', and by definition should therefore be infinitely reproducible. Yet that has not proved to be the case. Somehow, somewhere in the process, the base metal was turned to gold. The Monkees are a rare case of pop-cultural alchemy, involved in the ore of everything, yet distilled out into something entirely of their own; just them. Hey Hey, They're The Monkees!

GOOD TIMES?

In 2008, Glen Campbell, former Monkee session man and hit-maker extraordinaire, issued an album. Back on his spiritual home of Capitol Records, it was called, despite being his 60th long player, *Meet Glen Campbell.* It was produced and arranged by Julian Raymond, who in interviews before the album's release was reported as saying that the goal had been to make a 'real' Glen Campbell record. Listening to the tracks he produced for Glen, we can take that to mean a careful reconstruction of the kind of arrangement we find on Campbell's classic sides of the late 60s and early 70s, often on songs written by Jimmy Webb – intensely melodic but with a strongly melancholic wash, particularly in the strings. This model was applied to the songs chosen for the project, and indeed it does sound like a 'real' classic-era Glen Campbell album – all the musical signifiers are there – but one rebooted and made contemporary. It's the kind of album a Campbell fan would want him to make, and by putting himself in the hands of expert fans like Raymond, the two met in the middle. This is not exclusive to Glen – Brian Wilson and Cheap Trick are two other American musical institutions who have recently benefitted from reinventions such as this. The resulting records might be described as victory lap albums: the elder statesmen of pop being re-energised and directed back to source by their younger admirers and colleagues.

So it was with 2016's new Monkees album, *Good Times!* That it exists at all is cause for celebration and, as a less-partial friend said to me, 'It's so much better than it needed to be.' It was produced arranged and delivered by Adam Schlesinger of the band Fountains Of Wayne, a man with impeccable credentials for the job, with a CV covering movies, TV, and theatre music as well as his own band's output. He also wrote the title song for the underrated one-hit-wonder movie *That Thing You Do* with Tom Hanks. By any index, Mr Schlesinger knows what he is doing.

It's unlikely that anyone would claim that *Pool It!* or *Justus* rank in the upper reaches of Monkee albums, most notably because they faced the dilemma of their times – what does a new Monkee record in 1987 or 1997 sound like? *Good Times!* gets around this difficulty by setting out from the very beginning to be a conscious re-creation of the musical elements that made the original records so appealing and popular; it is a true victory-lap album, and if it does prove to be the valedictory record then it suits the role well. Crucially, all four are involved – Davy comes back to us on the issued-on-a-real-album-at-last 'Love To Love', one of the clutch of Neil Diamond Monkee tunes that was first recorded in 1967 and then set aside after 'the great revolt'. Like John Lennon's contributions to 'Free As A Bird' and 'Real Love' from the Beatle anthologies of the 90s, Davy's original vocal is woven into a boosted production, and he is joined by Dolenz and Tork vocals recorded in 2015.

The other revived oldie is Boyce & Hart's 'Whatever's Right', recorded in the flurry of activity in July 1966 and left without a vocal until Micky stepped up to the microphone for this album. The presence of this song on the album is in itself part of the richness and intertextuality of the record, as it keeps up the tradition of 'real' Monkee albums always having a Tommy and Bobby tune on there (the exceptions being the six-song *Head* and the reprised 'ev'ry stinkin' little note' philosophy of *Justus*). The title track is similarly allied to The Monkees' story – 'Good Times' is one of the songs Harry Nilsson presented as a demo for Colgems's consideration in 1967 from which 'Cuddly Toy' was chosen and kick-started his career. Dolenz joins his old comrade on the track, and via the miracles of technology they sing the song together – 'Go on Harry!' calls Micky at the song's climax, delighted to be reunited with him. I've heard something like that cry before, at Manchester's Royal Northern College of Music in October 2012, when Michael Nesmith encored with 'Thanx For The Ride' and, as the sample of O.J. 'Red' Rhodes's pedal steel solo rang out across the room, Michael called off-mic to no one and to everyone, 'Oh, there he is!' In both cases, it's humane and moving to hear. Peter finally gets to sing a song for *Easy Rider* – having had his own song 'Flower Child' rejected for inclusion in the movie back in '69 – as he takes the vocal over the backing track for 'Wasn't Born To Follow', recorded in 1968 and debuted on 2010's *The Birds, The Bees & The Monkees* boxed set. The song benefits from the wisdom of his years, sounding out from the far side of experience rather than imagining its leading edge.

Beyond such time-travelling, bespoke songs commissioned for the project are in their varying ways highly enjoyable – Schlesinger himself contributes 'Our Own World' and a co-write with Dolenz, who turns in a self-reflective piece employing a phrase he has been using onstage and in interviews for years: 'I Was There (And I'm Told I Had A Good Time)'. Rivers Cuomo sails close to the Brill breeze with 'She Makes Me Laugh', while Andy Partridge of XTC revisits his Dukes Of Stratosphear stylebook with the irresistible 'You Bring The Summer'. A second Partridge tune, 'Love's What I Want' (with Attraction Pete Thomas on drums), deserved better than to be tucked away among the scattering of extra tracks across various downloads and retailer-specific editions. 'Death

Of An Accidental Hipster', a loose co-write between Noel Gallagher and Paul Weller, just about qualifies as a song, but is better on texture than on structure. It's well sung by Nesmith, with assists from Micky and Coco Dolenz. Even Jeff Barry is here, with his Joey Levine co-write 'Gotta Give It Time'.

The album's surprise hit for me is 'Me & Magdalena', written by Ben Gibbard of Death Cab For Cutie – who took their name from a song performed by The Bonzo Dog Doo Dah Band (before they lost their Doo Dah) in the strip club sequence of The Beatles' own *Head*-like enigma, *Magical Mystery Tour*. Sung by Nesmith with help from Dolenz, it is more suggestive of an album like his own *Tantamount To Treason Vol. 1* than any Monkee record, but it is easily the best commissioned tune on the album. Hearing their voices lock together again (as on 'The Girl I Knew Somewhere' or 'Auntie's Municipal Court') also hints at what great music they could still make whenever they chose to get together.

Of the self-penned material, Peter Tork contributes 'Little Girl' (unrelated to Micky's tune of that title on *The Monkees Present*), which is a folk-pop beauty and could easily have been demoed at the sessions with Lance Wakely in 1968. Nesmith gives us 'I Know What I Know', a song originally made available as part of a download-only album *Around The Sun* via his website in 2012. Somewhat lost in the extra-track penumbra are Peter's version of his brother Nick Thorkelson's 'A Better World', Micky's vocal on Zach Rogue's 'Terrifying', and a busier variant version of 'Me & Magdalena'.

Good Times! was given a huge shove by Rhino, and so it should; the label had virtually wished it into being. The media blitz and the launch parties – all with a retro-eye on how it was done back in '66 – did a good job, and the album was their highest charting new release since 1968, reaching number 14 on the *Billboard* chart and number 29 in the UK.

A series of 'singles' came from the album – although not in a physical format – and were promoted with impressively witty and semiotically rich animated video clips. 'You Bring The Summer', directed by Jonathan Nesmith and Susan Holloway, goes to town with visual references to the band's history, and 'She Makes Me Laugh' reproduces the style of the

Monkee cartoon strips from the comics and annuals of their early days. It's ironic that these clips in some ways finally make Archies of them, but more truthfully they show the integrity of the band's representation across the 50 years, connecting the present with the past. The cover art for the album does something similar, festooned as it is with charming sketches of key objects in the band's story – the Monkeemobile, Gene Ashman's eight-button shirt – but also less obvious ones such as the flying saucer (referencing 'The Frodis Caper') and the unicycle. The value of listening is reinforced by the meaning of seeing, taking pleasure from picking out the references and enjoying the continuity of the symbols associated with the band. A victory lap album it may be, but it is one which deserves its billing.

The 50 years of The Monkees' lifespan is remarkable in itself for a group originally conceived to catch a wave that many industry insiders confidently predicted would simply be the next fad, replaced by something else in six months to a year. That's how the industry had always worked up until then. What their story also shows us is that 'manufacturing' pop music in the way that theatre or TV can be managed is an entirely unpredictable pursuit – it wasn't just any old four that made the magic happen: it was *those four*. Just as it was with The Beatles or R.E.M., groups who developed organically in the traditional way. The enduring success of The Monkees is proof that it cannot be faked. If it happens, it makes it real. So, regardless of how they came to be put together, it was the individuals who made it happen – the corporate machinery could have made it work in the short term, but it was the mixture of Dolenz, Jones, Nesmith, and Tork that made it become something else – something that has been taken on and made real by their fans over the five decades since the group's conception. Even attempts to undermine the band's own success and internal sensibilities, such as *Head* itself, have eventually only added to the lustre. The Monkees truly are the exception to just about every rule of the culture industries, and for that reason their career is as important to the history of popular music as any of the established founding mythologies.

It was television that first made The Monkees and, alongside the enthusiasm of their loyal fan following, it has kept their flame alive with successive generations of viewers discovering the joy of the show and, through this, the glorious pantechnicon of the music. The two cannot, finally, be separated, and in *Head* they attempted to find a way out of that 'black box' only to discover that, like the blues, or *Finnegan's Wake*, or the groove of a record, the end leads back to the beginning. In the 1997 TV special, their last bespoke piece of TV to date, Micky ponders out loud as the Monkeemobile heads for home one last time:

> I wonder if the general public knows that TV shows like ours never die, they just go on and on even though they're not being broadcast?

He is right. Even when it is not on the air, *The Monkees* does indeed just go on and on in the hearts and minds of their fans, and the music and moving images they made – caught in their prime – are immortalised on tape or disc. Having never quite fully existed onscreen or on record, they can never quite fully disappear, either. There's no one like The Monkees.

APPENDIX ONE

HERE WE COME

FOUR QUESTIONS ASKED ABOUT THE MONKEES BY DR. PETER MILLS FOR A BOOK HE IS WRITING ON THE SUBJECT OF THE MONKEES.

BY BILL DRUMMOND

WHAT ARE YOUR MEMORIES OF SEEING THE TV SHOW, AND HAVE YOU SEEN *HEAD*? IF YOU HAVE, WHAT DO YOU THINK OF IT?

Some context first:

1966 is the high water mark of Pop Music.

Or it is if you turned 13 years old in 1966. For me the sound of records made and released in 1966 were as close to perfection as pop records could ever be. At that stage there were no bands that I swore allegiance to. For me it was all about the sound and the record. And it had to be a seven-inch 45. I had no interest in long players, or where the band came from, or what they looked like, or what their last record sounded like. As for a band's influences or what direction they might be heading, I did not care. And I did not care who had written the song. And had no idea what producers were. Or even record companies.

What I can be certain about, at this distance in time, I was not bothered about The Beatles. To me The Beatles sounded dull and old fashioned, compared to The Rolling Stones, The Byrds, The Animals, The Small Faces, The Spencer Davis Group, The Kinks, The Lovin' Spoonful, The Yardbirds, The Who, The Troggs. I had also not seen either of the Beatles films, *A Hard Day's Night* or *Help*.

It was not until 'Penny Lane' / 'Strawberry Fields' was released in February 1967 that I fell under the spell of The Beatles.

Some more context:

Back in 1966 at teatime on Saturdays we would have the TV on. At 5:15 there would be *Dr. Who*. This was then followed by the national news, then the local news and then … I can't remember. But as 1966 turned the corner into 1967, *Dr. Who* was followed by a new series called *The Monkees*. I watched it because it was on. This programme did not inspire my imagination like *The Man From U.N.C.L.E.*, or *The Avengers*, or even *The Saint*.

But The Monkees were on, so I watched it.

I must have watched almost every episode as they were aired. That was unless we were away somewhere, staying at my granny's or off camping. There was nothing about *The Monkees* that particularly inspired me, but I would watch it. I knew they were not 'real' like the bands that I saw play on *Top Of The Pops* each Thursday evening. And I certainly knew they were nothing like The Beatles, who by the spring of 1967 I thought were the greatest thing in the world.

But I kept watching.

At some point I even saw *Head*, but I don't know where or how. It may have been when I first started art school in September 1970. It left no lasting impression on me.

I have never seen an episode of *The Monkees* since. Or re-watched *Head*. Until last night that is – but I will get to that later.

But over the decades I have thought about The Monkees, almost every week since. They have been a continual reference point in my head. Why this is the case I have no fixed reason. If I try to reason this at this distance, I may come up with some bogus attempt to intellectualise something that has no real substance – so I won't bother.

There is also something else that I do most weeks. That is quote, even if only to myself, a line that Davy Jones said at some point: 'Hey, don't pick on me, just because I am small.' I have just put the line into Google and nothing came up, so maybe I just imagined him saying it back in 1967, and I have been saying it ever since.

A LOT OF THE DISCUSSIONS AROUND THE MONKEES – OFTEN A SOURCE OF DISAGREEMENT BETWEEN THE FOUR INDIVIDUALS THEMSELVES – ARE TO DO WITH NOTIONS OF LEGITIMACY AND AUTHENTICITY. WHAT DO YOU THINK ABOUT THESE IDEAS OF AUTHENTICITY AND MANUFACTURE (OR THE REAL AND THE FAKE) IN MUSIC, AND IN YOUR VIEW WERE THE MONKEES AS A TV SHOW AND A POP GROUP 'REAL' OR 'FAKE' OR SOME OTHER THING?

Further context:

By the late 60s, I was into all the British blues bands – Chicken Shack, Fleetwood Mac, John Mayall, etc. They were for real. They meant it. They did what they did because they believed in it. It was not about having hits and being on *Top Of The Pops*. I was 16; this very much mattered to me as a 16-year-old lad.

Peter McMahon was a close friend of mine; he got into the band Creedence Clearwater Revival. As far as he was concerned they meant it more than any band in the world. They sang about things like bayous and levees, and riverboat steamers. They were for real, as real as you could get.

And to this day Creedence Clearwater Revival still sound real to me. But of course there was nothing real about either those British blues bands or Creedence Clearwater Revival. Those British blues bands that I so idolised were suburban lads from the Home Counties in England aspiring to play music made by middle-aged black men from Chicago who had been making their records back in the mid 50s.

As for Creedence Clearwater Revival, they were from San Francisco attempting to make music from some imagined version of the Mississippi Delta in Louisiana.

By the time I was 18 in 1971, I had lost interest in rock bands. All bands seemed to be faking it. They were all pretending to be something they were not. It was then that I started getting into black R&B records released on strange looking record labels from far-flung corners of the USA. These records sounded 'authentic' to me ears. This was for 'real' and it was now. 'Clean Up Woman' by Betty Wright was as 'legitimate' and 'authentic' as you could get, according to my ears.

Then, in October 1975, I went to see the band from Canvey Island in Essex called Dr. Feelgood at the Liverpool Stadium. I don't know why or how, but I went on my own. I had no idea what this Dr. Feelgood were going to be like. But they totally blew me away. They ripped the place apart.

At the age of 22, I must have been at least five years older than most of the audience. Dr. Feelgood were as 'authentic'-sounding as a band could be. But as a 22-year-old, I could see nothing about them was 'real'. They were a total fantasy of a band. A band pretending to be from another era that had never existed. Part Kray Twins, part something from the south side of Chicago, but mainly something that was just made up.

Without intellectually seeing this through, I knew from then on the whole thing about bands was they were never actually 'authentic' in the way that I maybe once had wanted bands to be. It was the inauthenticity of a band that made them what they were. The way they carried off their inauthenticity. The inauthenticity that they chose to weave. And the way they made it work with their music.

Within 12 months or so of watching Dr. Feelgood at the Liverpool Stadium I had seen both The Ramones and The Clash at Eric's, a club in Liverpool. Both of these bands were totally fantasy bands. Both pretending to be something from an era that had never existed and a place in the world that could only ever exist in your imagination.

It was the night that I saw The Clash play at Eric's that I decided to form a band. And I knew before we wrote our first song, we were never going to be for real – that 'authenticity' was just a made up thing. But it was that made up thing that somehow reached deeper into what it was to be human, to be an artist, to be alive, that really counted. We called ourselves Big In Japan, because it was a lie. Within a week we had played our first gig.

And I knew that whatever that was, it did not have to come directly from the band. It could come from all sorts of directions and people, but filtered through the band. The band – all bands – were merely the conduit. The band existed to be something for others to project onto and through.

It was sometime around then that The Monkees started to loom large in my understanding of the power of not only pop music but the band itself as an art form. As a medium. And that it was not a medium that could be used by the lonely artists struggling in their attic to be as true as possible. That somehow the medium of a pop group allowed for all sorts of individuals coming from all sorts of different directions with all sorts of agendas, to make something of creative value. Even if the proper art world thought it just to be throw away 'commercial' trash.

As I said earlier, I never went back and re-watched the Monkees television programmes. That was not possible anyway. This was in the days before VHS, and no one was re-running them at that time on television. It was all just in my memory. Today, obviously we can watch anything we want on YouTube and have our instant opinions. This is a different world. It is now easy to have opinions about anything that has ever been filmed or recorded. Back in 1977, all you had was your corroded memories of tea times on Saturdays ten years earlier.

I knew The Monkees were as manufactured as a band could be. They wrote none of their greatest songs. Hardly played on any of their hits. Did not write the lines they spoke in the television programmes. But somehow the overall thing had a power – a force. I knew The Monkees were great art, even though there was no one artist behind them with a burning vision. I knew it was all about ratings and exploitation and lowest common denominator and Davy Jones being cute for the prepubescent girls.

We as Big In Japan would talk about The Monkees in the van on the way to gigs. While other bands wanted to be Pere Ubu or Talking Heads, we wanted to be The Monkees – not actually The Monkees, but something that was distilled from them.

I have just put 'Big In Japan' and 'The Monkees' into Google to see what would come up. What I found straightaway on the Wikipedia page for Big In Japan was the following quote from our singer, Jayne Casey:

> We were all a bit too eccentric at a time when punk was quite

> macho and clear cut … a bit too much for people to handle. We always wanted to be like The Monkees or something. We wanted to be a cartoon …

Without any of us thinking this through, my guess is that we all knew that for the generation of bands and musicians that had been plying their trade in the first half of the 70s, The Monkees would have represented everything they hated most about the music business. Thus for us, the generation that came through with punk, we would have taken the opposite standpoint and embraced our childhood and early teen memories of watching *The Monkees* at Saturday tea times. We would like the fact that name checking The Monkees would piss off the old guard.

Then a couple of years later in 1979 the film *The Great Rock'n'Roll Swindle* came out. A film where Malcolm McLaren wanted to portray the Sex Pistols as somehow totally manufactured, and himself as the evil Svengali. In the film, the Sex Pistols perform a version of The Monkees song '(I'm Not Your) Steppin' Stone'.

There is so much that I both loathed and loved about that film, but the fact that it had the Pistols performing a Monkees song was and still is brilliant. There is no way any band in the first half of the 70s that wanted themselves to be taken seriously would have dared perform a song made famous by The Monkees.

It was around this time (1978/79), that I started to study how classic pop songs were structured. And these were not the songs written by bands or legitimate singer songwriters. No, these were the songs written by the craftsmen that had worked in the likes of the Brill Building in New York. I was also rediscovering again for myself the Phil Spector version of pop music. In 1978 I had bought a double album of all his greatest hits from the early 60s up to 'River Deep Mountain High' by Ike & Tina Turner. I broke all of these songs down. The chord structures; how the hooks worked; what the middle-eight did; and of course the sound of the snare and handclaps.

Although I had never been bothered about Carole King the early-70s singer-songwriter, I was totally in love with her previous incarnation as part of the songwriting team Goffin & King. I took each of their greatest hits from 'Will You Still Love Me Tomorrow' all the way through and deconstructed them. And of course they wrote a number of songs that were performed by The Monkees, including 'Pleasant Valley Sunday' (but more of that later). I even covered a version of their 'Goin' Down' on my *The Man* album in 1986.

But more important to The Monkees than Goffin & King were Boyce & Hart. Tommy Boyce and Bobby Hart wrote most of and produced all of The Monkees' hits. I might not have been as obsessed with Boyce & Hart as I was with Gerry Goffin and Carole King, but I must have broken down the chord sequences of every song they had written for The Monkees and then stored those chord structures somewhere in my head for future use.

After the failure of both Big In Japan and the subsequent failure of Lori & The Chameleons, I decided to concentrate my energies on managing and producing Echo & The Bunnymen.*

Echo & The Bunnymen were all about being 'authentic' in a very post-punk way. I don't think the Bunnymen and I ever openly or even privately discussed the great artistic merits of The Monkees. But somewhere in my head, I think, I thought I was managing a version of The Monkees.

For me a band had to be lot more than just four blokes that played music together. They had to have an attitude and outlook on the world. Something more than just touring and doing interviews and making records that got good reviews in the music papers. Having a pretty front man and a moody guitarist was not enough.

Behind the four members of the Bunnymen onstage, there were at least half a dozen of us putting all our creative energy into making them the best band that we could. It is not for the audience to know or understand this and maybe not even the band, let alone music

* Lori & The Chameleons were a studio band that I had with my colleague in many things Dave Balfe. We only released two singles. In my head we were some sort of futuristic Shadow Morton producing *Past, Present, And Future.*

journalists, but without that combined effort and belief and hunger, these things don't work. And that is why solo projects of band members hardly ever work.

In early 1981, we made a short film with the Bunnymen called *Shine So Hard.* It was a mixture of concert footage from the Pavilion Gardens in Buxton, Derbyshire, and footage of each of the four members of the band doing strange things on their own. In my head this was a sort of post-punk version of an episode of *The Monkees*.

At that time the Bunnymen rented a very large top floor flat of a massive Victorian house on the edge of Sefton Park in Liverpool. For me this was also the post-punk equivalent of the Monkees house on the oceanfront of Malibu.

The Monkees were maybe a manufactured group, in the sense they were all jobbing actors looking for a break. They all signed contracts to play parts. Thus from the puritanical idea of what a group is to 'proper', 'serious' musicians and music fans, they were 'fake'. But if you take a few steps back, you see and experience something that is not only very 'real', but also truly great art.

In a sense they were the flip of the coin that had The Velvet Underground on the other side. Both were part of a bigger picture. Both part of others visions, be that Don Kirshner or Andy Warhol. You could not have had one without the other. One was California and the other New York. And both of them had their greatest and most creative years at identical times – 1966 to 1968.

Both bands existed outside of the whole Haight-Ashbury / Woodstock thing of the mid-to-late 60s.

And both bands were hated or derided by 'real' musicians of the era.

Something else that I cannot pass without making my prejudices known – as far as I am concerned, Micky Dolenz has to have one of the greatest pop singing voices of all time.

And also – that aspect of the human condition that is drawn to the notion of the tortured genius being the true purveyor of great art, is the same human condition that is drawn to the charismatic dictator or divine right of kings. That need we have to elevate certain individuals to the pantheon is a weakness we seem not to cure ourselves of. Great art can be born out of the most muddled and compromised of situations with not a genius in sight, in the same way that great governance can be born from the most uncharismatic committee-led governments.

The fact that there was no tortured genius either in the ranks of The Monkees, or somewhere lurking in the background like a Phil Spector or even Joe Meek, removes nothing from the greatness.

ONE THING I LIKE ABOUT THE MONKEES IS HOW THEY SOUGHT TO UNDERMINE THEIR OWN SUCCESS, OR AT LEAST RENEGOTIATE IT ON THEIR OWN TERMS IN PURSUIT OF 'SOMETHING ELSE'. THEY DID THIS INITIALLY BY THE 'PALACE REVOLUTION', WHICH INVOLVED TAKING CONTROL OF THEIR OWN MUSIC, THE SECOND SERIES OF THE TV SHOW, AND LATER WENT OUT OF THEIR WAY TO SHATTER THEIR PUBLIC IMAGE IN *HEAD*. WHAT DO THINK ABOUT SUCH A DELIBERATE UNDOING OF THEIR COMMERCIAL SUCCESS?

As I think I have implied, I have never read anything about The Monkees, not even interviews with them at the time. I had no interest in them as individuals, or their attempts at subsequent careers. I was aware of Mike Nesmith's First National Band but what I heard on the radio sounded as dull as most other white bands of the time. That said, I love his song 'Different Drum' as performed by The Stone Poneys.

Hunter Davies's book on The Beatles is the only band biography that I have ever read. And I read that when it came out in 1968. Reading about bands has never interested me. I don't know why this is the case, because I have spent a lot of time thinking about bands and the way they work and interact with society. It might be that I have never trusted the motivations of music journalists.

I have lied.

I have just remembered that I did read *England's Dreaming* by Jon Savage, but that was because he was a friend.

So their 'palace revolution' is something that I do not know about. I do know that all bands – be they manufactured 'fake' ones or authentic 'real' ones, start to tear apart once they have success. The egos of young successful men almost guarantee this to happen – U2 are the exception that prove the rule. The added burden for a manufactured band is that once they are a couple of years older, they become embarrassed about their 'fakeness'. Their success and cute looks may have impressed the screaming pre-pubescent girls, but once those girls hit 16 or 17, they want 'real' authentic rock stars that write their own songs and play on their own records.

Being Davy Jones in 1969 must have been a really bad thing to have been. There is no way that he could have gone off to form Wings.

Last night I watched the first episode of the first series. This was the first time I had ever watched it or any episode since they were first broadcast in the UK, back in early 1967. Watching it left no major impression. Not even twinges of nostalgia.

I then watched *Head.* This blew me away. Although it is very much of its time – and the sexism was writ large in it – its radicalism and risk-taking leaves *Magical Mystery Tour* by The Beatles standing. It is a work of genius. *Magical Mystery Tour* just looks lazy compared to this; even though 'Porpoise Song' is trying to ape aspects of The Beatles, it is almost done in a knowing post-modern way. That said, I should add I have not seen *Magical Mystery Tour* since it was first broadcast on Boxing Day 1967. Maybe if I were to watch that now, it might 'blow me away' as well.

It is only in watching *Head* last night that I can see how they were party to their own destruction and shattering of their public image. Even Johnny Rotten could not have done that. I can only applaud them, even though the applause is 48 years after the event.

For a great band to be truly great, they must define an epoch, or at least an aspect of an era. Ideally, the epoch should last no longer than a couple of years. To do this they must not outstay their welcome, they must not soldier on, with compromised lineups and tours undertaken to pay mortgages and alimony. It is best that a band to achieve this greatness, they should go out in disastrous style. The Monkees did it with *Head.* Its complete commercial failure set against its artistic aspirations and achievements was the perfect ending for the ultimate manufactured band.

If you were to put *Head* in the ring with *Woodstock* (the movie), *Head* would win every time.

WHY DO SEVERAL KLF/JAMS RECORDINGS SHARE OR HINT AT MONKEES TITLES – 'LAST TRAIN TO TRANCENTRAL', 'PORPOISE SONG', 'HEY HEY WE ARE NOT THE MONKEES', THERE MAY BE OTHERS – AND WHY DID THE KLF WANT TO POINT OUT THAT THEY WERE NOT THE MONKEES RATHER THAN NOT THE BEATLES, BON JOVI, THE ANTI-NOWHERE LEAGUE, NEU, MUD, SUN RA, HANK WILLIAMS ...

I am not in a position to pass comment on the influence of The Monkees on The Justified Ancients of Mu Mu. Or even why we were not The Monkees. But I would like to draw your attention to the fact that you have not asked or passed comment on the fact that The Monkees had a car as part of their overall attitude and public image, as did The Justified Ancients of Mu Mu. We may be the only two bands that have ever existed where their vehicle of choice is central to who and what they are. They had the Monkeemobile, we had the JAMsmobile. The other thing you fail to mention is that we both had classic, era-defining signature riffs. Theirs was the guitar riff to 'Last Train To Clarksville'. Ours was the acid riff to 'What Time Is Love?'.

But your question does give me the opportunity to make you aware of something else that I had almost forgotten. In the mid 90s, my colleague Zodiac Mindwarp and myself, after attempting to place an icon of Elvis Presley at the top of the world, ended up in Helsinki inventing a singer-songwriter called Kristina Bruuk. This is not the time and place to explain all of the drama and tragedies of her sorry life. It is enough to say that she makes Nico seem like Lulu. We recorded a whole album of her 'originals'. We then allowed her to record one cover version of her choosing.

After we returned to the UK, and rumour was out about our adventures, numerous major record companies were keen to sign contracts with us for the fruits of our labours. The last thing I wanted to do was get back involved with the reality of the music business in

London. So we shelved the life's work of Kristina Bruuk. She became a distant and fading memory. I could not name one of the songs we had written for her, let alone the cover version.

Then last month I got an email from Helsinki. It was from one of the musicians that we had worked with over there on the sessions. He wanted to know if I had heard what we had done recently. I had not heard anything since we left the Helsinki studio back in late 1996.

Via the wonders of WeTransfer he sent me all 14 tracks. I played them on my iPhone speaker. I was staggered by them. When it came to the last track it was the cover version, and what should it be other than 'Pleasant Valley Sunday'.

This version of this song is the last song that I have ever gone into a studio to record afresh. It is also the bleakest record I have ever made.

Bill Drummond is an artist, musician, writer, and record producer best known for his work with The KLF.

APPENDIX TWO

ARCHIVAL ADVENTURER: BILL INGLOT

HOW DID YOU GET INTO THIS SIDE OF THE MUSIC INDUSTRY?

I got involved with what I did because I was interested in the music. Some people might think an engineer becomes an engineer because of an education or an ability that they have, but for me it was because I was a record collector. I got into the technical side from that record-collecting background. Just being enthusiastic about music. When I got hired at Rhino in the 80s, when they were primarily a reissue label, that was great. Because with engineers it's not so much about the catalogue they're working on; that's not really what they're focused on, they're focused on the technical side. I had an advantage because I was interested in both things. It made it easier for me to do research to find master sources and make sure they were the correct ones to use, and stuff like that. In all those years, that's sort of how I functioned as a content producer. I represented the music as well as the interests of the artists if they weren't in the room. In my mind, even though I was hired on by the label, I was working for the artists.

WHAT WERE YOU DOING BEFORE THE RHINO COMMISSION CAME ALONG?

Prior to that, I was in school, and then the first job I ever had after that was fixing turntables and cassette decks at a TV repair store. I didn't have an audio job before Rhino; it sort of starts with them. There was a Monkee compilation by a record label called Raven, and they did a package called *Monkee Mania* around 1982, a landmark compilation in the Monkees world. It was the first to have tracks and approach their music in a scholarly and reverential way. It had 40 tracks and at the time was widely imported into the States, and I imagine it probably made it over to the UK as well. I did some work on that, mostly just providing them with sources for some things they didn't have tapes for, out of my own record collection. So I was involved with bits and pieces before I was employed by Rhino, but it more or less started in 1982 when I did *Monkeemania*. All the work that's been done on the catalogue has been a constant effort to find better tapes that worked way after I was no longer with the label. I technically left Rhino in mid 2007. There was a large layoff. Some of us were asked to stay on a little bit longer, so even though I was out the door at the end of the year, I was actually made redundant in May.

HOW DID THOSE CHANGES COME ABOUT?

It's hard to say. They come about, as they say. I can't speak for how those decisions were made, but I was there in some form or another for 26 years. Rhino was a place where like-minded enthusiasts could gather. They were the first Stateside label to start initiating their own CD reissues. It was being in the right place at the right time, a place and time where you could have your foot in both disciplines. It was a good run; it'd be nice to still be working. I still do things for them from time to time as a job-for-job contractor. We did a lot of stuff at Rhino; at the peak we were putting out more than 20 titles a month. I wasn't doing expensive work on all of them, but it depended on the project. Most of them went through me in some way, but some were done by other people. It was a very busy time for all of us.

WAS THE FIRST RHINO MONKEES CD THE *MISSING LINKS* VOLUME?

That sounds right. Rhino were initially licensing the material from their business successors; they licensed the *Monkee Business* picture-disc from them. Possibly 1982. That began on Rhino's end with initial interest that I had suggested. We began an official licensing in Monkees albums in 1985 and it happened fortuitously before the explosion of the 1986 Monkees revival. Rhino was in a very good spot because we had already licensed the records. We had LP and cassette rights but initially licensors wouldn't grant CD rights in the CD era. So the first CD was *Missing Links*, I think, since the others didn't come until Rhino actually acquired the catalogue. We put all the items out eventually over the course. A few did come out prior to the '86 tour but the others came out during, because that was a time when The Monkees were on the charts. In the States they were massive; they were literally everywhere. I saw a show in Philadelphia and they filled the house with thousands of people. They were doing two shows a day at an outdoor venue. It was an explosion, unprecedented and unexpected by everybody.

WHERE WAS ALL THE MATERIAL STORED?

It was in all sorts of different places. It was distributed by RCA Records in the States. The tapes themselves: some of them were still in the RCA vault because of the licensing agreement, some of them ended up with the publishers because it was kind of an all-in deal. It was a division of Columbia Pictures. We found some things in the publisher's office, so to speak, and the RCA vault once the deal ended, that were transferred over to Bell Records … those returns are often done in good faith but they very seldom happen because people don't know what they're looking for. There's always five songs that everyone wants and then the others just get forgotten. That makes it hard to find the obscure ones.

HOW DID YOU DO THE DETECTIVE WORK WHEN YOU EMBARKED ON THE PROJECT?

It was all making phone calls. We had an advantage because the material owners – we had a lot of cooperation from people in their offices. We went to publishers, we went to RCA; we had to make sure they knew we weren't just people off the street calling in, we wanted to do business with them. That continues to this day; most of the music catalogue is owned by the Warner Music Group, which now owns Rhino. We're still finding materials, because The Monkees had a lot of unissued material from that time. One of the strengths of not always being the band that was playing on the record was that tons of stuff was cut. You could argue that The Monkees had one of the deepest wells in terms of unissued material, with what Rhino did and Rhino Handmade, etc. We put out three discs of unreleased material, a live record, and other bits and pieces as the reissue programme went along. The majority of the material from the Monkees era was recorded on tape for the most part, and then in late '67 they moved over to eight-track on the one-inch. The Monkees had their demise as an entity at the beginning of what would be the two-inch sixteen-track, there were very few Monkees recordings on that. Most studios were getting two-inch machines around 1970, and The Monkees weren't such a force by then.

WHAT DID THE CHANGEOVER TO MULTITRACK ADD TO THE 'NEW VERSION' OF 'DAYDREAM BELIEVER'?

It gave the advantage of being able to add strings and horns. Eight tracks gave people the power to expand the music without it necessarily being locked in. You could put in that extra guitar without erasing the one that was there before.

WERE THE TAPES IN GOOD CONDITION?

I mean, nothing was sitting under anybody's bed, because The Monkees were affiliated with large corporations who had large storage facilities and offices with shelves. There's no backstory there, really. They weren't deteriorated any more than other tapes from the time. For the most part, RCA handled the tapes, and a fair amount of them were recorded in the RCA studio, which meant there were rules about how things had to be documented. Very often you'll get a record and instead of having the title of the song it'll have the matrix code, like UBZ-3419 or something, so on one level you've got the firm bedrock information that it had to be on the tapes, but it's at the expense of organisational information that might have been there if the studio had not had such rigid rules. When looking through archives and doing archival work, it's a good idea to play everything anyway, which seems a little tedious but sometimes things get put in the wrong boxes because of the 'off the books' stuff that went on because of the rigidity of working with a union studio. They couldn't write them down. You could have a reel containing an acoustic run-through of a song that's just there, but it's not going to appear in the studio's forms and so it's not going to be written on the tape box. Same thing when you assign a matrix or serial number; the way RCA did things, the matrix number didn't disclose takes or versions, just the number for any recording of that song during that period of time. Normally there wasn't any extra detail on the box and that was down to the barebones method they had. You have to play everything. The Monkees were an anomaly because initially they were recording tracks recorded by others, then they became more involved with their own records, then they became insolvent, and then they became *individually* involved; you had Mike Nesmith recording songs, but there wasn't another Monkee within 1,500 miles of him. So you had these things kind of splitting off in different directions; a number on a box could represent either the group version of a song or a solo version without the other Monkees.

WHERE DID YOU LISTEN TO THE TAPES?

Things were very informal. When we did the *Missing Links* record the first time there was kind of a six-year arc between the first one and the last one. The publishers had a small studio, as a lot of them did at the time, and I went through the tapes in there. With Rhino, at that point I started doing packages for them; they were sending me stuff and I was going through them in those studios and in a long-term place called Penguin Recordings, about six miles away. We just did old tapes and went through them. After a while it just becomes work; I never got beside myself, never took things away with me; you don't leave things in the trunk of your car, you have to store them properly. Although while I was at Rhino, you never knew what might turn up on my kitchen table. I'm doing a series of reissues at the moment for a-ha, and it's sort of a side part to this. I'm pulling material from England, because that's where they were somewhat based, despite being signed on with an American record company and being in fact from Norway. In essence, they're not that different to the older tapes, only modern tapes are more difficult to go through. Because past 1987, you start dealing with a lot of things recorded in a digital format, which can literally be so obsolete you can't find a machine to play them on. Whereas other things, from as far back as 1947, you can put in a modern machine and just press play. You just have a lot of formats. If your analogue tape machine breaks, chances are there's someone around to fix it; if your digital machine breaks, you might as well throw it away because you can find a new one on eBay. There just aren't the parts, though it depends on the model. In a lot of ways, then, digital actually presents more challenges than analogue does. They all have their advantages and disadvantages, but it mainly comes down to digital having more specific issues that may need to be addressed, depending on the format.

WHAT WAS THE PROCESS TO CONVERT THE EIGHT-TRACK ONE-INCH TAPE TO A DIGITAL CD FORMAT?

We had the two-track master copy. It's not rocket science there; we just had the original tape we used when we did the boxed set in 1992. We did a mix from the eight-track because I wanted to match the character of the more guitar-dominated version. The idea was to try and match the character of the mono mix and do it in stereo; get a thicker, aggressive guitar sound. So it really depends: if you have multi-tracks, and there's a propensity for cleaning the things up, you do it. In the 30 years I've been doing this, I've wanted to 'mix the world', as it were, but sometimes it's just a thing you have to do. If you were faced with a package or artist and didn't have the masters, your alternative was dubbing from vinyl or doing a mix from the multi. I was generally going to focus on a multi mix and do my best to match it. You tried to do it to serve the music. We would always do better when we had all the tapes; we stopped once we had one of everything. We've done pretty good, but there's still a handful of things we don't have everything of. We don't have the multi of this, we don't have the multi of that. The list has always gotten smaller, but it's never been completely crossed off. It's a fairly small list at this point.

You have the two boxed sets, the '94-ish single-disc album-by-album series, you have the boxes of which I can't speak for the company's plans, but at this point there are probably one or two which will probably still happen. But it's fairly thin on the ground when you look at how much has already been done. With The Monkees, once you get past a certain point, some pieces are formed from outtakes of earlier records. You don't have 40 outtakes from *Pisces Aquarius* because they were reused. It's not like things have ever been intentionally held back. You put out the best product you can at the moment and save 'this one' for next time. That's the philosophy that was applied.

THE WAY YOU DID YOUR WORK HAS TRANSFORMED THE OUTPUT OF THE MONKEES PROJECT AND GILDED THE MUSICAL LEGACY OF THE GROUP. IF IT WEREN'T FOR YOU, SEVERAL RECORDS WOULD STILL BE LANGUISHING IN PUBLISHER'S OFFICES.

It's getting harder to do that kind of research, though. Things are getting more and more buried in all the different companies involved. Things get stored offsite. We're in the era now where nobody wants to use analogue tape; if it's not digitised, they get rid of it. There's a supposition that if it's on analogue, you can't work with it, while it's the other way around, like I said. You get a company who buys a smaller company and when they see they're storing analogue tape, they wonder why they're spending money on keeping this obsolete stuff in downtown Manhattan and suggest it be stored offsite instead in the middle of nowhere for five cents a month. Other things are removed entirely, removed from your eyes ... removed from the researchers; what I call the blind face of the spreadsheet. It's done with good intentions, but it's always going to be an inconvenience; it's a kind of editing. All it takes is one piece of information to be improperly imported or not documented properly and you're blinded because you're not holding that asset in your hand.

WHAT DO YOU THINK THE ASSOCIATION WITH THE MONKEES DID FOR RHINO AS A LABEL?

Certainly, we had a year that was phenomenal in terms of sales and profile. We had seven or nine spots in the Top 200 at the time. Rhino helped raise The Monkees' profile and their acceptability in the precincts of the non-believers. But Rhino was a company who had an incredible amount of good luck around that catalogue; it was a very fortuitous decision to license the rights to it. For us to sell 100,000 copies of an album back then was great; we would break out the party hats, and The Monkees did that for us. It was a priority because it grew the company and enabled Rhino to license things from other companies. We lived or died on licensing. Arista was doing us a solid by not pulling away the licensing rights once it was successful because they got a diamond record out of it. Everybody came out pretty good by the end of the deal. Don't think there were any losers.

OF ALL THE PROJECTS YOU'VE DONE, WHICH WAS THE MOST SATISFYING?

We did a lot of work, so it's hard for me to pick a favourite. The work we did with The Monkees did make a difference, and it was stuff I was happy to be involved with and improve the quality of. The '94 versions are great work by today's standards. We did them right. The first one, to be honest, was done with less effort and materials, but we got better in terms of repertoire and sound as we went along. That's not so much our brilliance as it is having brilliant material to work with. We tried to do a good job. There's tons of documentation of unissued stuff that's kind of a blemish on the record; also, we snuck a few things out on budget packages. They weren't the band's best day. But in the end it's a dialogue between the artist and the record labels. It doesn't mean that your opinions are any more valid than theirs; it's a working relationship, a collaboration, where you win some and lose some.

HOW MUCH INVOLVEMENT DID THE MONKEES HAVE IN THE CURATING OF THE BOXED SETS?

In terms of the repertoire, the answer is they haven't been very involved, and it's the modern way. They participated in some packages and they were aware what was going out, but it's not like they were getting lists of songs and being asked what they thought. They had courtesy approval. Once you work up a relationship with an artist, you gain their confidence; they're not gonna be looking over your shoulder constantly. In terms of the editorial work, they have been involved, but they weren't hanging out in the studio – at least not with anything I was involved in.

Bill Inglot is an audio-archive adventurer. For over three decades he has worked on countless projects to find, evaluate, and often redeem long-forgotten master tapes. His contribution to the Monkees issue/reissue campaign has been immeasurably significant, and Rhino was fortunate to have him on board for so long. His skills were by no means restricted to Monkee projects – a quick sweep through the CDs on a single shelf find his name on albums by R.E.M. and Television, a Stax/Volt boxed set, and even a very enjoyable Bob Newhart anthology. When we spoke, his most recent project was remastering the back catalogue of the Norwegian superior-pop outfit a-ha.

SELECTED DISCOGRAPHY

PRIMARY

The Monkees

The Monkees Colgems/RCA Victor, October 1966
More Of The Monkees Colgems/RCA Victor, January 1967
Headquarters Colgems/RCA Victor, May 1967
Pisces, Aquarius, Capricorn & Jones Ltd. Colgems/RCA Victor, November 1967
The Birds, The Bees & The Monkees Colgems/RCA Victor, April 1968
Head Colgems/RCA Victor, December 1968
Instant Replay Colgems/RCA Victor, February 1969
The Monkees Present Colgems/RCA Victor, October 1969
Changes Colgems/RCA Victor June 1970
Pool It! Rhino, August 1987
Justus Rhino, October 1997
Good Times! Rhino, May 2016

Live albums

Summer 1967 Rhino, July 1987
20th Anniversary Tour Rhino, July 1987
Live! no label, 1994 (sold only at concerts)
2001: Live In Las Vegas no label, 2001 (sold only at concerts)
Summer 1967: The Complete U.S. Concert Recordings Rhino, 2001

Individual album boxed sets

Headquarters Sessions Rhino, 2000 (3CD)
The Birds The Bees and The Monkees Rhino, 2009 (3CD)
Head Rhino, 2010 (3CD)
Instant Replay Rhino, 2011 (3CD)
The Monkees Present Rhino, 2013 (3CD)
The Monkees Rhino, 2014 (3CD)

Compilations, etc.

Monkeemania EMI Australia, 1979
Monkee Business Rhino, 1982
Monkee Flips Rhino, 1984
Missing Links Rhino, 1987
Missing Links Vol. II Rhino, 1990
Listen To The Band Rhino, 1991 (4CD)
Missing Links Vol. III Rhino, 1996
Music Box Rhino 4CD set, 2001

Variant reissue editions

The Monkees Rhino, 1994, 2006 (2CD)
More Of The Monkees Rhino, 1994, 2006 (2CD)
Headquarters Rhino, 1995, 2007 (2CD)
Pisces, Aquarius, Capricorn & Jones Ltd. Rhino, 1995, 2007 (2CD)
The Birds, The Bees & The Monkees Rhino, 1994
Head Rhino, 1994
Instant Replay Rhino, 1995
The Monkees Present Rhino, 1994
Changes Rhino, 1995

Selected best-of albums

The Monkees Greatest Hits Colgems, 1969
A Barrel Full Of Monkees Colgems, 1971
Refocus Bell Records, 1972
The Monkees Sounds Superb/Music For Pleasure, 1974
Then And Now Arista, 1986
The Best Of The Monkees Rhino, 2003

SOLO WORKS

Davy Jones

David Jones Colpix/Pye, 1964/1967
Davy Jones Bell Records, 1971
The Point MCA, 1978
Davy Jones Live JAL, 1981 (Japan only)
They Made A Monkee Out Of Me Dove Audiobook, 1987 (two cassette tapes)

Micky Dolenz

The Point MCA, 1978
Broadway Micky Kid Rhino, 1994
Demoiselle no label, 1998 (sold only at concerts)
King For A Day Gigatone, 2010
Remember Robo, 2012
The MGM Singles Collection 7A Records, 2015
A Little Bit Broadway, A Little Bit Rock And Roll Broadway, 2015

An Evening With Peter Noone & Micky Dolenz 7A Records, 2016

Peter Tork

Stranger Things Have Happened Beachwood, 1994

with James Lee Stanley:

Two Man Band Beachwood, 1996

Once Again Beachwood, 2001

Live/Backstage At The Coffee Gallery Beachwood, 2006

with Shoe Suede Blues:

Saved By The Blues CD Baby, 2003

Cambria Hotel CD Baby, 2007

Step By Step CD Baby, 2013

Michael Nesmith

The Wichita Train Whistle Sings Dot, 1968

And the Hits Just Keep On Comin' RCA, 1972

Pretty Much Your Standard Ranch Stash RCA, 1973

The Prison Pacific Arts, 1975

From A Radio Engine To The Photon Wing Pacific Arts/Island, 1977

Live At The Palais Pacific Arts, 1978

Infinite Rider On The Big Dogma Pacific Arts/Island, 1979

Tropical Campfires Pacific Arts, 1992

The Garden Rio Records, 1994

Live At The Britt Festival Cooking Vinyl, 1999

Rays Rio Records, 2006

The Wichita Train Whistle Sings/Timerider Edsel, 2008 reissue

The Amazing ZigZag Concert Road Goes On Forever Records, 2010 (disc five of 5CD set, comprising of April 1974 gig at London's Roundhouse for *Zigzag* magazine's fifth birthday)

Movies Of The Mind Pacific Arts/ Videoranch, 2014

with The First National Band:

Magnetic South RCA, 1970

Loose Salute RCA, 1970

Nevada Fighter RCA, 1971

with The Second National Band:

Tantamount To Treason Vol. 1 RCA, 1972

Dolenz, Jones, Boyce & Hart

Dolenz Jones Boyce & Hart Capitol, 1976

Concert In Japan Varese Sarabande, 1986

Boyce & Hart

Test Patterns A&M, 1967

I Wonder What She's Doing Tonite? A&M, 1968

It's All Happening On The Inside A&M, 1969

The Anthology: Boyce & Hart Polygram, 1998

Action! The Songs Of Tommy Boyce & Bobby Hart Ace, 2012

Bobby Hart

The First Bobby Hart Album 7A Records, 1979/2015

Tommy Boyce

Blown Away Chelsea Records, 1973 (as 'Christopher Cloud')

SECONDARY

The Beach Boys *Surfin' USA* Capitol, 1963

The Beach Boys *Pet Sounds* Capitol, 1966

The Beach Boys *Smiley Smile* Capitol, 1967

The Beach Boys *Surf's Up* Stateside, 1971

The Beatles *A Hard Day's Night* Parlophone, 1964

The Beatles *Revolver* Parlophone, 1966

The Beatles *Sgt Pepper's Lonely Hearts Club Band* Parlophone, 1967

The Beatles *Magical Mystery Tour* Parlophone, 1967

The Beatles *The Beatles* (aka *The White Album*) Apple, 1968

The Beatles *Yellow Submarine* Apple, 1968

The Beatles *Abbey Road* Apple, 1969

Tim Buckley *Happysad* Elektra, 1969

Tim Buckley *Starsailor* Straight, 1970

The Byrds *Mr. Tambourine Man* CBS, 1965
The Byrds *Younger Than Yesterday* CBS, 1966
The Byrds *Sweetheart Of The Rodeo* CBS, 1968
Clear Light *Clear Light* Elektra, 1968
Dexy's Midnight Runners *Don't Stand Me Down* Phonogram, 1985 (includes 'This Is What She's Like')
Neil Diamond *The Bang Years 1966–68* Columbia, 2011
Bob Dylan *John Wesley Harding* CBS, 1967
Bob Dylan *Nashville Skyline* CBS, 1969
The Fifth Dimension *The Essential Fifth Dimension* Sony, 2011
The Flying Burrito Brothers *Gilded Palace Of Sin* A&M, 1969
The Flying Burrito Brothers *Burrito Deluxe* A&M, 1970
Garland Frady *Pure Country* Countryside, 1973
Diane Hildebrand *Early Morning Blues And Greens* Elektra, 1967
Bert Jansch *L.A. Turnaround* Charisma, 1974
The KLF *The White Room* KLF Communications, 1991
The JAMMS *The History Of The JAMS aka The Timelords* TVT, 1988
The Leaves *Hey Joe* Mira, 1966
The Leaves *All The Good That's Happening* Capitol, 1967
The Lovin' Spoonful *Do You Believe In Magic?* Karma Sutra, 1965
The Lovin' Spoonful *Daydream* Karma Sutra, 1965
The Lovin' Spoonful *Hums Of Karma Sutra*, 1966
The Lovin' Spoonful *Everything Playing* Karma Sutra, 1967
The Lovin' Spoonful *Revolution: Revelation '69* Karma Sutra, 1969
Ian Matthews *Valley Hi* Elektra, 1973
Ian Matthews *Some Days You Eat The Bear, Some Days The Bear Eats You* Elektra, 1974
Ian Matthews with Plainsong *In Search Of Amelia Earhart* Elektra, 1972
The Modern Folk Quartet *Modern Folk Quartet* Warner Brothers, 1963
The Modern Folk Quartet *Changes* Warner Brothers, 1964
Van Morrison *Blowin' Your Mind!* Bang, 1967
Van Morrison *St. Dominic's Preview* Warner Brothers, 1972
Van Morrison *No Guru, No Method, No Teacher* Mercury, 1986
Nilsson *Aerial Ballet* RCA, 1967
Nilsson *The Point* RCA, 1971
Nilsson *Nilsson Schmilsson* RCA, 1972
Nilsson *Son Of Schmilsson* RCA, 1973
The Nitty Gritty Dirt Band *Uncle Charlie & His Dog Teddy* Liberty, 1970
Gram Parsons *GP* Reprise, 1973
Gram Parsons *Grievous Angel* Reprise, 1974
The Penny Arkade *Not The Freeze* Sundazed, 2014
Paul Revere & The Raiders *Midnight Ride* Columbia, 1966
Red Rhodes *Velvet Hammer In A Cowboy Band* Countryside, 1973
Kevin Rowland *My Beauty* Creation, 1999 (includes version of 'Daydream Believer' with different lyrics)
Pete Seeger *The Essential Pete Seeger* Sony, 2005
Shonen Knife *Happy Hour* Big Deal Records Japan, 1998 (includes version of 'Daydream Believer')
Charlie Smalls *The Wiz – The Super Soul Musical: Original 1975 Broadway Cast* Atlantic, 1975
The Stone Poneys *Evergreen, Volume 2* Capitol, 1967
The Turtles *The Battle Of The Bands* White Whale , 1968
The Turtles *Save The Turtles: Best Of* Manifesto, 2010
Various Artists *Easy Rider: Music From The Soundtrack* CBS, 1969

SINGLES

Monkees, etc.

Micky Dolenz 'Love Light' / 'Alicia' Chrysalis, 1979
Micky Dolenz 'To Be Or Not To Be' / 'Beverly Hills' Japan All Round Music Company, 1981
Micky Dolenz 'Tomorrow' / 'Fat Sam's Grand Slam ' A&M, 1983
Dolenz, Jones & Tork 'Christmas Is My Time Of Year' / 'White Christmas' Christmas Records, 1032 N. Sycamore Hollywood CA. 90038, 1976
Micky Dolenz, Christian Nesmith, Circe Link 'Porpoise Song' 7A Records, 2016 (7-inch EP)
The Monkees 'Steam Engine' / 'Rainbows' Relived Records, 1983 (limited-edition private pressing by Chip Douglas, sold at fan conventions)
Michael Nesmith 'Wanderin'' / 'Well, Well' Highness, 1963
Michael Nesmith 'How Can You Kiss Me' / 'Just A Little Love' Omnibus, 1965
Michael Nesmith 'The New Recruit' / 'A Journey With Michael Blessing' Colpix, 1965
Michael Nesmith 'Until It's Time For You To Go' / 'What Seems To Be The Trouble Officer' Colpix, 1965
Michael Nesmith 'Just A Little Love' / 'Curson Terrace' Edan, 1965
Peter Tork and the New Monks 'I'm Not Your Steppin' Stone' / 'Higher And Higher' Claude's Music Works, Vermont, 1981

Other

Dexy's Midnight Runners 'There, There My Dear' / 'The Horse' Late Night Feelings/EMI, 1980
Huddersfield Transit Authority (aka Tim Rice) 'Different Drum' / 'One Of The All Time Grates' Polydor, 1972
Simply Red & White 'Daydream Believer Cheer Up Peter Reid' / 'Karaoke Version' 13th Moon Records, 1996
This Mortal Coil 'Song To the Siren' / 'Sixteen Days' 4AD, 1984
Robert Wyatt 'I'm A Believer' / 'Memories' Virgin, 1974

SELECTED FILMOGRAPHY

PRIMARY

The Monkees

Head (dir. Robert Rafelson) 1968
33 1/3 Revolutions Per Monkee (TV special, dir. Jack Good) 1968
Heart And Soul Rhino VHS, 1991
Justus Rhino VHS, 1997
Hey Hey It's The Monkees (TV special, dir. Michael Nesmith), 1997
Hey Hey We're The Monkees (documentary) Rhino DVD, 1998
Live Summer Tour Rhino DVD, 2002
The Complete TV Series Rhino Blu-ray, 2016

Michael Nesmith

Elephant Parts (dir. William Dear) Sell-through VHS, 1981; DVD, 2003
TV Parts (NBC TV series, dir. Dolenz, Dear, Myerson, Nesmith) 1985
Live At The Britt Festival (dir. Nesmith) Starz/Anchor Bay, 1981

Dolenz, Jones, Boyce & Hart

Sing The Golden Great Hits Of The Monkees (TV special, dir. Larry White) 1976

Boyce & Hart

The Guys Who Wrote 'Em (dir. Rachel Lichtman) 2014

SECONDARY

About The Monkees

Behind The Music: the Monkees VH-1/Gay Rosenthal Productions, 2000

Daydream Believers: The Monkees Auditionees (dir. Ian MacMillan) 1997

Daydream Believers: The Monkees Story (dir. Neil Fearnley) 2000

Making The Monkees (dir. Brian Henry Martin) 2007

We Love The Monkees (dir. Gareth Williams) 2012

Other

America Lost & Found: The BBS Story – The Criterion Collection (six-disc boxed set including *Head*) 2010

Easy Rider (dir. Dennis Hopper) 1969

Every Day's A Holiday (dir. James Hill) 1965

Espresso Bongo (dir. Val Guest) 1959

Ferry 'Cross The Mersey (dir. Jeremy Summers) 1964

Five Easy Pieces (dir. Bob Rafelson) 1970

The Graduate (dir. Mike Nichols) 1967

A Hard Day's Night (dir. Richard Lester) 1964

Help! (dir. Richard Lester) 1965

I Love You, Alice B. Toklas! (dir. Hy Averback) 1968

The Jazz Singer (dir. Alan Crosland) 1927

Loving You (dir. Hal Kanter) 1957

Magical Mystery Tour (dir. The Beatles) 1967

A Mighty Wind (dir. Christopher Guest) 2003

Privilege (dir. Peter Watkins) 1967

The Point (dir. Fred Wolf) 1971

Repo Man (dir. Alex Cox) 1984

Singin' In The Rain (dir. Gene Kelly) 1952

Tapeheads (dir. Bill Fishman) 1988

The Girl Can't Help It (dir. Frank Tashlin) 1956

The Trip (dir. Roger Corman) 1967

This Is Spinal Tap (dir. Rob Reiner) 1982

This Is Us (dir. Morgan Spurlock) 2013

Timerider: The Adventure of Lyle Swann (dir. William Dear) 1982

Valley Of The Dolls (dir. Mark Robson) 1967

The Wrecking Crew (dir. Tommy Tedesco) 2008/2014

Who Is Harry Nilsson And Why Is Everybody Talking About Him? (dir. John Scheinfeld) 2010

Yellow Submarine (dir. George Dunning) 1968

BIBLIOGRAPHY

PRIMARY

Books

Adler, Bill *The Monkees Go Ape* (New York: Western Press, 1968)

Adler, Davis *Love Letters To The Monkees* (New York: Popular Library, 1967)

Baker, Glenn A. *Monkeemania: The True Story of the Monkees* (New York: St. Martin's Press, 1986)

Biskind, Peter *Easy Riders, Raging Bulls* (London: Bloomsbury, 1998)

Bone, Finn *The Monkees Scrapbook* (San Francisco: Last Gasp, 1986)

Boyce, Tommy *How To Write A Hit Song … And Sell It* (Los Angeles: Melvin Powers, 1974)

Bronson, Harold *The Rhino Records Story: Revenge Of The Music Nerds* (New York: Select Books, 2013)

Bronson, Harold (ed) *Hey, Hey, We're The Monkees* (Santa Monica: Rhino, 1996)

Chadwick, McManus, Reilly, Schultheiss *The Monkees: A Manufactured Image: The Ultimate Reference Guide to Monkee Memories And Memorabilia* (Ann Arbor, Michigan: Popular Culture Ink, 1993)

Dolenz, Micky, with Mark Bego, *I'm A Believer: My Life Of Monkees, Music, And Madness* (New York: Cooper Square Press, 1993/2004)

Falkenberg, Lise Ling *The Monkees – Caught In A False Image* Amazon Digital Services, 2012

Fawcett, Gene, *The Monkees* (New York: Popular Library, 1967)

Hart, Bobby, with Glenn Ballantyne *Psychedelic Bubble Gum: Boyce & Hart, The Monkees, And Turning Mayhem Into Miracles* (New York: SelectBooks, 2015)

Hickey, Andrew *Monkee Music* (lulu.com, 2011)

Johnston, William *Who's Got The Button?* (New York: Western Press, 1968)

Jones, Davy, with Alan Green *They Made A Monkee Out Of Me* (Beavertown PA: Dome Press, 1987)

Jones, Davy, with Alan Green *Mutant Monkees Meet The Masters Of The Multi-Media Manipulation Machine!* (New York: Click! Publishing, 1992)

Kubernik, Harvey *Canyon Of Dreams: The Magic And The Music Of Laurel Canyon* (New York: Sterling, 2009)

Lefcowitz, Eric *Monkee Business: The Revolutionary Made-For-TV Band* (Berkley: Last Gasp, 1985)

Massingill, Randi L. *Total Control: The Michael Nesmith Story* (Carlsbad CA: Flexquarters, 1997/2005)

Mitchell, Melanie *Monkee Magic: A Book About A TV Show About A Band* (CreateSpace Independent Publishing Platform, 2013)

Nesmith, Michael *The Long Sandy Hair Of Neftoon Zamora* (New York: St. Martin's Press, 1998)

O'Connor, Patrick *The Monkees Go Mod* (New York: Popular Library, 1967)

Parker, Scott *Good Clean Fun: The Audio And Visual Documents Of The Monkees 1956–1970* (CreateSpace Independent Publishing Platform, 2013)

Sandoval Andrew *The Monkees: The Day-By-Day Story Of The 60s TV Pop Sensation* (San Diego: Thunder Bay Press, 2005)

Velez, Fred *A Little Bit Me, A Little Bit You: The Monkees From A Fan's Perspective* (CreateSpace Independent Publishing Platform, 2014)

Wincentsen, Edward *The Monkees, Memories & The Magic* (Hamilton, Ontario: Wynn, 2000)

Magazines, periodicals, etc.

Mojo issue no. 103, June 2002 (article on *Head* pp.48–56)

Monkees Monthly UK, Beat productions: 32 issues February 1967–September 1969 (ed. Jackie Richmond)

Monkee Spectacular USA, *Tiger Beat* special magazine: 16 issues April 1967–August 1968 (ed. Ann Moses)

The Monkees Annual (London: Century 21 Publishing, 1967, 1968, 1969)

Shindig! issue no. 19, Nov–Dec 2010 (article on *Head* pp.42–53)

ZigZag issue no. 39, January 1974 (Nesmith interview, 'Just Roll With The Flow', pp.4–9)

ZigZag issue no. 40, February 1974 (Nesmith interview, part two, '283 Reasons To like Michael Nesmith', pp.9–14)

ZigZag issue no. 74, May 1977 (Nesmith interview, 'The Road To Rio', pp.16–20)

SECONDARY

Auslander, Philip *Liveness: Performance In A Mediatized Culture* (London: Routledge, 1999)

Bradley, D., and Werner, C. *We Gotta Get Out of This Place: The Soundtrack Of The Vietnam War* (Boston: University of Massachusetts Press, 2015)

Brode, Douglas *The Films Of Jack Nicholson* (London: Citadel, 2000)

Cohn, Nick *Awopbopaloobop Alopbamboom* (London: Paladin, 1969)

Cusic, Don *Roger Miller: Dang Him* (Chicago: Brackish Publishing, 2012)
GO Pop Annual (New York: Pyramid, 1968)
Higgs, John *The KLF: Chaos, Magic, And The Band Who Burned A Million Pounds* (London: Weidenfeld & Nicholson, 2012)
Holzman, Jac, and Daws, Gavan *Follow The Music: The Life And High Times Of Elektra Records In The Great Years Of American Pop Culture* (Santa Monica: First Media, 1998)
King, Carole *A Natural Woman* (London: Virago, 2012)
Leppert, Richard (ed.) *Adorno: Essays On Music* (Los Angeles: University of California Press, 2002)
Levy, Silvano *Decoding Magritte* (London: Sansom, 2016)
Lewisohn, Mark *The Complete Beatles Recording Sessions* (London: Hamlyn, 1988)
Marcuse, Herbert *The One Dimensional Man: Studies In The Ideology Of Advanced Industrial Society* (New York: Beacon Press, 1991 edition)
Mills, Peter *Hymns To the Silence: Inside The Words And Music Of Van Morrison* (London: Bloomsbury, 2010)
Nash, Graham *Wild Tales* (London: Penguin, 2014)
O'Dair, Marcus *Different Every Time: The Authorised Biography Of Robert Wyatt* (London: Soft Skull, 2014)
Perone, James *Songs Of The Vietnam Conflict* (New York: Greenwood, 2001)
Podolsky, Rich *Don Kirshner: The Man With The Golden Ear* (Milwaukee: Hal Leonard, 2012)
Ronstadt, Linda *Simple Dreams – A Musical Memoir* (New York: Simon and Schuster, 2014)
Seeger, P., and Rosenthal, R. & S. *Pete Seeger In His Own Words* (New York: Paradigm, 2012)
Shypton, Alvyn *Nilsson: The Life Of A Singer-Songwriter* (London: Oxford University Press, 2013)
Susann, Jacqueline *Valley Of The Dolls* (London: Cassell, 1966)
Taliaferro, John *Charles M. Russell: The Life And Legend Of America's Cowboy Artist* (Norman, Oklahoma: University of Oklahoma Press, 2003)
Tannenbaum, Rob, and Marks, Craig *I Want My MTV: The Uncensored Story Of The Music Video Revolution* (New York: Plume, 2012)
Wesley, Fred *Hit Me, Fred* (Durham, North Carolina: Duke University Press, 2002)
Wild, David *How I Learned To Stop Worrying And Love Neil Diamond* (London: Old Street, 2009)
Young, Neil *Waging Heavy Peace: A Hippie Dream* (London: Penguin, 2013)

ENDNOTES

CHAPTER ONE

1 Interview with Pat Thomas, October 29 2015
2 *Dolenz, Jones, Boyce & Hart* TV special, 1976
3 popcultureaddict.com/interviews/davyjonessi/
4 *Daydream Believers: The Monkees Auditionees*, 1997
5 *Monkee Spectacular*, January 1968, p41
6 Merrit-Jones, p.123
7 Dolenz, p.175
8 *16 Magazine*, July 1967
9 *16 Magazine*, April 1967
10 *Teen Set*, June 1967
11 Bronson, p.14
12 Sandoval, p.34

13 *Palm Springs Life*, January 2014
14 Sandoval, p.22

CHAPTER TWO
1 Jones, p.90
2 Jones with Alan Green *Mutant Monkees Meet The Masters Of The Multi-Media Manipulation Machine!*, p.112
3 Jones, p.56
4 Falkenberg, p.14
5 *The Monkees*, 'The Devil And Peter Tork' episode
6 Leary, p.174–75

CHAPTER THREE
1 Sandoval, p.36
2 *Monkees Monthly*, August 1967, p.7
3 *Monkees Monthly*, August 1967, p.15
4 *We Love The Monkees*, ITV, 2012
5 Liner notes to *Summer 1967: The Complete US Concert Recordings*, 2001
6 Liner notes to *Summer 1967: The Complete US Concert Recordings*, 2001

CHAPTER FOUR
1 *Hey Hey We're The Monkees*
2 King, p.90
3 *TV Guide*, September 9 1967, p.8
4 Hart, p.112
5 *TV Guide*, September 23 1967, p.9
6 *Monkee Music*, p.55
7 *Monkee Spectacular*, January 1968
8 Dolenz, p.132
9 Randy Smith, *Los Angeles Times*, September 25 2009
10 *Goldmine*, February 2013
11 Liner notes to *Instant Replay* reissue, 1994
12 Liner notes to *The Birds, The Bees & The Monkees* boxed set, 2009

CHAPTER FIVE
1 Liner notes to *Headquarters* reissue, 1994
2 Bronson, *The Rhino Records Story*
3 *Head* Blu-ray, 2010
4 *Hollywood Reporter*, November 7 1968
5 *Daydream Believers* commentary
6 avclub.com/article/bob-rafelson-48013
7 *Daydream Believers* commentary
8 *Mojo*, June 2002
9 *Mojo*, June 2002
10 *Mojo*, June 2002
11 Liner notes to *Head* reissue, 1995

CHAPTER SIX
1 *New Yorker*, November 16 1968
2 *Head* Blu-ray
3 *Head* script, p.3
4 *Head* script, p.4
5 *Head* Blu-ray
6 *Head* Blu-ray
7 *Head* script, p.9
8 *Head* Blu-ray
9 *Head* Blu-ray
10 *Head* Blu-ray
11 *Hey Hey We're The Monkees*
12 *Head* script, p.29
13 *Head* Blu-ray
14 *NME*, July 6 1968
15 *Head* Blu-ray
16 *Head* script, p.35A/36
17 Bronson (ed), *Hey Hey We're The Monkees*, p.145
18 *Head* Blu-ray
19 *Head* Blu-ray
20 *Rolling Stone*, December 27 1969, p.10
21 *Head* Blu-ray
22 *Head* script, p.41
23 *16 Magazine*, September 1967, p.62
24 *Head* script, p.49
25 *Head* Blu-ray
26 Marcuse
27 *Head* Blu-ray
28 *Flip*, August 1968
29 *Flip*, August 1968
30 *Flip*, August 1968
31 *Shindig!*, November/December 2010
32 *Head* Blu-ray
33 *16 Magazine*, August 1968
34 *16 Magazine*, August 1968
35 Reddit AMA session, April 2016
36 *Head* script, p.64

37 *Saturday Evening Post*, January 28 1967
38 *Head* Blu-ray
39 *Headquarters Podcast,* July 30 1988
40 *Head* Blu-ray
41 *Head* Blu-ray
42 See Lee Barron and Ian Inglis in Russell Reising (ed), *'Speak To Me': The Legacy of Pink Floyd's The Dark Side Of The Moon* (Routledge, 2006)
43 *Head* Blu-ray
44 Bronson (ed), *Hey Hey We're The Monkees*, p.63
45 *Headquarters Podcast*, July 30 1988
46 *Head* script, p.68
47 *Head* Blu-ray
48 *Head* Blu-ray
49 *Head* Blu-ray
50 *Head* script, p.75
51 *Head* script, p.80
52 *Head* script, p.89
53 *Head* script, p.90
54 *Head* script, p.92
55 *Head* script, p.99
56 *Head* Blu-ray
57 *Head* script, p.99

CHAPTER SEVEN

1 King, p.130
2 *Head* Blu-ray
3 Liner notes to *Head*, 1994
4 *Head* Blu-ray
5 *Head* Blu-ray

CHAPTER EIGHT

1 *Othello*, act III, scene 3, lines 90–92
2 Bronson, p.81–83
3 Harold Bronson, *Coast* magazine, September 1971
4 Bronson, p.160

ACKNOWLEDGEMENTS

There are many people to whom I owe a debt of thanks in the preparation and writing of this book. Firstly I'd like to thank Chip Douglas and Bobby Hart for so graciously giving me so much of their time and answering my very many questions with such patience and candour. I'd also like to thank Harold Bronson and Bill Inglot for their kindness in talking with me and discussing their own passion for music, which does a heart good, and their fascinating insights into the relationship between Rhino Records and The Monkees.

My hat is tipped to Iain Lee, the UK's number one Monkeemaniac. He very kindly facilitated introductions for this book but more broadly deserves the thanks of every fan of the group for his efforts to keep the band's name alive on his various radio programmes over the years and, more recently, via his '7A Records' project which has already delivered bounty to Monkee fans worldwide.

I would like to thank Bill Drummond, who made me very happy by granting one of only two interviews he will give in 2016 to me on the subject of The Monkees, and for giving me the exclusive rights to publish it. Thank you, sir.

To Tom Seabrook at Jawbone, thank you for commissioning the book, and then waiting for it.

Special thanks to Bobby Mills-Thomas for the interview transcriptions.

Thanks and greetings to Jonathan Lynas, John Jackson, Jonathan Wolstenholme, Tracey Thorn, Ben Watt, Laura Barton, Dave Evans, Chris Nickson, and a brotherly wave to my fellow Innocents Abroad, Steve Godrich, Stuart Hilton, Martin Malone, and David Skidmore, and 'Honorary Innocent' Chris Hobbs.

Thanks always to Gordon Johnston, who gave me a chance, and Lance Pettitt; much love to the indefatigable Pat Thomas, HP, and the ever-encouraging Russ Reising.

Alex King of the Leeds International Film Festival took my little dream of presenting Head as part of the Festival and made it happen; thanks to him, Head received its non-London UK premiere as part of the LIFF 28 on November 19 2014, proving such a success that it was rebooked for 2015. I had the honour of introducing the film on both occasions, and thank you Ceri Oakes for taking such beautiful photographs at the second of these events.

Finally, I'd like to thank all my students on the Media and Popular Culture/ Media Communication Culture degree programmes at Leeds since I began teaching there in 2002; as part of their degree, every last one of them had the chance to see Head. By my reckoning there are now over a thousand young people out in the world who have seen and studied the movie who otherwise most likely would never have encountered it at all. Now that's job satisfaction. Some loved it to bits, some ran screaming, and some were happily puzzled. I was meant to be teaching you, which I hope I did, but on the quiet you were teaching me. Thank you all.

To Charlotte, Bobby, and Eva.

INDEX

Unless otherwise noted, words *in italics* are album titles, and words 'in quotes' are song titles.